To Walk the Earth Again

RELIGION IN AMERICA

Harry S. Stout, General Editor

Recent titles in the series:

A PARADISE OF REASON
William Bentley and Enlightenment Christianity in the Early Republic
J. Rixey Ruffin

EVANGELIZING THE SOUTH
A Social History of Church and State in Early America
Monica Najar

A REPUBLIC OF RIGHTEOUSNESS
The Public Christianity of the Post-Revolutionary New England Clergy,
Jonathan D. Sassi

THE LIVES OF DAVID BRAINERD
The Making of an American Evangelical Icon
John A. Grigg

FATHERS ON THE FRONTIER
French Missionaries and the Roman Catholic Priesthood in the United States, 1789–1870
Michael Pasquier

HOLY JUMPERS
Evangelicals and Radicals in Progressive Era America
William Kostlevy

NO SILENT WITNESS
The Eliot Parsonage Women and Their Unitarian World
Cynthia Grant Tucker

RACE AND REDMEPTION IN PURITAN NEW ENGLAND
Richard A. Bailey

SACRED BORDERS
Continuing Revelation and Canonical Restraint in Early America
David Holland

EXHIBITING MORMONISM
The Latter-day Saints and the 1893 Chicago World's Fair
Reid L. Neilson

OUT OF THE MOUTHS OF BABES
Girl Evangelists in the Flapper Era
Thomas A. Robinson and Lanette R. Ruff

THE VIPER ON THE HEARTH
Mormons, Myths, and the Construction of Heresy
Updated Edition
Terryl L. Givens

THE LIFE AND DEATH OF THE RADICAL HISTORICAL JESUS
David Burns

MORMONS AND THE BIBLE
The Place of the Latter-day Saints in American Religion
Updated Edition
Philip L. Barlow

MISSIONARIES OF REPUBLICANISM
A Religious History of the Mexican-American War
John C. Pinheiro

SYMPATHETIC PURITANS
Calvinist Fellow Feeling in Early New England
Abram C. Van Engen

A DIVINITY FOR ALL PERSUASIONS
Almanacs and Early American Religious Life
T. J. Tomlin

THE ORIGINS OF AMERICAN RELIGIOUS NATIONALISM
Sam Haselby

HOUSES DIVIDED
Evangelical Schisms and the Crisis of the Union in Missouri
Lucas Volkman

CLERGY EDUCATION IN AMERICA
Religious Leadership and American Public Life, 1785 to 1935
Lawrence A. Golemon

TO WALK THE EARTH AGAIN
The Politics of Resurrection in Early America
Christopher Trigg

To Walk the Earth Again

The Politics of Resurrection in Early America

CHRISTOPHER TRIGG

OXFORD
UNIVERSITY PRESS

Oxford University Press is a department of the University of Oxford. It furthers
the University's objective of excellence in research, scholarship, and education
by publishing worldwide. Oxford is a registered trade mark of Oxford University
Press in the UK and certain other countries.

Published in the United States of America by Oxford University Press
198 Madison Avenue, New York, NY 10016, United States of America.

© Oxford University Press 2023

All rights reserved. No part of this publication may be reproduced, stored in
a retrieval system, or transmitted, in any form or by any means, without the
prior permission in writing of Oxford University Press, or as expressly permitted
by law, by license, or under terms agreed with the appropriate reproduction
rights organization. Inquiries concerning reproduction outside the scope of the
above should be sent to the Rights Department, Oxford University Press, at the
address above.

You must not circulate this work in any other form
and you must impose this same condition on any acquirer.

Library of Congress Cataloging-in-Publication Data
Names: Trigg, Christopher Peter, author.
Title: To walk the Earth again : the politics of resurrection in early
America / Christopher Trigg.
Description: New York, NY, United States of America : Oxford University Press, [2023] |
Series: Religion in America series |
Includes bibliographical references and index.
Identifiers: LCCN 2022040704 (print) | LCCN 2022040705 (ebook) |
ISBN 9780197652756 (hardback) | ISBN 9780197652770 (epub)
Subjects: LCSH: Resurrection—Biblical teaching. |
Protestantism—United States—History—17th century.
Classification: LCC BS2545.R47 T74 2023 (print) |
LCC BS2545.R47 (ebook) | DDC 232/.5—dc23/eng/20221116
LC record available at https://lccn.loc.gov/2022040704
LC ebook record available at https://lccn.loc.gov/2022040705

DOI: 10.1093/oso/9780197652756.001.0001

1 3 5 7 9 8 6 4 2

Printed by Integrated Books International, United States of America

For Kate
I found it in you

Contents

Acknowledgments ix

Introduction: Resurrection in the New World 1

1. Resurrection, Selfhood, and the Church 15
   Eschatological Innovation in the Seventeenth Century 15
   Robert Baillie's Attack on Resurrection Theology in New England 17
   Conversion as the "Cominge of Christ": Anne Hutchinson's
      Realized Eschatology 22
   "Men Think It Easie to Believe a Resurrection": John Cotton's and
      Thomas Shepard's Responses to Hutchinson 28
   No Sacred History: Samuel Gorton's Realized Eschatology 38
   The Inner Light Is the Risen Christ: Quaker Resurrection Theology 51

2. Cotton Mather and the First Resurrection 59
   Collective Life after Death 59
   The Greatest Work of Christ in America: Resurrection in the
      Magnalia Christi Americana 65
   Mather and the Science of Resurrection 74
   The Imperial Politics of Mather's Millennialism 84
   The Bones of Joseph: Mather, Benjamin Colman, and the First
      Resurrection 94

3. Resurrection's Racial Politics 100
   Protestant Evangelism and the Development of Racial Difference 100
   "Can the Ethiopian Change His Skin?": Samuel Sewall, Resurrection,
      and Race 109
   "The Obedient Nations": Non-Europeans in Cotton
      Mather's Millennium 116
   John Beach and Immaterial Resurrection 123
   Race, Resurrection, and Revivalism 130
   "The Heaven of Comparative Freedom": Radical Black Eschatologies 138

4. Thomas Prince and the Resurrection of the World 143
   Prince's Globalism 143
   "Perpetual Spring throughout the Earth": Prince and the
      Millennial Transformation of the Planet 149
   Revivalism and Immortalism 159
   The Resurrection of Other Worlds: Prince and William Torrey's
      Brief Discourse 170

viii CONTENTS

5. Secular Resurrections   179
   Reworking and Rejecting Protestant Eschatology   179
   Resurrection as Metaphor   183
   Natural and Social Resurrection   190
   Debating Literal Belief in Resurrection   200
   Spiritualism, Sentimentalism, and Materialism   208

Coda: Resurrection Hereafter   222

Notes   229
Works Cited   271
Index   293

Acknowledgments

This is a book about eschatological beliefs in colonial America. But the long path to writing it began with my undergraduate studies in the heroes and saints of medieval Ireland, Wales, and England. I will always be grateful to the faculty of the Department of Anglo-Saxon, Norse, and Celtic at the University of Cambridge, especially Oliver Padel, Máire Ní Mhaonaigh, and Rosalind Love. Their intellectual curiosity, scholarly rigor, and generosity of spirit continue to inspire me all these years later.

As a graduate student at the University of Toronto, I was fortunate to receive mentorship from many great thinkers, writers, and teachers, including David Galbraith, Brian Stock, Lynn Magnusson, Paul Stevens, Sarah Wilson, Nick Mount, Nicholas Terpstra, Elizabeth Harvey, Andrea Most, Will Robins, Derek Allen, and Michael Cobb. Special thanks must go to Neal Dolan and Andrew Dubois, whose wit, warmth, and unbridled enthusiasm for literature remain inspirational. In Paul Downes, I found the best PhD supervisor one could possibly hope for. His insightful advice and comments are still invaluable to me, and he was an essential reader of my work for this project. Many thanks are due to my fellow students, in particular Ira Wells, Dale Barleben, Joel Goldbach, Christopher L. Hicklin, Timothy Perry, Donald Sells, and Ross Hawkins. Mark Colborne and Rory Hanchard gave me a musical education that I draw on to this day. My studies at the University of Toronto were generously funded by the Connaught International Scholarship, the Commonwealth Scholarship, and the Ontario Graduate Scholarship.

After receiving my PhD, I was lucky to receive funding to attend the School of Criticism and Theory at Cornell University. I would like to thank Amanda Anderson, then director of the program, for her kind support. The seminars I took with Hent de Vries were a miracle that I often return to. I am grateful to Ian Patterson and Mary Newbould for enabling me to return to Cambridge to teach in these years.

I never imagined that my career would bring me to Southeast Asia. I began work on this book after taking up a position in the Division of English at Nanyang Technological University, Singapore, which has proved a wonderful place to teach and research. I am indebted to all my colleagues here, particularly Neil Murphy, C. J. Wee Wan-ling, Terence Dawson, Shirley Chew, Boey Kim Cheng, Graham Matthews, Jane Wong, Richard Barlow, Guinevere Barlow, Kevin Riordan, and Barrie Sherwood. Thanks also to my students, whose eagerness to learn about the literature of places long ago and far away is a wonder, and to the administrative staff who do so much to make the School of Humanities what it is. Special thanks to my brilliant graduate students Charlotte Hand, Aaron Tang, Tejash Kumar Singh, and Ellice Wu. Aaron Tang and Olivia Djawoto contributed indispensable research assistance. The research for this book was supported by the Ministry of Education, Singapore, under its Academic Research Fund Tier 1 RG142/19 (NS).

I arrived at a specialization in early American literature comparatively late in my career, after finishing my doctoral studies. Attending my first Society of Early Americanists conference in my hometown of London in 2014 opened up a new world of scholarly inspiration, community, and friendship. At subsequent SEA conferences in Chicago, Tulsa, St. Louis, and Eugene, I presented the work that has culminated in this volume. Without the encouragement and inspiration I received there, writing this book would have been impossible. Many thanks to Zachary Hutchins for sharing his insightful and as-yet-unpublished research on the Sewall family and slavery, which is cited in chapter 3. I am particularly grateful to (and for) Hannah Wakefield, Kris Bross, Dan Walden, Alex Mazzaferro, Chris Philips, John Miles, Jay David Miller, Bryce Traister, Michelle Burnham, and Sarah Rivett. Reiner Smolinski's unparalleled and freely shared expertise in Protestant millennialism has been fundamental to my development as an early Americanist. I am obliged to the attendees of the first "Salon Beyond the Wall" in central Vermont for their fellowship, as well as their feedback on the first stirrings of *To Walk the Earth Again*: Laura Stevens, Meredith Neumann, Ana Schwartz, Jason M. Payton, and Lara Rose. Our magnanimous host Jonathan Beecher Field is the heart and soul of the SEA. Last, I have benefited immeasurably from the kindness and wisdom of Abram Van Engen, whose guidance was central to the completion of this book.

Publishing in *Early American Literature* is a rite of passage for early Americanists and I would like to thank editors Sandra M. Gustafson and Marion Rust, as well as the journal's anonymous reviewers, for their helpful recommendations on my work. Portions of chapter 3 were published in my article "The Racial Politics of Resurrection in the Eighteenth-Century Atlantic World," *Early American Literature* 55.1 (2019): 47–84. I am also grateful to the staff of the Massachusetts Historical Society, the American

Antiquarian Society, the British Library, and Cambridge University Library, where I carried out research.

I owe a huge debt of thanks to Cynthia Read and Harry Stout for believing in this book. Thanks too to the anonymous readers for Oxford University Press for their detailed and supportive comments, as well as to Chelsea Hogue, Theo Calderara, and Laura Santo for their editorial support.

Last, love and gratitude to my family. If I have anything valuable to say, it is because my parents Lynn and Jonathan Trigg have urged me to follow my curiosity wherever it takes me. Their love and many accomplishments are my wellspring. My siblings Nick and Louise never cease to bring me laughs and joy. Thanks to them and my sister- and brother-in-law Pippa and Elliott, I have four wonderful nephews and nieces: Sam, Sophie, Rafferty, and Méabh. Love and thanks to my inspirational father- and mother-in-law David Mulroney and Janet Wakely, whose encouragement and example I could not do without. This book describes the community of the living with the dead. I am sorry that my grandparents Peter and Marjorie Trigg, and Dennis and Iris Hannen are not here to see it into print, but they are still with me nevertheless. *To Walk the Earth Again* is dedicated to my wife Kate Wakely-Mulroney. Your love is the lamp that lights my way.

Introduction

Resurrection in the New World

Crossing the Atlantic took seventeenth-century English settlers away from death as they knew it. Not only were they now distant from the churchyards in which their forebears lay (and in which they would have once expected to be entombed themselves), but the dangers of the voyage itself and the difficulty of establishing new homes in a hostile environment exposed them to the threat of disorderly burial. During Jamestown's early years bodies were frequently interred quickly, without a presiding clergyman, and often on private farmsteads rather than near places of worship. Conflicts with the native inhabitants of Virginia and Massachusetts saw both settler and Indian corpses subject to mutilation and exhumation.[1] On the disease-ravaged plantation islands of the Caribbean, meanwhile, the life expectancy for the incoming English, as well as those given over to bondage, was extremely short.[2]

The doctrine of the future resurrection of the dead helped to assuage settlers' fears about untimely death and burial far from home. When in August 1620 the *Speedwell* was forced to abort its attempt to carry English separatists to New England, Robert Cushman wrote to a friend in London, complaining of his own ill health and of his fears that his party's pious endeavor would be thwarted. "If ever we make a plantation, God [will have] work[ed] a mirakle," he observed, adding that he and fellow passenger William King were competing as to "who shall be meate first for the fishes." Despite these gloomy prospects, Cushman professed his faith that both he and the putative colony would be saved, linking these two fortunes through his expectation of a second bodily existence: "But we looke for a glorious resurrection, knowing Christ Jesus after the flesh no more, but looking unto the joye that is before us, we will endure all these things and accounte them light in comparison of that joye we hope for."[3]

The funerary practices that the various colonies developed addressed both aspects of Cushman's anxiety, enacting the permanence of the English body politic in the New World by securing the remains of individual believers. Virginia replicated English customs fairly closely. Following the funeral rite of the Anglican Book of Common Prayer, ministers committed bodies to the earth "in sure and certain hope of the resurrection to eternal life, through our Lord Jesus Christ."[4] As the seventeenth century progressed, Virginian authorities attempted to curtail burial on private land, urging colonists to choose interment in the churchyard.[5] Behind this policy lay the old belief that the dead of each parish ought to rise together on the last day. Puritan New England managed death differently. Burials took place in graveyards that were unaffiliated with any particular church. Memorial sermons were generally delivered at the next religious meeting after funerals (addresses spoken in the presence of the corpse were seen to be suggestive of Roman Catholic prayer for the dead).[6] The doctrine of predestination and the assumption that the number of the elect was much smaller than that of the damned meant that "sure and certain hope" of salvation could not be articulated.[7] In practice, however, mourners were usually confident that their loved ones were bound for heaven. Furthermore, Puritan writing regularly invoked the resurrection of saints as a symbol of the eschatological victory of Reformed Christianity over its doubters and persecutors.

Faith in resurrection also allowed settlers to draw ethnic distinctions between themselves and other groups, reinforcing their sense of their own superiority over Native Americans and enslaved Africans. Though English and Anglo-American writers asserted that indigenous peoples' belief in life after death was evidence of their humanity, they often commented on Indian confusion or skepticism toward the resurrection of the flesh. In his late sixteenth-century survey of Virginia, Thomas Hariot noted that the local natives thought that the colonists at Roanoke held a magical power over diseases and therefore supposed "that wee were men of an old generation many yeeres past then risen againe to immortalitie."[8] In the 1640s, Roger Williams's guide to Algonquin language and culture observed that "though the Natives hold the Soule to live forever... they die, and mourn without Hope," because they do not expect "Resurrection."[9] Advocating for the conversion of the enslaved people of Barbados, Anglican royalist Richard Ligon noted that the island's black population were "not altogether of the [afterlife-denying] sect of the *Sadduces:* For, they believe a Resurrection, and that they shall go into their own Country again, and have their youth renewed."[10] This conviction was a potential source of resistance and rebellion, as the slaves could threaten their owners with suicide, safe in their conviction that death would improve their lot. Although such superstition ostensibly confirmed Ligon's presumption that Africans were inherently intellectually inferior to Europeans, he also framed it as a standing reproach to the English Barbadians who allowed their enslaved people to persist in their ignorance.

But belief in and about resurrection did more than just delimit the boundaries between Christian and pagan, "civilized" and "savage." Throughout the American colonial period, devotional, controversial, and speculative writing on the subject addressed questions of religious, social, and political identity. The translation of the church itself from earth to heaven was a mainstay of all varieties of Christian eschatology. Building on this principle, Protestant ministers described the persistence of more narrowly defined corporate bodies and affiliations into the next world. In the 1630s and 1640s, Massachusetts Puritans John Cotton and Thomas Shepard imagined institutional and theological continuities between their own New England Congregationalism and the eschatological church triumphant. Around the turn of the eighteenth century, Cotton Mather reconfigured their vision. Now that New England was more closely integrated into the English/British empire, it was less expedient to picture the kingdom of God along Puritan lines. But while he portrayed the perfected church of the millennium as an evolution of global Protestantism, rather than of one denomination in particular, Mather still insisted that New England's unique story would outlast the end of secular time. The spirit of Congregationalism would live on through the resurrection of the colonies' many departed saints, who (along with their counterparts from other countries) would serve as the governors of the New Earth. Mather thought that these believers would take on a luminescent appearance when they returned from the grave. Some of his friends and colleagues (including Boston magistrate Samuel Sewall) wondered instead whether resurrection would lighten the skin of African saints. The assumption that black bodies were incompatible with immortality reflected a widespread reluctance to offer Christians of color religious and political equality in this life. Toward the end of the eighteenth century, some of the first African writers to be published in English contested this prejudice, insisting that black people would be admitted to heaven.

Controversy over the nature of resurrected existence was nothing new. The patristic and medieval eras produced a wide variety of interpretations of the Bible's often confusing pronouncements on resurrection.[11] But colonial authors, as one would expect, were more directly influenced by the English and European Protestants who overturned eschatological convention at the beginning of the seventeenth century. By arguing that the thousand-year reign of Christ described in the book of Revelation was yet to begin, these theologians enabled new ways of understanding the general resurrection's place in sacred history. Revelation's prediction that some of the dead would be resurrected a thousand years before the rest (in the "First Resurrection") was particularly evocative, apparently referring to the revitalization of the church or the literal resurrection of some or all of the righteous departed long before the damned were summoned to face their doom. These millennialist beliefs were held by a significant number of those who took the parliamentary side in the British and Irish civil wars (and were especially popular among Oliver Cromwell's New Model Army). American Puritans who shared these opinions were enthused by the possibility that they might gain more ground in England, Scotland, and Ireland.

More troublingly, the virtual suspension of government censorship in England during the Interregnum facilitated the circulation of a variety of heretical views, including the idea that the resurrection was an allegory for the spiritual elevation of the true believer, rather than an event that would take place after death.[12] Civil and ecclesiastical authorities could not prevent the spread of similar ideas in the colonies. Enlightenment materialism posed a different, but equally dangerous threat, questioning received distinctions between humans, animals, and machines. Radical philosophers attacked the fundamental principles of Christian eschatology and soteriology, denying that humankind possessed a soul that was separate from the body, or even refuting the very possibility of immortality itself.[13] Some Protestants believed that straightforward restatement of biblical teaching was the best way to rebuff these attacks. Others developed innovative defenses of orthodoxy, combining theology with experimental science in an attempt to prove that it was entirely reasonable to believe that dead matter could return to life.[14]

Cosmopolitan colonial ministers followed these debates closely. When, as at Salem, they encountered unusual phenomena that appeared to prove the existence of an invisible world of spirits, they produced empirical studies for the benefit of the wider scientific community.[15] But American resurrection theology was also informed by the general demands of life in the New World. Settled in a far-flung region suspected to be inimical to European life, Protestants meditated on the promise of resurrection to redress their fears about the corporeal degradation and disintegration of individuals and communities. Although many scholars have projected US exceptionalism back onto Puritan writing, colonial eschatologies generally characterized

America's role in the end times in defensive terms. In most accounts of the millennium, the continent was to remain a provincial territory of God's kingdom, rather than a metropolitan center. In the late eighteenth century this would change. The American Revolution encouraged both Protestant theologians and secularists to hope that a global resurrection of political society was taking shape in the new republic.

To Walk the Earth Again explores developments in American Protestant resurrection theology between the 1630s and 1860s. While it discusses a broad range of texts, including histories, funeral sermons, epic and lyric poetry, novels, and eschatological tracts, much of the material assembled in this study is drawn from the New England Congregationalist tradition. The resurrection of the dead was a particularly important concept for Puritans since they saw it as the culmination of the eschatological trajectory by which the true church would emerge from the alleged corruptions of Roman Catholicism. It was also linked to personal conversion: by accepting God's free gift of grace, believers passed from a state of spiritual death to life, prefiguring their future ascension to bodily immortality. Puritan writing on resurrection forms a rich and neglected archive of political-theological thought. Works that considered the mysteries of corporeal life after death addressed the relationships of individual to community, subjects to government, white bodies to bodies of color, humanity to nature. As we shall see, these issues were of special concern for English settlers in the New World. Contemplating the unity and integrity of individual and collective bodies in the world to come helped Anglo-Americans to make sense of their place in a changing and uncertain global order.

This book also examines more unorthodox approaches to resurrection. Seventeenth-century radical sectaries (Anne Hutchinson, Samuel Gorton, and the Quakers) valued conversion's anticipation of the next life so highly that they downplayed the importance of the body's deliverance from the grave. For them, resurrection became a spiritual process that could be completed in the course of mortal existence. Some even suggested that Christ's own conquest of death was less a historical event than a spiritual change that took place within each of his children. The idea that the Bible's eschatological prophecies had been accomplished inevitably shaped its proponents' political views. Those who believed they had already been resurrected within challenged civil government's jurisdiction over religion, claimed the right to establish their own religious communities where they chose, and even (in Gorton's case) denied that the church had or would be ideologically and institutionally purified through historical time. During the colonial revivals of the 1740s and 1750s, a number of itinerant preachers would adopt comparable attitudes, sometimes declaring besides that they would never taste corporeal death at all. Where these religious radicals claimed that a select few had been resurrected without dying, the next generation's political commentators and reformers (including some of the founders of the United States) speculated that the republican reconfiguration of society following the Revolution would eventually offer all Americans moral perfection and long life, secular equivalents of resurrection's advantages.

My analysis of resurrection's transformations in colonial and early national America produces two key insights. First, I challenge the scholarly assumption that early modern Protestantism maintained a largely theocentric and otherworldly view of the afterlife.[16] The abolition of purgatory and proscription of prayers for the dead did lead Protestants to emphasize the remoteness of heaven.[17] At the same time, the belief that humans would return to the flesh presupposed other contiguities between mortal and immortal life. Most obviously, the premise that the same body that had lived on earth would be rewarded or punished throughout eternity was held to reinforce social order. But the prospect of living in a resurrected community on the millennial earth or in heaven structured Protestant political attitudes in other ways as well. If the policies of the British government (including the exclusion of Nonconformists from public office) did not always seem calculated to protect the interests of Congregationalists in America and Independents in England, the resurrection of the church during the millennium guaranteed the survival of the Puritan way. When Christ reigned over the world, these formerly marginalized groups would be given the influence they deserved. Meanwhile, speculative theories about the whitening of bodies of color through resurrection sought to vindicate the potentially controversial evangelization of enslaved Africans. Some white Protestants were worried that slaves would claim that their conversion and/or baptism was grounds for emancipation. The idea that black Christians would not be fit for immortality until the putative stigma of their complexion had been removed justified keeping them in a subordinate position in both church and society in the meantime. For their part, radicals questioned the Puritan claim that Congregational church structure, discipline, and worship prefigured the religious practice of saints after the resurrection. Since the convert's inner spiritual experience was the only true link between earth and heaven, the survival of religious institutions into the next world was moot and their authority in this one was compromised.

In recent years, historians have questioned the long-standing narrative that the Reformation decisively separated the dead from the living. Peter Marshall and Thomas Laqueur have argued that English and European Protestantism retained many of the Roman Catholic burial and memorialization practices that stressed the continuing social presence of the dead.[18] Writing on colonial America, Erik Seeman has shown how Protestants conversed with departed loved ones in various ways. The dead offered counsel directly through dreams and ghostly appearances, as well as figuratively by means of elegiac poetry and headstone inscriptions written from their point of view.[19] This book charts resurrection theology's contribution to this culture of fellowship with the dead, showing how new political developments occasioned different treatments of the relationship. John Cotton, one of the leading theologians of the first cohort of Massachusetts ministers, urged the faithful to identify closely with the saints who had gone before them. Each individual conversion, he insisted, contributed to the ongoing resurrection of the church, signaling the wider adoption of Puritan principles. Two generations later, challenges to Congregationalism's preeminence in New England led Cotton Mather to take a more personal, rather than institutional, approach. Adapting the scientific concept of an ethereal substance that linked matter and spirit, he attempted to explain how the souls of the dead were able to move, act, and recognize each other in heaven. Though physically divided from living saints, they were part of the same community, praying, worshiping, and eagerly anticipating the completion of their redemption through corporeal resurrection. In the nineteenth century, sentimentalist authors and Spiritualists would present their domestic and social visions of the afterlife as a break with austere Puritan eschatology. But while their lack of emphasis on judgment and damnation did distinguish them from their Calvinist forebears, their preoccupation with the celestial reunion of friends and family was part of a long Protestant tradition.

This book's second pivotal claim relates to Protestant resurrection theology's legacy. I contest the persistent idea that Puritanism was especially instrumental in the desacralization and secularization of Western society. Max Weber's criticized but still widely cited analysis of Reformed Christianity's impact on modernity argues that "genuine Puritan[s]" removed all ritual from the burial of the dead to symbolize the inefficacy of all "sacramental forces" with regard to "salvation."[20] This antipathy to magic, combined with a stress on "the corruption of everything pertaining to the flesh," supposedly helped to establish the "disillusioned and pessimistically inclined individualism" that Weber associated with the "worldly asceticism" of Protestant early capitalists.[21] *A Secular Age*, Charles Taylor's monumental overview of secular modernity, makes the related claim that Puritanism's attack on relics and sacraments helped to create a new "buffered" form of selfhood. Where the medieval self was "porous"—open to the invasive influence of spirits and humors—the modern individual is prone to emotional detachment "from everything outside the mind," and consequently more capable of rejecting the existence of the divine altogether. For Taylor, as for Weber, Puritanism's rigorous spiritual discipline and insistence on making productive use of time is at least partially responsible for modernity's *this-worldly* ethos.[22]

To the contrary, I demonstrate that the "heretical" eschatologies of seventeenth- and eighteenth-century religious radicals parallel the secular-modern outlook on death more closely. Since Hutchinson, Gorton, the early Quakers, and the evangelical Immortalists believed that the eschaton had been realized within believers, their teachings on the afterlife and the end of the external, material world were vague and inconsistent. While the Puritans continued to frame a person's last hours on earth as a period of high religious drama, the radicals emptied it of spiritual significance: there was no reason to worry about the destination of the soul of the departed when he or she had already received the full benefit of salvation in life. Denuded of that final mystery, death could be subjected to human comprehension and mastery. Secular moderns, equipped with different tools (advanced medicine and psychological counseling), aspire to exercise a comparable control over the end of existence. Today, the act of dying is seen as essentially meaningless in itself, but open to any interpretation we may choose to place upon it (as well as subject to our medical manipulation). In our secular age, mortality is therefore an essentially personal phenomenon, just as it was for the religious radicals of the 1600s and 1700s.

For all its supposed individualism, mainstream Puritanism typically envisioned mortality along much more communal lines. Puritans may have scorned the Roman Catholic practice of entombing holy relics beneath the altars of churches, but they attributed a tremendous spiritual significance to the risen form of every saint. Although these bodies obviously could not be immediately present in the way that relics were, Puritans strove to bring them near through their writing, as well as in their public and private devotions. That endeavor sometimes involved close contemplation of the material process of resurrection. It was important for believers to have a clear sense of how their victory over death would transpire, since the resurrection of the individual Christian would be the vehicle for the reassembly of a variety of collective bodies (denominational, cultural, national, and ethnic) in the next life. Resurrection could be framed scientifically, but it was also a source of enchantment, imbuing certain polities (the Puritan colonies), identities (white Reformed Christian), and even times (the sabbath) with special holiness. Weber's and Taylor's secularization narratives overlook this dimension of Puritanism, emphasizing instead its apparent anticipation of modernity's aversion to the numinous. This book, by contrast, stresses the distance between the Puritans and us on questions relating to death. Counterintuitively, such an approach is best placed to make their debates on resurrection come alive, opening unfamiliar perspectives on the politics of human mortality.

My journey through Protestant resurrection theology begins with the reaction to the so-called Antinomian Controversy of the 1630s, during which Boston radical Anne Hutchinson claimed that the prophecies of Christ's Second Coming and the future resurrection were fulfilled in each act of conversion. As Revolutionary England debated the direction of its ecclesiastical reformation, Scottish Presbyterian Robert Baillie adduced Hutchinson's heretical ideas to support his contention that the Congregationalist system of church government generated dangerous, socially disruptive beliefs. In defense of American Puritanism, John Cotton and Thomas Shepard suggested that Hutchinson was an exception: Congregationalism's institutional emphasis on gracious conversion produced orderly communities that brought the eschatological purification of wider Christendom closer. Chapter 1, "Resurrection, Selfhood, and the Church," considers the significance of resurrection in these ministers' responses to Hutchinson's provocations. Her claim that conversion was a spiritual resurrection modeled a self-sufficient (or "buffered") sainthood: as conduits of the power of the risen Christ, true believers had little or no need for ministerial direction. In response, Cotton and Shepard set out soteriologies that emphasized (in Charles Taylor's terms) the porosity of the Christian self. They argued that resurrection bound the individual to his or her fellow Christians, to the church, and to dead saints.

The chapter also addresses two other varieties of realized eschatology that challenged Puritan orthodoxy in seventeenth-century New England. Like Hutchinson, the early Quakers and Samuel Gorton maintained that conversion was a spiritual resurrection that accomplished Christ's eschatological return. I explain how Gorton developed what might be called a proto-secularist theology from this premise, denying the legitimacy of religious institutions and even rejecting the concept of sacred history. God had no reason to select particular denominations, nations, or colonies as agents of his will—his providential plan was constantly being accomplished in a sphere entirely disconnected from worldly politics. The Quakers, meanwhile, would eventually moderate the anti-institutional impetus of their eschatology. As they turned their revolutionary movement into a respectable Protestant denomination and planted their own American colony, Quakers claimed (somewhat misleadingly) that they held conventional eschatological beliefs. In so doing, the Quaker leadership conceded that faith in a future corporeal resurrection of the dead and Second Coming was essential for the maintenance of political order.

Chapter 2, "Cotton Mather and the First Resurrection," discusses Mather's adaption of Puritan resurrection theology around turn of the eighteenth century. Scholarly consensus holds that the Puritans did not believe that political identities would be carried over into the next life: nations would only be collectively rewarded or punished for their piety or lack of it within the course of secular history. This assumption makes it easier to identify continuities between Puritan political ideas and their modern counterparts. Taking the opposite approach, I focus on an aspect of Mather's political thought that is more alien to contemporary sensibilities. The revocation of Massachusetts's old charter and the enforced toleration of other Protestant groups left him less certain of Congregationalism's immediate prospects than his forebears had been and consequently less inclined to invest the preservation of its institutional forms with eschatological significance. Instead, he emphasized personal connections between New England's saints and the global kingdom of Christ he believed would be established in the millennium. Reading a key biblical prophecy (Revelation 20:4–6) literally, he claimed that the beginning of the end times would see every elect person among the dead physically resurrected to serve as the ruling elite of the millennial earth. Even if Congregationalism could no longer take its influence over Massachusetts society for granted, it could find solace in the thought that an exceptionally high proportion of its departed members would take part in this First Resurrection. When these saints returned, they would serve as a living link between the experimental piety that had been practiced in the Puritan colonies and the church of the New Earth.

Mather claimed that human life during the millennium would be radically different—there would be no sin and no death then. Nevertheless, he also stressed the contiguity of this world and the next. While the dead elect were physically absent, they were vital members of every community of living saints. With them added to the count of the faithful, things did not seem so bleak for the Reformed Protestant cause. Throughout his career, Mather reminded Congregationalists in America and Nonconformists in England that though they might seem peripheral to the present order, they were members of the "party" that would go on to rule over the planet. As I demonstrate, this denominational perspective was much less pronounced in the eschatological rhetoric of Benjamin Colman, minister of Boston's Brattle Street Church and a leading figure in the next generation of New England pastors.

Chapter 3, "Resurrection's Racial Politics," shows how Protestant eschatology responded to the hardening of legal, political, and social distinctions between Africans and Europeans across North America and the Caribbean over the eighteenth century. This development coincided with renewed efforts by Anglican, Presbyterian, Congregationalist, and Quaker missionaries to convert enslaved Africans (as well as Native Americans). Typically, advocates stressed that the baptism of the enslaved would not alter their socioeconomic status in this world: only in the next life would they receive spiritual equality. Contemporary scholars have tended to accept this rhetoric at face value. While the legal and scientific discourses of ethnic difference gradually coalesced into the modern concept of biological race, they argue, Protestants continued to believe that divergences between different peoples would be transcended in heaven and through resurrection. I question that assumption, through close readings of works by Cotton Mather, his friend Samuel Sewall, and John Beach, a Connecticut Anglican associated with the English Society for the Propagation of the Gospel. Even when these authors explicitly insisted that racial difference would be of no consequence in the world to come, the details of their eschatological and millennial schemes implied otherwise. Each of them suggested, in strikingly different ways, that it was impossible to imagine that a resurrected body could be black, thereby underlining the subaltern standing of Christians of color in mortal life.

The chapter also outlines how the first black writers to be published in English responded to racialized constructions of salvation (which the evangelical revivalism that developed in the middle of the century continued to employ). Poets Jupiter Hammon and Phillis Wheatley adopted the traditional Christian rhetoric that associated blackness with sinfulness, but they did so advisedly, insisting that people of any complexion could be in thrall to spiritual darkness. Other authors, including Ottobah Cugoano and Ignatius Sancho, explicitly contested the notion that black bodies would not be welcome in heaven. As they suggested, the doctrine of resurrection would have to be recast for a truly inclusive model of global humanity to be established.

Extending the exploration of revivalist theology begun in chapter 3, chapter 4, "Thomas Prince and the Resurrection of the World," focuses on the extensive and varied writings of Boston minister Thomas Prince (1687–1758). Although he was a prominent promoter of the awakenings of the 1740s, Prince had misgivings about the evangelical approach of some of his colleagues, including George Whitefield and Gilbert Tennent. These influential preachers linked conversion and resurrection so closely that some of their auditors were inspired to literalize their metaphor, coming to believe that it was possible to be corporeally resurrected through spiritual conversion. For his part, Prince urged the faithful to adopt a broader soteriological perspective and accept that no individual's regeneration would be complete until the planet itself had been environmentally purified at the beginning of the millennium. He hoped that this approach would not only lessen the chances of an ecclesiastical schism between moderates and radicals but would also give Christians a fuller sense of their relationship to the rest of God's creation. To that end, he encouraged his parishioners to take a close interest in the physical processes by which both their own resurrections and the renovation of the earth would take place.

I show how this fascination with the transition from this world to the next distinguished Prince from some of his clerical contemporaries in Boston. In common with Benjamin Colman, Thomas Foxcroft, and Ebenezer Pemberton, he celebrated the extent to which the British Empire and the wider Protestant interest was seemingly making the globe a more orderly and productive place. But where these other ministers tended to identify sinful behavior as the primary disruptor of this improvement, Prince placed an equal weight on the debilitating corruption of the earth's natural environment. In eschatological tracts and funeral sermons, he therefore considered the latest scientific explanations of how the Fall and the Flood had distorted the earth's orbit and degraded its atmosphere. For him, he best way to navigate the disorienting exigencies of an ever-changing earth was to set one's sights on its resurrection, when globalization's haphazard course would be definitively corrected. Prince's career, I argue, represented the high-water mark for this kind of physico-theological speculation in America. In the nineteenth century, theologians such as John Nelson Darby and Joseph Smith would continue to connect individual salvation with the eschatological transfiguration of the planet. But where Prince was determined to understand the formation of the New Earth scientifically (as far as was possible), they were prepared to trust in God's mysterious power to transform the world in an instant.

Chapter 5, "Secular Resurrections," investigates the conceptual afterlives of corporeal resurrection in the early national and antebellum eras. As American writers and politicians considered the future of their young country, they repurposed the doctrine's promise that fragile, fallible bodies would be integrated into a triumphant, enduring collective. Many of them expected that the rationalization and democratization of economic and social structures would bring about a biopolitical enhancement of the US citizenry, lengthening lives and perfecting mental capacities. But there was disagreement as to how this secular progress related to the Protestant eschatological tradition. According to Thomas Jefferson, Benjamin Franklin, Tom Paine, and other radicals, Americans needed to move beyond belief in corporeal resurrection to reach their full secular potential. Benjamin Rush, conversely, insisted that the republican principle of social and political resurrection was fully compatible with Protestant teachings about the afterlife. John Adams, meanwhile, adopted an intervening position. His attempt to balance political progressivism and conservatism was mirrored by his trade-off between universalist and conventional Protestant eschatologies: though he was certain that heaven was real, he denied that the dead would need to exchange mortal vileness for resurrected glory to be worthy of eternal life.

The chapter concludes with a discussion of Spiritualist, sentimental, and materialist treatments of resurrection in the middle of the nineteenth century. During this period, sentimental novelists and Spiritualist theologians contrasted their accounts of heaven with Calvinism's supposedly impersonal afterlife. Nonetheless, I show that their respective emphases on the heavenly reunion of family and friends and the eternal expansion of human capabilities have close analogues in earlier Puritan texts. Literary authors Henry David Thoreau, Edgar Allan Poe, and George Lippard frequently described bodies that were dismembered, decaying, or trapped between life and death. Poe's short stories and Lippard's novel *The Quaker City* also featured misguided or fraudulent attempts to return the dead to life artificially. These writers' fixation with the material afterlife of the corpse appears to register a skepticism toward theological and secular claims that the body can be perfected. But with Poe and Lippard in particular, the compulsive depiction of cadavers that refuse to rest quiet suggests the lingering influence of the old Protestant yearning for corporeal life after death.

In the early twenty-first century, faith in human immortality is still central to many people's understanding of the world. But modern secularism has narrowed the scope of religious belief. Salvation tends to be framed as an individual—or familial—concern. Ideas about heaven are assumed to reflect personal conviction, or adherence to a particular cultural tradition, rather than to constitute a perception of objective truth. The survival of one's soul is therefore disconnected from the future of humanity as a whole or the fate of the planet. Belief in bodily resurrection has also waned among Christians. By the end of the nineteenth century, Protestants were increasingly inclined to take it for granted that God would carry them safely into the next life—they were no longer overly concerned by the corporeal nature of celestial existence (cremation became more socially acceptable as a result).[23] That attitude is now entrenched: very few of those who profess to believe in resurrection would consider it expedient to produce a plausible explanation of the process. The perpetuation of consciousness is all that is necessary for immortal life. As Fernando Vidal observes, the prevalence of this view betrays the modern sense that "our bodies are ... things we own, not entities we are."[24]

Then why study resurrection's history today? The coming years are set to transform attitudes to death, as people around the world experience mortality along progressively unequal lines. Climate change and global pandemics will shorten the lives of the earth's most vulnerable and impoverished populations. Meanwhile, the digital revolution will continue to transform healthcare in wealthy countries, promising to extend lives significantly while offering more control over how people die. Though the notion of an eternal corporeal existence may seem hopelessly outdated, critical engagement with early American resurrection theology may help to elucidate the current situation. The conviction that they would rise again in bodily form forced seventeenth and eighteenth-century Protestants to contemplate death as a collective and political phenomenon. Their discussions of resurrection and depictions of the world to come were inevitably flawed, indicative of contingent denominational, national, and racial biases. Yet their insight that death ties us to other people, as well as to the world around us, remains valuable. The uncertain future of human mortality demands that this perspective be adopted again.

1
Resurrection, Selfhood, and the Church

Eschatological Innovation in the Seventeenth Century

In the first four decades of the seventeenth century, the next world changed forever. Across Europe, and especially in England, a considerable number of Protestants came to believe that the thousand years of Christ's rule over the earth predicted in Revelation 20:1–10 were yet to begin. Through the 1500s, most (but not all) exegetes had accepted St. Augustine's claim that the millennium was already in progress and that Christ reigned spiritually within the hearts of believers. But the writings of Thomas Brightman (1562–1607), Johann Alsted (1588–1638), and Joseph Mede (1586–1638) encouraged Protestants to expect a future period in which their church would triumph over its Roman Catholic enemy and the global political scene would be transformed.[1]

This fresh eschatological approach brought with it new understandings of the future resurrection of the dead. Up until then, Protestant (and Catholic) orthodoxy had followed Augustine's argument that every human being, the righteous and the wicked, would be corporeally resurrected on Judgment Day.[2] Yet the new millennial models suggested the possibility that there might be more than one time of resurrection. Revelation 20:4–6 spoke of a "First Resurrection" of martyrs that would take place a thousand years before "the rest of the dead" would return to their bodies. Augustine assumed that this passage described the saints' conversion during mortal life.[3] By contrast, Brightman believed that it referred to a period in which the church would be regenerated as "more cleare truth . . . returne[d] to the world."[4] Alsted and Mede, meanwhile, claimed that the martyrs would be physically resurrected at the beginning of the millennium, to enable them to rule over the world as Christ's representatives (the rest of the elect would be resurrected on Doomsday).[5] More variations of these two models would emerge as the seventeenth century progressed.

Any theology that split the future resurrection into different parts was potentially socially and politically disruptive. Those who followed Brightman in anticipating a regeneration of the church might become too precisionist in their ecclesiology, excluding those who failed to meet their standards of spiritual purity. Meanwhile, the corporeal First Resurrection and political reign of saints described by Alsted and Mede could incite violent insurrection, as believers fought to establish God's rule or else die as martyrs. Subscribers to either interpretation could seek wide-ranging ecclesiastical and legal reform in an attempt to anticipate the ways of the coming kingdom. Finally, a diverse range of radicals who understood resurrection as an internal, spiritual event sought to overturn social conventions. Following a path established by sixteenth-century Anglo-German mystical sect the Family of Love, these groups claimed that resurrected perfection could be achieved individually within this life.

Radical eschatological ideas flourished during the British and Irish civil wars of 1638–1653, not least due to the collapse of the print-licensing system that had operated through the Stationers' Company with episcopal and government supervision.[6] From 1645, beliefs that a political and/or supernatural millennium was imminent circulated within Oliver Cromwell's New Model Army. During Cromwell's Protectorate, a group of radical soldiers and Parliamentarians known as the Fifth Monarchists pressured him to establish a fully theocratic government of saints in England.[7] At the Westminster Assembly (1643–1653), ministerial debates over the ongoing reformation of the Church of England were closely informed by eschatological ideas.

As the delegates considered the best way to structure the church, appoint its clergy, and rewrite its liturgy, they were presented with millennial theories by both English Independents and Scottish Presbyterians.[8] The ecclesiastical polity of New England was also scrutinized as a possible model for a church that aspired to millennial purity. Independents Thomas Goodwin and Philip Nye endorsed John Cotton's explanation of the Congregationalist system as a "*Middle-way*" between Presbyterianism's hierarchical church government of regional and national assemblies and Independency's autonomous local congregations.[9] Scottish Presbyterian commissioner Robert Baillie fiercely criticized Cotton's scheme, arguing that it facilitated the dissemination of heretical opinions: once "a few persons" had "locked themselves up within the narrow walls of one Congregation... [and] made themselves uncontroulable by any or all upon the earth," they "open[ed] a wide doore to any erroneous spirit, to mislead them towards what ever fancy can enter into any cracked braine."[10]

Though he was concerned by eschatological fancies in particular, Baillie had some millennial hopes himself. The dedication of *A Dissuasive from the Errors of the Time* (1645), his critique of Congregationalism, concluded with his expectation that Britain's churches would soon be bathed in a spiritual "brightnesse."[11] Crawford Gribben clarifies that like most Scottish Covenanters Baillie believed that the Jewish people and most of the rest of the world would eventually convert to Christianity, and that the wider adoption of the Presbyterian model of ecclesiology would help to make this possible.[12] Yet Baillie was wary of any claim that a totally pure church could be established on earth. And as we shall see, he was especially suspicious of some of the claims that Congregational eschatology made about the resurrection of the dead.

Taking Baillie's attack as its starting point, this chapter will explore the resurrection theologies produced by Puritans and other radical Protestants across the seventeenth-century North Atlantic, with a special focus on New England. The authors I will discuss include members of New England's Congregationalist standing order (John Cotton and Thomas Shepard), as well as a range of more unconventional thinkers (Anne Hutchinson, Samuel Gorton, and various Quakers) who challenged Puritan orthodoxy by arguing that the prophecies of the resurrection of the dead had already been realized. I will consider in detail how these competing eschatological beliefs represented different approaches to the organization of religious and civil communities in colonial America. But I will also address their longer-term significance. Puritan theology has often been seen as formative of secular-modern attitudes toward selfhood and mortality. I will argue, however, that it was the Puritans' radical adversaries (or progeny, according to Baillie) who anticipated contemporary perspectives on these issues more closely.

Robert Baillie's Attack on Resurrection Theology in New England

Baillie attempted to identify Congregationalism with two dangerous misreadings of the doctrine of resurrection. First, he seized on the 1636–1638 controversy in Boston over the teachings of Anne Hutchinson. Citing

John Winthrop's recently published account of Hutchinson's civil trial and examination by the ministers of the Bay Colony, Baillie set out the several ways in which her teachings broke with conventional theologies of salvation and resurrection. Saints, she believed, had both a "fleshly" and a spiritual body. In the instant of conversion, the latter was "united" with Christ, making its owner no longer capable of sin. Hutchinson therefore denied that Christ's physical form had ascended into heaven: rather than sitting at the right hand of the Father, he was mystically present within the men and women who comprised his church on earth. This conflation of the ordinary work of sanctification with the incarnation of the godhead was troubling for several reasons, not least because it threatened to render belief in judgment and life after death redundant.

Though Baillie highlighted the formerly close relationship between Hutchinson and her mentor John Cotton, "the greatest promoter and patron of Independency,"[13] he stopped short of claiming that all Congregationalists held unorthodox views. Instead, he claimed that they subscribed to another eschatology that was in some ways opposite to Hutchinson's. "Our Brethren[]," he alleged, believe that "in the year 1650, or at furthest, 1695, Christ in his humane nature and present glory is to come from heaven unto Jerusalem where he was crucified" (224). "At the same time," he added, "all the Martyrs, and many of the Saints both of the Old and New Testament are to rise in their bodies[,] [and] the Jewes from all the places where now they are scattered shall return to Canaan" (224–25). Once Christ had violently subdued "all the disobedient Nations," he would reign for a thousand years before the "second resurrection of all the dead good and bad for the last judgement" (225). During that millennium, Baillie affirmed, Congregationalists expected "to live without sinne[,] ... [enjoying] great worldly delights, begetting many children, eating and drinking and injoying all the lawfull pleasures which all the creatures then redeemed from their ancient slavery can afford."

This millenarianism outlined a corporeal resurrection that was yet to come, while Hutchinson described a spiritual return to life that saints had already accomplished. Yet Baillie objected to these contrary perspectives for the same reasons. As he saw it, each took an exclusive, elitist attitude toward resurrection. Hutchinson and others of her mystical persuasion allegorized the doctrine, characterizing it as something that only those who had been spiritually amalgamated with Christ could understand. Millenarians may have expected all of humanity to rise again on the day of judgment, but (in his account) they reserved the reward of a second life on earth for the martyrs and notable saints who would participate in the First Resurrection at the beginning of the millennium. Resurrection, Baillie insisted, was not a "rare and singular . . . priviledge," but the destiny of "all the Godly" (227), who would "rise immediately to a Heavenly Glory" on Doomsday (228). "Christs Marriage with his Church," he added, "is not solemnized with a part of his Elect, but with the whole bodie at the generall resurrection" (234). This point was linked to Baillie's objection to a major aspect of Congregationalist discipline. He thought that overly discriminating attitudes to church membership that required a convincing profession of saving faith from newcomers were doomed to produced fragile congregations prone to schism. Like most Presbyterians, Baillie believed that as "long as [the church was] upon the earth," it would remain "a mixed multitude, of Elect and Reprobate, good and bad, . . . a company that hath neede of the Word and Sacraments, [and] of Prayer and Ordinances." Only the resurrection and judgment at the end of the world would separate these two groups.

Baillie's highly partisan summary overgeneralized and misrepresented Congregationalist eschatology. Far from all English Independents and New England Puritans believed that Christ would return in person at the beginning of the chiliad, and some, including Cotton himself, saw the millennium as a period of "brightening" when the church would return to the purity of the apostolic era, but would still have to contend with the sinfulness and frailty of humanity's fallen condition. Nevertheless, Baillie was right to draw a connection between conventional Puritan and unorthodox radical theologies, insofar as both sought to reshape church and society on the basis of claims about who would be or already had been resurrected as a saint. Although most seventeenth-century Protestants, including Laudian Anglicans, described spiritual rebirth in this life as a kind of preview of the future glories of resurrection,[14] Congregationalists and Independents were inclined to restrict church membership to those who had experienced such a foretaste of life eternal. In this respect, their soteriology was indeed analogous to that of various "heretical" groups they sought to distance themselves from (and in some cases found it necessary to persecute). While the term "realized eschatology" is most commonly used to describe the beliefs of Quakers, Familists, and other radicals, some orthodox Puritans also employed rhetoric that suggested that individual conversion spiritually fulfilled certain aspects of the Bible's eschatological prophecies.[15] Furthermore, some Puritan varieties of ecclesiology were premised on the notion that Congregational worship and governance was particularly consonant with the way in which the church would be organized during the millennium and even in heaven itself.

According to Baillie, his Independent/Congregationalist rivals were at once too secular and too supernatural. Their belief that a pure church would be established on earth during the millennium led them to focus too closely on worldly politics in a misconceived attempt to hasten that eventuality. On the other hand, their overly expansive understanding of the spiritual transformation worked by conversion encouraged them in the delusion that saints on earth already dwelt in a spiritual paradise. Some of the most influential modern studies of the Reformation have followed this lead, arguing that Puritan eschatology decisively shifted the borders between the secular and sacred spheres of Western culture. Max Weber hypothesized that Puritanism sanctified economic productivity in order to relieve the sense of soteriological isolation created by its abolition of purgatory and doctrine of predestination. Since they could no longer ease their anxieties about the next life through donations to "religious institutions" such as chantries and monasteries, or via participation in the "magic" of sacramental ritual, Reformed Christians searched for signs of their election in their material successes.[16] More recently, Carlos Eire has cast early modern Calvinists as "avatars of modernity" in their attitude toward mortality and the sacred. The Puritans, he claims, stressed the radical otherness of the supernatural plane to mortal existence and conceived of death as "an unbridgeable metaphysical and ontological chasm in time and space."[17] These positions set the stage for the disenchanted world of the present. Furthermore, Puritanism's emphasis on the special providential role played by the elect prefigured the modern tendency to find quasi-religious significance in secular success. As "God's agents on earth," saints were imbued with "an aura of divinity" that sacralized their religious and civil endeavors.[18]

The readings that follow contest this account of Puritanism's role in the secularization of the West. My analysis of works by John Cotton and Thomas Shepard will demonstrate that New England Congregationalists were more closely attuned to traditional Christian attitudes to death and the afterlife than Weber and Eire suppose. It is certainly true that some Congregationalists used resurrection as a symbol of the self-sufficiency of the converted saint. Accentuating the connection between conversion and resurrection was a means of defending Congregationalism's lack of higher ecclesiastical officers (if church members were already halfway to heaven, then congregations and their ministers would not require supervision from an extensive disciplinary hierarchy). But Puritan authors also argued that resurrection linked Christians to the living, the dead, and those yet to be born.

In the texts I discuss here, Cotton and Shepard are concerned with the communal and institutional aspects of mortality. Both ministers described individual conversion as a kind of resurrection of the soul. They curbed any antinomian sentiment that might arise from that analogy by underscoring the limitations of the mortal human body. Because the soul was tethered to a frail lump of flesh, the hard road to heaven was not one that could be walked alone. Though they rejected the Roman Catholic belief that saving grace could only be received through the ministrations of the church, Congregationalists still held that those searching for salvation required the support of ministers, peers, and textual example. The prospective resurrection of believers was therefore framed as a public concern, their risen bodies as testaments to the other saints who had watched over them in life. Cotton and Shepard were also concerned with the resurrection of the church itself. On this topic they had their disagreements—Shepard did not share his colleague's conviction that the regenerated church of the millennium would be entirely composed of true believers. Yet each identified eagerness to rise together with the saints on Judgment Day as a key marker of vital, genuine faith.

This was, in part, a defensive measure, necessitated by the proliferation of unorthodox eschatologies in the middle decades of the seventeenth century. My discussion of these heretical theologies will reveal that it was their adherents, rather than the Puritans as a whole, who prefigured the modern, secular approach to death. Anne Hutchinson, Samuel Gorton, and the Quakers all understood the rebirth of the converted believer differently (George Fox, for instance, saw the growing number of men and women turning to Quakerism's "inner light" as evidence that a new holy age was at hand, whereas Gorton denied that there could be any such thing as a novel development in sacred history). Yet they all thought that spiritual resurrection elevated the individual above conventional remedies for anxiety about mortality (for Catholics, the church's sacramental rites, for Protestants, its ministry of the Word). This internally accomplished eschaton provided the radical saint with an unmediated and personal link to God and the heavenly sphere, thereby anticipating one of the key features of Charles Taylor's model of secular modernity: the individual's "direct access" to sources of transcendent meaning and authority.[19] Furthermore, the possibility of rising from the grave in the course of mortal life denuded the deathbed of much, perhaps all, of its spiritual significance. Orthodox Puritans viewed the weeks, days, and hours before death as a critical time in the saint's journey to salvation, as an ordeal that often (but not always) indicated whether he or she would reach that destination.[20] Radicals, conversely, contended that the final moments of life were not particularly important from a religious point of view, since the true convert had already conquered mortality. Their concept of inner resurrection was therefore analogous to the secular precept that wherever possible each individual should have control over the terms of his or her death.

Baillie claimed that Hutchinson's influence over the Boston church had left the Massachusetts Bay Colony "in a clear hazard of utter Ruine."[21] Though Cotton and Shepard unsurprisingly did not share that view, their responses to the so-called Antinomian Crisis and to the growth of other radical theologies underlined the political danger that realized eschatology posed to Christian commonwealths. Understandably, they were particularly concerned by the possible attenuation of ministerial influence in New England: the bold claims that Hutchinson, Gorton, and the Quakers made about the spiritual power granted to those who receive eternal life without dying signaled their determination that laypeople should be respected as religious leaders.[22] Yet the battle between heretical and orthodox resurrection theologies also held wilder implications. The Puritans' commitment to resurrection as a collective phenomenon reflected their sense of heaven as a place in which earthly communities of the elect would be reconstituted. While the radicals also sought to build religious associations of various kinds, they could not imagine them carrying over to the next life in the same way. Hutchinson and Gorton were more focused on the spiritual joys of the believer in the present; the early Quakers suggested that it was possible to win eternal life without belonging to any type of church at all. Their rhetoric of individual self-sufficiency may have been couched in transcendental, eschatological language, but it nonetheless anticipated the modern propensity to value personal fulfillment in this life above all else.

Conversion as the "Cominge of Christ": Anne Hutchinson's Realized Eschatology

Anne Hutchinson's challenge to the patriarchal authority of the government and clergy of Massachusetts Bay has occupied a prominent place in historical and literary studies of colonial America. Nineteenth and early twentieth-century scholars enshrined her as a martyr for what they saw as the quintessentially American cause of freedom of conscience and religion.[23] More recent work has cited Hutchinson's defiant performance in her trials as evidence of resistance to Puritan orthodoxy on a range of topics, including rules of representation in language, gender relations, and the economics of trade.[24] Bar a few notable exceptions, commentators have tended not to dwell on Hutchinson's unconventional opinions about resurrection, concentrating instead on her claim to have received immediate instruction from the Holy Spirit or her argument that she could alter her descriptions of her beliefs without being said to have altered the beliefs themselves.[25]

However, the summary of her church trial at Boston in March 1638 makes it clear that the ministers accusing her of heresy saw her views on resurrection as among her most dangerous: the first four charges of the sixteen that were brought against her on the first day of the proceedings directly concern resurrection theology. Thomas Shepard, minister of Cambridge, alleged that Hutchinson had said:

1. That the Soules ... of all men by Nature are mortal.
2. That those ... that are united to Christ have 2 Bodies, Christs, and a new Body and you knew not how Christ should be united to our fleshly Body.
3. That our Bodies shall not rise ... with Christ Jesus, not the same Bodies at the last day.
4. That the Resurrection mentioned [in] 1 Corinthians 15 is not of our Resurrection at the last day, but of our Union to Christ Jesus.[26]

A little later in the hearing, Thomas Savage (who would later marry one of Hutchinson's daughters and join the family in exile) complained that the assembled church members ought to be given more time to deliberate over the allegations relating to the accused's beliefs about the resurrection of the body and the immortality of the soul. Minister John Wilson strongly disagreed. "It was usuiall in the former Times," he observed, "whan any Blasphyemie or Idolatrie was held foreth," for the people "to rent thear Garments and tare thear hare of thear heads in signe of Lothinge. And if we deny the Resurrection of the Body than let us turne Epicures. Let us eate and drinke and doe any Thinge, tomorrow we shall dye" (357). Delivering a formal admonition at the end of the first day of the trial, John Cotton expressed a comparable sentiment, claiming that Hutchinson's beliefs "set an open Doore to an Epicurism and Libertinisme; if this be soe . . . than let us nayther fear Hell nor the loss of Heaven; than let us beleve thare is nayther Ayngelles nor Spirits" (372).

Why, exactly, were these ministers so disturbed by what they gathered from their examination of Hutchinson? In the course of the trial, it emerged that Thomas Shepard's accusations were broadly accurate: the accused held that men and women did not possess immortal souls at birth but were granted everlasting life in the instant of their conversion (in her words, "*The Soul is immortall by Redemption*") (359). Hutchinson described this process both as a "Resurrection" (351) and as a "Cominge of Christ" (358) through which the soul of the saint was spiritually unified with the Son of God. The "Graces," or refined religious capabilities and sensibilities that believers exhibited after their conversion, she believed to "*flow from Christ*"—to emanate directly from the soul's union with God, rather than from the saints themselves (this implied that the outward behavior of a Christian was no likely sign of his or her salvation) (375). While Hutchinson did not deny that saints would be corporeally resurrected on Doomsday, she insisted that they would be granted entirely new forms, since their "fleshly Bodies" were not worthy of being joined to Christ (364).

These ideas were not new, being comparable to the ancient heresy of mortalism (which held that the soul dies with the body) as well as the beliefs of the Family of Love (who also described conversion as an amalgamation of the soul with the Godhead). Though modern scholars have often followed the Puritans' official narrative of the trials in ascribing Hutchinson and her followers an exceptional status, the unconventional eschatological and soteriological views she expressed in the trial were not uncommon in early Massachusetts and would attract many new advocates in the ideological ferment of the British and Irish civil wars.[27] The colonial church establishment, then, was so exercised by Hutchinson because they knew that beliefs like hers were not particularly unusual, and indeed were a particular temptation for Protestants raised in the conversion-centered Calvinist tradition. Their response was typical. Throughout the seventeenth century, orthodox ministers would make the same point as they did about the political danger posed by challenges to the doctrine of resurrection. If the people were encouraged to doubt the idea that the body they occupied would be punished or rewarded for their actions in this life, they would be much less inclined to obey civil and religious authorities.

As the interlocutors at Hutchinson's church trial recognized, making the saint's transcendence of mortality something that happened in this life, rather than after it, utterly undermined the church's soteriological and moral purchase over the individual believer. Resurrected Christians had no need of the disciplinary regime of the Puritan Sunday, as they were already living in the blessedness of an eternal sabbath.[28] Nor were they subject to the law of wedlock. Peter Bulkeley told Hutchinson that "if the Resurrection be past than Marriage is past" (362), alluding to Christ's saying that those who "rise from the dead . . . neither marry nor are given in marriage" (Mark 12:25). The logical outcome of her realized eschatology, therefore, was the principle of "*the Communitie of Weomen*"—the idea that men and women could freely share sexual partners, which Bulkeley, John Winthrop, John Cotton, and John Davenport all associated with the sixteenth-century Familists.[29] Hutchinson responded that she "*abhor*[red] *that practice*" and implied that she would therefore reconsider her claims about resurrection (362). On the second day of the hearing, moreover, she claimed that she now saw that she had been "deceaved" and recognized that her "opinion" on the subject "was very dayngerous" (375). Thomas Shepard, however, was unconvinced by this change of heart. Though we must be wary of uncritically accepting his conclusion, the balance of evidence does indeed suggest that Hutchinson had not actually renounced her previous position.[30]

Modern interpreters of the trials have generally agreed that Hutchinson's defiance of her questioners modeled a distinctive and innovative form of selfhood. Some have argued that she embodied a cohesive personality defined by fidelity to the conscience rather than conformity to established norms.[31] Others have suggested instead that Hutchinson acted as if the self was split, and that there was no fixed relationship between her external words and deeds and what she really felt and believed.[32] Bridging these two approaches, Bryce Traister argues that her performance "separate[d] the credible, internally apprehended self from its falsification in a public order."[33] Hutchinson's insistence that her spiritual experience could not be articulated in conventional theological language foreshadowed the ethical sovereignty of secular personhood, as well as the modern separation of private religious faith from civic life. Traister also describes the historiographical process by which her unruly and mystical female subjectivity has been transformed into an icon of American political liberty.[34] As he notes, Hutchinson's body (the "monstrous birth" it issued after her exile; the supposed incompatibility of its female gender with religious leadership) has played a significant symbolic role in this narrative.[35] During her church trial, however, her accusers were more preoccupied by her beliefs about the eschatological location of Christ's body (and of the resurrected bodies of the elect). As I will demonstrate now, her position on this subject was central to the secularizing potential of the religious identity she performed.

The sixth of Thomas Shepard's charges to be laid against Hutchinson at the outset of her trial ran as follows: "That you had no scripture to Warrant Christ beinge now in Heaven in his humane Nature" (352). The examiners would repeatedly return to variations on this issue. Did Hutchinson believe that the saints who rose again when Christ was resurrected were now in paradise in "the same Bodies that wear dead and layd in thear Graves"? Were "the *very Bodys of Moses Eliah and Enoch . . . taken up into the Heavens*, or no?" (364). Though Hutchinson obfuscated, it eventually became clear that she thought that the elect would be granted entirely new spiritual bodies and souls when they entered heaven. Furthermore, she did indeed doubt that Christ was corporeally present in heaven, emphasizing instead his spiritual communion with the converted. As John Davenport recognized, these were "not slight matters." In his view, Hutchinson's opinions shook "the very foundation" of the Christian "fayth."

Davenport was right. Not only did her ideas undermine the key doctrines of the incarnation and future resurrection of the dead, but they also contested the church's pastoral guidance of believers. While Congregationalists rejected the Roman Catholic claim that salvation depended on participation in the sacramental rituals enacted by the church, they retained a strong sense of the duty of ordained ministers to preside over religious ordinances and supervise the religious and moral lives of their parishioners. Though Christ ruled providentially over the whole of creation, ministers exercised a personal control over the church on his behalf, until his return. But if Christ's body were not actually in heaven, and was instead spiritually dispersed among the saints, then the church's vicarious application of his authority was superfluous.

Hutchinson did not attempt to overthrow the church of Boston. Before excommunication and exile were forced upon her, she did not even try to separate from the congregation. Nonetheless, her enemies suspected that she sought the same level of influence as the town's ordained ministers. In the private theological discussion meetings (or "conventicles") that she held at her home, she railed against all of the Massachusetts clergy (with the exception of John Cotton). Hutchinson and her allies (who included the governor of the colony, Sir Henry Vane) also attempted to have her brother-in-law

John Wheelwright installed as one of the ministers of the Boston church.[36] Though this attempt failed, at least one of her followers saw her as the foremost spiritual figure in New England at the time. In his 1650 history of the colonies, Edward Johnson noted that a man had told him that Hutchinson "Preaches better Gospell then any of your black-coates that have been at the Ninneversity," adding that he "had rather hear such a one that speakes from the meere motion of the spirit, without any study at all, then any of your learned Scollers."[37] As the man's remarks suggest, lay ministry was a logical extension of Hutchinson's theology. The resurrected Christ moved within her—that fact alone gave her the power to preach and to lead.

Though Hutchinson laid claim to religious authority, her challenge to the Boston ministry possessed a transformative, secularizing potential. According to Charles Taylor, modernity presupposes that each individual is (theoretically) "equidistant" from the central institutions around which his or her political community revolves—the government, citizenship, society, humanity itself. By contrast, premodern polities were hierarchical in a symbolic as well as a socioeconomic sense: certain privileged figures (quintessentially the king and the clergy) were the nodes through which those lower down were connected to the fundamental "order of things." The erosion of this system of "mediated access" to meaning helped to produce what Taylor describes as the "buffered self" of secular modernity—an individualist subjectivity that is not necessarily isolated from the outside world but cherishes the possibility of "disengaging" from it emotionally and intellectually.[38]

"This self" is inclined to "see itself as invulnerable, as master of the meanings of things for it," as "giving its own autonomous order to its life." A buffered person, furthermore, assumes that her "emotional life" takes place "in an inner, mental space." In the premodern period, a "porous" kind of selfhood predominated. A porous person conceives of his individuality in more material terms, as something that is closely tied to his body. Since his "inside . . . is also [an] outside," physical substances (the sacramental host, the four humors) and external agents (angels or demons) are able to alter the way in which he experiences the world.[39]

Hutchinson's denial "that Christ Jesus is united to [the] Bodies" of believers in the course of conversion demonstrates that she subscribed to the buffered model of selfhood (362). Conversion was entirely an inward, mental process. Once it had taken place, no outside force—the ministry, the world, the flesh—could loose the mystic bond between the saint and her Christ. The ministers' claim that this position opened the way for libertinism was halfway true. Hutchinson's approach was entirely compatible with fervent faith and rigorous spiritual self-discipline (Taylor insists that buffered people can still be religious).[40] But the untouchable self that she described could equally be driven by entirely secular ambitions—power, fame, desire. And while she professed to believe in a future resurrection, her insistence that the resurrected body was not the same as the mortal frame threatened to subvert faith in the world to come. Removing this material link between the present life and the next could be the first step toward rejecting the idea of an afterlife altogether. Moreover, the conviction that a saint's salvation was fully accomplished here and now seemed to render postmortem glory superfluous.

John Cotton and Thomas Shepard's longer-form responses to the radical ideas that Hutchinson and others had espoused therefore emphasized the porosity of the Christian individual. Mortal men and women would always be vulnerable to sin, hypocrisy, and mental and physical distempers. Conversion ameliorated this exposed condition, but only to a certain extent. It worked a real change within the elect persons, transforming both their experience and their behavior, but it could not eradicate their flaws and weaknesses altogether. Only at the resurrection of all the dead would that perfecting transformation take place. In the meantime, Protestants had to learn to see their own salvations as part of a bigger narrative that included the ongoing reformation of the church, a millennial period in which ecclesiastical institutions would be purer than ever before, and the ultimate triumph of God's people following the Last Judgment. During his admonition of Hutchinson, Cotton warned that to deny that all men and women would be resurrected in "thease very Bodies" to face that Day of Doom was to destroy religion as a collective phenomenon, rendering worthless "all our preaching and your hearing and all our sufferings for the faythe" (371). Where she portrayed resurrection as a closed circuit between savior and saved, he and Shepard insisted that it tied prospective participants to each other, to the church, and to the righteous dead.

"Men Think It Easie to Believe a Resurrection": John Cotton's and Thomas Shepard's Responses to Hutchinson

After her church trial, Hutchinson, her husband, and several of her supporters left Massachusetts for the island of Aquidneck, in Narrangansett Bay, not far from Roger Williams's Providence Plantations. But it was only after her 1643 death at the hands of Siwanoye Indians on land claimed by the Dutch colony of New Netherland that the leadership of the Bay Colony sought to disseminate an official account of her place in its history. Governor John Winthrop assembled a series of documents relating to the trials of Hutchinson and other "Antinomians," which was published in London in August 1644. The tract was quickly reissued in a second edition entitled *A Short Story of the Rise, Reign, and Ruine of the Antinomians, Familists, and Libertines*, with the addition of a contextualizing preface by Thomas Weld, the London agent of the colony (Robert Baillie's attack on Congregationalist radicalism would draw its account of Hutchinson's beliefs primarily from this version). Winthrop and Weld's propagandistic text was intended to encourage the highly misleading perception that the recent outbreak of theological error in New England had been clustered around Hutchinson and her advocates and had now been definitively contained.[41] In fact, unconventional ideas about free grace and resurrection could still be found across the colonies, and not just among openly rebellious figures such as Samuel Gorton, who contested Puritan orthodoxy through a series of writings in the 1640s and 1650s.[42] Indeed, New England's two most prominent theologians spent the next decade writing sermons and tracts that sought to pivot American Puritanism away from the radical spiritual individualism that Hutchinson and others had championed.

The controversy over Hutchinson's claims and behavior had put John Cotton and Thomas Shepard in very different positions. As her one-time religious mentor, Cotton initially hoped that the members of his church would find a way to avoid excommunicating her.[43] Shepard, however, had had a private discussion with the accused in which she had supposedly admitted to holding heretical beliefs. He therefore "account[ed] her a verye dayngerous Woman" liable "to sowe her corrupt opinions to the infection of many."[44] What is more, he had come to suspect that Cotton's unsound preaching on conversion and sanctification had encouraged Hutchinson and her party in their unorthodox opinions. To satisfy this misgiving, he had helped to lead a ministerial inquiry into his colleague's soteriological views that culminated in a conference held in August 1637, three months before Hutchinson's civil trial.[45]

Despite this tension, and the significant theological disagreements between the two of them, Cotton and Shepard adopted comparable strategies in their writings against the radical threat. Both stressed the historical/teleological dimension of Christian life that Hutchinson's realized eschatology occluded. Personal justification and sanctification, they insisted, must always be understood with reference to the future resurrection of the dead and the apocalyptic victory of the true Church. Gracious devotion could give the elect a foretaste of the world to come. But human fallibility meant that this experience should be complemented by active involvement in a community of believers and respect for ministerial guidance. Cotton and Shepard differed on the extent to which individual saints and particular congregations could anticipate the blessings of heaven. Cotton was convinced that believers could come to a full assurance of their election. For this reason, he was much more confident that churches of pure Christians could and were being founded in the present. Shepard, on the other hand, worried that even the most apparently sincere professors might turn out to be religious hypocrites. He therefore emphasized just how difficult it was to maintain faith in the coming resurrection of the dead. Only through intensive spiritual discipline and pious participation in collective acts of worship could believers attain the briefest preview of paradise.

Because it is uncertain when Cotton's published sermons were composed and delivered, it is not easy to trace the development of his thought after the Hutchinson trials.[46] But it is clear that he never renounced the aspect of his theology that had attracted Hutchinson to it: his sense of conversion as a sudden transformation in which the "faculties and affections" of a previously "dead" soul were "quickened and made alive to God." At the same time, he was careful to contradict the radical claim that the process made Christ and believer one ("the things united are distinct from the bond by which they are united; Christ is one thing, the soul is another, the Spirit of God that uniteth them is distinct from both"). He also specified that converts were only figuratively new creatures. Conversion created "new spirituall gifts of grace," but "the substance of the soul and body" remained "the same ... [as] before."[47]

Cotton's eschatological tract *The Churches Resurrection*, published in London in 1642, is unlikely to have been composed long before that date, as it alludes to the settlement of the Hutchinson party on Aquidneck. With those radicals and Roger Williams's settlement in mind, Cotton critiqued those who thought that personal redemption and sanctification were enough to tie a Christian community together. "If we could have large elbow-roome enough, and meddow enough," Cotton imagined these discontents saying, "though wee had no Ordinances, we [could] then goe and live like lambs in a large place." To entertain this fantasy of individualist autonomy was to prove New England's critics right, by confirming that the wide reaches of America attracted those who wanted the freedom to live and worship in whatever fashion suited them. Those who prioritized their personal tastes in this way might be participating in a "Reformation of Churches" but that was no guarantee that they would have a "part in the Resurrection of Christ Jesus." There were two sides to taking one's place in that eschatological event. Saints had to be "sincere"—their hearts and minds had to have been "raised againe from death to life" by God's grace. But they also had to be mindful that this conversion integrated them into a wider "spirituall community" of all the elect. Truly regenerate men and women would not be satisfied with the "loose frame[s]" of church discipline that prevailed on Aquidneck and at Providence. Rather than following the lights of their individual consciences, they would join together in a "Church body" that "[bore] witness against all Antichristianisme [i.e. Roman Catholicism] in doctrine, Worship and government."[48]

It was New England's scheme of ecclesiastical organization and spiritual discipline that could best serve this end. During the millennium (which Cotton believed would likely start in 1655),[49] Congregationalism would spread across the world. This development would fulfill the prophecy of the First Resurrection, as "men of the same spirit" as the first martyrs and early Protestants would "have the Judicature and Government of the Church."[50] At present, New England was closer to that ideal than was any other place on earth. Cotton boasted that "many pretious soules throughout the Countrey" had undergone the "Resurrection" of conversion.[51] Yet he also conceded that the resurrection of the church as a whole was far from complete in the colonies. On the one hand, there was too much "resting in the World."[52] People who were "*weary*" of the hard labor of living in a godly society were contemplating a return to England. On the other hand lay the temptation of religious enthusiasm, with its concomitant assumption that converted saints need not form orderly congregations under the supervision of trained ministers. People of that opinion (including the Hutchinsonians) had recently gone "to the west part of this Country" to live "without [church] Ordinances." Like a sugar syrup, New England needed to be "boyled up to a full consistence." Though it had the best system of church government, it could not rest "secure." If the colony was to maintain its expected position with the pure church of the millennium, its inhabitants had to live up to high standards of both piety and obedience.[53]

According to Cotton, those who attempted to do so would need to adopt a porous kind of selfhood. True Christians would not be content to enjoy the fruits of their faith within "their hearts and Families" only. Nor would they "rest [themselves] in [their] outward Profession of Church Fellowship," or the religious "priviledges" of belonging to a pure congregation. Instead, they would recognize that their personal and local struggles were part of a much bigger narrative of reformation that was leading to a millennial "Resurrection" of churches across the planet. That realization would, in turn, lead them to a closer relationship with the righteous dead, who had once overcome the same challenge. Though seventeenth-century Protestants would not necessarily be faced with a literal choice between life or God, they would follow the "Martyrs" by preferring death "rather than sinne," refusing, that is, to compromise their religious principles for worldly advancement.[54] Then, during the millennium, they would start to finish the work that the martyrs and apostles had begun.

Despite their orientation toward an imminent chiliad, Puritans were not radicals set on overthrowing the current political order. In his response to the criticisms leveled by Baillie and other critics, Cotton insisted that English Independents and New England Congregationalists did not seek to "cast off" ecclesiastical and civil authority, but rather to "professe the Kingdom of Christ in the government of each holy Congregation of Saints within themselves." Though their reforms might be "dangerous" to "the Catholick cause," they posed no threat to the rest of "the Christian world."[55] On a similar theme, *The Churches Resurrection* observed that the elect would still have worldly affairs to attend to. Cotton observed that when saints made a financial transaction, they did so "as if [they] bought not," mindful that the "Sovereign good" or end of their trade was not their own enrichment.[56] "Whatever your businesse put you upon," he told his readers, "you are not besmeared and entangled with it, but you look to Christ, verily you are risen with Christ, you are high."

This last statement demonstrates why Cotton's thought appealed to radicals, despite his attempt to distance himself from them. *The Churches Resurrection* argued that individual conversion was inextricably connected to the institutional revitalization of the church. Reformed congregations could not exist without "godly persons, raised againe from death to life."[57] Equally, regenerate men and women must look to join a saintly collective. Yet at the end of the tract Cotton also noted that it was possible to participate in the coming millennium without belonging to a pure congregation or even living to witness the dawning of the new age for yourself. If you "stand fast in Christ," he proclaims, then "you have your part . . . . in his Resurrection" now, even if you "should have a thousand formall Christians on your right hand, and a thousand on the left."⁵⁸ For Cotton, the doctrine of resurrection did not describe the transcendence of religion's external forms, but rather guaranteed their preservation and perfection. However, his argument that the eschatological prophecies were "accomplished in some degree" among "the faithfull of... every age" could be distorted by those who thought, with Hutchinson, that Christ's coming was already complete in every saint.

Thomas Shepard certainly recognized that possibility. In two sermon cycles preached during and after the controversy around Hutchinson's party, he argued that true Christians were defined by their heightened awareness of human weakness, warning against the spiritual overconfidence of many of those who presumed themselves to be elect. *The Parable of the Ten Virgins*, delivered between 1636 and 1640, and published posthumously in 1659, warned that Congregationalist churches were particularly vulnerable to that sin of "Carnal Security."⁵⁹ Consciences that had been kept alert by the challenges of "liv[ing] under Antichristian pollution" might grow docile in a pure or "Virgin" church (2:4). Sure of their salvation, these conceited Christians would overlook the significance of religious and moral discipline, equating the "liberty of a Christian" with the sovereign freedom "of a Prince to be lawless" (2:24). Although radicals who believed that the "Resurrection [was] past" were the most obvious example of this dangerous propensity, any Protestant inclined to view conversion as a transformation of an essentially passive soul by the Holy Spirit was at risk of making the same mistake (2:113). If they did, they would be shut out of heaven, just as the foolish virgins were excluded from the wedding feast in the parable. *Theses Sabbaticæ* (preached sometime after 1647 and published in 1649)⁶⁰ presented the discipline of the sabbath, the weekly commemoration of Christ's resurrection, as the best remedy for such spiritual lethargy.

Like Cotton, Shepard believed that the millennium would see the defeat of the Roman Catholic Antichrist and the establishment of Reformed churches across the planet.⁶¹ He therefore followed his colleague in encouraging believers to see their own journeys toward salvation in an eschatological light (his exegesis of the parable of the virgins explained that the arrival of the bridegroom symbolized both the death of the individual and the Last Judgment of all humankind). Yet Shepard placed a special emphasis on the likelihood there would be Christians falsely convinced of their election even at the very end of the millennium.⁶² Focusing on the recurrent appearance of these hypocrites in every Protestant community allowed him to underline his central argument that the personal quest for assurance was inevitably long, repetitive, and far from certain to succeed. While Cotton addressed individual salvation in relation to the incremental purification of the church, Shepard claimed that what linked saints together above all else was their participation in cyclical patterns of spiritual self-examination.

That constant discipline was necessary because it was very difficult for Christians to arrive at a genuine faith in the future resurrection of the dead. In a series of sermons preached in England before his emigration (later published without his consent as *The Sincere Convert*), Shepard had observed that "every man is born stark dead in sin," their "bodies" nothing more than "living coffines to carry a dead soule up and down in."[63] Natural, unconverted people would always remain in this "carrion" state, unable to see the "wrath of the Almighty" or the "glory of Heaven," and unwilling to contemplate their eternal fate.[64] *The Parable of the Ten Virgins* would return to this point at length, in support of its author's assertion that many Christians who professed to be sure of their salvations were in fact mistaken.[65] "Men think it easie to believe a resurrection, and a second coming of Christ for that end," Shepard noted there, "but an hoverly sleight work is quickly done, and an hoverly [tenuous] Faith is quickly wrought" (1:91). "When a man comes to look considerately," he continued, "Is there such a day indeed? Is there one now in the third Heavens that will fire this whole world, and gather his Saints to his Glory?" Bridging the divide between a superficial acceptance of this doctrine and a genuine reckoning with its implications was almost as difficult as the passage from death to second life itself. Nonetheless, there were "eye-witnesses" to the truth of the coming resurrection currently living "in the world," a "Generation" of people who "verily look for this day and see it, and have the first-fruits and beginnings of it already in their souls."

Shepard described an existential distinction between these saints and the rest of the world: on the "last day" the "bodies of the Saints" would be "different" from those of others; Even now, their "souls" were divergent, having been already "rais[ed] ... from the Dead" (1:132). He was careful, though, to draw his reader away from the potentially antinomian implications of this conviction. Saints, he explained, possessed a "double being" (1:66). While their "subsistence in Christ" indicated that they were bound for heaven, their selfhood per se remained "dead, guilty, damned, [and] weak." That put paid to the radical claim that the believer's soul was already fully resurrected through union with Christ. But Shepard also needed to confute the buffered self-sufficiency of the sainthood to which Anne Hutchinson had laid claim.

To that end, he underlined that sanctification—the transformation of ethical outlook and action—was the most telling sign of election. Shepard argued that "nothing makes so firm an union between man and man" as the "holiness and grace" displayed by sanctified people (2:56). Yet this proof of conversion was easily (and often unwittingly) counterfeited by those who displayed a mere "*form of godliness* before men." For that reason, Protestants needed firm pastoral guidance. Ministers were to act as "Physitians," nursing their charges through the trauma of their "first conversion" in which "the horrour and smart of sin" were initially revealed and directing them through the lifelong project of maintaining their gracious relationship with God.[66] In return, the people were to submit to the clergy's disciplinary power, accepting that they were right to be highly discriminating when admitting new members into their congregations. To one another, believers were to offer sympathy, encouragement, and example.[67] They were also urged to "shew kindness" to those on the margins of their church communities, to "non-members," "poor families," "discouraged hearts," and "strangers" (2:61). Shepard reminded his audience that salvation could not be granted by proxy, for simply "being in the fellowship of the wise, . . . having got good by them, and imitated them" (2:61–62). But he also argued that "the fellowship of God's people" was a common "instrument[]" by which "Christ . . . convey[ed] Grace" to the elect (2:90).[68]

The most obvious way in which the church helped God to save souls was in the celebration of Christ's resurrection that took place on the sabbath. Shepard's *Theses Sabbaticæ* underlined the key importance of Sunday worship and devotion in the context of the continued growth of radical sects in England in the decade since the Boston panic over Hutchinson. The sermon cycle singled out the ideas of John Saltmarsh (d. 1647), a chaplain in the New Model Army, as particularly dangerous. Saltmarsh's *Sparkles of Glory* (1647) argued that the "outward *Ordinances* and *Duties*" of religion, including worship, "faith," "self-denial" and "repentance," led to only "shadowed and clouded" knowledge of God, as compared with the clarity of insight that accompanied direct and "*inward*" spiritual experience. The division between the sabbath and the other days of the week, Saltmarsh asserted, was a symbol of the distinction between these two levels of religious practice: the "six dayes" were "a *figure* of the Christian in bondage" to merely external forms; Sundays represented the "*eternall* every-day *sabboth*" that the more advanced, "Spirituall Christian" dwelt in.[69]

Shepard identified Saltmarsh's claims as an attack on entire moral and religious order of Christian society. The "constant and continued holinesse" of the sabbath was the cornerstone of an orderly religious life—though believers were expected to "take some time for converse with God" on other days, it was inevitable that "worldly occasion[s]" would "soon call [them] off" from this purpose.[70] *Theses Sabbaticæ* also cautioned that disdain for Sunday worship, "under pretence of more *spiritualnes* in making every day a Sabbath," would lead to a secularization of the weekly round. People with "bold consciences" such as Saltmarsh would be content to commune with God internally, while those with "loose consciences" would spend their Sundays in self-indulgent leisure. American Christians, Shepard observed, ought to find this prospect particularly alarming. As exiles "in a strange land, and in an evill world," they were especially in need of the "special fellowship" that observation of the sabbath provided.[71]

Saltmarsh's critique of sabbath-keeping also held extremely troubling theological implications. If the Mosaic commandment to remember the sabbath could be interpreted as referring exclusively to the convert's "inward" communion with the divine, then "the Ordinances of Christ in the New-Testament" were equally vulnerable to being "allegorized and spiritullized out of the world."[72] Sure enough, *Sparkles of Glory* explicitly advanced an argument that Hutchinson had flirted with during her church trial. Christ's physical incarnation, death, and resurrection, Saltmarsh maintained, "were so many discoveries as to us in the flesh, of the whole mystery of God in the Saints"—corporeal signifiers of each Christian's transcendence over "the life of nature" and accession "into glory."[73] Shepard unsurprisingly abhorred this relegation of Christ's life and ministry to "a meere forme." In his eyes, the mysteries commemorated by the sabbath were predicated on the unity of "Christ in the flesh and Christ in the Spirit." Spiritually, the first Easter had accomplished the justification of every saint's soul and the redemption of his or her body. But as an incident that had taken place at a particular juncture in historical time, it remained "materially and formally" separate from both their "sanctification" and their "resurrection and glorification at the last day."[74]

Worship on a Sunday, in short, was a weekly reminder that one's salvation was not yet fully worked out. In the ferment of Revolutionary England, this truth was in danger of being forgotten. At the close of the final sermon in the *Theses Sabbaticæ* series, Shepard notes that the kingdom's Puritan congregations had once shown more respect for the sabbath than had "any other ... Churches in the World."[75] What is more, they had once endured great persecution from the leadership of the Church of England for this commitment.[76] But now that the Revolution presented an opportunity to enforce stricter standards of observance, the Parliamentary cause appeared to have been hijacked by radicals who considered "almost all Gods Ordinances" beneath them.[77] This sorry circumstance, together with an apparently comparable situation in New England, led Shepard to worry that only a "remnant" of the Protestant Atlantic would be allowed to "enjoy" the "great blessings" of the coming millennium.[78] To forestall that eventuality, he recommended that "Civill Magistrate[s]" should strictly enforce observation of the sabbath.[79] Mandating worship on Sundays was conducive to the political health of commonwealths, as it curtailed the influence of socially disruptive theologies such as Saltmarsh's.[80] Even more importantly, the day's special holiness provided mortal men and women with the best possible means of "casting aside the world and getting out of it" for a time.[81] It is on the sabbath, Shepard observes, "that the Lord comes down from Heaven to us in his ordinances, and thereby makes himself as near to us as he can in this fraile life." The day's "speciall" immediacy of the divine presence must be conserved.

Shepard believed that the Congregationalist system was most likely to achieve that end. In a posthumously published work that defended the New England way against its English and Scottish critics, he wrote of the "blessed priviledge" of belonging to a covenanted church in which one's spiritual progress would not only be subject to close ministerial supervision but also to "judgment" by lay members "of wisedome, grace, and experience."[82] This sentiment reflected Shepard's distinctive resurrection theology. Though he urged individual believers to meditate on the eschatological return of Christ the bridegroom, he did not encourage them to see their spiritual lives as a proleptic participation in the First Resurrection, as John Cotton did. Though they might have been spiritually resurrected, saints' "victory" over sin would always remain "incompleat" in this life (indeed, some of those who had been made new through grace would not even be fully aware that this rebirth had taken place).[83] Shepard was therefore also particularly repulsed by those heretics who preached a realized eschatology. While those who were truly elect could never forfeit their salvation, the spiritual growth of the convert ("the new creature" within them) could still be "decayed," their piety "suspended."[84] Real, saving faith in the resurrection to come was something that needed to be constantly worked at. It was not embodied in the overconfident independence of those who believed they had already been raised from the dead, but in those who gathered each sabbath to bear collective witness to their desire to transcend their fallibility.

No Sacred History: Samuel Gorton's Realized Eschatology

In *Culture and Redemption*, her study of the Protestant characteristics of modern American secularism, Tracy Fessenden argues that despite their respect for the sabbath the colonial Puritans sought to create a society in which religious devotions were equally observed across the rest of the week. In support of this thesis, she cites a tract by John Eliot calling for Reformed Christians to keep "many Sabbaths more" between Monday and Saturday— not only in reading the scriptures and personal and family prayer, but also in "all 'civill callings' and 'employment[s]' ('we buy and sell, and toil; yea we eat and drink, with some eye both to the command and honour of God in all')."[85] Fessenden also quotes historian John Gillis's argument that the American Puritans, as "Radical Protestants,"

> demanded that the sacred be brought into everyday life, into history itself; and to do so they abolished the separation of holy from secular days, insisting that the divine leave its old haunts—churches and pilgrimage sites—to become a part of the workplace, the household, to be identified with the history of peoples (at first reforming sects, later with whole nations) chosen by God to carry out his divine purpose in secular time and space.[86]

Shepard's *Theses Sabbaticæ*, far more representative of Congregationalist consensus than Fessenden's quotations from Eliot are, suggests that this claim is overdrawn. Though mainstream New England Puritans rejected what they saw as the overblown and unscriptural pageantry of Anglican ceremony, they were firm proponents of the spiritual importance of properly conducted ritual (especially the Eucharist). And while Puritans may have called for intensive religious observances throughout the week, they retained a strong sense of the special importance of Sundays.

Gillis's contention that the Puritans' ultimate aim was "the deinstitutionalization of religion and its internalization in the hearts and minds of all believers" is also misleading. As I have argued, seventeenth-century Puritan writing about resurrection reveals a heavy investment in the eschatological significance of Congregationalist institutions of worship, discipline, and ecclesiastical organization—where John Cotton anticipated the global adoption of the Congregationalist system during the millennium, Thomas Shepard stressed the value of collective profession of faith in resurrection on the sabbath. However, the small community that developed around lay theologian Samuel Gorton at Shawomet on Narragansett Bay did indeed advocate the deinstitutionalization of Christianity. Critique of the sabbath and belief in an internally accomplished resurrection were fundamental to this attempt.

Gorton did not altogether reject the idea of reserving Sundays for religious observations. But he strongly denounced the soteriological and ecclesiological meanings with which Congregationalists like Shepard invested the practice. In a 1656 letter to Quakers imprisoned in Boston for attempting to proselytize there, he characterized the settlers of Massachusetts Bay as a people "in bondage under their Sabbath."[87] By placing too high a value on the external ordinances—the "bodily exercises"—they enacted each week, the Puritans "set up" Sundays as "a God of time," a false deity "of four and twenty hours continuance." The true sabbath, he argued, was "not bounded by evening and morning." Nor was it celebrated by separating oneself off from the rest of Christendom into exclusive congregations supervised by conceited ministers. It was, instead, an unceasing operation in which the blessings of "Christs Kingdome" received their fullest realization in the spiritual experiences of the individual saint.[88] In eschatological terms, the true Christian was already distinguished by "all those glorious ornaments of that new heaven and earth wherein righteousness and peace dwels forever." Mainstream Protestants, he suggested elsewhere, had been seriously misled by exegetes such as John Cotton, who delineated a gradual resurrection of the church during the millennium. It was not Christian, but worldly, to assume that there was "still some Fast to keepe, some Sabbath to sanctifie, some Sermon to preach, some Battel to fight, some Church to constitute, some Officers to raise up, or Orders to reforme and re-edifie" before the final victory of the saints could be won.[89]

Throughout his dealings with the Puritan establishment in New England, Gorton strove to put the anticlerical implications of this realized eschatology into practice. In the autumn of 1643 he was sentenced to hard labor in Charlestown for his criticisms of the Bay Colony and his supposedly heretical opinions. From prison, he wrote to the ruling elder of the church there, defiantly asking to be allowed to celebrate "the Lords day" in his own way. Like the "seamlesse coat" of Jesus in John's Passion, Christianity's "priviledge[s]

[and] prerogative[s]" could "not be divided." It followed, therefore, that if Gorton was to be expected to listen to sermons in the course of a Sunday service or "ordinary Lecture," he ought in turn to be granted the "liberty to speake and express the word of the Lord in the publick congregation freely [and] without interruption." To reserve the right to preach for ministers, even to appoint clergy in the first place, was to sanction the "*piece mealing of the things of God.*"[90]

This robust interpretation of the Protestant principle of the priesthood of all believers, like every other aspect of Gorton's religious thought and praxis, was governed by a complex resurrection theology, which proclaimed that the elect had already risen from the grave through spiritual union with Christ. Anne Hutchinson, as we have seen, made the same claim, and this shared conviction had undoubtedly contributed to Gorton's (ultimately short-lived) sojourn at Aquidneck (later Portsmouth), the settlement established by Hutchinson, her husband William, and other "Antinomian" exiles from Massachusetts.[91]

But while we must rely on the records of her trials for brief insights into Hutchinson's take on resurrection, Gorton set out his views in significant detail in a range of textual venues, including the correspondence with John Winthrop that led to his 1643 trial in Boston, and two lengthy explications of his idiosyncratic beliefs that he published in the 1650s. These theological works are certainly difficult, but they are by no means incoherent. They each have the same, powerful idea at their center—the full sweep of sacred history is accomplished within each believer. For Gorton, as we shall see now, this premise had both civil and ecclesiological implications. Not only did it subvert the Puritan narrative of the resurrection of the church (especially as conceived by John Cotton), but it was also the grounds of a unique approach to political and social life in England's American colonies.

Scholars continue to disagree about the extent to which Gorton should be categorized as a political radical. Michelle Burnham has connected his critique of the ministerial claim to monopoly over biblical exegesis with the Levellers' attack on the economic monopolies exercised by trading companies and merchant guilds.[92] Like this populist English faction, Gorton favored a "consensual" rather than appropriative "model of political authority," a theory he put into practice in his dealings with the Narragansetts, from whom in 1642 he and his followers purchased land to establish their own community of Shawomet (later renamed Warwick).[93] Jonathan Beecher Field notes by contrast that when the struggle to preserve Shawomet's independence from Massachusetts led Gorton to travel to London, the Parliamentarians whose support he secured were ranged "across a broad political spectrum." Operating in a "sphere... almost entirely distinct" from the extremely radical religious groups he associated with during his four-year residency in the metropolis, Gorton presented himself as a "loyal English subject" who considered his American settlement to be under the jurisdiction of the Westminster Parliament and the common-law tradition.[94]

My reading of Gorton's work will steer a course between Field's and Burnham's. Rather than seeking to establish entirely new forms of government and/or economy, as his contemporaries the Ranters, Diggers, and Fifth Monarchists did, Gorton advocated for an alternative mode of relation to existing structures of authority. He did not call for Christians to extricate themselves from their political allegiance to worldly regimes, as Anne Hutchinson would in her years of exile.[95] But he did ask that they disengage spiritually from the civic realm. In other words, Gorton urged saints to stop investing their political or even their ecclesiastical affiliations with religious significance. Any institution that was structured around "relations . . . between creature and creature," was no more sacred than the herds and flocks formed by the "naturall instincts" of "the beasts of the field, and fowles of the ayre."[96] As a result, the Puritan fixation with founding and maintaining pure churches was just as misguided as the high Anglican conception of the sanctity of kingship, or the idea that England, or any nation, was specially favored by God. The only "Edicts and Institutions" that had spiritual meaning were those that were "established between God and man" through the "conjunction" of the believer's soul with the resurrected Christ.[97] To focus on the preservation of particular "Ordinances" or exclusive congregations was to tie oneself to "a dead carkasse of Religion," a "dead bulk or body" of corrupted exegesis.[98]

Gorton's skepticism toward the urge to build and conserve religious institutions did not prevent him from fighting for to secure his settlement's independence from Massachusetts so that he and his followers could worship in their chosen fashion. Having secured Parliament's confirmation that the 1644 charter granted to Roger Williams for Rhode Island included Shawomet, Gorton returned to New England in 1648. He would go on to serve in a variety of roles in the government of Rhode Island, including president (in 1651) and deputy to the General Assembly (in 1664–1666 and 1670).[99] Although this might appear to be a surprising development, given the irreverent attitude toward political authority he had exhibited earlier in his life, he insisted that his mysticism was not at all incompatible with respect for worldly hierarchy. In *Saltmarsh Returned from the Dead* (1655), the definitive statement of his theology, Gorton noted that "the order set in nature in point of sexe, age, gifts, place, &c." was "created" for God's "use and service"—not least as "significant intelligencers [or symbols] of higher, and more noble and durable things" (149). It was insulting to "the spirit and power of God," he added, to suppose that its influence over Christians would not "preserve [them] in modesty, chastity, gravity, and moderations in all things" (173).

Yet this tract also claimed that the eschatological time in which all secular dominion was to be abrogated had been fully realized within each believer. The elect recognized that "the *world to come*" had arrived and Christ's "kingdome" had been established within (150). The various manifestations of worldly government—its "Schools, Libraries, and Records," its "Law[,] ... policy, ... and force of arms"—retained their own "proper sphear" of influence, but they no longer held any ideological power over the saint. Whatever the Puritans might think, the great divide between true Christians and those preoccupied by worldly affairs could not be adequately represented by political actions such as an institutional separation from corrupted churches. It was, instead, a mystical process, in which Christ's incarnation, death, and return to life, Adam's fall, the conversion and resurrection of the individual, and the creation and destruction of the cosmos itself were constantly and ceaselessly accomplished together.

This amalgamation and internalization of the events of sacred history was the foundation of Gorton's theology. *Saltmarsh Returned from the Dead* sets out its bold implications by means of a commentary on the fifth chapter of James, in which Gorton radically reworks the Calvinist doctrine of predestination. Writing to Jewish Christians in the first century, the author of James likens those who are not ready for the "coming of the Lord" to people who have "condemned and killed" an innocent man (James 5:5). In Gorton's explication, this murder stands for reprobate men and women's rejection of saving grace. By indulging "the corrupt desire of the flesh" for "things which are transitory and fading," the wicked participate in a travesty of Christ's death and resurrection that ensures their damnation (34). All humans are "naturally mortall," but are made immortal through an admixture of the divine principle and their souls. By becoming one with his saints, Christ dies "unto the flesh" (18) and is resurrected with them into an "eternal life" of "excellency and purity" (17). But in his conjunction with "the men of the world," he dies "unto the spirit" (18), giving life to "lusts and corruptions" that condemn them to "eternal death" (17). It was a terrible mistake to insert these opposed experiences into any kind of temporal sequence. The wicked did not repudiate their savior because of some predisposition to do wrong that had been handed down through the generations from humanity's first parents. Their false union with Christ was their personal original sin. It was also their very own hell. The "state of man-kind with respect unto God," Gorton noted, "is in one act and for ever" (15). To live sinfully now, in repudiation of spiritual resurrection, is to have faced the last judgment and been found wanting, to be enduring endless punishment already. Likewise, to live righteously is to have received one's eternal reward: the "salvation of the just" is "really present in the act of expectation, . . . [s]o that in patient waiting, we possesse" it completely (53).

One of Gorton's primary theological complaints about his Congregationalist neighbors was that they had failed to learn this last lesson—a point he underlined in the first dedication of *Saltmarsh Returned from the Dead*, addressed to his radical friends in London. There, he criticized the Puritan investment in the "restauration of the Church" during an earthly millennium (n.p.). This prospective orientation denied Christ his "present being" within his saints, failing to recognize that the work of redemption was already complete. By deferring the total accomplishment of God's plan to a future time (no matter how close at hand), the Puritan clergy sought to appropriate for themselves the sacred authority that belonged to every Christian. Yet this attempt would inevitably fail (just as the Bay Colony's attempt to claim jurisdiction over Shawomet had failed), because it was grounded in false assumptions about the nature of spiritual power.

Despite their professed aversion to ecclesiastical hierarchies, Congregationalists appointed ministers and elders to administer their churches on God's behalf. They also assumed that godly rulers, such as John Winthrop, could act as vehicles for providence in the civil arena. In claiming these deputations, Gorton warned Winthrop in a 1642 letter, "You limit, and so destroy the holy one of Israel."[100] Christ, he insisted, had always and would always be the same. To set up clerical or political leaders to rule as his representatives "in one time or place" was to suggest that his nature and influence were malleable and divisible. In a later letter written to his wife during his imprisonment in Charlestown, Gorton noted that it was equally wrong to speak of particular "ministrations"—whether the primitive apostolic church or a resurrected church to come—that were, or would be, especially favored by God for their purity.[101] As he had reminded Winthrop, this position did not necessitate rejecting all worldly authority (the "same spirit" of overreaching could be found in "the basest Peasant" as in "the greatest Princes of this world").[102] But it did require saints to be very cautious about wielding institutional power in the name of their faith. If the savior's resurrection was always taking place in the souls of the elect, then so was his death.[103] Following him meant bearing witness to both these events—acknowledging the political "weaknesse of Christ," his death in the flesh, as well as his religious supremacy, or resurrection in the spirit.[104]

Gorton's celebration of those who are "cut off from being supported by any earthly power, carnall policy, or any temporal glory" was transparently influenced by his long fight against the comparative might of Massachusetts.[105] In the dedications to *Saltmarsh Returned from the Dead* he noted that even in 1655 there were still those in the colonies who considered "the place of our bodily abode" to be "a *non ens*," with "no [legal] being" (n.p.). Yet he also made it clear that spiritual aversion from worldly affairs was more than a compensatory consolation for those who were obliged to take refuge in a "remote wildernesse." His message was of urgent importance for every Christian since it demanded nothing less than a total reassessment of conventional Protestant beliefs about reformation, salvation, and the afterlife.

In the first place, Gorton totally dismissed the idea that there could be any kind of institutional continuity between this world and the next. As we have seen, he viewed the practice of forming social, political, and even religious collectives as a worldly expediency that had no purchase at all on eternity. While the Puritans and other Reformed Protestants claimed to have cleansed their churches of sacramentalism, they were in fact just as guilty as Roman Catholics were of blending immaterial spiritual concepts with material structures, rituals, and symbols (Gorton disgustedly compared those who tied their faith to "forms of earthly Governments, forms of Churches, forms of ordinances, and exercises" to priests who enacted "carnall copulations, with bread, wine, and water, oyle, spittle, and cream" [31]). The Catholic Church proclaimed that the ceremonies over which it presided were the only way to heaven. The Puritans held that their method of worship, mode of church government, and model of personal conversion were the closest approximations of the protocols that would be adopted across the world as a purer church was constructed during the millennium. Each of these assertions made the mistake of tying God's word to a corporate body that was subject to "decay."[106]

Like the Roman church that it excoriated as the Antichrist, Congregationalism could be aptly compared to those "States-men and Politicians" who sought to extend their influence beyond their natural lifetimes, "lay[ing] plots and platforms ... to ... achieve things, which they know can never be done in their dayes, that their wisdom and policy may live and be in use when they are gone."[107] Indeed, the Puritan aspiration to contribute to Satan's defeat through reforming the church around the world was in itself Antichristian, a product of the perverted confederation of the Son of God and the damned. "The Almighty," Gorton explained, had imbued the human soul with a "variety of operations and excellencies" that were of divine origin, including the intellectual capacity to "compose the earth, and comprehend all things, and find out the causes, relations, and operations of them." While these abilities had their legitimate uses, it was as sinful to employ them to "eternize" particular religious practices and affiliations as it was to use them to seek earthly fame. The Puritans styled themselves as world-deniers, but their eschatological beliefs confirmed that they were world-perpetuators. All they could offer was a false, immanent eternity, a projection of the creaturely will to endure and conquer onto the heavenly sphere.

This claim was controversial enough, as it tended to undermine any narrative of ecclesiastical regeneration, not just the Puritan millennium. But Gorton's unconventional soteriology had even broader and more iconoclastic implications. His unrelenting focus on the spiritual union of Christ and saint meant that there was no place for corporeal resurrection in his system. Still he went further. It was dangerously misleading, he suggested, to claim that elect men and women would be granted independent, individual immortality. Christ's death and resurrection did not save "the life of a meer creature," but that of "the Son of God" himself (196). There was no "life in man-kind," no singular self, that was worth preserving for its own sake: that which was safeguarded for eternal blessedness was the conglomeration of Christ and saint that had been formed through the work of conversion.

This was arguably the most radical of Gorton's interventions, since it called into question several axiomatic Christian principles. The distinction between animal and human biological life, for instance, fell away before it (only spiritual union with God allowed human existence to "transcend the life of all other creatures"). Gorton's soteriology also undermined the traditional view of redemption as something that had to be secured or discovered. He maintained that the saints' "Salvation" had already been "perfect[ed]," that they had already been integrated into the eternal "fullnesse of Christ" (those who argued "that a Christian [could not] be perfect in this life" because he or she was still subject to "natural infirmity" were still stuck in the Antichristian mindset that mistakenly associated "terrene things" with the "glory of God").[108] Perhaps most importantly, Gorton critiqued the deeply engrained supposition that the end of an individual's physical existence held a particular significance for the fate of their soul. *Saltmarsh Returned from the Dead* cautioned against prayer for a spiritually painless passing: "If you speak of death," Gorton urged his readers, speak of the "death [of] all transitory and carnall things in Christ, or else [the] death [of] all spirituall and durable things in Antichrist" (168). The physical fact of mortality carried no religious weight with him—the annihilation of one's religious attachment to worldly things and ways of thinking was all.

To what extent does his attitude toward death make Gorton a protosecularist thinker? It is certainly true that his descriptions of the afterlife tend to be brief and oblique. Though his writings insist on the eternal nature of the bond between the elect and Christ (and the damned and Antichrist), they make little or no comment on what postmortem existence might be like as an experience. Such is Gorton's emphasis on the nonsurvival of anything other than the combination of God and man that the modern reader is left to wonder whether he included individual consciousness among the carnal aspects of being that would be left behind at the end. The disparaging remarks he made about mortalists in *Saltmarsh Returned from the Dead* suggest that Gorton probably did believe that saints would be mindful of their persistence through eternity (32, 176). Nevertheless, his lack of interest in the notion of heaven as a *place* brings him closer in some respects to secular moderns than to most of his contemporaries.

Gorton's disengagement with the end of life as a spiritual event connects him to another aspect of secularism. Talal Asad has argued that one of the signs of the emergence of secular subjectivity was a growing tendency to contest the symbolic value with which religion often invested pain, and to recast suffering as a "scandal" that "every human being . . . has the inalienable right" to seek to avoid.[109] Modern Christianity, Asad contends, has been significantly affected by this development: the faithful now see bodily suffering "as an evil to be fought against and overcome" rather than as a "mode of participating in Christ's [passion]."[110] He attributes their new attitude to the Enlightenment's emphasis on "belief as a state of mind rather than . . . [an] activity in the world."[111] Gorton's insistence that Christian theology, devotion, and practice should be disentangled from earthly endeavor, from "stately buildings, large quantities, & breadth of lands, great revenews, learning, [and] trade" certainly seems to fit this narrative. His strict separation of religious and civil spheres did technically leave a space for broadly secular approaches to medicine, science, law, and governance to emerge. However, like his contemporary and rival Roger Williams, Gorton was more concerned with purifying Christianity from association with "the wayes of the world" than he was with developing secular models of knowledge and praxis.[112]

The most direct parallel between Gorton's theology and modern secularism is his disavowal of the concept of sacred history. According to Charles Taylor, secular, "direct access" society is not only characterized by the diminution of mediating figures who channel access to sacred meaning, but also by a propensity to view time as essentially (though not exclusively) linear, flat, and empty.[113] Premodern Euro-Christians certainly had a strong sense of "ordinary time" as the temporal course in which most people lived their daily lives.[114] Yet they recognized another kind of chronology as well, in which instances of "higher" or "gathered" time brought them especially close to sacred events and periods in the past (Christ's death and resurrection; the Age of the Apostles) or even to eschatological occurrences that were yet to come (the Day of Judgment). The observation of the sabbath, a day that was supposed to commemorate the Easter mystery and to offer a foretaste of heaven's eternal peace, is a particularly obvious example of this logic. Just as important for most Protestants was the narrative of Reformation, which held that certain nations and/or congregations were moving closer toward, or had already arrived at, an approximation of the uncorrupted Christianity of the early years of the church, before the consolidation of excessive papal power.

Gorton contested both these forms of higher time. Refusing to acknowledge any temporal fluctuation, whether weekly or generational, in the degree of intimacy and sympathy between God and his saints, he insisted that those who did recognize such a pattern made "Christ a momentary and transient thing, saying, that now he is one with mans nature, but the time was when he was not one with it, nor had any use thereof."[115] Gorton's Puritan rivals were deeply concerned by this position on a theological level, since it undermined the soteriological significance of the death and resurrection of the historical Jesus and effectively erased the distinction between the time before and the time after his incarnation.[116] Its social implications were also alarming. To reject sacred history was to abrogate the authority of the ordained ministers who were entrusted with the task of leading the church back to its primitive purity and were supposed to keep their congregations mindful of the higher time of eternity.

What is more, Gorton's conviction that Christian perfection arrived fully formed in the moment of conversion obviated the need to chart a personal religious narrative of improvement.[117] Encapsulated within the saint's interior relationship to God, eternity could not be synchronized with any secular timeframe. As Gorton put it, "The word of God only terminates [within] it self [i.e., in the spiritual union of converted individual and Christ], and not elsewhere, as in any other Creature whatsoever in Heaven or Earth: for all the rest of the Creatures are but as the hand in the Dyal, or sound of the Clock, which proclame and point at time, which they themselves are not, but may give true or false intelligence according to the skill of him who hath the ordering of them."[118] It was impossible, that is to say, for any carnal individual, practice, or concept to point out the way to salvation. Gorton's Christian is therefore left in a position comparable to the person of faith in Taylor's theorization of secular modernity: connected to transcendent meaning through individual spiritual experience and participation in communities of fellow believers, but no longer integrated into broader public chronologies of religious commemoration, inheritance, and development.[119]

What kind of legacy, then, could Gorton hope to leave? In 1771, future Yale president Ezra Stiles visited a "Mr. John Angell" of Providence. This eighty-year-old claimed to be a "Gortonist," and could trace his affiliation with the faction back to his grandfather, "Thomas Angell," who had "c[o]me from Salem to Providence with Roger Williams."[120] Gorton, John Angell told Stiles, "wrote in Heaven, and no one can understand his writings, but those who live in Heaven, while on earth." Because of this obscurity, Angell was the last "disciple" left; Gorton "live[d] now only in him." In the political arena, Gorton's career had a much more significant impact. It was partly thanks to his advocacy for Shawomet in Revolutionary London that the Colony of Rhode Island and Providence Plantations (which brought together the settlements at Shawomet / Warwick, Providence, Portsmouth, and Newport) survived as an autonomous polity, despite the objections of the powerful Bay Colony.

Gorton's intervention on behalf of Rhode Island had long-term religious consequences, too. The colony's lack of an established church attracted a religiously diverse range of settlers, including Quakers, Baptists, Huguenots, and even some Jewish families. Though Evan Haefeli rightly emphasizes the role of metropolitan government (both Revolutionary and Restoration) in securing Rhode Island's tolerant constitution,[121] it is likely that Gorton's correspondence with the Quakers imprisoned in Boston in 1656 and his broad sympathy with the ideology of the Society of Friends were important factors in the establishment of sizable Quaker communities in Warwick and Providence.[122]

But while Gorton would have been sympathetic to any group that was skeptical of external religious ordinances and professed the presence of Christ within the believer, he evidently had little desire to convince Quakers and other religious seekers to join a sect of his own. As he reminded the jailed Quakers in one of his two letters to them, those who were preoccupied with establishing their own "tract" of earthly influence would always see his teachings as "a formless confusion." Gorton's writings might bear "witnesse against the world," but they could not articulate what it meant to be spiritually raised out of it to men and women who were still sunk in its corruption. It would have been entirely futile, therefore, for him to establish a school of thought or a persistent community organized around his ideas. Spiritual "life from the dead" ("as honourable an office, as ever a Saint can attain unto") sprang up wherever it would, with no regard for worldly conceptions of power, influence, and collective continuity.[123]

Gorton would reiterate this point in a 1669 letter to Nathaniel Morton, whose *New Englands Memoriall* (published earlier that year) had cast him as "a proud and pestilent Seducer, . . . deeply leavened with blasphemous and Familistical Opinion."[124] In particular, Gorton objected to the elegies included in this history of the Puritan colonies. When Morton's text arrived at the death of a particularly prominent minister or civil leader, he had appended one or more of the poems that had been composed by their colleagues to mark the occasion. These verses invariably celebrated the certain ascent of their subjects to heaven, identifying them as exemplars for those who hoped to follow them there. In this way, they suggested that the individual's search for salvation was part of a larger story of collective redemption. For example, Benjamin Woodbridge's elegy for John Cotton (presented alongside John Norton's effort), used imagery more normally associated with the Roman Catholic cult of the saints to suggest that the deceased continued to discharge his pastoral duty from the next world:

> Nor from himself, whilst living doth he vary,
> His Death hath made him an Ubiquitary:
> Where is his Sepulchre is hard to tell,

> Who in a thousand Sepulchres doth dwell;
> (Their Hearts, I mean, whom he hath left behind,)
> In them his Sacred Relique's now Enshrin'd.[125]

Gorton strongly criticized Morton for reproducing acts of "Canonization" like this. Who had given him the "authoritie" to proclaim that his church's departed leaders were now in "the ranke and number of [the] Saints" (especially when they had been "persecutors" of Quakers, Hutchinson's party, and of Gorton himself)?[126] Such presumption, Gorton continued, revealed that Morton was a "sectary" rather than an "Orthodox Christian." In common with the Roman Catholics whose rhetoric he imitated, he was only concerned with the salvation of those who belonged to his own church. This partiality idolatrously associated that which was "temporary"—certain approaches to worship and ecclesiastical organization, a particular theological and pastoral tradition—with eternal divinity.

The whole premise of celebrating exceptional ministers, of preserving the story of the church of a given polity was anathema to real Christianity. In telling the story of Gorton's quarrel with Ralph Smith, a Plymouth clergyman and Gorton's landlord during his brief stay there in the 1630s, why had Morton not favored Smith with a biographical "Canonization"?[127] "Of my knowledge," Gorton mischievously declared, "[Smith was] as pure and precise in your religion as any of you all[.] What, was he not rich enough, or was he not honourable enough, or had neither himself nor his poets made enough verses to bring him into the ranke[?]" As this omission suggested, Morton was really in the business of memorializing worldly glory, not spiritual integrity.

In the title of *Saltmarsh Returned from the Dead*, Gorton had performed a memorialization of his own.[128] Though it was unclear whether he knew John Saltmarsh personally, there were obvious connections between their religious views. Like Gorton, Saltmarsh was skeptical of outward religious ordinances, and described conversion as a mystical participation in Christ's resurrection.[129] Yet Gorton's decision to name a tract after Saltmarsh was more than an acknowledgment of his theological influence over him, as the text's first dedication reveals. There, Gorton describes having recently "received letters" from the English capital that had mentioned Saltmarsh. "That name," he continued, "*is an oyntment poured out*, causing the parties to whom it appears, to fall in love therewith, carrying in it a spirit which can produce a reall presence, where there is an absence in bodily respects."

This is the only reference to Saltmarsh in a 220-page book titled after him. Gorton's conceit was that the Yorkshireman did not stand in need of the kind of elaborate textual monument that Morton constructed for his Puritan subjects. Saltmarsh had reached a considerable degree of prominence within the New Model Army and the wider English radical movement and had had a letter of his read out at the 1647 Putney debates on the future of the nation's constitution.[130] But these outward achievements were of little consequence compared to his inner union with God.

True saints, Gorton implied, had no use for panegyric elegies. Nor did they require the consolation that John Cotton had offered them: the revival of their denomination's fortunes during the millennium. Having been created anew in their lifetime, the elect continued to live through and in Christ. There was no instructive or exemplary narrative that could be told about their personal experience of salvation. Nor was it necessary to register the hope that people like them would exert more influence over the world in the future. The full title of *Saltmarsh Returned from the Dead* revealed that it was written by one residing "in a despised Village remote from ENGLAND, but wishing [the nation] well, and heartily desiring [its] true prosperity."[131] In truth, however, it mattered not whether Rhode Island crumbled or the revolution in the old country faltered. Resurrection, which knew no history, would continue to unfold in the eternal present.

The Inner Light Is the Risen Christ: Quaker Resurrection Theology

The English Quaker movement developed around the itinerant preaching of layman George Fox in the late 1640s. By the second half of the 1650s, Quaker missionaries were targeting New England. The government of the Bay Colony greeted them with violent persecution: between 1659 and 1661 four Quakers were executed in Boston, and many more were whipped and mutilated. Nonetheless, they were able to establish communities at Salem, Cape Cod, and Aquidneck/Rhode Island. In Rhode Island, the movement attracted converts from those who had left Massachusetts with Anne Hutchinson.[132] As Michael Winship observes, "the more esoteric [Quaker] doctrines" that challenged conventional resurrection theology would have seemed familiar to Hutchinson's followers and associates.[133] Quaker beliefs also paralleled Samuel Gorton's teaching in many respects. John Angell told

Ezra Stiles that when Fox visited Rhode Island in 1672 he made a point of visiting Gorton at Warwick (Angell added that Gorton's speculations had got far closer to the truth about God than Fox and the Quakers ever had).[134] Though the veracity of this story is uncertain, Gorton was unquestionably supportive of Quaker settlement around Narragansett Bay and on Aquidneck.

In common with Hutchinson and Gorton, Fox preached a realized eschatology that contested the authority of professional ministers. Those who expected that God and his saints would "Reign upon Earth [for] a Thousand Years" in an "Outward" or literal sense, were blind to the fact that "Christ is come, and doth dwell in the Hearts of his People; and Reigns there."[135] These converts had learned to recognize Christ's "inner light" within themselves and were thereby incorporated into the mysteries of his incarnation and resurrection. As vessels of the living God, every believer possessed a spiritual prestige far outmatching that of a Cambridge, Oxford, or Harvard degree. Fox therefore proclaimed "the End of the Old Priesthood, whose Lips were to preserve Knowledge." He and the other friends of the light were "come to witness that, we need not any Man to Teach us to know the Lord, having his Law written in our Hearts, and his Spirit put in our inward parts."[136] According to Nathaniel Morton, members of this "pernicious Sect... affirmed" that Christ was not bodily present "in Heaven" and "denied the [future] Resurrection from the dead."[137] Fox and other Quaker leaders insisted, as Hutchinson and Gorton had, that acknowledging the possibility of spiritual resurrection here and now did not preclude faith in the historical Jesus or belief in life after death.[138] Nonetheless, the perception that Quakerism undermined Christian orthodoxy on the Last Judgment and other eschatological matters continued to shape perceptions of the sect as a social and political threat until the end of the seventeenth century.

After the reestablishment of the Stuart monarchy and the concomitant rise in religious persecution, Fox and his fellow Quakers were forced to change tack. In the 1650s, Fox had argued that a new phase in sacred history was at hand (this was a key difference between his theology and Gorton's). By propagating his message he conducted what he called "the Lamb's War"—an apocalyptic, nonviolent struggle against coercive religion and social injustice and inequality that was destined to transform the world in a short space of time.[139] In the mid-1660s, however, he urged Quakers to shun more extreme forms of religious witness ("quaking, offering prophesies, dressing in sackcloth and ashes," going naked in public) and reorganized the movement into a more respectable and hierarchically structured "Society of Friends."[140]

Quakerism's eschatological beliefs were adapted accordingly. Rather than striving for global change, Friends focused instead on the ways in which their own circumscribed communities had already established the kingdom of God on earth.[141] This inward turn was accompanied by an extensive apologetics campaign, in which Quaker theologians such as George Whitehead, Robert Barclay, George Keith, and William Penn attempted to convince the wider public that Friends believed in the fundamental tenets of Protestant Christianity, including the future resurrection of the dead.

The Society of Friends' efforts to present their eschatology in a more conventional light placed Quakerism at the cusp of the two Protestant approaches to resurrection theology discussed in this chapter. The doctrine of the inner light declared that the Second Coming of Christ and the resurrection of the dead were fully accomplished in the individual believer. Fox taught that following the light would carry men and women "out of the world which hath an end" (the secular world) and "into the world which is without end" (transcendent eternity).[142] Yet his claim that saints had no need of "church-made-faith" since they had personal "access to God" via their "pure conscience[s]" underlines the strong resemblance between Quaker identity and Charles Taylor's buffered secular selfhood.[143] This position was far more likely to lead to the secularizing "deinstitutionalization of religion" described by John Gillis than Congregationalism ever was. As a result, the apologetics campaign that attempted to repair the movement's reputation in the wake of its divisive beginnings had to balance the self-sufficiency of the children of the light against traditional Protestant soteriology. Seeking to reshape Quakerism into something closer to a Protestant denomination, Friends theologians emphasized the relationship between the inner Christ and the historical Jesus, as well as the connection between the resurrection of conversion (or turning to the light) and the corporeal resurrection that was still to come. If Quakers were going to join or create political communities that incorporated both Friends and conventional Christians, as they would in Pennsylvania, it would be necessary to moderate the radical ethos of realized eschatology.

Quaker attitudes toward biological death were one of the most likely sources of conflict between Friends and conventional Protestants. Like Samuel Gorton, Quakers played down the religious importance of the end of life. The more fundamental existential distinction was not between the living and those who had passed on, but rather between those who were "quickened, and made alive by Christ," and those who were "Dead in Adam," as Fox put it.[144] Therefore, death should hold no fear for saints. William Penn underlined this point in the brief biography included in his preface to Fox's *Journal* (published in 1694). The first Friend had died exactly as he had lived, "feeling ... in his last Moments" the "same Eternal power that had raised and preserved him" throughout his life.[145] "So full of *Assurance* was he," Penn claimed, "that he *Triumpht* over Death; and so *even* in his Spirit to the last, as if Death were hardly worth *Notice* or a mention." Quaker funeral and burial practices, which were more austere than their Congregationalist equivalents, reflected this conviction. Fox himself critiqued the gifting of memorial rings, which was customary even at Puritan funerals; Penn noted that Friends carried their dead to the burial ground "*in a plain Coffin, without any Covering or Furniture* upon it and observed that they followed "no set Rites or Ceremonies on those Occasions."[146]

Some modern scholars have argued that Fox and the early Quakers believed that spiritual resurrection during life was accompanied by a physical alteration. Though the external form of saints' bodies might not be changed, the inner substance became one with the "celestial flesh" of the risen Christ.[147] However, Fox's theology was far from systematic, and, as William Frost has noted, the suggestion that he posited a literal, material transformation of the living believer must be set against his "extreme spirit-body dualism" as well as his tendency to associate human physicality with "sin and corruption."[148] In fact, Fox often accentuated the *discontinuity* of the saints' flesh and the spiritual forms they would inhabit in the afterlife. Citing 1 Corinthians 15, he pronounced that "to fools that say, *That this Body of natural flesh and bones shall be raised*; I say, *That body which is sown, is not that Body that shall be.*"[149] Every individual who would be saved carried "the Seed of Christ," but that seed was intangible—the product of believers' decision to accept their savior. Together, the disembodiment of the next world and the doctrine of the inward light prefigure the modern sense of mortality as an essentially psychological and radically singular phenomenon, something that it is within the grasp of each individual to come to terms with and thereby define the personal parameters of his or her life.

Though their seventeenth-century critics might have been ignorant of the longer-term implications of the Quaker disregard of death, they were all too aware of its immediate political consequences. The conviction that the resurrected Christ lived eternally within them empowered Quakers to defy civil authorities who attempted to curtail their evangelism. In October 1659, William Robinson, Marmaduke Stephenson, and Mary Dyer were sentenced to death by the General Court of Massachusetts for ignoring the colony's ban on Quaker proselytization (Dyer was granted a last-minute reprieve but would be arrested and executed for the same offense the following summer). Contesting the court's justification of its condemnation of the three missionaries, George Bishop's 1661 tract *New England Judged* mocked the judges' observation that the law had proved "*insufficient to restrain their Impudent, and Insolent Obtrusions.*" "Insufficient indeed," Bishop fulminated, "against *Him* who *made the Earth and the Sea, and all that there is,* Who giveth unto *Man, Life, and Breath, and Moving*; Whose *time* being come for the *sounding* of *His* Everlasting Gospel to *those who sate in Darkness* . . . in *your* Jurisdiction." Bishop had already objected that Massachusetts had no legal right to prevent "free Denizen[s] of *England*" from visiting or residing in any of the kingdom's "Dominions." But it was especially foolish, he suggested, to exclude and persecute those who "bear in their Bodies *the marks* of the Lord Jesus."[150]

Accepting the inward light taught Quakers to look beyond (and in the early years of the movement, openly defy) laws and customs that tried to separate one place from another. In fact, Quaker teaching promised to collapse spatial distance entirely. As Matthew Pryer suggested in 1677, the time when God would gather all his saints together had arrived. Though he was on Long Island and his correspondents (the English missionaries Alice and Thomas Curwen) were in Barbados, they were "both [as] dear and near unto [him], as [his] own Life."[151] Christ's "unspeakable Love," Pryer continued, has "gathered us near unto himself, and near one to another, but the Arm of his endless Power, which reaches over Sea and Land, and reaches to his own, wherein we have true Fellowship one with another in the Spirit of Truth, where the World knows us not."

Two documents relating to the settlement of Quakers in the New World are illustrative of the Society of Friends' later attempt to downplay the sovereignty and mobility of those who walked in light. Following his 1671 visit to the nascent Quaker community in Barbados, George Fox published a rejoinder to criticisms of his teachings made by the Anglican clergy of the island. At the end of this tract, he appended a letter for the attention of "the Governour And His Council & Assembly," in which he summarized his defense of his theology and insisted that his followers were no threat to the stability of the English colony and its slaveholding economy (this text is now known as "The Barbados Declaration"). The implicit premise of the letter is that denying the historical reality of the incarnation and resurrection of Christ might be construed as just as much of a political danger as "*teach*[ing] *the* Negars *to Rebel*." To forestall this attack, Fox maintained that Friends believed that the Son of God really had been "Crucified for us in the Flesh, without the Gates of Jerusalem," and that he was now seated "at the Right Hand of God" the Father in heaven. The Easter mystery, he insisted, was still at the heart of Quaker belief: "We have no Life, but by him; For he is the Quickening Spirit, the Second Adam, the Lord from Heaven, by whose Blood we are cleansed . . . that we might serve the Living God." Theological differences notwithstanding, the Friends remained loyal, dutiful, and productive citizens of Barbados because they believed in the same future reckoning as did any other Christian—the "Day . . . of the Resurrection, both of the Good and of the Bad . . . When the Lord shall be Revealed from Heaven with his Mighty Angels, in Flaming Fire, taking Vengeance on them that know not God" (here Fox suggested that those inhabitants of the island who had failed to instruct the black and Indian enslaved people in their households would then be held to "Account" for this sinful omission).[152]

William Penn's *Frame of Government of the province of Pennsilvania*, issued in 1682, also drew a connection between political order and soteriology. The document's preamble declared *"Government"* to be *"a Part of Religion itself, a Thing sacred in its Institution and End."*[153] In a fallen world, disciplinary power was needed to curb *"the Effects of Evil."* But hierarchical social organization would still have been necessary even if "Adam never fell." And now politics' *"Care and Regulation"* of civil *"Affairs"* could help *"Men on Earth"* reach *"the highest Attainments they may arrive at,"* by maximizing the restorative impact of *"the Coming of the blessed Second Adam, the* LORD *from Heaven."* In the case of Penn's new proprietary colony, that would involve affording residents liberty "in Matters of Faith and Worship."[154] But while his proposed laws represented a major "Advance" on the constraints imposed on "Quakers and other dissenters" in England at the time, Penn did not offer colonists total religious freedom.[155] Only those prepared to "confess and acknowledge the One Almighty and Eternal GOD" would be able to exercise "their religious Persuasion" without persecution. Furthermore, the rights to hold public office and to vote would be restricted to those men who "profess[ed] Faith in *Jesus Christ*."[156] In this way, Penn tied political participation to belief in the incarnation and resurrection.

This position was in keeping with the apologetic tracts he had been publishing since his conversion to Quakerism in 1667. Though he disagreed with the orthodox Christian position that the Passion was the direct cause of the remission of humanity's sins,[157] Penn sought to reassure non-Quakers that Friends did indeed believe that Christ's life, death, and return from the tomb played a hugely significant role in the salvation of those who received "his Light in [their] Conscience."[158] And while he followed Fox in stressing the lack of material connection between the "Carnal" body that would be buried and the "Spiritual" one that would rise again,[159] he also underlined Quaker faith in the future resurrection and the life to come ("*though we own the Beginning of Heaven and Hell to be in the World . . . yet* [these spiritual states are] *but Earnests of that Compleat Joy or Torment that Men* [will] *receive as their Eternal Reward or Recompence hereafter*").[160] Penn held that differences between Friends and other Christian groups over the details of Christology and eschatology should be accepted—better to preserve a civil "Unity and Amity" based on a broad but shallow religious consensus than to search for an "unattainable" or "unsincere . . . Uniformity."[161]

In truth, Penn underplayed the gulf between Quakers and conventional Protestants on these issues (similarly, Fox had a propensity to edit his real views when defending his ideas in public).[162] Debates over the relationship of the inner light to Christ and resurrection theology remained a source of division within the Society of Friends. In 1692, the Philadelphia Meeting underwent a serious schism over the question, as high-profile Scottish Quaker George Keith accused the city's religious establishment of undermining Christian orthodoxy on a range of related matters, including the presence of Christ's risen form in heaven, the corporeal nature of resurrected bodies, and whether "the inward rising of the Soul from the Death of sin" could properly be termed a resurrection.[163] Like Robert Baillie nearly fifty years earlier, Keith warned of the social and political consequences of realized eschatology. As he saw it, the erroneous opinion that conversion brought the believer into a state of resurrected perfection in this life could encourage Friends to become spiritual tyrants, certain of the sanctity of their religious judgment (this was a particular problem in a colony where Quakers made up the elite).[164] Keith would form his own rival meeting of "Christian Quakers" that attracted a significant number of middle- and lower-class Friends from across Pennsylvania.[165] He would later complete his journey back to Protestant orthodoxy by receiving an Anglican ordination—between 1702 and 1704 he would return to the colonies as missionary for the Society for the Propagation of the Gospel.[166]

Keith's eventual break with Quakerism should not disguise the fact that both Penn and Fox had shared his central concern. "The Barbados

Declaration" and the *Frame of Government of the province of Pennsilvania* each conceded that Quakers needed to balance the doctrine of the inner light with belief in the historical Jesus and an eschatological scheme that had yet to be fully accomplished. That view betrayed the prevalent notion that collective faith in a future resurrection and judgment was necessary for the preservation of public order. In the seventeenth century only freethinkers or radical sectaries such as Hutchinson, Gorton, and Saltmarsh thought differently (even the archmaterialist and skeptic Thomas Hobbes required citizens of his ideal commonwealth to profess that "Jesus is the Christ"—though he did not require them to believe so).[167] By the beginning of the eighteenth century, however, challenges to this assumption were more widespread and even somewhat respectable (especially in elite circles).

Scholars continue to debate how this transformation and the further secularization of Western society that followed took place. Some (Peter Harrison) emphasize the rise of natural science.[168] Others (Jonathan Israel, Margaret Jacob) point to the growing influence of materialist philosophers such as Baruch de Spinoza.[169] Charles Taylor, Carlos Eire, and Brad Gregory present variations on Max Weber's thesis that the Reformation was the primary driver of secularization.[170] While registering his suspicion of overly generalizing narratives of religion's decline, Dominic Erdozain describes how "Christian" radicals (including Luther, Spinoza, Fox, and Voltaire) loosened orthodoxy's hold by elevating conscience over conventional belief.[171] However that bigger picture is framed, the particular contribution of seventeenth-century Puritanism to the development of modern secularity must continue to be reassessed. Protestant innovations—the rejection of purgatory, the denial of the power of relics, and the revival of millenarianism—unquestionably had a significant effect on approaches to mortality and the sacred. But only thinkers on the fringes of Reformed religion saw death in terms comparable to how it is viewed today.[172] These radicals claimed that resurrection was at the heart of their theologies. But by characterizing it primarily as a spiritual process they disconnected it from the postmortem survival of individual subjectivity and religious community. Mainstream Puritans, on the other hand, strove to preserve faith in corporeal resurrection, associating it closely with the eschatological victory of the church. In the eighteenth century, Cotton Mather would continue this fight, facing political circumstances that were particularly difficult for Congregationalism as well as an emboldened philosophical challenge to its resurrection theology.

2
Cotton Mather and the First Resurrection

Collective Life after Death

Do countries—and colonies—have afterlives? Will different national identities mean anything in the world to come? According to John Tillotson, archbishop of Canterbury under William and Mary, the answer to both of those questions was no. In the next world, he insisted, "All those public societies and combinations, wherein men are now linked together under several governments, shall be dissolved."[1] On Doomsday, he continued, "God will not . . . reward or punish nations, as nations; but every man shall then give an account of himself to God, and receive his own reward, and bear his own burden."

New England Puritan ministers tended to agree. Sermons delivered on annual election days afforded the clergy the opportunity to comment on the relationship between the church and civil society. In the late seventeenth and early eighteenth centuries, several preachers used the occasion to advance views like Tillotson's. In 1706, John Rogers quoted the late archbishop's sermon to support his belief that God would reward "Righteous Nation[s]" and punish "Wicked People[s]" in the course of "this Life."[2] In 1694, Samuel Willard likewise maintained that nations that professed to be Christian but fell away into "Apostasy" would be chastened in "this Life and World." "The future Judgment of the Great Day," he added, would "not be of Communities as such, for there will then be an end of them, but every one there and then must personally answer for himself."[3] In 1668, William Stoughton made the related point that God only favored nations conditionally—"on terms."[4] Though individuals predestined for heaven by the "purely spiritual Covenant" of personal salvation would always be filled with God's grace until the end of their lives, "A Body of People" could at any time be stripped of the divine favor that sustained them materially.

In the 1950s, Perry Miller quoted all three of these texts as he attempted to outline the secular afterlife of Puritan New England in the United States. The thesis of his hugely influential book *The New England Mind: The Seventeenth*

Century was that American Puritanism's constraint of the awful sovereignty of the Calvinist God with covenantal theology was both its making and its undoing. Stoughton's, Willard's, and Rogers's sermons may have warned that God might withdraw his temporal blessings from New England, but they ultimately reinforced the promise that the colonies would prosper.[5] This rhetoric of a "national covenant" gave the Puritans the confidence to establish a stable polity and assured them that their economic profits were God-given. Yet Miller also suggests that it was the vehicle for the gradual secularization of their society. Convinced by their success of their infallible righteousness, the Puritans lost touch with the self-searching piety that had led them to Massachusetts Bay in the first place. Their holy city on a hill gave way to America's commercial and military empire.[6]

Scholars now reject Miller's account of the Puritan origins of the United States for both its American exceptionalism and its occlusion of the contribution of other "peoples, geographies, contacts, cultures, and literatures spread throughout North and South America."[7] However, some recent studies have adapted his approach to Puritan covenantal theology. Miller identified the assumption that "a nation, as such, has no life beyond this world" as a key problem for those who attempted to make Massachusetts a saintly society.[8] Was there any guarantee that even a settlement of those who were bound for heaven would endure through secular time? Michael Winship argues that the Puritans developed a "godly republicanism" to address this issue. By limiting the franchise to church members, the Bay Colony sought "to create a rough approximation between the body politic and the body of Christ," and thereby to build a lasting community. Winship critiques Miller's assumption that the Puritans believed they were certain to succeed in this effort. "Even at their most active," he observes, "they retained a core of anxious fatalism, for they knew that God disposed as he wished." But while he stops short of the direct connection Miller drew between Puritanism and the American national character, Winship does find parallels between godly republicanism's attempt to constrain the power of the civil executive and the American Revolution's critique of arbitrary authority.[9] Nan Goodman, meanwhile, links the Puritan emphasis on the periodic renewal of collective ecclesiastical and social covenants to the fabrication of provisional treaties between nations. She claims that covenant-making took on different connotations in soteriological and political contexts. Individual covenants with God were oriented toward the unchanging heavenly sphere; corporate covenants were aligned with the changeable and "contingent" world of international "relations."[10]

Like Miller, Winship and Goodman take the election sermons' rhetoric for granted, assuming that the Puritans saw political communities and identities as temporary affiliations that would not survive the end of secular history. But what if we read against the grain of Samuel Willard's insistence that life after the end of the world has no collective dimension? This chapter will show that the writings of Cotton Mather are particularly compatible with such an approach. Unlike John Cotton or Thomas Shepard, Mather interpreted the book of Revelation's prophecy of the First Resurrection literally. He believed that the present dispensation would conclude with three transformative (and more or less simultaneous) events: the First Resurrection, the Second Coming of Christ, and the immolation of the globe predicted in 2 Peter 3:10. This "Conflagration" would kill all wicked people and reshape the planet into a terrestrial paradise, free from death and sin. During the ensuing "millennium" (Mather actually thought this period would last for much longer than a thousand years) the New Earth would be governed by those brought back from the dead in the First Resurrection (the "raised saints"). Their subjects would be the righteous men and women alive at the time of the Conflagration, who would be spared from the inferno by being raptured into the sky and then returned to the ground in new, immortal bodies. While these "changed saints" would all be citizens of the universal kingdom of God, they would still be organized into "*Cities* and *Nations.*"[11] Mather agreed with Willard's, Stoughton's, and Rogers's conviction that individuals, rather than nations, churches, or other associations, would be judged on Doomsday. But his vision of a supernatural earthly millennium whose inhabitants would reside in distinct communities complicates the notion that Puritans rigorously distinguished personal from political salvation.

Mather was not the only New England Puritan to subscribe to the theory that the First Resurrection would see the dead saints rise from the grave at the beginning of the millennium, long before the Day of Judgment. While many of his colleagues interpreted the prophecy allegorically, his father Increase, and John Davenport of New Haven, also took it literally.[12] Nonetheless, Mather's eschatological writings are notable for their singular commitment to thinking through in some detail what it would mean for political and communal life to continue into the end times. As I will argue, there were two reasons why he was particularly interested in this subject.

First, Mather's ministerial career coincided with a transitional time for the Massachusetts Bay Colony. In the middle of the seventeenth century, Cotton and Shepard had suggested that New England Congregationalism's institutional structure and rigorous spiritual discipline might serve as a blueprint for the purified church that they believed would be gradually established around the world in the millennium. At the century's end, that narrative was no longer plausible. The new charter that Increase Mather negotiated with the government of William and Mary stipulated that the province of Massachusetts Bay would be ruled by a governor appointed by the Crown and that it must afford all Protestant Christians freedom of religion. The strong association between membership of a Congregationalist church and political participation was attenuating. New England's future lay in fidelity to England's Protestant succession and closer integration into the British Empire.

Second, Mather's thought was deeply impacted by the Enlightenment's reconfigurations of science, philosophy, and biblical criticism. The new approach to natural science associated with London's Royal Society opened up the possibility of hyperliteral explications of the Bible's miracles and wonders, both those already accomplished and those yet to come.[13] So it was that physico-theologians such as Thomas Burnet (c. 1635–1715) and William Whiston (1667–1752) developed scientific accounts of Noah's Flood and the apocalyptic Conflagration. Yet new learning could also undermine long-held beliefs. By the turn of the eighteenth century, for instance, the doctrine of the resurrection of the flesh was viewed increasingly skeptically by many among Europe's intellectual elite. Cambridge Platonists Henry More and Ralph Cudworth had both contended that the bodily resurrection described in the Bible was a metaphor for the human individual's return to life on Doomsday. Rather than being united with their material bodies, the souls of the saved would be given new, ethereal forms.[14] Under the influence of the Jewish philosopher Baruch de Spinoza, freethinkers such as Pierre Bayle, John Toland, and Charles Blount interrogated every aspect of Christian teaching about the afterlife, variously rejecting the possibility of the immortality of any kind of body and even questioning the existence of life after death itself.[15] Perhaps the most damaging challenge to orthodoxy, however, emerged from John Locke's philosophy of mind. Despite his own faith in corporeal resurrection, Locke paved the way for the psychological, disincarnated self of secular modernity, by tying personhood to memory and consciousness rather than either body or soul.[16]

Responding to these uncertain political and intellectual times, Mather placed great emphasis on the intimacy of the living and the dead. He published detailed speculations into the condition of the saints in heaven as they waited to return to their bodies at the First Resurrection. He urged his congregation and his readers to contemplate the blessings of the holy dead. He encouraged living believers to consider themselves as belonging to the same political community as the departed elect. Finally, he developed a scientific theory that he thought could explain how the souls of the dead could be conscious outside of the body, how the process of corporeal resurrection would work, and what resurrected life would be like. Mather was consistently scornful of Roman Catholic belief in purgatory and veneration of relics. Yet his resurrection theology did harken back to Catholic teaching and practice in certain respects. Mather warned against praying for the dead (as there was nothing that the living could do to alter their destiny), but he insisted that it was possible to enter a meditative "*Communion*" with them.[17] He also suggested that the presence of the bones of great saints could make a particular region holy. Of course, Mather denied that bones or other relics had any literal supernatural power. However, his interpretation of the eschatological prophecies meant that the interment of large numbers of saints in a given polity was far from insignificant. If New England was fortunate enough to have many great Christians buried beneath its soil, then it could expect to play a significant role in the events of the next age. When the millennium dawned, they would return to lead the living into glory.

In different ways, Miller, Winship, and Goodman all seek to make Puritan political theology more familiar to modern readers. By highlighting the distinction New England preachers drew between the eternal destiny of the individual and the contingent fate of the collective, they attempt to isolate those aspects of Puritan thought that are recognizably political from a modern point of view. Even if the Puritans themselves never saw civil affairs as strictly secular, their conviction that corporate bodies would be rewarded or punished in the present life can be straightforwardly translated into the secular language of twentieth- and twenty-first-century politics. Episodes that the Puritans understood providentially can be reframed as part of the development of individualism, republicanism, or cosmopolitanism. Treating the dead as an active part of one's community and attempting to understand resurrected existence on a supernaturalized planet earth are not so easy to render in modern terms. Accordingly, my reading of Mather does not attempt to mitigate his strangeness and acknowledges how difficult it is to place him in the history of changing attitudes toward death and the afterlife.

Protestant theologians who interpreted the prophecy of the First Resurrection allegorically generally believed that the millennium would be realized through the reformation of the church, the institutional body of Christ. Mather, by contrast, placed his hope in the physical bodies of the dead saints who would rule over the earth once it had been cleansed of death and sin. This eschatological shift appears to anticipate the evangelical modernization of Christianity, whereby religious devotion is expressed primarily through individual piety rather than by subscription to a certain denominational confession or membership of a particular church. At the same time, Mather doggedly resisted the modern tendency to dematerialize postmortem existence (as we shall see, that proclivity was already evident in the thought of his Boston contemporary Benjamin Colman). Yet rather than take scriptural accounts of resurrection for granted or argue that the process was entirely beyond human comprehension, he formulated the quasi-scientific concept of the Nishmath-Chajim ("breath of life"), a semiphysical, semispiritual substance that linked soul and body in life and would facilitate their eventual reunion. By demonstrating the continuity of the mortal and the resurrected bodies, Mather hoped to discredit Cartesian dualist and Hobbesian materialist approaches to the relationship of mind and matter.

The Nishmath-Chajim had political implications, too. It helped Mather to show that civic, public life did not end with the death of the individual or the destruction of the present world. In his account, the political scene of the millennial earth would mirror that of his own time. When they returned from their disembodied sojourn in heaven, the saints of the First Resurrection would participate in a perfected iteration of eighteenth-century imperialism. As the planet was rebuilt and repopulated after the Conflagration, they would be seconded from the metropolis of the celestial New Jerusalem to lead the various peoples of the New Earth. Their relationship with those living saints would therefore be like that of colonial governors and officials to colonial settlers, only much more harmonious. Although Mather always remained loyal to Britain's Protestant succession, his later eschatological writings are notably negative about the state of Christianity in the island kingdom and its empire. Nevertheless, he did not see the millennium as a period in which America would inherit the leadership of the earth. New England's afterlife would still be colonial. But it would also be a vindication of all the ministers and laypeople who had attempted to realize the purest form of religion there.

As *Magnalia Christi Americana* (1702), Mather's monumental chronicle of New England, made clear, their resurrection from the dead would carry the colonies' history into the next world.

The Greatest Work of Christ in America: Resurrection in the *Magnalia Christi Americana*

Cotton Mather was a necromancer. In one of the several prefatory poems to the *Magnalia*, Benjamin Thompson marveled at the book's ability to bring New England's worthies back from the dead:

> Is the Bless'd MATHER *Necromancer* turn'd,
> To raise his Countries Father's Ashes Urn'd?
> *Elisha*'s Dust, Life to the Dead imparts;
> This Prophet, by his more *Familiar Arts*,
> *Unseals* our *Hero*'s Tombs, and gives them Air;
> They Rise, they Walk, they Talk, Look wond'rous Fair,
> Each of them in an Orb of *Light* doth Shine,
> In Liveries of *Glory* most Divine.[18]

Nicholas Noyes, meanwhile, claimed that the book's many histories of notable ministers and statesmen had "made a *resurrection of the just.*" Puritan biographies often claimed that writing about the dead allowed them to "speak" to the living from beyond the grave.[19] But in the introduction to his life of Governor William Phips, published separately in 1697 and incorporated into book 2 of the *Magnalia*, Mather explored the analogy between necromancy, resurrection, and life writing in much more detail than was conventional.

First, Mather discussed alchemical attempts to revivify vegetable matter. Through "*Maceration, Fermentation*, and *Separation*" a plant was reduced to its essential salts.[20] Applying a "*Soft Fire*" to a glass container in which those salts were "Hermetically sealed" would supposedly cause the plant to rise from its ashes, thereby providing "a notable Illustration" of the resurrection of the dead. Mather then moved on to the work of "Borrellus" (the French scientist Pierre Borel), who had apparently claimed that animals could be returned to life in a similar way. In *Biblia Americana*, an extensive commentary that reinterpreted the scriptures in line with the latest exegetical and scientific theories, Mather confessed his interest in these attempts to simulate resurrection, but added that he viewed them "not without great Suspicion."²¹ In his life of Phips he was less respectful, mischievously noting that a scholar could use the process to create "the whole *Ark* of *Noah* in his . . . Study" or to raise up "any *Dead* Ancestor from the Dust" without resorting to "any Criminal *Necromancy*." After these witticisms, Mather took a more serious tone. Biography was by far the best way of producing "an *Anticipation* of [the] Blessed *Resurrection*." "*Book*[s]" were much better vessels for raising the dead than alchemical "*Glass*[es]" were because texts could reveal the "true *Shape*" of the departed: the moral and religious qualities that were "*Memorable* and *Imitable* in them."

There are several other places in the *Magnalia* that make similar distinctions between grossly literal and fruitfully figurative approaches to human remains. In his prologue to book 4's life of Joshua Moodey, for example, Mather bemoans Augustine's boast that the "reliques of the Martyr *Stephen*" had "Wonderful Effects" on the sick people who visited them.²² "The best sort of *Reliques*" were not physical bodies, but religious biographies that provided a genuine physic for "Spiritual Maladies." Meanwhile, the introduction to the life of John Eliot in book 3 describes a curious episode in the middle of the seventeenth century when Maronite shepherds supposedly found the tomb of Moses on Mount Nebo in Jordan. The story was in fact a concoction of the English natural philosopher Sir Thomas Chaloner (1595–1660), who wanted to highlight the absurdities of biblical literalism.²³ But for Mather it was indicative of Catholic idolatry (he believed that the Jesuits had taken possession of the grave "*by Tricks and Bribes*," only to find it empty [3:172]). Introducing Eliot as an American analogue of the biblical patriarch, he insists that his textual recapitulation of "*the* Life *of such a* Moses" is incomparably more valuable than the contents of any "Grave." At the conclusion of the biography, Mather disparages the "Ancients" who held "the Reliques of the *Dead Saints*, to be the *Towers* and *Ramparts* of the Places that enjoy'd them" (3:208). If only such "Dust" could indeed provide "Protection" from one's enemies, New England would "not [be] without it." But rather than trust in superstition, the colonies would be better served by "rais[ing] up" a new generation of leaders to replace Eliot and their other fallen heroes.

Notwithstanding this abstracting, metaphorical rhetoric, *Magnalia Christi Americana* is closely concerned with the spiritual meaning of material bodies, both corporate and individual. The biographies of ministers and politicians that comprise books 2 to 4 are preoccupied by the manifold ways in which the mortal form can sicken and die. Thomas Shepard, one of the greatest ministers of the Bay Colony's first generation, succumbs to a sudden "Distemper" years before his time (3:88). William Phips, who rose from his birth in the remote trading post of Nequasset to become the royal governor of Massachusetts, succumbs to a "*Malignant Feaver*" (2:71). Book 6, which catalogs extraordinary examples of divine providence that have occurred in New England, features multiple examples of the human frame at the mercy of supernatural forces, good and evil: pious sailors preserved from peril at sea, withered limbs miraculously healed, men and women possessed by demons or tormented by a witch's invisible weapons. The *Magnalia* itself—a different kind of material body—is also figured as a kind of prodigy. The prolix, reduplicative style attempts to represent everything that is significant about the Christian experience in America, at the risk of assembling a disorderly, garrulous monster of a text. But all these wonders are subordinate to the greatest feat that Christ will work in America: the resurrection of its dead saints at the beginning of the millennium.

The *Magnalia* repeatedly invokes that eschatological miracle as the moment that will make sense of the political trials and physical sufferings of the people of God in New England. Mather claims that the full history of the "many good Services" that Edward Winslow performed as an agent for Plymouth in the English Commonwealth would not be revealed "until the *Resurrection of the Just*" (2:6). Remarking on Samuel Newman's generous hospitality, he drew a parallel with the welcoming angels who conveyed the spirits of the dead "unto the Regions, where they must attend until the *Resurrection*" (3:115). Describing the death of Jonathan Mitchell, who had suffered from infirmity in later life ("Of extream *Lean*, he soon grew extream *Fat*"), Mather looked forward to the day when Mitchell's body would "become [more] impenetrable and invulnerable" than that of "Achilles" (4:184). He also commended Thomas Parker's patient response to problems with his eyes: "*Well, they'll be restored shortly, at the Resurrection*" (3:144). Furthermore, Mather highlighted the writings of New England ministers themselves on the future resurrection of the dead. For instance, he notes that Samuel Danforth's last sermon was on Luke 14.14 ("Thou shalt be recompensed at the resurrection of the just"), adding that Danforth was now waiting "*all the days of his appointed time*" for the "*Change*" that would take place "at that Resurrection, when our Lord Jesus Christ shall *Call*" (4:155).[24] Likewise, he quoted extensively from his brother Nathaniel Mather's private meditations on the regeneration of "the *Body of Sin*" that would accompany the saint's return to life (4:217). Finally, he observed that two ministers of the Old Plymouth Colony, the celebrated John Davenport and the less well-known Thomas Walley, both agreed with his literal interpretation of the First Resurrection, "as in the Times of more Illumination Learned Men must and will" (3:223).[25]

As was typical of Puritan memorial sermons, the *Magnalia*'s biographies urged the reader to emulate the piety of their subjects (indeed, more than a few of the lives collected in the text had been originally composed on the occasion of the subject's funeral). Moreover, Mather frequently returned to the common theme of the elect's exemplary fortitude and piety in the face of death. In the introduction to the first section of book 3, which dealt with five of the most significant ministers of the first generation, he claimed that his own contemplations of these great figures (John Cotton, John Norton, John Wilson, John Davenport, and Thomas Hooker) had made him more joyful at his own "hastening Death" (3:13). "Through Grace," he hoped to enter "that State" where "the *Spirits* of these *Just Men made Perfect*" had been "*Gathered*." That introduction also used another standard Puritan technique: a warning that the passing of a church's prominent leaders might presage its general degeneration. Mather hoped that the "*Care*" he was taking "to preserve the *Memorables*" of New England's "*First Settlement*[s]" would prevent their Laudable *Principles* and *Practices*" from being "utterly... lost" in the "Apostasies" of the present generation. Statements such as this have led some notable readers to categorize the *Magnalia* as a lament for the colonies' declension from true Puritan standards. However, most scholars now view the text as ambiguous, expansive, and essentially optimistic.[26] While Mather is undoubtedly anxious that what he sees as New England's exceptional religious purity should not go to waste, he also repeatedly expresses his confidence that the rising generation will preserve that tradition. Indeed, the *Magnalia*'s biographies often draw attention to genealogical continuities in the colonies' civil and ecclesiastical leaderships, as grandees such as John Winthrop and John Cotton are succeeded by their sons and grandsons (Thomas Hooker, moreover, is described as "living [on] in his worthy Son, Mr. *Samuel Hooker*").[27]

Mather, then, is just as interested in the afterlife of New England as he is in the salvation of its individual inhabitants. In the *Magnalia*, he considers this subject from two perspectives. In the first place, he addresses the immediate future of the colonies as part of the wider British Empire. Despite the loss of autonomy entailed by the revocation of the original Massachusetts Bay charter, Mather insists that New England will retain its distinctively Puritan character. Yet the region's new political circumstances also led him to stress its ecumenical credentials. "The Churches of *New-England*," he claimed, "make no Difference between a *Presbyterian*, a *Congregational*, an *Episcopalian*, and an *Antipaedobaptist*, where their *Visible Piety*, makes it probable, that the Lord Jesus Christ has received them" (3:12). Though persecution from Anglican bishops had driven the founders of their plantations across the ocean, the colonists had never denied that the Church of England had always retained some true Christians. If the metropolitan government continued to respect their religious freedom, there was no reason why American Puritans might not take their place in "the *True Protestant Reforming Church* of England," which "contain[ed] the whole *Body of the Faithful*, scattered through the *English* Dominions."

But the longer-term future of New England was also at stake. Mather's history poses an eschatological question: what will become of the Puritan colonies in the next age of the world, when the resurrected saints will govern the planet in Christ's name? The very beginning of the text insists that the successful translation of "*Pure and Undefiled Religion*" to the New World must have an apocalyptic significance (1:n.p.). Plymouth, Massachusetts, and Connecticut had established churches in a "*Wilderness*" that had previously only known "*Heathenism, Idolatry,* and *Devil-Worship.*" Surely this was a fulfillment of the prophecy that in the "*Last Age*" of secular time the gospel would be brought to the "*Ends of the Earth*"? The *Magnalia* seeks to rebut the suggestion that New England would be excluded from the blessings of the millennium in any case.

The Anglican exegete Joseph Mede (1586–1638) had strongly influenced Mather's literalist interpretation of the First Resurrection. But Mede had argued that the earthly kingdom of God would be limited to the territories of the old Roman Empire. Furthermore, he had suggested that the native inhabitants of America would form the satanic armies of Gog and Magog, who according to the book of Revelation (20:7–8) would make a doomed attempt to destroy Christendom at the end of the millennium. Mather summarized and rejected Mede's theory in book 1's general history of New England. The godly society that had been founded in New England was an attempt (however "*feeble*") "to anticipate" the glory of the millennium. Mather was confident enough in the triumph of that mission to append a dryly sarcastic remark. If the "*Posterity*" of the founding generation went on to join

Mede's American Indians in "the *Legions* of the *Grand Apostate*," then those who dismissed the Puritan colonies would be proved right.[28]

While this critique of Mede is prominently placed near the beginning of the work, the *Magnalia*'s most powerful statement about New England's eschatological destiny is in the structure of its biographical center, books 2, 3, and 4. As we have seen, Thompson, Noyes, and Mather himself identify resurrection as the book's method. Introducing his lives of the colonies' ministers, Mather distinguishes his approach from the "Prosopopœia" employed by classical authors such as Archilocus and Cicero, who offered advice and chastisement by ventriloquizing the dead fathers of their addressees. His biographies of "*the* Fathers *of* New England" would employ no such "*Fiction, or Figure of Rhetoric*" (3:1). In true Puritan style, he would communicate "*their* Fatherly Counsels" by simply telling "*the plain* History of *their Lives.*" The *Magnalia* is notoriously anything but a "plain" text. Its closely set, two-columned pages are dense with literary, historical, and biblical allusions, learned digressions, and baroque flourishes. So while Mather does indeed eschew prosopopoeia for the most part, his biographies employ a range of other rhetoric tricks to make their subjects come alive. In addition to his much-discussed propensity to compare New England's great and good to other famous figures, Mather sometimes quotes from their diaries to dramatize their spiritual struggles. But the most important trope that he employs is prolepsis. The biographies do not only frequently reference the First Resurrection, but also seek to recreate it in advance. By gathering the colonies' ministers and magistrates in one book, Mather simulates their reunion in the flesh.

This simulation is dependent on volume for its effect. The complex arrangement and minute detail of the *Magnalia* make it hard to determine exactly how many biographies it contains. For instance, should the total include the extremely brief reference to three Connecticut politicians ("Mr. *Willis*, Mr. *Wells*, and Mr. *Webster*") about whom the author admitted to knowing very little (2:25)? Indeed, Mather deliberately cultivates the impression that it is difficult both to number and to classify the sheer number of exceptional men that the colonies have produced. Having covered five of the most important clergy in the first part of book 3, he opens the second part with a discussion of how its lives of thirty lesser figures should be ordered (having rejected "*rank*[ing]" the ministers *according to their Merits*" lest it cause offense, Mather settles on arranging them by year of death [3:70]). Similarly, part 4, which treats even less prominent figures, begins with a Latin quotation from Swiss-Italian Calvinist theologian François Turrettini to the effect that the Reformation has produced so many and so great religious leaders ("tot tantosq[ue] . . . Viros") that properly thanking God for calling them to action would take all eternity (3:212).[29] On the following page, Mather presents his own astronomical variation on this theme. New England's churches, he suggests, are just like its skies: "so Clear" (or pure), that even the "*smaller Stars*" stand out (3:213). Nevertheless, he concedes that it would be foolish to attempt to write full biographies of all of them.

The Magnalia has been criticized for its lopsided structure and rhetorical magniloquence since its publication. Yet Mather's biographical catalog of New England's ministers is self-consciously convoluted and awkward. Textual necromancy might have been far preferable to misguided attempts to replicate the miracle of resurrection in the laboratory or through witchcraft, but it, too, was compromised by human fallibility. While it might be easy to identify the importance of men like John Winthrop and John Cotton, categorizing the colonies' many less prominent leaders was extremely challenging. And even a work as voluminous as the *Magnalia* was too brief to give them all their due.[30] Mather's repeated emphasis on the limitations of his attempt reminds his readers that only the First Resurrection itself would arrange these saints in their true order of precedence. Furthermore, his book's deficiency was also a cause for pride. It was especially difficult to write about New England's elect because there were so many of them. Despite their struggles, the colonies were home to "a *larger* number of the *strictest* saints" than was "any other" country "on the face of the earth" (5:86). This would be made fully apparent at the beginning of the millennium, when Mather's "Spot of *American* Soyl" would "afford a rich Crop" of resurrected believers (3:208). Those immortalized men and women would guarantee New England's participation in the world to come.[31]

Mather's claims about the millennial significance of the colonies should not be overstated. Sacvan Bercovitch's strong misreading of the *Magnalia* argues that the book audaciously presents American secular history as the arena in which the prophecies of the earthly kingdom of Christ would be fulfilled. According to Bercovitch, "Mather was the first major writer to infuse [the word "American"] with the imaginative power it has carried ever since."[32] By synthesizing "sainthood and nationality," he made America into a symbol of the progress of all humankind. Another school of thought contends that Mather eventually moved past the *Magnalia*'s concern with New England's eschatological fate. Jan Stievermann rejects Bercovitch's assumption that Mather believed that the colonies were the primary referent of the millennial prophecies. At the same time, he argues that the *Magnalia* portrays America "as the realm of a new experience in which the inward and outward reformation of church as well as society are progressing well beyond anything known in (ecclesiastical) history."[33] Over the course of Mather's career, however, his "ecclesiology [and therefore his millennialism] became increasingly less corporate, more individualistic, pietistic, and ecumenical."[34] John Erwin, likewise, maintains that by the 1720s Mather had forsaken the "nationalistic millennialism" of the *Magnalia* in favor of a soteriological concentration on "the individual's soul."[35]

My reading of the *Magnalia* complicates this narrative of a later turn away from political eschatology. The history's fixation with the death and resurrection of New England's politicians and clergy allows Mather to address corporate and individual salvation simultaneously. On the one hand, he gathers evidence that the colonies will find it very difficult, if not impossible, to recapture the ecclesiastical purity and social cohesion of their early years. The loss of the founding generation, the "considerable number of loose and vain" young people who chafe against "the Congregational Church-Discipline" (n.p.), and the persistent threat posed by French Canada and hostile Native nations all suggested as much. On the other hand, Mather's general introduction professed his faith that the Congregational way "was not far from a glorious resurrection." He meant this both figuratively and literally. Those who believed (as he did) that Puritanism was the most scripturally sound form of Christianity would seek to restore Congregationalism's influence over New England society. More importantly, the church would triumph definitively when its dead saints returned to rule over the millennial earth. Although it begins with a general history of the foundation of the colonies, the *Magnalia* places greater rhetorical weight on the lives and deaths of their political and spiritual rulers (Mather only arrives at book 5's archive of the synods and assemblies of New England Congregationalism after three books of biographies). But this focus on the fate of individuals does not occlude the critical question of New England's collective future. Mather's introduction states that his subject will be "a *Peculiar People*" who, under the influence of "the *Spirit* of God," have lived "like *Strangers* in *this World* . . . in Expectation of a *Kingdom*" to which they would be "advanced" in "another and a better *World*." The biographical core of his book clarifies that it will be through the physical resurrection of the elect that this corporate body will live on.

Problema Theologicum, an unpublished tract composed the year after Mather's great historical work was published, explained this eschatological theory in more detail. There, he justified literal reading of Revelation 20:5–6 on the grounds that the unquestionably literal nature of the "*Second Resurrection*" on Doomsday meant it was inconsistent to "make a Meer Metaphor of the *First*" at the beginning of the millennium.[36] He also identified an important pastoral reason for preferring this exegesis. The allegorical interpretation favored by John Cotton was potentially "very destructive to the Consolation of the ffaithfull [sic]" who were struggling here and now for the Reformed religion's cause (407). If the First Resurrection were understood as the approaching reformation, and eventual perfection, of ecclesiastical and civil government, then only future generations, living many years from now, would see it completed. It was far more equitable, he argued, to conclude that "the very Individual Sufferers for our Lord" (by which he meant all of the dead elect, not just those who had been literally martyred) would return "in their own Persons," and go on to rule over the millennial earth (408, 407). In any case, the inherent corruption of the "Present Evill World" would inevitably frustrate any attempt to achieve social and religious perfection in the present dispensation (408).

Mather's sense of when the millennial prophecies would be realized was subject to fluctuation. *Problema Theologicum* predicted that the Second Coming would take place in 1716, and in the run-up to that year Mather was hopeful that an evangelical revival would unite the world's Protestant churches before the end times began.[37] In the 1720s, he did indeed grow more pessimistic, anticipating a period of war and persecution before Christ reappeared.[38] Sometime between 1714 and 1724 he came to reject his earlier belief that the end of secular history would be preceded by the Christian conversion of the Jewish nation and their restoration to Israel.[39] But his fundamental eschatological approach remained consistent. Though he continued to believe that Congregationalism was the best system of church government, he did not assume that its adoption in England and across the world would help to bring about the millennium. Whenever that new age began (and whether it was heralded by a religious awakening or by a period of bitter conflict), it would be subject to the personal authority of saints from all kinds of churches, rather than to the strictures of a particular confession.

The *Magnalia* makes this point most succinctly in its biography of John Davenport. His New Haven church was an early pioneer of a practice that would later be widely adopted in New England: requiring prospective members to "make . . . a Public Profession of their *Faith*" (3:55). By this measure, and through his "more than ordinary Exactness" in the discipline of his congregation, he "did all that was possible, to render the Renowned Church of *New-Haven*, like the *New Jerusalem*." In the end, however, "The Lord gave him to see that in this World, it was impossible to see a *Church State*, whereinto there *enters nothing which defiles*." This realization, Mather implies, was not unrelated to Davenport's "true Notion of the *Chiliad*"—his conviction that the dead elect would rise to rule over the world "a thousand years before *the rest of the Dead* [would] *live again*" (3:56). The connection between imperfect Reformed congregations and the millennial church, Davenport realized, would be primarily personal rather than institutional. Mather underlined the importance of this insight with the closing sentence of his biography, which pictured the clergyman "resting in hope, to *stand in his Lot*" with the other New England saints at the First Resurrection (3:57).

This image, evoked many times across Mather's book, helps to explain why he was so interested in the state of the soul after death, as well as in the physical process of resurrection. The *Magnalia* might be scornful of misguided belief in the miraculous power of holy corpses, but it does not dismiss the significance of human remains altogether. For Mather, the "dust" of dead believers was more precious than the historical survival of the denomination to which they had belonged. Saintly bones were precious insofar as they constituted a material link with life after the Conflagration. The *Magnalia* addressed the historical ramifications of this belief: whatever happened in the next few years, New England's legacy to the millennial earth was secure. Mather would explore its scientific and philosophical corollaries elsewhere.

Mather and the Science of Resurrection

At the end of the *Magnalia*'s book 3, Mather mounted a defense of the immortality of the human soul. Rather than a biography as such, the book's final section was his 1697 funeral sermon for John Baily, minister at Watertown, Connecticut, and latterly assistant pastor at the First Church in Boston. Shortly before his death at the comparatively young age of fifty-four, Baily had been drafting a sermon on Psalm 31:5—"Into thine hand I commend my spirit." Taking the same verse as his text, Mather took it upon himself to approximate what his "dead Friend" might have had to say about it (3:226). He began, for once, with some prosopopoeia: "Could that Mouth, which is this Day to be laid in the Dust, once more be opened among us, I know what Voice would issue from it: . . . *Man, Thou has a Soul, Soul within thee; a Soul that is to exist throughout Eternal Ages*." Mather then launched into a line of argument he would repeat many times in the years to come—to deny that "Man ... has ... a *Rational Soul* in him, which is of a very different Nature from his *Body*," was "monstrous *Unreasonableness*." There was extensive evidence in the scriptures for the indestructibility of that soul—both Paul and Christ himself had testified to it. The materialist model of consciousness, moreover, was inherently ridiculous ("Meer *Body* cannot *Think*; and I pray, of what Figure is a *Rational Atom*?"). Human individuality, Mather concluded, resided in "our *Spirits*" rather than in "the Ruines of our *Bodies*." It was therefore entirely logical to be more preoccupied by heavenly things than with what would "become of our Lives, our Names, [and] our Estates."

As the eighteenth century went on, Mather worried that skepticism about the soul and the invisible world of spirits was on the rise. In the 1710s he published several sermons defending Protestant soteriology and resurrection theology on rational grounds. In *Reason Satisfied and Faith Established* (1712) he employed probabilistic reasoning to establish the historicity of Christ's resurrection. If Jesus had not actually risen from the grave, he insisted, it was safe to assume that "His Enemies" would have "brought out [his] *Dead Body* immediately." In the same tract, Mather noted that the direct experience of "Hundreds of people" in New England (most notably during the Salem witch crisis) "render[ed] it altogether unquestionable, That there are *Invisible and Intellectual Agents* within our Atmosphære." What is more, he attributed the apparent rise in "*Infidelity*" in the colonies to the "*Energy of Evil Spirits*."[40] Alongside apologetic writing like this, Mather continued to develop his physico-theological theory of a "plastic spirit" that mediated between immaterial and material substances. In 1695, Mather told skeptic Robert Calef that this putative force could explain how the witches active at Salem had acted on the bodies of the afflicted.[41] By the early 1720s he had a name for it: the Nishmath-Chajim, or breath of life. In *Coheleth* (1720), *Comfortable Chambers* (1727), and two unpublished manuscripts (medical tract *The Angel of Bethesda* and eschatological study *Triparadisus*), he claimed that the Nishmath-Chajim linked the soul to the body, was the means by which sin could cause physical disease, and played a crucial part in corporeal resurrection.

Mather's theory of the breath of life was by no means original. It drew on the work of the French physician Jean Fernel (1497–1558), the Flemish chemist Jan Baptista Van Helmont (1579–1644), and the Cambridge Platonists Henry More (1614–1687) and Ralph Cudworth (1617–1688).[42]

More described a "spirit of nature" that animated the entire physical world; Cudworth a "plastick spirit" that formed and moved material bodies. These concepts were developed in opposition to the apparently atheistic materialism of Thomas Hobbes, whose *Leviathan* (1651) and *De Corpore* (1655) denied the existence of incorporeal substances.[43] But like Fernel and Helmont before them, More and Cudworth were influenced by longer tradition of alchemical and Kabbalistic attempts to understand the generation of life.[44] Mather's formulation of the Nishmath-Chajim was similarly shaped by both natural science and mysticism. Sarah Rivett has shown that the theory was also an extension of a distinctively American-Puritan "science of the soul," which sought to measure the transformative effect of grace on the individual believer with empirical precision. Thomas Shepard had collected the religious testimonies produced by members of his congregation, creating an archive that allowed him to study the psychological ramifications of supposed conversion. Mather's speculations into the breath of life provided a means of understanding the mechanics of the process.[45]

What was distinctive about Mather's version of the plastic spirit thesis was the way he employed it in every area of his ministerial work. As well as investigating the Nishmath-Chajim in his more scholarly writings (his medical tract, millennial treatises, and biblical commentary), he invoked it in pietistic and pastoral texts aimed at a more general audience.[46] Scholars have also identified political motivations behind the theory. Margaret Warner reads Mather's formulation of the Nishmath-Chajim as an attempt to protect the authority of Puritan ministers amid a "creeping secularization" of New England that subjected them to increasing "disrespect." By explaining the spiritual world through the principles of medicine and natural philosophy, he hoped to show that the clergy could still play an important role in maintaining individual and societal health, despite the growing prestige of professional medics.[47] Similarly, Louise Breen argues that the Nishmath-Chajim allowed Mather to demonstrate "the preponderance of spirit over matter."[48] Although the breath of life was "self-regulating" under normal circumstances, it could not protect itself from the extraordinary "assaults" of serious disease, sin, demonic influence, and witchcraft. To counter these "life-threatening" threats, ministers needed to call upon a "Godly science" that "reveal[ed] itself through the ... soul." Mather put this idea into practice through his championing of inoculation against smallpox in the face of significant opposition. Building on Breen's analysis, Cristobal Silva claims that this advocacy, together with the associated concept of the Nishmath-Chajim, led Mather to develop a new understanding of the relationship between the biological body and the body politic. Previously, New England ministers had called for "communal penitence" during deadly epidemics. By undergoing inoculation, however, men and women appeared to put their own health ahead of that of the community. To defend that choice, Mather highlighted the connection between solicitude for one's physical well-being and personal piety. Just as individual spiritual discipline contributed to society's godliness, inoculation safeguarded the health of the collective.[49]

As I will show now, Mather's work on the Nishmath-Chajim was also concerned with the connection between individual and collective salvation. In the *Magnalia*, he had dramatized the historical stakes of the First Resurrection: in rising from the grave, the dead elect would effect the regeneration of the embattled churches they had belonged to in their earthly lives. The Nishmath-Chajim imbued this narrative with a greater material heft, detailing how that process would take place and allowing Mather to imagine what the immortal corporeal existence that followed might be like. These were difficult and obscure subjects, certainly, but he hoped that his ideas would make them more accessible. Mather also applied it to a related theme that became increasingly prominent in his later writing: cultivating a solidarity between living and departed saints. The Nishmath-Chajim explained how the souls of the dead could continue to praise God while they awaited their reunion with their bodies. It also clarified how individual likenesses would persist through that disembodied state and into the resurrected form. Though it was generally not possible to communicate with those who had passed on, acknowledging the dead's ongoing devotional practice and enduring personal identities made it easier to comprehend how they could continue to participate (however indirectly) in living religious communities.

The question of the status of souls during the interval between death and resurrection was related to the long-standing Protestant controversy around the heresies of psychopannychism and mortalism. The former claimed that the spirits of the dead were unconscious or "sleeping" until their bodies rose from the grave. The latter held that human beings were not naturally immortal and would receive that gift only when resurrected. During the British and Irish civil wars and the Commonwealth, several high-profile English authors, including Thomas Hobbes, John Milton, and the Leveller Richard Overton had advanced mortalist views.[50] In the early eighteenth century, a group of Anglican clerics advocating for the further reformation of the Church of England defended mortalism, on the grounds that it constituted a decisive break with the Roman Catholic doctrine of purgatory.⁵¹ At the same time, mortalist and psychopannychist arguments continued to be aired in the ongoing philosophical debates about the plausibility of immaterial substances and the inherence of vitality in matter.⁵² The second edition of John Locke's influential *Essay Concerning Human Understanding* (1694) proposed that selfhood rested solely on the persistence of self-reflexive perception ("as far as consciousness can be extended backwards to any past Action or Thought, so far reaches the Identity of that *Person*").⁵³ As Locke's detractors saw, this theory not only effectively endorsed mortalism, but also removed the need for any kind of material or even spiritual continuity between the individual who had lived on earth and the individual who would live on into eternity.⁵⁴ Because belief in postmortem reward and punishment was still considered to be integral to the preservation of social order, works that challenged the existence of the soul more directly than Locke had risked official censure. In 1704, for example, the House of Commons ordered mortalist texts by physician William Coward to be burned by the state hangman.⁵⁵

Mather's writings on the soul and the Nishmath-Chajim directly reject psychopannychism and mortalism on moral and political grounds. *Coheleth* argued that the soul's "*Natural Tendency . . .* towards God"—its longing for eternal life—was "the Ground of all the *Natural Honesty*" in the world and therefore the only thing that kept human society "in any comfortable or tolerable Circumstances."⁵⁶ *A Midnight Cry* (1692) attacked those who thought that souls "fall into the Sleep of a *Senseless Condition*" after death or else denied that humans possessed a "Never-dying Soul" altogether. Those who held such "vile" beliefs made men and women into "beast[s]."⁵⁷ *Triparadisus* (written 1726/27) likewise asserted that "*Desire* of *Immortality*" was essential to human nature.⁵⁸ This inclination, which could be found "even [in] the rudest *Pagans*," was not the product of "Fancy" or of "*Tradition*," but was "Engraven" in the soul by God himself.

Contesting the immediate social impact of unconventional beliefs about the soul was undoubtedly expedient. Yet Mather was focused on another task: proving that the collective aspect of human existence did not expire with mortal life. He presented the dead as a functioning political community—united by pious affection, engaged in communal labors, and acutely aware of their place in the sweep of sacred history. While decoding the Bible's obscure references to this heavenly community was a task for learned exegetes like him, Mather also held that all regenerate Christians could gain an insight into its circumstances through their own encounters with God's grace. I therefore disagree with Warner's claim that the development of the Nishmath-Chajim was primarily intended to bolster the supposedly waning social authority of the Puritan clergy. Instead, the theory is best understood with reference to Mather's faith that the regeneration of the church would be accomplished through the corporeal resurrection of individual Christians (rather than through institutional "resurrection"). Where the *Magnalia* explored the special connection between the living and the dead in New England, his work on the breath of life presented a general account of how and why maintaining a link with departed saints was crucial for any pious collective.

The first premise of that account was that the spirits of the dead would be capable of activity. Mather presented his most comprehensive treatment of this point in the middle portion of his millennial treatise *Triparadisus*, where he described the particular section of heaven that had been "praepared [sic] . . . for the *Departed Souls* of Good Men" to occupy before their resurrection.[59] Though this "Second Paradise" (the first being Eden, the third the "New Heaven and Earth" that would be formed after the Conflagration) was the dead's primary residence during this interstitial period, they were nevertheless sometimes permitted to visit their living friends and relatives. Mather cited several incidents of that nature in support of his argument. For instance, he claimed that during a trip to London a "Worthy Friend" of his named John Watts had been surprised by the appearance of a "Beloved Sister" whom he had left behind in Boston.[60] She told him "That she was *Expir'd*, but *Happy*" and proceeded to give him advice about how to live "a Life of *Serious Piety*." Later, Watts had discovered that his sister had died shortly before visiting him in London. The authenticity of this account and other similar stories was not to be doubted—ever the empiricist, Mather claimed that they were as "unquaestionable as the *Matters of Fact*" established by "the most undoubted *Histories*." But scriptural evidence was obviously more consequential. The most relevant biblical passage was the visionary ascent to heaven Paul described in 2 Corinthians 12, which Mather discussed in *Triparadisus* and in several other places. The Apostle had "*heard unspeakable words*" during his trip to the celestial sphere.[61] It was obvious, then, that "the *spirits* in the *chambers* above, do *hear*; and therefore they *speak*; and therefore they *do* other things." While paradise would afford dead saints a restful opportunity to reflect "on the Holy *Aims* and *Cares*" of their earthly lives, they would not "*Lose* [their] *Labours*" entirely.[62] Instead, they would be constantly serving and worshipping God. As Mather put it, the elect would enjoy "a *Rest* from *Sorrows*," though "Not a *Rest* from *Hallelujahs*."

Specialist tracts *Triparadisus* and *The Angel of Bethesda* revealed that it was the breath of life that would enable departed spirits to move and speak. In the latter text, Mather claimed that it was "probable, that when we dy, the *Nishmath-Chajim*" leaves the corpse behind to serve "as a Vehicle to the *Rational Soul*" and then "continues" to function as the "Instrument" of the disembodied soul's "Operations."[63] He added that this was presumably how Paul had "*heard Words*" and had been "*Sensible* of Occurrences" while possibly "*Out of his Body*" during his vision.[64] Mather made the same observation in a text aimed at a wider audience: *Comfortable Chambers*, his funeral homily for the Reverend Peter Thacher, and the last sermon he would ever preach. There, Mather was reticent about the precise nature of the tasks that would be entrusted to dead saints in heaven ("*I cannot tell, God knows*," he conceded, echoing Paul's uncertainty about the nature of his visit to paradise).[65] It was more important, in any case, for his hearers to realize that for all its mystery the realm of the dead was not entirely unlike the world of the living. Though freed from sin, the elect would still have their work to do. A little more than seven weeks later, on February 13, 1728, Mather would find out what that work was himself.

In *Cœlestinus*, a series of essays written in the autumn of 1723 during his father Increase's last days, Mather reflected on the paradise of departed souls from a different perspective. *Comfortable Chambers* discusses that area of heaven primarily to reassure individual believers about the destination of their spirit immediately after death. The second section of the earlier text focused instead on the souls who were already there. Though he is understandably wary of recommending any devotional technique that might seem to parallel the Catholic practice of praying for the spirits of the dead in purgatory, Mather insists that cultivating a "*Communion*" with the deceased "is so far from . . . being *Unlawful* . . . that our Sanctity . . . lies very much in the Study of it."[66] The primary means of realizing this communion is a deliberative exploration of the situation of the souls of the righteous dead, closely grounded, of course, in pertinent scriptural passages. The dead might "have *nothing* to do with us," Mather observed, but "we have *something* to do with them" (it was rhetorically convenient for him here to overlook his belief that the dead sometimes appeared to the living in ghostly form) (2:40). By meditating on "what and how [the faithful] do" in heaven, Christians could transform their lives on earth.

Here Mather was more forthcoming about the work of the holy dead than he would be in *Comfortable Chambers*. At the beginning of *Cœlestinus*'s third essay he noted that the dead did the same things that living believers did, only with "less *Imperfection*" (2:54). The departed worshiped God more fervently, loved each other more fulsomely, hated sin more vociferously, and renounced the world more totally. By approaching each of these duties with this example in mind, the living could bring the mortal sphere closer to paradise and prepare the way for their own "Translation" to the celestial plane (2:40). Adopting this mental exercise would remind saints that they were pilgrims who did not belong to the mortal world—Mather urged his readers to imagine that they were *"taking a step into the Heavenly World"* each time they began their own acts of worship (2:56). But contemplating the activity of the righteous departed was more than an act of pious self-discipline. Mather stressed that rigorous meditation on that subject would result in spiritual influences ("*a Fire of* GOD") descending from heaven (2:42). The elect above were the kin of those below. "The *Saints*, whose *Bodies* are *Laid in the Earth*," he insisted, "are the Noblest Members of the *Family*, which we our selves in a *Lower State* belong unto" (2:40). As ever, he demanded that Protestants think carefully about the practical implications of the eschatological prophecies. After the First Resurrection, those who were resting in paradise now would walk the earth again, forming a tangible community with those they had once left behind.

If that millennial reunion was to be meaningful then saints would have to be able to recognize each other. The semispiritual, semimaterial nature of the Nishmath-Chajim helped Mather to detail how this would be possible. The tiny "Particles" of the breath of life extended throughout the whole human frame.[67] Since it was "commensurate" with the body, it was logical to assume that it was the same shape. Therefore, if a given person's Nishmath-Chajim were separated from the person's corporeal form, and were visible to the naked eye, it would resemble that individual's physical appearance. When it carried a believer's soul to heaven, Mather concluded, the breath of life would indeed render that soul identifiable to the other spirits there. *The Angel of Bethesda* and *Triparadisus* cited classical and patristic authors who shared this supposition. Plato spoke "of those that are punished in *Hell*, as having such Members and <u>Faces</u> as they had once upon the Earth." Homer made the same assumption in the *Odyssey* (Odysseus is able to recognize the shades of his mother and his comrade Elphenor, as well as other spirits).[68] Church fathers Irenaeus and Tertullian, meanwhile, extrapolated from the parable of Dives and Lazarus (Luke 16:19–31) "that the Souls which have putt off their *Bodies*, do yett . . . preserve the *Shapes* of the Bodies, to which they were united."[69] Ghost stories such as that of John Watts's sister provided further confirmation of this fact, as did accounts of dying people desperate to visit a distant location but confined to their sickbeds being "actually Seen at the *Place*" in question."[70]

The persistence of personal outward appearance following the separation of body and soul would be pointless if resurrected bodies were not recognizably individual as well. Here again, the Nishmath-Chajim was put to work, building a new body out of the ruins of the old, and thereby ensuring that there was a material continuity between the two. The desiccated corpse would be filled with an "*Ethereal Matter*" that was "fitt for . . . Coelestial Employments and Enjoyments."[71] Mather stressed that the resulting form would be visually different from the mortal frame in many ways. The risen body would be "*luminous*."[72] It would be denuded of sexual difference, as well as of any deformity.[73] He most likely thought that it would also be stripped of any of the physical markers (such as skin color) that in eighteenth century were increasingly associated with racial difference (see chapter 3 for more on this subject). Yet the risen saints would retain something of "their *former figure*" and aspect.[74] Though now "*One* with GOD," they would not "become the *Same* with GOD," or with each other.[75] This preservation of "*Individuation*" would allow them "to Remember who and what their Friends were."[76] Mather was careful to specify that relationships between these "*Children of the Resurrection*" would not take exactly the same shape as they had before—there would be no "*Carnal Affections*" in the next world.[77] Yet he was also clear that the continuation and perfection of old associations from mortal life would be one of the things that made the life to come so fulfilling.

By outlining how souls retained consciousness and agency in paradise as well as confirming that the resurrected body was materially and perceptibly connected to the mortal body that preceded it, the theory of the Nishmath-Chajim sought to demonstrate the reality of three connected relationships: of the living to the dead, of the dead to each other, and between the raised and the changed saints of the earthly millennium. The first two of these were defined by a shared longing for resurrection. The souls of the elect in heaven were undoubtedly in a much happier and more harmonious state than were their counterparts on earth, not least because there were "no *Reproaches*" and "no *Discords*" between them. Yet insofar as they were disembodied, they were "not in a *Natural State*."[78] So they waited with "quiet Expectation" for their salvation to be completed through the restoration and transformation of their physical forms.[79] Mather often returned to this yearning in his writings as he knew it was something that his readers, laboring as they did under various bodily infirmities, could easily empathize with. To emulate the intensity of the dead's "*Thirsting*" after resurrection was to live as if one were already a citizen of heaven.[80]

Mather's fascination with the state of mind of the souls of the departed reflects his belief that personal religious experience was essential to accurate scriptural exegesis. While he always recognized the importance of scholarly erudition, he was increasingly convinced that only those who had undergone spiritual regeneration could fully understand the Bible's truths. As Jan Stievermann points out, this "hermeneutics of experimental piety" combined the "empirical verification" advocated by the "new sciences" with the personal testimony of inward religious "affections" and outward altruistic practice.[81] In *Cœlestinus* Mather argued that the experience of conversion was among the "Ungainsayable *Proofs*" of the reality of the "HEAVENLY WORLD" (2:4). Christ's resurrection and ascension, the most important proofs of all, were historical events attested by the Bible and observed by "a Number of as credible *Witnesses* as ever were found among the Sons of Men" (2:9). But these mysteries—and the spiritual realm to which they pointed—were also evident in measurable intellectual, emotional, and behavioral changes that took place in those who truly followed him. The self-renouncing piety displayed by regenerate men and women was so out of place in the fallen world that it could only have been "implanted" from heaven (2:36). By extension, this holy way of living provided an insight into the exertions and sensations of the dead elect. "*Their Joys*," Mather insisted, "must be *Ours*" (2:53). By carrying out the same "*Motions of* PIETY" as the departed, Christians could be "assured of . . . coming to dwell in the same [temporary paradise]" as them (2:68). Elsewhere he noted that following the path of righteousness could help believers see even further into the future. Through being "*a Blessing in the World*," they could "a Little anticipate the *Life*" that both they and the souls in heaven were "to Live at the *Resurrection of the Dead*."[82]

If Reformed Protestants had always believed that conversion and resurrection were linked, Mather's version of the plastic spirit thesis attempted to provide a scientific basis for this assumption, showing how the same person could perform similar religious duties across three modes of existence: as a mortal, as a disembodied soul in heaven, and as a resurrected being in the new heavens and earth. Mather presented his work on the Nishmath-Chajim as a riposte to those extreme materialists who, like Hobbes, denied the existence of the soul altogether (in *Triparadisus* he memorably dismisses this group as "*Epicurean Sadducees*" and "*Soul-killing Swine*").[83] Yet he also wrote in opposition to thinkers (such as Locke) who were comparatively more orthodox but embraced mortalism or psychopannychism. Mather rightly realized that these positions separated the material realm of the living from the incorporeal domain of the dead. Such a partition was intolerable, since it threatened Puritan providentialism that he subscribed to throughout his life. The founding and maintaining of godly congregations were premised on the external legibility of internal grace. The belief that God rewarded or punished individual and corporate bodies during their secular existence was likewise dependent on spiritual forces—whether divine, angelic, or demonic—being able to influence the physical world.

But the theory of the breath of life was more than a defense of tradition. It also reflected Mather's creative adaptation to the changing fortunes of Reformed religion in New England and further afield. Mather never stopped scrutinizing the high affairs of state and machinations of rival kingdoms for eschatological significance. Yet as he grew older, he was less optimistic about the ability of governmental intervention to make the world a godlier place. Rather than aiming at specific political outcomes, his millennialism therefore was increasingly oriented toward the formation and conservation of a particular political identity: pietistic, ecumenical, and evangelical. The uninterrupted consciousness and unimpaired individuality of the dead saints in heaven reassured him that this ethos would endure, no matter how marginalized it appeared to be on the earth below. When the time was right, the Nishmath-Chajim would restore them to their bodies so that they, in turn, could bring the church—and the world—back to life.

The Imperial Politics of Mather's Millennialism

What would the New Earth be like? What institutional forms would its churches and nations adopt? How would the radically altered physical forms of the raised and changed saints affect their daily routines? While he addressed these concerns most extensively in his late tract *Triparadisus*, Mather had always been fascinated by them and returned to them regularly in his public and private writings. Though his view of various significant particulars fluctuated, he invariably described the millennial world in imperial terms. The saints who returned to life in the First Resurrection would serve as the governors of the kingdom of God (unlike some other millennialists, Mather did not think that Christ would rule over the planet in person during the chiliad).[84] Since their resurrected bodies would enable them to fly like angels, these saints would commute between their home in the heavenly New Jerusalem and the region of the globe that was under their command. Their subjects would be the men and women who had been preserved from the Conflagration by the Rapture and returned to earth in immortalized, but still more familiarly human, form. Mather was (generally) convinced that the changed and raised saints would coexist in perfect harmony, with the latter able to move back and forth between the celestial metropolis and the surface of the planet almost instantaneously. In this way, he imagined the millennial world order as an adaptation and perfection of the flawed imperial governance of the present.

Reading Mather's New Earth as an imperial afterlife (or an afterlife of empire) contests the once prevalent and still persistent notion that his millennialism partakes of an incipient American nationalism. As my discussion of the *Magnalia* has shown, Mather's writing about the next world was certainly preoccupied by America's place in it (especially with rebutting Joseph Mede's claim that the earthly kingdom of Christ would not reach the Atlantic's western shore). Moreover, it is not unusual to find invocations of the rights and liberties of New England in his millennial works. Yet Mather was just as invested in the rights of Reformed Protestants in Britain. Furthermore, the imperial cast of his eschatology may reflect his frustration that the British Empire was not powerful enough—at least when it came to the military defense of its North American colonies from the French and other rival powers, and to fostering Protestant piety across its possessions. More generally, my approach cuts across modern scholarship's (entirely understandable) propensity to focus on Puritan millennialism's legacy to secular history. Studies such as Nan Goodman's, which explores millennialism's contribution to the development of cosmopolitanism, are invaluable insofar as they demonstrate that anticipation of the kingdom of Christ was not a historical dead end, of no relevance to our secular age. But they tend to pass over the question that literal interpretations of the apocalyptic scriptures like Mather's demand of us: what did it mean to believe that one would live a second earthly life as an immortal? Considering Mather's ideas about the transition between the two worlds opens up neglected perspectives on his politics and his theology.

In his last years, Mather was especially fixated on the experience of living through the end of this dispensation and the beginning of the new one. His previous hope that the millennium would be preceded by a worldwide revival of evangelical Christianity and an ecumenical union of Protestant denominations faded away from the late 1710s (this change of heart was linked to his concern at the spread of the Arian heresy among Nonconformists in England).[85] At the same time, he expressed his frustration at the slow progress of missionary efforts across British possessions—not only among America's indigenous peoples and the "*Africans* [who were] treated like meer *Beasts of Burden*" in colonial plantations, but also with the residents of "the [rural] corners of *England*, the Highlands of *Scotland*, [and] the boggy Recesses of *Ireland*."[86] In this context, Mather accentuated a suspicion that had always been present in his eschatological work. The apocalypse would find the world, and much of the church, asleep. Infidelity and Christian complacency would intensify, earthquakes would become more frequent, before the Conflagration overturned every human nation and empire to prepare the way for the kingdom of Christ.[87] It was highly likely that people living now would witness these seismic events for themselves.

As he prepared *Triparadisus*'s treatment of this theme and comprehensive survey of the millennial earth, Mather prominently featured apocalyptic sentiments in his other writings. In 1726, for instance, he published a handbook for young men preparing "for the Work of the Evangelical MINISTRY." *Manuductio ad Ministerium* offered them practical guidance on personal devotions, university studies, sermon writing, pastoral duties, and maintaining bodily health. Mather framed this advice eschatologically. When Christ returned, he would not only "*shake . . . the Earth*"—overturn secular geopolitics—"*but also Heaven*"—totally reshape the church. All that would remain of Christianity then would be "those *Things that cannot be shaken*," or the three key "MAXIMS of the *Everlasting Gospel*." For that reason, young ministers were to take a radically ecumenical attitude to their work. Since there was so little time left, any attempt to construct an institutional "*Union among the Professors of Christianity*" was bound to "come to nothing." Instead, they should embrace a "*Unity of the Spirit*" by permitting all "Godly" Protestants (whether "*Independent*, . . . *Presbyterian*, . . . *Episcopalian*, ... *Antipedobaptist*, [or] *Lutheran*) to take communion in their churches.[88]

The book's Latin preface presented a starker view of the eschatological weather. The end of the current era was near. Soon, the Antichristian power of the Roman Church would be defeated and Christ would return in triumph. Though he prayed that this "Day of the Lord" would come soon, Mather warned that it would also be "a Day of Wrath, a Day of Anguish, [and] a Day of Devastation."[89] When it arrived, the globe would be "almost void of true and lively Faith (especially of Faith in [Christ's] Coming) (67)." Most of the church would be "like a dead Carcass, . . . miserably putrified" with worldliness. Only the prophesied Conflagration could "purge" this impurity (77). Just before the blaze was ignited Jesus would "send his Angels" to "rescue the Elect . . . from all Parts of the Earth" (87). These people would be found "in the midst of wicked and perverse Nations," where in the face of widespread apostasy they would still be "humbling themselves, and walking with their God." As the planet burned, they would be kept safe in heaven. When the New Earth was ready, they would descend again, to live in peace with the resurrected saints. While that apocalypse approached there was still much to do. Before the "Ruler of the World" came back to take possession of it, he would "send Fore-runners" to spread word of "his Approach" (65). Mather encouraged his readers, candidates for the ministry, to accept this role. The hour was getting late, so there was no place for large-scale religious, social, or political reform. Instead, they were to fight for each and every soul, by making it plain that the coming inferno was not an allegory, and that only those who exhibited "serious and sincere Piety" would escape the flames. "No Business art thou charged with but this," Mather concluded (97).

Manuductio ad Ministerium is particularly notable for pessimism about the state of Protestantism in Britain and its empire. The tract was dedicated to the students of Glasgow University, New England's two colleges, and the English Dissenting Academies that had been "forced into" the homes of "private Families" by the Crown's and Church of England's intolerance.[90] The inference was clear: the imperial metropolis was not adequately supportive of evangelical ministry. Mather's claim that the treatment of English Nonconformists echoed the Roman emperor Julian's "Persecution" of Christians reinforced the sense that this was a pivotal moment in the history of religion.[91] All over Europe, the institutions that trained clergy were impure or in decline. In England, the universities produced priests who aspired to exercise "Tyranny over Mens Consciences" by punishing Dissenters and had in some cases supported the Jacobite challenge to the "more moderate" and tolerant Hanoverian line (109). Moreover, theologians and preachers were becoming too eager to reconcile faith with social politeness. As a result, they hid the truth of the apocalyptic scriptures behind allegories and "Metaphors," scorning those who held fast to literal interpretations as "vain Dreamer[s]" or enthusiasts (81, 69). From the edge of empire, Mather warned that the corrupt center would not hold much longer. The elect would soon be "freed from the Slavery and Vanity to which" they were "now subject," and a global "Nation of the Righteous" would uphold "the Liberty of the Children of God" (89).

Since it was concerned primarily with propagating Mather's literal interpretation of the prophecies of the Conflagration and First Resurrection, the Latin preface doesn't discuss the nature of millennial life in great detail. But together with the main text it does provide a glimpse into that mystery. Mather notes that the raised saints would be "more spiritualized" in their bodies and thus "superior to the Inhabitants of the new Earth" (91). They would therefore "descend frequently" from the celestial city to lead "the Administration of the heavenly kingdom" on the regenerated globe. That privileged assignment (which approximated the role fulfilled by angels in the present) was the special "Reward" of all those faithful who had gone to the grave (Mather even called the millennium the "Time of the Dead") (73).

Though he thought it probable that the young men he was addressing would live to see the end of the world, Mather highlighted the parallels between the evangelical task they needed to fulfill in the present and the governorship that would be entrusted to saints who had and would die before the millennium. He told them: "'Tis even the *First born* of my Wishes for you, That you may be one of those *Angels* that shall *fly through the midst of Heaven*, with the *Everlasting Gospel*, to *preach* it unto them who *dwell on the Earth*."[92] At the same time, he emphasized the key differences between the situation they faced and the better circumstances of the chiliad. In the world to come, Christians would not fight among themselves over "*lesser Points*" of doctrine and practice.[93] Even more importantly, the elect would no longer be so largely excluded from political influence. For the time being, Mather claimed, ministers were better off staying away from party politics: "If any *Factions* arising in the *Commonwealth*, sollicit your Imbarcation in them, keep close to the Business of your *Ministry*, and say, *I am doing a great work, so that I cannot come down; Why should the work cease, while I leave it, and come down to you*?"[94] There were just two political positions that young clergymen needed to adopt—remaining "forever Loyal and Faithful to the *Protestant Line* [of succession to] "the British Scepter," and defending the "*Civil Rights*" of Christians to worship however they wished, as long as they were "Faithful *Subjects*," "Honest *Neighbours*," and "Inoffensive Livers."[95]

Mather's support for the house of Hanover never wavered. In his 1727 sermon on the death of George I, he noted that the king's accession to the throne had been more popular in New England than in any other part of the empire. The colonists had rightly recognized that the German prince would defend the Nonconformists' right to worship as their consciences dictated, and Mather was certain that his son and successor would continue that wise approach. He also expressed his confidence that George II would protect the privileges of Congregationalism in New England, given that its founders had "improved an horrid *Wilderneß* into a *Fruitful Field*, and enlarged the *British Empire* in *America* . . . from whence . . . Returns are very year made unto Great *Britain*."[96]

Nonetheless, *Triparadisus*, written toward the end of George I's reign, is highly critical of Britain and its treatment of Dissenters. Accordingly, the tract describes the millennial polity as a correction of the limitations of the kingdom and its empire. Though Britain was widely seen as "*The Glory of all Lands*," its corrupt government and law courts, impious universities, hellish prisons, and scandalous theaters made it "ripe for the *Conflagration*."[97] And while it was supposed to be the leader of the global "*Protestant Interest*," the island had done much to hinder the cause of Reformed religion. Not only had previous regimes "Afflicted, Ruined, [and] Murdered" many "*Witnesses* of GOD," but the present government excluded them from public life. Mather noted that the screams once produced by "The *Fires* of your *Smithfield*, are not all the cries that have gone up to Heaven against you" (235). The primary source of present injustice was the 1678 Test Act that, despite William and Mary's 1689 Act of Toleration, continued to prevent Nonconformists in England and Wales from political office and other "*Employments in* profitable *Places*" (263). This law, Mather complained, might as well have been "aim'd at the *Establishment of Iniquity*." Men whose piety would have made them the most "*Faithful Officers*" in the country were "shutt out," to the great detriment of "*Humane Society*."

Just as in the Latin preface to *Manuductio*, Mather presents participation in the First Resurrection as a compensation for these saints' struggles. Following that event, England's Nonconformists would occupy "more Honourable *Offices*, than any of those that [were] now denied [them]" (264). Here, though, there was room to consider at length what those offices entailed. The home of the raised saints would be the heavenly Jerusalem, which Mather believed would be suspended in the sky above its worldly original. In contrast with London, this metropolis would know "no Dissensions" and "no Divisions" (252). Each of its resurrected citizens would be assigned a greater or lesser degree of honor, depending on their spiritual attainments in mortal life (258). That hierarchy would cause no resentment, as the faithful from different eras and diverse regions would delight in each other's stories of perseverance, sacrifice, and grace (261). They would also benefit from an ever-expanding comprehension of the natural "*Mysteries*" of the universe and the "*Secrets*" of the scriptures (253). While there was therefore plenty to occupy them in the celestial sphere, the resurrected elect would often be required to descend to the New Earth to offer guidance to its inhabitants.

Mather's earlier model of the millennium assumed that they would also have to discipline them. In *Problema Theologicum* (written 1703), he speculated that the raised saints would have to exercise an especially vigilant control of those "Nations in the Remoter Skirts of the World," who would "not be under so high a Dispensation of Christianity" as the countries of Europe and the Levant.[98] This suggestion reflected his belief at that time that the denizens of the millennial earth would still be mortal and thus fallible. But even Mather's later millennial scheme (adopted sometime after 1714), in which the population of the New Earth were to free from death and sin, assumed that their resurrected counterparts would have plenty to teach them.[99]

Triparadisus explains that despite their immortalization, the changed saints would have the same biological and social needs as fallen men and women: they would still eat and drink, cultivate crops, build houses, marry, and have children.[100] The raised saints would presumably instruct them how to harmonize these appetites and requirements with their obligation to further God's glory. In the early years of the millennium, the changed saints' primary duty would be to rebuild a devastated world. Mather stressed that the Conflagration would utterly consume the surface of the planet, killing most of the global population (189). The "*empty*" earth would be a desolate wasteland. Only in Europe would there be "any considerable Number" of people saved from the inferno by the Rapture (at this point, Mather interpolated a prayer that his "poor *American* Countrey" would be permitted to contribute some survivors to the total figure). When the flames receded, the planet would need to be replanted and repopulated (272). Though he did not say so explicitly, Mather imagined this task as a sanctified reiteration of the European colonization of the New World. In the sixteenth century, Spanish and English writers had sometimes imagined the Americas as a kind of sinless paradise. In the millennium, their fantasy would become reality: freed from the curse of Adam's sin, the earth's "*Wilderness*" would become "*like Eden.*" The world would also be rid of the evil of slavery that had blighted the European Atlantic empires (Mather mentions the "*Iniquity*" of the enslavement of Africans as one of the reasons why the coming Conflagration would be just) (236). Last, there would be no pagan peoples left to resist the Christian settlement of the planet's further reaches. In these superior circumstances, the mostly European and Euro-American changed saints would set out to reclaim the earth for God. Leading and supporting them in this task, the raised saints would serve as the equivalent of the royal governors and colonial officials of the Mather's time. But rather than reporting back to flawed human parliaments and monarchs (Mather revels in the prospect that "there will be no *Carcases of Kings* in the *New Earth*" [287]), these leaders would implement directives straight from the heavenly throne.

In many ways, then, the afterlife that Mather envisioned for New England would repeat the region's history to date. The colonies would not be the center of the world to come, but an outpost of empire. Sometimes Mather appeared to make more expansive claims about the millennial significance of his hometown and its hinterland. *Theopolis Americana*, an address he delivered to the Massachusetts General Assembly in 1709, featured an eschatological prediction that God would establish a "Holy City in AMERICA; a *City*, the street whereof will be *Pure* Gold."[101] Sacvan Bercovitch wrongly assumed that the sermon foresaw the establishment of the New Jerusalem, the capital of the millennial world, in New England.[102] In fact, *Theopolis Americana* presented a variation on the same theme Mather would explore in *Triparadisus*. America would not be the hub of the next earth, but it would be fully integrated into the kingdom of Christ. It would be "impossible," Mather observed, "for the *Holy People*, and the *Teachers* and *Rulers* of the *Reformed World* in the other *Hemisphere*, to leave *America* unvisited."[103] Through their efforts, the New World would be subject to a "conquest . . . ten thousand times more glorious, than all that ever any *Cortez* pretended unto."[104] Before glorious campaign began, Bostonians had another fight on their hands. As a colonial trading center, their town inevitably faced strong social pressures: commercial competition, alcohol abuse, and the presence of enslaved Africans. In 1709, Mather had little faith that the Crown's representative, Joseph Dudley, would be of much help in dealing with these issues: he had long resented the man he privately called "our wicked Governour" for mismanagement of the war against French Canada and support of the expansion of the Anglican Church in America.[105] And so he called for the people to display the honesty and piety required to preserve New England's place in the perfect empire that was promised.

Several scholars have detected a growing "otherworldliness" in Mather's mature writings on piety and the end of days. Disappointment with his declining standing among New England's ruling class supposedly led him to prioritize the contemplation of the next world over engagement with the government of this one. Disenchantment with the progress of the Protestant Interest fueled his appetite for the imminent destruction of the global status quo.[106] Yet this narrative of eschatological aversion from political affairs depends on a presentist disjuncture of the secular realm from the millennium and the afterlife. As Mather described it, the New Earth would perpetuate the politics of its antecedent in several respects. In particular, the circumstances of the changed saints would seem familiar to those who knew what it was like to be subject to an authority whose seat was thousands of miles away. The principal task charged to those saints would likewise be recognizable to white Christians who had attempted to domesticate the planet's wild frontiers (I will have more to say about the racial dynamics of this aspect of Mather's eschatology in the following chapter). The divine empire of the millennium would utterly outstrip British colonialism, but without obliterating its legacy entirely. The *Magnalia* suggested that ministers and politicians who had labored for New England would not be fully recognized and requited until they rose again in the First Resurrection.[107] *Theopolis Americana* and *Triparadisus* made it clear that the reward for their work would be for it to continue, only in very different conditions: during the millennium, the resurrected elect would not have to reckon with obstructive crown officials or an ungrateful populace any longer.

In the earlier text, Mather used a term taken from feudal law to underline the continuity between the English settlement of New England and America's situation in the world to come. The people of the Puritan colonies had "made a *Seisin* of *America*, on behalf of [their] Glorious LORD"—in other words, they had taken legal possession of the territory.[108] Mather noted that the "*Seisin in Fact*" (a claim of ownership supported by physical presence) they had established over New England constituted a "*Seisin in Law*" (a claim of ownership through legal right not yet asserted de facto) "for all the rest" of the New World. When Christ came into "*Actual Possession*" of the Americas in the chiliad, this effort would be commemorated. Mather's legal language here was more than a metaphor. The Puritan colonization of New England was the real beginning of an American dominion that would only be fully established in the millennium.

Rhetorically, *Theopolis Americana* was the most optimistic of Mather's eschatological writings. The sermon's text, Revelation 21:21, claimed that the streets of the New Jerusalem would be of "pure gold." Mather explained that this meant that "the *Business* of the CITY, [would] be managed by the *Golden Rule*"—"without *Corruption*" and "*Base* Dealing."[109] He then observed that in terms of "*Purity*" of preaching, there was nowhere "upon the Face of the Earth" that came closer to the standard of that golden city than New England did.[110] Despite this boast, even *Theopolis Americana* does not describe Boston as a beacon to the rest of the world, a shining city on a hill that perfectly embodies the values of the approaching millennium. Though its ministers were exemplary and its judges and politicians wise, New England's purity was vitiated by its involvement in financial speculation and commerce (especially the slave trade).[111] Mather's use of the terminology of feudal conveyancing at the end of the sermon underlines the provisional nature of the colonies' title to participation in the millennium. Legal claims can always be contested. There were more than enough miscreants in New England (those who cheated their clients or partners, abused enslaved Africans, and exploited "*Christianized Indians*") to endanger its eschatological inheritance.

If Mather was confident that God's claim to the Americas through the Puritan colonies would be upheld in the end, it was not because of the economic improvements that the settlers had made, or even the pure churches they had established. Instead, it was the saints who had lived and died there who validated the deed: "The Blood of the *Martyrs* here, is an Omen That the Truths for which they Suffer are to Rise, and Live, and carry all before them, in the Land that has been so *Marked* for the Lord." Mather certainly believed that the colonial settlements of New England and the British imperial power that defended them had substantially improved the social and material conditions of the New World. But he ultimately viewed both colonies and empire as vehicles for the sowing of elect men and women in American soil. Only when one remembered those who were waiting for the resurrection did the politics of imperial Britain make sense. *Triparadisus* observed that "most of the more *Learned* & more *Splendid* People" then in the world seemed to belong to "*Satan*, and his *Party*." Mather therefore advised the faithful to "Look up to *Paradise*." In heaven, "The Holy Ones [made] a Party far from *Inconsiderable*[,] . . . *an Exceeding Great Multitude, which no Man* [could] *number*." These righteous dead were "on [their] Side enow to weigh against all the Foolish & Brutish People" who thought that the colonization of distant lands was about personal enrichment or national prestige.[112]

The Bones of Joseph: Mather, Benjamin Colman, and the First Resurrection

The work of Benjamin Colman (1673–1747) offers a helpful foil for identifying what was distinctive about Mather's resurrection theology. The older minister initially resented the new Congregationalist church at Brattle Street at which Colman was installed as minister in December 1699. Mather objected to the church's adoption of several Anglican conventions, including the reading of passages from scripture without ministerial interpretation, keeping an open communion table, and allowing all baptized adults (rather than just communicants) to select ministers.[113] In an anonymous 1701 pamphlet, he would accuse Colman and his congregation of forsaking Puritan tradition in an attempt to seem more British, polite, and fashionable in their worship: he was particularly exercised by their "Elegant[] *Scoff*[s]" at the convention that candidates for church membership should give an account of "the *Operation* of the Holy Spirit, . . . in their Conversion to God."[114] Mather would eventually reconcile with his younger colleague, who had previously been a member of his own church.[115] Yet he and Colman would always have their theological disagreements, including with regard to eschatology. As I will demonstrate, Colman's contrasting approach to the doctrine of the future resurrection spoke to his divergent understanding of the place of New England in the British Empire.

Colman's memorial sermon for Mather, *The Holy Walk and Glorious Translation of Blessed Enoch* (1728), reveals several similarities between their theologies of resurrection. Like Mather, Colman distinguishes between the dead saints who would return in the First Resurrection and the believers who would still be alive at the Second Coming (he notes that "Christ will raise his dead Servants before the great Change passes on them whom he shall find alive").[116] Moreover, his repudiation of mortalism echoes Mather's position. Here, as in *Triparadisus*, the dead saint's "soul" is separated "from the body" in order "to be present with the Lord" in spiritual form until the resurrection (the sermon also clarifies that "The *Spirits of the just made perfect* are in the same Heaven, . . . where *Enoch* and *Elias* are in their Spiritual bodies").[117] Yet

Colman's decision to honor Mather by means of a comparison with Enoch highlighted their disparate approaches to postmortem life.

According to the conventional exegesis of Genesis 5:24 ("And Enoch walked with God: and he was not, for God took him"), the biblical patriarch had been deemed pure enough to be physically translated into heaven without dying. Colman noted that all those who "walk[ed] in *Enoch's* faith and piety" would also be taken to the same place.[118] However, they would not be carried "bodily" there, but would instead have to pass through death's "dissolution" and a subsequent resurrection first. Even though Enoch's direct ascension to heaven was not typical, Colman often alluded to it in his discussions of the afterlife because framing resurrection as a process akin to an instantaneous translation to paradise suited his eschatological scheme.[119] In common with many other Protestants, he envisioned the millennium as a special period within secular history during which the church would experience unprecedented "*Peace and Tranquility, Purity and Holiness*" before undergoing a decline once more.[120] At some point during this latter age of spiritual complacency and "*Unbelief*" Christ would return in person and the resurrection of the dead would take place. In his sermon for Mather, Colman specified that this Day of Resurrection would also be the Day of Doom. Immediately after the raised saints returned to life and the changed saints were given their new spiritual bodies, both groups would be "caught up to meet the Lord in the air."[121] Christ's judgment of them, and of the damned, would ensure directly. After this all the faithful would ascend with him "to the *Third Heaven*," where, "glorified in soul and body," they would "*walk...in white* for ever more."

According to Colman, therefore, the elect would have no second life on earth after the resurrection. In a 1742 sermon, he specified that all the dead would "awak[e] from their long *Sleep* in the Dust" at the same time, ready to witness the descent of Christ "with their *restored* Eyes of *Flesh*, in *spiritual* Bodies." Shortly afterward, the saved would be raptured into heaven—pictured as an "*Æther of Light*"—whereas the damned would descend into hell's "*Cavern* of Smoke and *Gloom*."[122] As these descriptions suggest, Colman's delineation of the afterlife was spiritual and somewhat insubstantial, even though he insisted on the literal and corporeal nature of the resurrection. His writings give very little sense of the celestial city *as* a city, or of the church in heaven as a political body. Moreover, the tutelary relationship between the raised and changed saints, so critical to Mather's understanding of the politics of the millennial earth, is entirely absent from this model. Since both the living and the dead would ascend into heaven together, worldly political concerns, indeed, the very concept of politics itself, would be swiftly set aside.

Colman was nonetheless convinced that political developments this side of the apocalypse held eschatological meaning. Since he was sure that it was impossible for mortal humans to develop any clear sense of the specific timetable of "the Dissolution of all Things,"[123] he disapproved of attempts to invest specific events with detailed prophetic significance. Yet he was more than willing to ascribe a general eschatological importance to the Protestant struggle against the French and Jacobite forces of the Catholic Antichrist.[124] Great Britain therefore stood at the center of his providential conception of history. Colman could see a millennial promise in certain developments in the New World, including New England's ongoing missions to the Native Americans, the 1722 conversion of a Jewish Harvard instructor to Christianity, and the colonial revivals of the 1740s.[125] But the most valuable contributor to the coming of the kingdom was the house of Hanover, to which he urged "near-total obedience."[126] Following the failed Jacobite rising of 1715, Colman insisted that there was a higher purpose behind the rebels' defeat. George I, he prayed, would "live to be the *Glorious Instrument in the Hand of* GOD" who effected "*Reformation* in every Respect" across the empire.[127]

This fervent faith in the king's spiritual mission illustrates Colman's especially strong tendency to equate political and social stability with divine providence. While he valued "Piety and Charity" just as much as Mather did,[128] he was far less inclined to assume that practicing these heavenly virtues would bring Christians into conflict with worldly authority. "DISORDER," he argued, "is as much the *Misery* & Ruine as it is the *Deformity* of Societies, private or public, civil or religious."[129] Since the "*Order* that there is in the World" was providentially "Establish[ed] [by] GOD for our present & future Well-being," Christians should "be very careful to preserve it in our places, and to do what we can to promote it everywhere." Until the "*Day of the Resurrection of all things* . . . put an *End* to all the *Disorders* that Sin and Death have bro't into the World," the saints would be best served by creating earthly approximations of the "Peace, Purity and perfect *Order*" that would prevail in heaven.[130] On that day, "the united Loveliness of All Saints" would be collapsed into "One Body," "the Light of All Ages . . . contracted into One Point of dazling Lustre."[131] Colman's "catholick" churchmanship (which did not require a profession of saving faith from new members) and pro-Crown politics were modeled after this frictionless transition into "solemn [and] glorious *Order*."[132]

Characteristically, Colman's primary eschatological treatise culminated with a warning about the social effects of preaching that the millennium was imminent. Although "They that *love the Lord and his appearing* are ready to think that he can't come too soon," this "excess of Desire" was potentially "of very ill Consequence, leading us into Error, staggering the Faith of some, and hardening others in Infidelity, while it provokes their Scoffs."[133] Instead of dwelling on the "General Judgment-Day" which was probably "many Ages off," believers would be much wiser to meditate on their own deaths, which were "certainly very nigh."[134] Mather, too, used his apocalyptic writings to urge his readers to remember the brevity of their lives.[135] But the closing section of *Triparadisus* also encouraged Christians to consider their places in the wider drama of the millennium. Since the earth was soon to be "condemned *unto* Flames," they ought to treat it "with the *Contempt* which is due to such a Wretched Object." There was no danger that adopting this attitude would lead to the radical political excesses of the "Hare-brained *Fifth-Monarchy Men*."[136] Believers should continue to engage in "the Honest and Proper *Business* of *This World*" as if the planet "might yett stand for *Many Years*."

In a certain sense, it would. In contrast to Colman, Mather did not expect time to stop following the resurrection of the dead. Year would still follow year on the millennial earth. Generational differences would matter. New saints would be born, and older saints would be translated to heaven (as Enoch was) to make room for them.[137] Because time would still be significant, so would space. The immortalized elect would spread out across the globe until it was "incomparably better peopled" than the old earth had been.[138] Though there would be no wars or secular states, there would still be "*Nations*" of people that were demographically connected to the countries and colonies of the first earth. Mather's obsession with discrediting Mede's exclusion of America from the kingdom of God is indicative of his belief that the changed saints would begin their new lives in the same place they had ended their previous ones. That conviction always distinguished him from Colman, even though he came to share the younger man's ecumenical attitude toward the broader Protestant Interest.

Mather was far more critical of Britain's treatment of English Dissenters and its attitude toward Congregationalist New England than Colman ever was. This was because he was worried about the standing of the colonies and the imperial metropolis in the millennium. Only those who had fully accepted God's grace would number among the raised and changed saints of the next world. While Mather knew that in most supposedly Christian countries there were "but *a Few*" of these *Chosen* Ones,"[139] he still sought to ensure that Britain and New England were as well represented in the coming kingdom as possible. From his perspective, less apocalyptically minded colleagues such as Colman prized peace and order in the present too highly. Protecting the legacy of Anglo-American Protestantism in the next age sometimes necessitated political and theological critique. As he warned English Nonconformists fighting against Arianism in their ranks, forbearing from urgent criticism in order to preserve "*Secular Friendship*" would only lead to the "Desolation" of British interests in the eschaton.[140]

The divergence between Mather's and Colman's resurrection theologies also anticipated a longer-term shift in Protestant attitudes toward the afterlife. For both ministers, belief in the future resurrection was tied up with filiopiety toward dead believers. *The Bones of Joseph*, Colman's 1720s funeral sermon for Joseph Dudley, echoed Mather's treatment of this theme. Through his title and text (Hebrews 11:22), Colman compared Dudley's burial place in Roxbury, alongside his father Thomas (another former governor of Massachusetts), and the resting place of the remains of the biblical Joseph, supposedly carried out of Egypt by Moses (Exodus 13:19) and later buried in Canaan (Joshua 24:32). The patriarch's remains were treated with such reverence and care because of his faith in corporeal resurrection: "For why should he ... be concerned with what became of [his] *bones*, if they were never to *rise* again?"[141] "But if there be a Resurrection of the Just," Colman continued, "then there is a kind of Communion which the mix'd dust of Saints enjoy in the Grave." For this reason, Joseph wanted to be buried in the Promised Land. His father, Jacob, similarly, had asked his sons to bury him "*in the Cave that is in the field of Machpelah*," alongside his grandfather Abraham, his father Isaac, and his first wife Leah. "As to bring the matter near to our selves," Colman asked his congregation, "Who would not desire to ly and rise with such as our *Eliot* of *Roxbury*, our *Hobart* of *Newton*? or, among our Governours ... our *Bradstreet* and *Stoughton*?"

This question called to mind the same image that Mather invoked repeatedly in the *Magnalia* and throughout his career: the extraordinary number of notable saints who would rise from New England's ground at the First Resurrection. Yet immediately after raising this prospect, Colman dismissed its significance. He insisted that "it matters not at last where our bones are scattered, if we by faith are united to CHRIST, and in him unto all his Saints; for all the dust of Saints all the world over makes but *one body* of CHRIST, whereof [all] Individual[s] are *Members in particular.*" In the absence of an earthly millennium, the afterlife of distinct political collectives is largely moot. For Colman, the only corporate body that is to be translated into the next world is the aggregate of all the faithful. Insofar as it downplayed the importance of the specific location in which saints were buried and would rise again, this perspective was compatible with the gradual disembodiment and dematerialization of the afterlife that followed the Enlightenment. Though Colman himself defended the reasonableness and scientific plausibility of the corporeal regeneration of the same body,[142] his depiction of resurrection as an instantaneous ascent to the spiritual world foreshadowed the later Christian tendency to view heaven as a realm entirely apart from our own.

Conversely, without ever underestimating their radical disparity, Mather saw this world and the next as part of a contiguous whole. His writings on millennium and the celestial city repurposed the pre-Reformation tradition of viewing the dead as ongoing participants in particular communities (as well as in the wider church). His description of resurrection as a return to earth, rather than a direct flight to heaven, contests the modern sense of what salvation means. For him, it did not constitute a straightforward transcendence of the challenges of human existence, but a re-engagement with them under different conditions. In the next chapter, we shall see how Mather and other eighteenth-century Protestant eschatologists employed the resurrected body to address an issue that was newly emergent in their time—the pseudo-science of racial difference.

3
Resurrection's Racial Politics

Protestant Evangelism and the Development of Racial Difference

Early modern Protestants knew that every human being possessed an immortal soul. On Judgment Day, that soul would be reunited with the body to stand before God's throne. Saints would rise in glory, the damned in corruption and disgrace, regardless of their status and origin on earth. This universal resurrection was seen as a symbol of the ultimate unity of the human race, who were assumed to have an innate desire for eternal life. Though Africans, Native Americans and other pagan peoples were often thought to worship the Devil, missionaries, explorers, and ethnographers identified echoes of Jewish and Christian doctrine in their beliefs about the afterlife: Roger Williams and John Hariot noted that the Algonquian nations were certain of the immortality of the soul; John Ogilby observed that faith in an eternal reward led Egyptians to live "honest and vertuous" lives.[1]

Finding these resonances was important, because the "discovery" and ongoing colonization of a New World unknown to the Bible had overturned traditional assumptions about global geography and demography.[2] This momentous development led some authors, most notably French Calvinist Isaac La Peyrère (1596–1676), to argue that humanity was not one—in a widely read and translated 1655 treatise, La Peyrère claimed that Native Americans and most other non-Europeans were the posterity of a people created before Adam. Nonetheless, polygenetic anthropologies were widely rejected in the seventeenth century, with most scholars preferring to believe that the inhabitants of the Americas could trace their lineage back to some European or Asian group.[3] One controversial theory, popularized in England by Thomas Thorowgood, claimed that Native Americans were descended from the lost tribes of Israel. One of the proofs that Thorowgood assembled for this claim was that South American Indians apparently believed in corporeal resurrection ("for that cause," he explained, they are "careful in burying their dead; and when they saw the Spaniards digging into Sepulchers for gold and

---

To Walk the Earth Again. Christopher Trigg, Oxford University Press. © Oxford University Press 2023.
DOI: 10.1093/oso/9780197652756.003.0004

silver, the Natives entreated them not to scatter the bones, so that they might with more ease be raised againe").[4]

During this transitional period, the question of the eschatological end of human diversity developed in parallel to the related matter of its origins. As La Peyrère's English critic Edward Stillingfleet pointed out, the "universal effects of the fall of man" depended on Adam's position as the first parent.[5] If his Fall did not communicate original sin to all humankind, then Christ's sacrifice on the cross could not be the source of redemption for every man and woman. So it was that Anglican missionary Morgan Godwyn described the proselytization of Africans and Native Americans are part of the "War . . . *against Sin* and *Infidelity*." Differences in "Condition, Country, Complexion, [and] Descent," had no bearing on the destination of the believer's soul. "There is the same Heaven and Salvation," Godwyn insisted, "proposed for the conversion of Slaves, as of more illustrious *Grandees*."[6]

But would people of color enjoy equal status in the next life? Protestant evangelists of every stripe insisted that they would. As he attempted to convince English settlers in Barbados to cooperate with the Christianization of the people they enslaved, Godwyn maintained that "Slave" and "Master" should hold "*equal hopes*" about their eternal fate.[7] In his 1727 history of the mission on Martha's Vineyard, Experience Mayhew approvingly quoted the words of the Wampanoag preacher Hiacoomes at the 1684 funeral of Tackanash, another Native religious leader. On the day of resurrection, Hiacoomes had noted, "it shall not be . . . as you see it is now; now every one is diversely apparelled, some after one manner, and some after another, but all after a pitiful mean sort; but the Righteous at the Resurrection shall have all one uniform Glory."[8] In an anonymous 1743 tract, English Baptist Anne Dutton made a comparable claim to African bondsmen and women who had been recently converted in South Carolina. On the last day, Dutton promised, Christ would take every variety of gentile, "even *you despised Negroes*, and join [them] into *one Fold*" alongside "his peculiar People," the Jews.[9]

Modern scholarship has taken a keen interest in this promise that racial scholarship would be transcended in heaven. Even as they have traced the myriad ways in which Christian mission could facilitate the oppression of Native American and African converts, historians have tended to assume the good faith of seventeenth- and eighteenth-century proselytizers who spoke of heavenly equality. Vincent Brown, for example, argues that "equality in the afterlife" was "a central tenet of [the] Christian teaching" that enslaved Africans encountered in colonial Jamaica.[10] Meanwhile, John Wood Sweet notes that the idea that "salvation would eradicate racial difference" in the next world was a common belief among New England Protestants, even though the history of the region in the eighteenth century reveals that "racial divisions were not in fact reconciled by religious conversions but rather reinforced and made to seem more natural."[11] The equal status of different ethnicities in heaven is also implicit in the frequently repeated claim that colonial Protestant missionaries offered people of color "spiritual equality," rather than liberty or social parity in life.[12]

However, some eighteenth-century Protestants did in fact suggest that racial distinctions would continue to be significant in the world to come. In the previous chapter, I showed how Cotton Mather imagined the survival of New England Congregationalism into the millennial age through the participation of its departed elect in the First Resurrection. Through his theory of the Nishmath-Chajim, Mather sought to establish a scientific basis for his conviction that dead and living saints formed part of the same political community. This part-spiritual, part-material "breath of life" allowed departed believers to continue to serve God in paradise as they awaited their resurrection. It also guaranteed the postmortem preservation of distinguishing individual characteristics, ensuring that old friends would be able to recognize each other when reunited on the New Earth. Here, by way of contrast, I will be primarily concerned with resurrection as a marker of political *discontinuity* and *distinction*. I will show how certain Protestant authors—including Mather himself—suggested that saints of color would need to undergo an extra supernatural transformation before they would be able to assume their places in heaven.

While speculations into the racial dimensions of the afterlife might seem fanciful today, they were of real significance in the late seventeenth and eighteenth centuries. The discussion as to whether ethnic identities would be carried over into the next world was part of the increasingly acrimonious controversy regarding the social, political, and religious status of Native Americans and Africans in the British Atlantic. Mainstream scientists and theologians insisted on the genealogical unity of humankind but began to emphasize African divergence in particular, offering a number of explanations for the darker skin tones of African peoples. Similarly, authorities on the next world stressed that men and women of every nation would be resurrected and judged, then saved or damned. But they also developed theories that suggested that Africans would require special treatment during this process, including the whitening of their skin. Even those who denied that this alteration would be necessary sometimes set out visions of heaven or the millennium that privileged those of European descent. In so doing, these authors were not simply suggesting that the question of racial identity was a worldly problem that would be "transcended" in heaven. Instead, they were actively participating in the construction and coalescence of racial difference, as well as outlining the terms on which those newly marked as racially other should be integrated into Christian communities in the present.

By the early eighteenth century, Protestant eschatology was already bound up with assumptions of (northern) European cultural superiority.[13] But two new developments in the period combined to intensify this association. First, English colonies began to codify racial distinctions more strictly. In Virginia, the marriage of English to African had been illegal since 1662, but a 1705 statute (An Act Concerning Servants and Slaves) stipulated that unlike their "christian white" equivalents, African and Native American servants were subject to perpetual, heritable enslavement, as well as harsher disciplinary measures.[14] While the numbers of enslaved men and women in North America and the Caribbean continued to increase, other jurisdictions passed legislation that not only delineated the terms of slavery, but also described a widening gap between Africans and Euro-Americans in general.[15] In New England this legal division was not as broad as it was farther south—both free and enslaved Africans could give evidence against white people in court, for example.[16] The small number of slaves in the North meant that they and their enslavers "were densely enmeshed in the overlapping relationships that formed local communities."[17] Nevertheless, slavery there was still characterized by the principle described by Orlando Patterson as "social death"—although they were present within the body politic, enslaved people were not full members of it, being barred from serving in the militia and from marrying whites.[18] This exclusion extended to the grave—Africans were usually buried in a "separate section of [a town's] burial ground," and in some places this proviso was legally compulsory.[19]

The perceived racial gap between Anglo- and Native Americans was also widening. In New England, King Philip's War (1675-1678) had led many settlers to conclude that "the categories of 'Christian' and 'Indian' were inherently incompatible."[20] All across British North America, the colonial occupation of tribal land in the decades that followed led Europeans to insist ever more strongly on the physiological, mental, and cultural inferiority of the Native Americans they sought to dispossess.[21] By the middle of the eighteenth century, these distinctions were beginning to coalesce around the racial marker of "red" skin (though Nancy Shoemaker points out that different Native groups were from the 1720s already referring to themselves as "red men" in opposition to white Europeans).[22] Sharon Block reminds us that "skin colour" was not "consistently . . . privileged as *the* sign of racial identity" until "the beginning of the nineteenth century."[23] However, the central opposition between "white" Europeans and "black" Africans was taking shape in the Caribbean and Southern American Colonies by 1700, and in New England and the rest of the North East by the 1730s.

In the same period that this racial hierarchy was emerging, Anglican, Presbyterian and Nonconformist clergy were insisting that English Protestants should take the conversion of Africans and Indians more seriously. The Society for the Propagation of the Gospel, founded in 1701, was primarily concerned with ministering to Europeans in colonies without an established Anglican church, but its leadership in London also encouraged missionaries to attempt to convert Africans and Native Americans in the Caribbean and North America. In 1730, the Presbyterian Society in Scotland for the Propagation of Christian Knowledge, hitherto focused on bringing English-speaking Protestantism to the Gaels of the Scottish Highlands and Isles, established missions to Native peoples in Connecticut and New York.[24] Meanwhile, Congregationalist clergy in New England continued to call for the conversion of the region's Indians, even though King Philip's War had undone most of the earlier work of John Eliot and the other New England Company missionaries. They also paid increasingly close attention to the proselytization of enslaved and free Africans, as the population of the former increased sharply across both southern and northern colonies in the first two decades of the new century.[25] Members of the Quaker Society of Friends, finally, were particularly strong proponents of mission to bondsmen and women, gradually exchanging their earlier advocacy of Christianized slavery for a consistently abolitionist position by 1761.[26]

As several recent studies have noted, the conflicting demands of inclusive evangelism and exclusionary racial codification occasioned a series of debates about the baptism of people of color. Heather Kopelson and Rebecca Goetz have shown how enslaved people across North America and the Caribbean asserted that the Christian liberty that attended baptism entitled them to civil liberty too. While they could appeal to the Protestant conviction that all Christians were equal members of the collective "body of Christ," this claim had to compete against the widely held belief that Africans (as well as Native Americans) were constitutionally predisposed to be impervious to the spiritual and social transformation that accompanied true conversion and were therefore trapped within what Goetz calls "hereditary heathenism."[27] Focusing on Barbados and the Danish West Indies, Katherine Gerbner describes a gradual shift from a regime of "Protestant Supremacy" that generally denied enslaved people baptism, to one of "Christian Slavery" that integrated a limited number of Africans into Anglican and Danish Reformed congregations while denying them the legal and political privileges reserved for their white equivalents.[28] Similarly, Travis Glasson's history of the SPG shows how the society eventually settled on the position that the baptism of the enslaved did not necessitate their release, since spiritual and political freedom were separate.[29] By 1706, Maryland, Virginia, North Carolina, South Carolina, New York, and New Jersey had all passed laws that stipulated the same thing.[30] Although the various New England jurisdictions would not join them, the principle was affirmed by Cotton Mather and other Puritan clergy.[31]

Writing and thinking about the fate of bodies in the afterlife and the millennium was another means by which eighteenth-century Protestants negotiated the troubling spiritual implications of the emerging rhetoric of racial difference. Ethnic and religious distinctions were crucial to the eschatological and millennial models that had been developed in the sixteenth and seventeenth centuries. Many early modern Protestants (though not Calvin) adopted Augustine's view that there would be a national conversions of the Jews before the end of time.[32] Frustrated by the persistent threat of the Ottoman Empire, Puritan and Anglican ministers alike predicted that the last days would also witness the end of Islamic power in the Levant.[33] The proclamation of Matthew 24:14 that the gospel will be preached to every nation before Christ's return charged English colonialism in North America and the West Indies with eschatological importance. For instance, although the theory that Native Americans were descended from Tartars predominated in the Bay Colony, some Massachusetts authors, including missionary John Eliot and prominent judge Samuel Sewall, were strongly attracted to the lost tribes theory, hoping that the conversion of Native Americans might help to accomplish the prophesied Christianization of Israel.[34] Moreover, some Protestants, including Cotton Mather, saw a providential significance in the slave trade's importation of so many Africans into colonies where their souls might be claimed for Christ.[35]

As the concept of race as biological distinction slowly took shape, this eschatological optimism collided with anxiety about the disruptive social impact of growing numbers of nonwhite Christians. For the writers discussed in this chapter, the salvation of Africans, in particular, was both a desired outcome and a potentially disconcerting development. Cotton Mather, Samuel Sewall, and the SPG missionary John Beach all insisted that men and women of any provenance could be selected to join the resurrection of the just; at the same time, they were reluctant to imagine that risen bodies could be bodies of color.

Each articulated this reluctance in a different way. Like many of his contemporaries, Sewall wondered if Africans might be turned white through their resurrection. For his part, Mather insisted that the bodies of all risen saints would be comprised of spiritualized matter, both epidermically luminous and robed in white garments. While he therefore rejected the possibility that black bodies would need to be literally whitened, Mather nonetheless characterized the spiritual education of Africans as an especially arduous task. Furthermore, his descriptions of the earthly millennium strongly implied that the great majority of the raised saints—those returned to life by the First Resurrection to serve as the rulers of the next world—would be of European origin. Because they would be converted just before the millennium, the greater part of saved Africans and other former pagans would be numbered among the changed saints who would need to be tutored by their resurrected counterparts before being deemed worthy to ascend to heaven themselves. Where the old Puritan fathers (and mothers) would be ready to assume command as soon as the millennial age arrived, most people of color would continue to be subject to religious instruction. Beach, finally, argued that the resurrection of Christian believers took place individually, rather than collectively, immediately following each saint's demise, rather than at the end of time. As a result, neither the resurrection of the flesh nor the earthly millennium had any place in his system: after their deaths, saved men and women would immediately enter heaven, where they would be given new, entirely spiritual bodies. By denying that resurrected saints would have a material form at all, Beach entirely obviated the troubling question of whether African believers would be spiritualized and empowered in resurrected nonwhite bodies.

None of these authors subscribed to the modern idea of race as biological distinction. But as they set out the terms on which it was possible to imagine enslaved people and other Africans living forever, they reinforced an association between black bodies and human frailty that would only become stronger as the concept of biological racial difference solidified. The

Christianized slavery that Mather and Beach advocated was premised on the idea that bondsmen and women could be brought into the church on less than fully equal terms (broadly the same structure was at play in Sewall's understanding of the place that Africans in general occupied within New England society). This inequitable approach to evangelization attributed an inferiority to black believers that was only partially balanced by the prospect of their postmortem integration into the elect.

By depicting the conversion of people of color as a difficult undertaking that demanded careful oversight, Protestants risked eternalizing the imputed characteristics that African Christianization was supposed to redress: carnality, ignorance, recalcitrance. Most of all they linked the black body to mortality, in some cases implying that blackness was not compatible with eternal life. In so doing, they anticipated a later development described by Andrew Curran, whereby French Enlightenment thinkers admitted Africans into the category of the human, only to ascribe a morbid "materiality" to their physical forms.[36] Achille Mbembe's conceptual history of Africa and blackness from the age of Atlantic slavery onward delineates a similar process, through which the figure of "the Black Man" in the abstract comes to symbolize mortality, suffering, and "the scandal of humanity."[37] Sewall's, Mather's, and Beach's concern about the place of Africans in the world to come was an early example of this qualification of African personhood. Before black skin was a definitive marker of social and political exclusion in this world, it was a sign of qualified and contested acceptance in the next.

Native American salvation was also a controversial subject in the colonial Atlantic. The broad failure of most Protestant missions in the seventeenth and early eighteenth centuries led some to wonder if Indians were congenitally resistant to Christian conversion.[38] Even those who insisted that the conversion of Native Americans was possible and desirable recognized that it must necessarily be a long and difficult undertaking. John Eliot organized the Massachusetts Indians he proselytized into "Praying Towns" because he believed that they would need to adopt English standards of civility, labor, and social organization before they could be properly instructed in Christian doctrine.[39] Cotton Mather, who boasted that Eliot and his colleagues had been the first to bring "the Pure Gospel to the *Americans*," characterized that mission as a work of "*Humaniz*[ing] . . . Miserable *Animals*."[40] When the number of Native Protestants increased following the mid-eighteenth century revivals, converts were still confronted with the assumption that " 'Christian' and 'Indian' " were opposed "identities."[41]

Nevertheless, the possibility that a Native American body might be granted eternal life did not trouble Euro-Christians to the same extent as the resurrection of an African body. This fact reflects the different social and political expectations attached to Indian and African conversion. Though the early colonizers of Virginia may have formulated an ambitious plan to create an "anti-Catholic Anglo-Indian commonwealth,"[42] it was more typically assumed that Christianized Natives would continue to live in separate communities, like the "praying towns" established by Eliot. Converted Indians were effectively offered a parallel, politically separate, passage into heaven. African converts, whether free or enslaved, were more closely dependent on Euro-American settler society. Furthermore, the continued growth of the slaveholding economy necessitated the development of a more extreme discourse of black racial inferiority. Because Africans in the Americas were perceived to be *particularly* abject people whose fates lay under white control, some Protestants came to believe that their integration into the eternal company of saints might require special measures.

The chapter's closing two sections consider how the black evangelical and literary cultures that developed from the late eighteenth century responded to this condescending view of African redemption, which was perpetuated by leading white revivalists such as George Whitefield. Many of the first generation of black authors in English adopted the traditional Christian rhetoric that linked blackness with damnation and whiteness with redemption. However, several of them (including Phillis Wheatley, Ignatius Sancho, Ottobah Cugoano, and Prince Hall) directly contested the idea that eternal salvation would require saints of color to shed their ethnic identity. Black skin, they insisted, had no bearing on either conversion on earth or life in heaven. Some writers—Sancho and, later, David Walker and Frederick Douglass—sought to reconfigure the concepts of resurrection and salvation in various ways. Where Sancho undermined the association between Christianity and whiteness by denying that the damnation of unconverted pagans would be eternal, Walker and Douglass emphasized immediate, self-determined redemption out of slavery over the prospective resurrection of the flesh. These soteriological transformations support my contention that in the eighteenth century heaven and resurrection had never been entirely racially neutral concepts. Although most missionaries and evangelists stopped short of imagining that bodies of color would be literally whitened as they rose again, their assumption that Christianization also involved a degree of

Europeanization certainly impacted their understanding of what life after death would be like.

"Can the Ethiopian Change His Skin?": Samuel Sewall, Resurrection, and Race

On April 3, 1711, Samuel Sewall had dinner with his fellow justices of the Massachusetts Superior Court. He noted in his diary that the company "Spake much of Negroes" that day.[43] In the course of their discussion, Sewall raised the problem of whether Africans "should be white after the Resurrection," prompting a vigorous debate at the table. John Bolt maintained that the question was inherently "absurd, because the [resurrected] body" would be translucent, and therefore "void of all Colour." Sewall retorted that Bolt "spake as if it [the resurrected body] should be a Spirit," reminding him of the risen Christ's words to his disciples in the Gospel of Luke (24:39): "Behold my hands and my feet, that it is I myself: handle me, and see; for a spirit hath not flesh and bones, as ye see me have." Sewall's diary entry on the conversation ultimately abstains from offering a firm conclusion on the whitening of resurrected black saints, although it does suggest that he considered it a serious possibility.

Twelve years later, Sewall's son Joseph preached a sermon that touched on the same idea. In April 1723, Boston was panicking over a series of arsons that had begun on March 30 and would continue for several weeks. Following a second fire three days later, "in Leverett's Lane[,] near the Quaker's Meeting House," the *Boston News Letter* reported that "a Negro Man Servant" had confessed to starting the blaze.[44] More fires followed, including one on April 13 that very nearly spread to "the Wooden part of Judge *Sewall's* dwelling House."[45] Enslaved men were assumed to be behind these further incidents, and Samuel Sewall himself counseled Governor William Dummer to advertise a reward for information leading to the apprehension of those responsible.[46] It was in this context that Joseph's homily addressed the African inhabitants of the city, encouraging them to confess to the crimes or to identify the perpetrators. As Zachary Hutchins observes, Sewall junior linked this cooperation in the investigation to the remission of sins and a prospective setting aside of the "burdens" of their "black bodies." "The terms of forgiveness," Hutchins continues, "are framed by Sewall in the racialized language of Isaiah 1:18—'Come now, and let us reason together, saith the

Lord: though your sins be as scarlet, they shall be white as snow; though they be red like crimson, they shall be as wool.'" The language of Joseph's sermon stressed that accepting Dummer's offer would mean receiving enough money to purchase one's freedom. Hutchins explains that this prize is figured as a kind of "social ascension" or resurrection: by quoting Philippians 3:21 Sewall suggests that the African servant can exchange the "vile body" of the enslaved for the "glorious body" of the free man. The prospect of a literal blanching after death, I would add, was also in play.

These two episodes in the history of the Sewall family sit somewhat uneasily with Samuel's later reputation as an opponent of slavery. In 1700, a dispute between an enslaved man named Adam and the Boston merchant John Saffin, led Sewall to publish a short tract titled *The Selling of Joseph*. This essay, still widely read today, has been cast as one of America's first articulations of antislavery sentiment.[47] However, it is more accurate to describe the pamphlet as a critique of the slave *trade*, rather than the practice of slaveholding *tout court*. Sewall's primary contention was that "the specific form of slavery practiced in the American colonies" was both morally questionable and financially risky, since it could not easily be established that the enslaved were legally taken captives of war.[48] *The Selling of Joseph* also rejects the then common justification that the enslavement of Africans might help to effect their conversion.[49] "Evil must not be done," Sewall explains, "that good may come of it.[50]" Indeed, he worried that the growth of slavery in England's colonies would hinder the Protestant mission to the nations. In 1705, he arranged for the Boston reprinting of an issue of the London *Athenian Oracle* that claimed that the trade was "a Disgrace to Christianity, and makes the Name of Christ to be blasphem'd amongst the Gentiles, and (in all likelihood) hinders the Propagation of the Christian Faith in the World."[51] As many scholars have noted, *The Selling of Joseph's* argument against the slave trade was also rooted in ethnic prejudice.[52] Sewall opposed the idea of increasing numbers of Africans (whether free or in bondage) being brought into English colonies because he worried that people of color were "unchangeably inferior."[53] This intolerance, I will argue now, was also reflected in his view of the millennium and the afterlife.

In common with many of his Protestant peers, Sewall believed that the conversion of growing numbers of Africans, Native Americans, and other pagans would be one of the key signs of the advent of Christ's kingdom on earth. Indeed, the Christianization of America's indigenous peoples was particularly important to him, given his emphasis on the eschatological importance of the global West.⁵⁴ His millennial treatise *Phaenomena Quaedam Apocalyptica* (1697) identified the Catholic or "Antichristian Interests in the New World" as the referent of Revelation's prophecy that "the great river Euphrates" (16:12) would need to be dried up before the final triumph of God's cause.⁵⁵ Sewall therefore eagerly scrutinized events across both North and South America for evidence that Protestants missions and colonies were prospering at the expense of their Roman rivals.⁵⁶ Once the pope and his French and Spanish allies were definitively defeated, the Jewish people would realize their mistake, and embrace, en masse, the true Protestant faith. These converts would then gather in Mexico, where a global capital, the New Jerusalem, would be established. The stage would then be set for a progressive Christianization of the planet and the salvation of most of its inhabitants. Not only would existing churches "in Asia, Africa, Europe, and America" be brought back to "Life from the dead,"⁵⁷ but pagan peoples around the planet would be "rescue[d] . . . from that palpable Darkness and Death into which they are plunged."⁵⁸

Unlike his friend Cotton Mather, Sewall did not believe that this New Earth would be populated by a new, supernaturally transformed type of human being. He held that the resurrection of the dead would take place at the end of the millennium, rather than at its beginning. But while life would continue along the same existential and biological lines, the geopolitical order of the planet would be completely overturned. The Americas, formerly the "Uttermost *parts of the earth*" would form the center of a global community of saints,⁵⁹ extending to the four corners of the planet. Barbados and Jamaica, formerly hubs of the slave trade, would become staging posts for English pilgrims visiting the city of God. Needless to say, there would be no slavery at all during the millennium: all military conflicts, the primary drivers of legitimate enslavement, would have ceased.⁶⁰ Sewall was therefore inclined to see the gradual diminution and eventual abolition of slavery as a way of preparing for the new age. Writing to the American secretary of the English Society for Promoting Christian Knowledge in 1714, he noted that there would "be no great progress in Gospellizing" until the "wicked practice of Slavery" was ended.⁶¹

How can this cosmopolitan millennialism be reconciled with the idea of resurrection as whitening that Sewall raised at that dinner in 1711, or with the prejudicial account of African personhood he outlined in *The Selling of Joseph*? First, it is important to recognize that like John Cotton, Sewall parsed the First Resurrection allegorically, taking it to refer to the religious, political, and social transformation of the earth. Whereas the resurrection at the end of the world would elevate all saints to spiritual and physical perfection, its millennial equivalent would merely reform their way of living: "The Beauty and Grandeur of the *New Jerusalem*," Sewall noted in 1727, "will chiefly consist in Humility, Purity, Self-denial, Love, Peace, and Joy in Believing."[62] Second, it should also be noted that the *Phaenomena* readily acknowledges that not every part of the millennial world would be of equal importance or virtue. Mexico's new city of God, of course, would be preeminent among the nations for power, influence, and holiness. London, the tract implies, would continue to be an important center, while New England itself would be comparatively marginal.[63] Most strikingly of all, Sewall believed that after the final defeat of the papacy, the city of Rome itself would be excluded from "the Privileges of Christ's Kingdom."[64] That spiritual "*Babylon*" would be either literally or politically destroyed, subject to "an absolute Desolation," or a "cursed, and hatefull" existence.

Together, these points indicate that for Sewall there would have been no contradiction between offering African saints a place in the international community of saints that would exist during the millennium and simultaneously setting a hard limit to their integration into that collective. For if men and women of color really were set to become "white after the [literal] Resurrection" that would take place at the end of the millennium, then black skin would have remained the marker of a certain inequality between their race and the others, even after the abolition of slavery and a thousand years of peace and unity.

Sewall did not view dark complexions with the same degree of contempt as did the other Protestants who speculated that Africans might be resurrected white. He rejected the position taken by the English physico-theologian William Whiston, who held that blackness would have to be "taken off" at the beginning of the millennium, following Africa's "general conversion to Christianity," because it was the product of a curse placed on Lamech, the murderous scion of Cain mentioned in the fourth chapter of Genesis.[65] He also stopped short of the aesthetic argument offered by the editor of the *Athenian Mercury* (forerunner of *The Oracle*), who suggested that "the colour of Night" was so objectively "frightful ... and horrid" that it would have to be left "behind ... in the darkness of the Grave." Africans were not cursed to be slaves by scripture, Sewall insisted. They were just as much "the Offspring of GOD" as were any other ethnic group.[66]

Nonetheless, he cast black skin as a symbol of inferiority. *The Selling of Joseph* (now notoriously) insists that physiological differences, "disparity in ... Conditions, Color & Hair," would prevent them from forming "orderly Families" within New England, and thereby contributing to the "Peopling" and civilizing "of the Land" (2). This supposed incompatibility made him opposed to the proliferation of enslavement and the growth of the free black population in New England. "Few" white Christians, he claimed, "can endure to hear of a Negro's being made free" (he added that emancipated slaves "seldom use their freedom well" in any case). Liberated Africans would be an alien and debilitating presence within the colonies, "a kind of extravasat Blood" diverted into the wrong part of the "Body Politick." The social and political problems Sewell associated with out-of-place people of color would be more or less solved during the millennium: the slave trade would be ended, and a Christianized Africa would offer black people a suitable home. Yet even then, something of their troublesome otherness would remain: why else would he entertain the possibility that black bodies would need to be blanched to enter heaven?

In the course of making its case that "*Ethiopians*, as black as they are," ought to be afforded protection from "the Rigor of perpetual bondage" under natural law (3), *The Selling of Joseph* cites the first clause of a famous verse from the book of Jeremiah (13:23): "Can the Ethiopian change his skin, or the leopard his spots? then ye may also do good, that are accustomed to do evil." Jeremiah poses these questions rhetorically, suggesting that Judah is as tethered to its sinful ways as the Ethiopian and leopard are tied to their appearances. Yet Sewall implicitly answers the first query in the affirmative, notwithstanding his claim that "Black Men ... have been distinguished by their Colour" for "time out of mind" (2). Figuratively speaking, Africans could change their skin—or else have it changed for them. Though their supposedly different constitutions allegedly made it difficult for them to live along Europeans, their "Conversion" to Christianity in large numbers was "Promised" and "to be prayed for."

For the time being, Sewall approved of and participated in attempts to bind the black inhabitants of Boston more closely to Puritan social conventions. In 1711, he noted with pleasure that two "Negro women" had been among the recent intake of new members into his church. Their "Relations" of their spiritual experiences, he observed, had proved "very acceptable."[67] When, in 1705, the Massachusetts government drew up a bill banning the "fornication, or Marriage of White men with Negros or Indians," he objected, fearing that it would prove "an Oppression provoking to God."[68] In mitigation, he managed to "g[e]t the Indians out of the Bill" altogether, and had a clause added that prevented masters from forbidding their slaves to marry someone of their own "nation."[69] After trusted local servants died, Sewall remarked on their positive qualities.[70] Following the demise of his own black servant Boston in 1729, he prepared a "good Fire" and bottles of "Sack" for the mourners.[71] The "long Train" that "follow'd [the coffin] to the Grave" on the day of the funeral numbered "about 150 Blacks, and about 50 Whites" (including "several Magistrates, Ministers, [and] Gentlemen")—testament to the "general Love and Esteem" in which the judge's employee was held.[72]

But Sewall's diaries also make frequent note of murders, infanticides, suicides, and arsons involving the African residents of Massachusetts. These sad events, which in his capacity as a magistrate he was often obliged to pass judgment on, would have served to confirm him in his opinion that people of color were not well adapted to life among white Christians.[73] Furthermore, he would play a prominent part in the events leading up to the legislation of a stricter Boston city slave code. During the civil unrest in the spring of 1723, the Sewall family home on Newbury Street would twice nearly be burned down—the second attack, Zachary Hutchins observes, occurring on the evening of Joseph's provocative lecture on the "burden" of blackness.[74] The following day, April 19, new laws were passed that tightly controlled the ability of black slaves and servants to associate with each other. The Bay Colony's government seemed to have come round to *The Selling of Joseph*'s point of view: bringing more people of an apparently lawless disposition into a Christian society was dangerous and disruptive and did little to bring most of them any closer to God.

Come the millennium, Sewall knew, there would be no need for restrictive legal codes that singled out people of a particular ethnicity. Then, men and women of color would collectively pass from spiritual death to life, from barbarity to civilization. And yet he was prepared to set a limit to African integration into Christendom even in that blessed time, suspecting that total incorporation into celestial eternity would require the shedding of the black skin that had always symbolized death and disorder. In the celebrated "Plum Island Passage" he positioned toward the end of the *Phaenomena*, Sewall employed the beauty and ecological harmony of the natural landscape around his childhood home at Newbury as an emblem of the quiet persistence of the Puritan way of life right up to the end of the present dispensation. "As long as the Sea-Fowl shall know the Time of their coming," he observed, "As long as any free and harmless Doves shall find a White Oak, or other Trees within the Township, to perch, or feed, or build a careless Nest upon . . . So long shall Christians be born [in Massachusetts]."[75] He also predicted that New England would endure throughout the millennium, ready to offer refreshment to saints travelling from London to visit "the City of the Great KING" in Mexico.[76] When the Anglo-American inhabitants of the region rose again at the end of the thousand years, therefore, it would be the culmination of a long collective tradition of piety and devotion. The bodily resurrection of African Christians, on the other hand, could be seen as a final break with a history of suffering and subjection.

A peculiar passage in Sewall's journal for 1701, where a racially inflected insult is loaded with eschatological significance, serves to support this conclusion. In October of that year the judge was feuding with the Mather family over Increase's controversial presidency of Harvard. In common with the Massachusetts General Court and the College's Corporation, he believed that Increase was neglecting his duties in Cambridge by commuting back to Boston to minister to his congregation there.[77] On the twentieth of the month, Cotton very publicly claimed that Sewall, who "pleaded much for Negroes" and their rights, "had used his father worse than a Neger" in this matter.[78] Sewall was greatly put out by this, but resolved to make amends. Sending Mather Senior "a Hanch of very good Venison," he archly noted in his diary that he hoped this generosity did not constitute another instance of "treat[ing]" the minister "as a Negro."

Despite his eagerness to reconcile with his friends, Sewall also wondered whether the Mathers' harsh treatment of him might not have a deeper spiritual significance. Cotton had made his accusations from inside Richard Wilkins's bookshop, but his loud voice had carried into the street. Did this mean that Sewall had been "slain" in the street, like the two witnesses whose death and resurrection were described in Revelation 11? If this were so, then he could expect to enjoy a renewed influence in New England affairs following this humiliation (after lying dead in the road for three and a half days, the Bible explained, the witnesses would receive "the Spirit of life from God," and "[stand] upon their feet" again [Revelation 11:11]).[79] Perhaps his argument with the Mathers was a sign of the imminence of the millennium, as the slaying of the witnesses was often understood to be.

Given this context, it is striking that Sewall's lofty sense of his own potential should be closely linked to the pejorative power of the word "Neger" or "Negro." If that term denoted social death and spiritual exclusion, then it was only fitting that Sewall's resurrection "as one of Christ's Witnesses" should follow an unjust accusation that he dealt with Africans more fairly than he did his friends. Only at the end of the millennium that the slaying of the witnesses heralded would the blemish of blackness be removed. For now, Sewall believed, it was important to maintain a clear distinction between those who were marked by that stigma, and those who were not.

"The Obedient Nations": Non-Europeans in Cotton Mather's Millennium

The Negro Christianized (1706), Cotton Mather's primary statement on the conversion of black slaves and servants, also associated unconverted Africans in New England with social and spiritual death. As he chastised white enslavers in the province and across England's empire for their lack of progress in gospelizing their enslaved charges, he warned them that "a SOUL . . . that neither knows nor likes the Things that are Holy and Just and Good . . . is in *Great Folly wandering down to the Congregation of the Dead*."[80] "The uninstructed *Negroes* about your houses," he continued, "appear like so many *Ghosts* and *Spectres*," accusing their masters of spiritual manslaughter, of spilling "the *Blood* of [their] *Souls*."[81] Mather's solution to this problem was significantly different from Sewall's. Though he too had some reservations about the practice of enslavement and slave trading, Mather disagreed with the judge about the potential for Christianizing the institution of slavery.[82] If owners would only recognize that the religious education of their slaves was their responsibility, then the unfortunate situation in which the enslaved found themselves could be sanctified. This process, he explained, would require the head of the household to approach the religious education of his slaves and servants in more or less the same way as he would that of his own children.[83] Yet Mather also stressed that conversion and baptism would not entitle enslaved men and women to emancipation.[84] Indeed, he suggested that Christian slaves would be much more "*Serviceable*, . . . *Obedient*[,] and obliging" toward their masters.[85]

Mather had ambitious plans for his pamphlet. As well as attempting to place the text "in every Family of New England, which has a Negro in it," he sent copies "unto the most eminent Persons, in all the Islands" of the English

Caribbean.[86] He was confident that his evangelical plan, which emphasized catechistical instruction, the inculcation of practical piety, and slaves being permitted to keep the sabbath properly, was well suited to the task of awakening enslaved Africans across the Atlantic world. A few months after the tract's publication he wrote to Sir William Ashurst, president of the Nonconformist missionary organization the New England Company, ambitiously hoping to "procure an *Act of Parliament*" for the promotion of his particular "Design of Christianizing the *Negroes.*"[87] Although the main body of *The Negro Christianized* itself does not make a direct reference to the millennium, Mather believed that the conversion of the enslaved (and of Africans in general) was rich with eschatological significance. In 1721 he would suggest that a more concerted Protestant effort to save the pagan peoples of the world, including those "treated like meer *Beasts of Burden* . . . in the Plantations of cruel *Americans*", would help to usher in the millennial time when "the *Gentiles* would *walk in the Light* of the *New Jerusalem!*"[88]

But would Africans exist on equal terms with saints of European descent in the next world? One important early reader of *The Negro Christianized* believed that they would need to undergo a phenotypical transformation before they could be admitted to heaven. On August 15, 1706, a few weeks after the publication of the tract, Reverend Nicholas Noyes of Salem wrote to Mather in response to the latter's request for a tally of the families in the town with African servants. In addition to his answer ("about 27"), Noyes included a poem in praise of Mather's book and of his mission to the black servants and slaves of New England. The first half of this composition runs like this:

> You plant like Paul, you Water like Apollos,
> You set fair Coppyes, happy he that follows.
> You bid fair for it, let Heaven make it doe;
> And by your hands, wash the Æthopian toe.
> Christs grace & blood applyed, makes white within,
> And clenseth from the Guilt & Stain of Sin.
> The resurrection whiten will the Skin;
> The great refiner & the blessed fuller,
> Will one day make the Saints all of a coler.
> And all be blacker than the Sons of Cham,
> That are not Whitned by the Spotless Lamb.[89]

Here Noyes compares Mather to Paul and Apollos, who carried the gospel to the gentiles in the early years of the church. Picking up on *The Negro Christianized*'s reference to the Greek proverb about washing an Ethiopian, he describes Mather's evangelization of New England's African inhabitants as a kind of internal cleansing, in which "Christs grace" leaves slaves spiritually "white within." For Noyes, however, this sanctification foreshadows their literal, physical whitening at end of time, when God will "make the Saints all of a coler."

The second half of the poem underlines Noyes's sympathy with one of the primary messages of the text: masters who "use their Slaves as if they had no Soules" risk their own soul's damnation. Like Mather, Noyes holds that slavery is acceptable for the moment, but also warns slaveholders that after the end of the world the distinction between master and slave will no longer hold. Then, Noyes points out, election and reprobation will cut across social classes and ethnic groupings:

>And they of all men only shall be free,
>Christ bought, & brought out of Captivity.
>The Slaves of Sin & Satan then shall stand
>Bound hand & foot, though here they did command.
>The pious Master and the pious Slave,
>The Liberty of Sons of God shall have.[90]

These lines propose that the injustices and inequalities of secular history will be resolved in the next life—the pious slave will then be rewarded, the wicked master punished. However, Noyes also suggests that the color distinctions that were increasingly important to the practice of slavery in England's empire would continue to be significant. Although those who were masters in this life might be consigned to captivity in hell while their charges were granted the freedom of heaven, whiteness would remain the marker of liberty, blackness the sign of bondage. What is more, Noyes's admission that it was difficult to convince most owners ("Mammons fools") to take the conversion of enslaved Africans seriously suggested that the final number of black men and women who would be saved was in danger of being comparatively small. Noyes hoped that Mather's campaign would redress this issue (his own eschatological writing maintained that Revelation's First Resurrection referred to a "time of Reformation" toward the end of human history, when the "Elect" would be drawn "from all parts, and Quarters of the World").[91] But his poem ultimately underlined his belief that it was impossible for Africans to be saved *as* Africans—only white bodies would be admitted into the kingdom of heaven.

Much of *The Negro Christianized*'s rhetoric appears to contradict Noyes's reading of the text. Mather declares that "the God who *looks on the Heart*, is not moved by the colour of the *Skin*; is not more propitious to one *Colour* than another."[92] He also argues that it is absurd to assume that "none but *Whites* might hope to be Favoured and Accepted with God" when "it is well known, That the Whites, are the least part of Mankind." Furthermore, the transoceanic emigration of European peoples appeared to be complicating received notions of ethnic appearance. "The biggest part of Mankind," Mather observed, are *Copper-Coloured*; a sort of *Tawnies*. And our *English* that inhabit some Climates, so seem growing apace to be not so much unlike unto them."[93] Elsewhere, Mather suggested that saints' bodies would be "luminous" after their resurrection.[94] Drawing on rabbinical tradition, he proposed that this radiance could be seen as a restoration of a glowing quality possessed by the bodies of Adam and Eve before their Fall.[95] If that were indeed the case, he implied, it would be reasonable to expect the luminescence of the resurrected to have a reddish, rather than white, hue. "Jewish Tradition," he explained, called the "*Garment*" of light that shrouded the first parents' bodies the "*Vestis Onychina* . . . from its Resemblance to an *Onyx* in the Colour of it." Accordingly, the extensive entry on the Creation in his scriptural commentary *Biblia Americana* claimed that Adam's body "shone like the *Ruby*" in its "*Primitive Glory*" (before the Fall), formed as it was from "a Red, Rich, Rosie, and *Shining* Sort of Earth."[96]

For Jan Stievermann, these remarks indicate that it is wrong to assume that Mather's views on Africans and Native Americans were informed by racial prejudice, as several scholars did in the twentieth century.[97] Stievermann claims that Mather resisted the developing Enlightenment tendency to "divide[] humanity into a hierarchy of racial groups inherently unequal in their abilities and capacities," adding that he also opposed more traditional attempts to account for ethnic variation, which centered around the idea that peoples of color had degenerated from "an original state of whiteness."[98] Mather's support for the institution of slavery was therefore not grounded in "racism," but rather was premised on a variety of political and theological positions, including reluctance to disrupt a "social hierarchy" that "depended on . . . unfree labor," and unwillingness to question the parts of the Bible "where slavery was accepted under certain conditions."[99] Stievermann concludes that the underlying message of Mather's mission to enslaved people was that "old differences in earthly station," including those related to ethnicity, "would be abolished" in the world to come.[100]

While Stievermann is right to argue that Mather's thought does not reflect the "modern type of racial essentialism" that gained ground in the later eighteenth century, I disagree with his claim that racial difference played no role in Mather's vision of the world to come. Certainly, Mather believed that race and ethnicity were no obstacle to salvation. *Triparadisus*, his definitive statement of his late eschatology, contends that it is "very Contradictory to the *Language* of our *Gospel*" to believe "that the Glorious GOD *of the Spirits of all Flesh*, has a *Distinguishing* Regard for the Offspring of the *Flesh*, of One Ancestor more than another."[101] Yet he also expected that the Second Coming, First Resurrection, and global Conflagration that would begin the millennium would take place soon, likely only in a few years. That conviction alone lent his eschatology a racial cast.

Stievermann observes that Mather's belief in an imminent end time helps to contextualize his decision to advocate for the "conversion of slaves" rather than "their release."[102] Since they were living in the last days, enslavers should not feel too much "guilt" at keeping Christians as slaves, while enslaved Christians could be assured that they would not have to endure their lowly status much longer.[103] However, Mather was also aware that there was little time left to affect the conversion of pagans, enslaved or otherwise. He had to concede that there were "many *Ungospelized Plantations*" in British North America.[104] Even in a sermon celebrating the prospect that saints would be found "*in all the Nations of the Earth*" he could only bring himself to claim that "the *Indians*, and the *Negro's*" would afford "some Subjects for the Kingdom of GOD."[105] The great majority of those who dwelled in that kingdom, though, would be of white European origin. In a commentary on the book of Isaiah, Mather noted that when Christ returned, only in "*Europe, and the western Parts of the World* [presumably New England]" would there be "any [great] Number" of elect to greet him.[106]

Mather's description of how the millennium would unfold from that point also held racial implications. As discussed in chapter 2, he envisioned the politics of the chiliad in distinctly imperial terms. The raised saints brought back to life at the beginning of the millennium would fly from their home in the celestial Jerusalem to serve as the governors of the earth below, their subjects the changed saints who had lived to see the end of the former world. Mather suggested that the former group would be entirely divested of their ethnicity, as well as of their gender (they would "so Putt on CHRIST," that there would "be neither Male nor Female, nor any more Difference, between them, than between Jew and Greek").[107] But while the latter would be rendered sinless and immortal at the dawn of the new era, their lives would otherwise continue along (somewhat) familiar lines: they would work the soil, construct houses and communities, produce offspring, and belong to different countries.[108] Since the large majority of Africans, Native Americans, and other formerly pagan peoples who would receive eternal life would be converted in the latter days of secular history, they would generally number among these changed saints (who would have not died before the Second Coming). As a result, they would continue to occupy a subordinate position in the millennial world. Organized into what Mather called "the Obedient *Nations,*" they would serve as the students and subjects of the resurrected, quasi-angelic believers who would rule the planet on behalf of their heavenly king.[109] Mather may not have proposed, as Samuel Sewall did, that resurrected bodies would have to be whitened in order to be worthy of eternal life, but he still offered Africans and other people of color a qualified position within global Christendom. Through the course of the millennium, they and their descendants would be subject to the correction and guidance of the raised saints, most of whom would have originally been European.

There would be many white people among the changed saints too. But it is not hard to see that Mather would have viewed the raised saints' rule over the New Earth as an extension of the abortive and underfunded missions to the pagans of his own time. This is evident in an earlier eschatological tract, written before he came round to the opinion that the believers alive at the Second Coming would be made sinless and deathless in the instant of their rapture. There, Mather speculated that the full Christianization of the planet during the millennium would take several years because "the [formerly pagan] Nations in the Remoter Skirts of the World" would require more guidance from the resurrected "*Rulers* of the New World."[110] On "Occasion," the raised saints would have "to Employ a *Rod of Iron*" to discipline these people of color.

The punitive aspect of the millennial government inevitably receives less emphasis in Mather's later eschatology, which stresses the perfected nature of the New Earth's population. Yet his late tract *Triparadisus* likewise alludes to the "*Rod of Iron*" (Revelation 2:27) with which the raised saints would rule. That text also considers the possibility that non-European resistance to Christian leadership might resurface at the end of the millennium. As he ruminates on the origins of the armies of Gog and Magog who would assault the kingdom of God in the final days of the chiliad (Revelation 20:8), Mather discusses a theory developed by the Anglican minister Thomas Staynoe (d. 1708). Before the resurrection of the damned on Judgment Day, Staynoe suggested, another resurrection would take place, consisting only of those pagans who had never heard the gospel. These men and women would then be given the chance to accept Christ "& be admitted into the *Camp of the Saints*."[111] "Most" of them would "*Refuse*" and join the Devil's ill-fated attempt to overthrow the New Jerusalem. Mather ultimately favored another explanation of how Gog and Magog would come to be.[112] Yet it is telling (and unsurprising) that he was attracted to Staynoe's account of the enduring recalcitrance of the pagan nations.

Esoteric questions such as the ethnic makeup of the changed saints or the provenance of Gog and Magog would have been of more interest to eschatological specialists than they were to many of Mather's parishioners. However, the racial inflection of his resurrection theology is also apparent in his pastoral writings on the salvation of individual believers. When addressing the deaths of white ministers or church members, he presented their place among the raised saints as a continuation of, and reward for, their Christian work in this life. These reassuring words, taken from his 1705 funeral sermon for the poet and minister Michael Wigglesworth, are typical in that respect: "Be patient, O faithful ones! God intends an inconceivable advancement for you.... Highly advanced shall [you] be, when you [will be made] companions of angels, and be raised out of the dust, and be set with those princes and nobles.... Oh! how highly advanced, when all [your] faithful endeavors and achievements will be proclaimed with honor in the city of God."[113]

By contrast, Mather framed the salvation of Africans as the escape of a potentially white and pure soul from a benighted, sinful, and suffering body. In *A Good Master Well Served* (1696), he informed black slaves and servants that "though your *Skins* are of the colour of the *Night*, yet your *Souls* will be washed *White* in the *Blood of the Lamb*; and be Entitled unto an *Heritance in Light*."[114] *The Negro Christianized* similarly claims that "they that have been Scorched and Blacken'd by the *Sun* of *Africa*" need "to have their Minds Healed by the more Benign *Beams* of the *Sun of Righteousness*."[115] Alluding to an ancient Greek proverb (as well as to the verse from Jeremiah cited by Sewall), the pamphlet concedes that it might "seem, unto as little purpose to *Teach*, as to *wash an Æthiopian*," but adds that "the greater their *Stupidity*, the greater must be our *Application*.[116] Last, *Advice from the Watch Tower* (1713) demands "that more pains [be] taken, to show the *Ethiopians*, their *Sin*, which renders them so much *Blacker* than their *Skin*."[117] African conversion, the text continues, necessitates "a *Change* of *Soul*, which is much better than," but still closely analogous to, "a *Change* of *Skin*." Even though Mather did not associate the resurrection of black men and women with a literal whitening of the skin, he still suggested that black bodies had to work harder before their souls ("as white and good," in his eyes, "as those of other Nations") would be ready to receive salvation.[118] Where the resurrection of Euro-American Christians would serve as the ultimate endorsement of an identity that they had always already possessed, African converts would be born again into a strikingly different selfhood.[119]

This distinction shaped Mather's expectations of white and black believers in the present. His pietism demanded that "the *Kingdom of* GOD must be first set up" in the hearts and minds of prospective saints, before they could be "*Received* into His *Heavenly Kingdom*"—only through devoting their lives to practical, philanthropic godliness could Christians hope to participate in the resurrection of the just.[120] That standard applied as equally to the enslaved as to their enslavers. But while Anglo-Americans were encouraged to adopt the "MAXIMS of PIETY" through the practice of self-control, slaves, and by extension all black people, needed European mentors to "*Form & Mould* their Souls for the Kingdom of God."[121] Although Mather's Christian universalism stressed Africans' humanity, it also suggested that they needed to be civilized and disciplined to be included within the global community of saints.

John Beach and Immaterial Resurrection

While the Society for the Propagation of the Gospel saw the conversion of Anglo-American colonists to Anglicanism as its primary remit, it was also exercised by the goal of Christianizing enslaved Africans across the British Atlantic. If Mather and Sewall expected that the millennial Christianization of the planet would begin in earnest relatively soon, SPG affiliates were more likely to assume that it would take many more years to achieve much significant progress in that venture. Each February, the annual sermon preached to the society by a senior Anglican clergyman referenced the belief that Reformed Christianity would take hold in every part of the planet before the end of the world. But the speaker usually equated the coming of Christ's kingdom with the general health and growth of the Protestant church, rather than with the advent of the millennium itself.[122] Preachers closely associated Protestant mission with the gradual consolidation of English (and, later, British) imperial authority. Like the SPG as a whole, they were wary of offending the slaveholding interest that was becoming integral to the empire's prosperity.

As the society's missionaries struggled to convince plantation owners to permit the religious education of their bondsmen and women, they grappled with the same question that troubled Mather and Sewall: what was the relationship between the liberty promised to the enslaved in the afterlife and their present status as human chattel? Shortly after the SPG's inception, most of its members settled on a strategy of insisting that the baptism of the enslaved did not compromise the legality of their bondage. As the first half of the eighteenth century progressed, the society continued to emphasize the alignment of its interests with those of enslavers (from 1710, it would become a slaveholding institution itself, as it inherited a sizable sugar plantation on Barbados from Christopher Codrington). Yet many owners would resist its mission, particularly in colonies such as South Carolina and New York which were home to large numbers of enslaved and/or free black people. These regions were confronted with a problem that was much less of an issue in New England, with its comparative low population of Africans: the potentially disruptive presence of large congregations of black Christians, many of whom might be able to read.

Anxiety about slave conversion centered on social upheaval, but also extended to misgivings about the status of black Christians in the next world. As a result, SPG members often found themselves reminding others of the spiritual equality of all believers. In 1711, William Fleetwood, bishop of St. Asaph, attacked recalcitrant masters for denying the plain truth that their charges were "equally the Workmanship of God, with themselves; endued with the same Faculties, and intellectual Powers; Bodies of the same Flesh and Blood, and Souls as certainly immortal: [a] People . . . made to be as Happy as themselves, and . . . as capable of being so."[123] Similarly, Thomas Wilson's *Essay towards an Instruction for the Indians* (1740), which became "the Church of England's standard handbook for promoting the conversion of black and Native American people," scorned those enslavers who attempted to convince their charges that "they [had] no Souls."[124] Wilson worried that this cynical behavior would lead men and women to commit suicide "to free themselves from Slavery."[125] "All Men," Wilson insisted, "shall rise again from the Dead with their own Bodies, and give Account of their own Works."[126] Therefore, "all Christians" must be reminded "that this Life is the Time to choose where and what they are to be for ever."[127] Reporting back to London from South Carolina, missionary Francis Le Jau reported a troubling episode that confirmed the SPG's suspicions that some slaveholders struggled to accept these equitable visions of postmortem existence. One of his female "Neighbours," he informed the Society's secretary, had asked him if it were "possible that any of [her] slaves could go to heaven, & must [she] see them there?"[128]

On the other hand, Le Jau was even more concerned by an episode that had occurred the previous February, when "the best Scholar of all the Negroes in my Parish" informed "his Master" that he had read of a coming time when "the Moon wou'd be turned into Blood" and the land would be covered in "darkness."[129] Although Le Jau was able to convince the man in question that it was dangerous for him to develop his own interpretation of the Bible in this way, a rumor spread among the local enslaved people that "an Angel" had spoken to him and "he had heard a Voice, [and] seen fires &c." Le Jau's anxiety that conversion was leading some slaves to claim a spiritual authority that was above their station foreshadowed the response of alarmed enslavers to the colonial awakenings of 1740s. Writing in the *South Carolina Gazette* in 1742, one author complained that rather than "teaching [Africans] the Principle of Christianity" New Lights were "filling their Heads with a Parcel of Cant-Phrases, Trances, Dreams, Visions, and Revolutions."[130] These instructional sessions, he added, were taking place "without public Authority, at unseasonable Times, and to the Disturbance of a Neighbourhood." By this time, many SPG missionaries were slaveowners themselves and were therefore equally disturbed by what they saw as the disruptive enthusiasm of the revivals.[131] Anglicans believed that the ways in which African Christians accessed the spiritual world needed to be tightly regulated, and reports of black men and women preaching to racially mixed congregations contributed to the decision of most SPG affiliates to oppose the New Lights.[132]

The contested relationship between the Society's mission, colonial social order, slavery, and Christian liberty in the world to come forms the context for the next work that I want to discuss: *A Modest Enquiry into the State of the Dead* (1755), an eschatological tract by Connecticut SPG missionary John Beach. A Yale graduate and former Congregationalist minister, Beach had converted to Anglicanism in 1732 and traveled to London for ordination by the bishop of London.[133] Upon his return to New England later that year, he took up a position as missionary to Newtown and Redding (he had previously been minister to the Congregationalist church at Newtown). As an Anglican priest in New England, Beach's primary charge was to win converts among the Anglo-American inhabitants of the region (Cotton Mather had complained about this aspect of the SPG's activities in 1715, noting that the Society "send[s] forth . . . their missionaries . . . to maintain confusion in towns of well-instructed Christians," while ignoring entire "plantations in the southern colonies that are perfectly paganizing").[134] Yet it was also Beach's duty to pay special attention to the salvation of the enslaved Africans who lived in his district. Writing back to the secretary of the SPG in 1749, he noted that his "parishioners [were] poor, and [had] but few negro slaves," before adding that those that he had converted "appear[ed] to be serious Christians."[135] By 1769, he could report further progress: Newtown and Redding were now home to "about fifty negroes, most of whom" he had baptized.[136] However, Beach's most notable contribution to the conversation over the Christianization of people of color was a provocative claim made in the course of an intervention in a different controversy.

As noted in chapter 2, the Church of England continued to be troubled by the heresies of mortalism and psychopannychism in the 1700s. Eighteenth-century mortalists and psychopannychists argued that Protestant eschatology had been insufficiently purified of Roman Catholic beliefs. In particular, they held that the spiritual states of reward and punishment in which the souls of the saved and the damned would await reunification with their bodies on the Day of Doom were too similar to the Catholic idea of purgatory. Their solution was to revive an idea that had been popular with radical Protestants in the seventeenth century: between the hour of death and the end of the world, the human soul would "sleep" (or alternatively fall out of existence entirely); on the last day, each man and woman would return to consciousness through the resurrection of the body, in preparation for judgment and eternity.[137] Mainstream Anglicans vehemently opposed mortalism on the grounds that it undermined the key Christian tenet of the natural immortality of the soul (immortality, for mortalists, was a contingent quality that would be bestowed on the material body following its resurrection). They were also worried about its rejection of immediate postmortem retribution for sinful behavior, as they believed the moral order of the world depended on the understanding that wickedness would be punished directly after death.[138] Beach, for his part, was especially exercised by this second point—so much so, that in making his critique of the mortalist heresy he traveled far beyond the limits of orthodoxy himself.[139]

In *A Modest Enquiry* he made three proposals that were as boldly simple as they were heretical, by the standards of the time: "there is no *intermediate State*" between the death of the individual and his or her personal resurrection; each saint would be given an entirely spiritual, rather than physical, body when raised again (immediately following his or her death); there would be no general resurrection of the dead at the end of the world. Beach "freely" conceded that he was "singular" in holding these "opinion[s]."[140] Yet he also explained that this was to be expected, since Roman Catholic resurrection theology had not been properly "examined" and reassessed "since the Reformation." A careful consideration of the scriptural evidence would reveal that immediate resurrection was the teaching of the Apostolic Church: St. Paul, for instance, "expected . . . that Christ would give him the *Crown of Righteousness*" on the very day that he died (20). Another Pauline text (1 Corinthians 15:50) provided justification for Beach's claim that the resurrection of each saint was noncorporeal: "*Flesh and Blood cannot Inherit the Kingdom of God*" (24). While most authors, including Cotton Mather,[141] took this verse to mean that resurrected bodies would be composed of a purified and spiritualized matter, Beach used Paul's words to support his conviction that the saints would be raised as insubstantial spirits and would never return to the material world after their deaths.

In this way, he repudiated one of resurrection theology's most widely accepted principles: the resemblance between Christ's resurrection and the general resurrection of the dead. Jesus, he explained, was raised into a physical body as his redemptive mission required him "to tarry some time on Earth, . . . but we have no reason to think that our Flesh and Blood will rise again, unless we are to come and live upon Earth again."[142] Indeed, Beach made it quite clear that there would be no such return to life on earth, either before or after the Second Coming, which would "put an end to this present world" (15). His eschatological system left no room for the establishment of a redeemed society of saints that would retrospectively compensate for the vagaries of secular, fallen politics—a central premise of both Mather and Sewall's scripts for the millennium. Instead, Beach stressed the alterity of life after death. Straight after their demise, saints would awaken in heaven, which he described as "another world" (2) and a "foreign Country" (1), "invisible" to those still living on the earth.

The central politico-theological thrust of this argument was that belief in immediate postmortem judgment would produce a more orderly society. Beach explained that the conventional notion that souls would "wait for [their] Resurrection and Judgment until the End of the World, as Prisoners wait for their Trial till the Time of the *Sessions*," was likely to breed dissension and immoral behavior, "for the farther off an Event is, the less it influences us" (37). But his heretical ideas also held significant implications for the racial politics of the next world.

As I have argued, Protestant eschatologies that featured a millennium on earth tended to make an issue of the conversion of Africans—the assumption being that their integration into the global community of the elect would require special measures. In Beach's system, however, the world to come was equally alien to all mortal men and women. To reinforce this point, *A Modest Enquiry* stipulated that the spiritual bodies the saints would possess in heaven would have none of the "present Properties" of their mortal forms (26). "In the Resurrection," Beach claimed, "we shall neither be *Male* nor *Female*; neither be Tall, or of low Stature; neither have Hands, Eyes, or Feet, or any other of these earthly Members." Differences in pigmentation would also be redundant: "Our resurrection Bodies will not be white, nor black, nor brown, nor of any other Colour, consequently not Flesh and Blood, nor visible to men in an earthly Body." Beach may have intended the three colors mentioned in this statement to stand for nothing more than skin tone or humoral complexion. But the immediate context, which includes the negation of gender noted above, strongly implies that he had more fundamental questions of personal identity in mind. In so far as he treats skin color as a contingent "property" of human bodies, rather than as a marker of essential, biological difference, Beach is typical of authors writing before the development of modern racial theory. Nevertheless, the fact that he even brings up the possibility of the persistence of skin tone in the next world, if only to reject it, is emblematic of the eighteenth century's growing preoccupation with racial distinction. It was impossible to even *imagine* "a Body of Flesh . . . and Blood" that had "no Colour or Stature," he insisted (27).

Beach was formally reprimanded for his unorthodox theories at a meeting of Anglican ministers held at Stanford, Connecticut, in October 1757.[143] He claimed there, somewhat disingenuously, that he had not intended to disavow the resurrection of flesh. Though the local Congregationalist ministers continued to taunt him with the charge of heresy, Beach was soon reconciled with his Anglican colleagues, and settled back into the task that occupied him for most of his authorial career: arguing questions of soteriology, liturgy, and ecclesiology with his Congregationalist rivals. But his advocacy of an immaterial resurrection deserves to be seen as more than a curious episode in one man's career. While his unorthodox eschatology was condemned on all sides, it offered a solution to a problem that vexed Anglicans and Nonconformists alike: how could the Christian obligation to evangelize the nations be squared with the concern that converted Africans, enslaved and free, would demand greater social and political freedoms?

In *A Modest Enquiry*, Beach argued that the prospect of an imminent and personal Doomsday would encourage believers to focus on eternity, rather than on secular concerns. "What Folly is it," he asked, "for me to contend fiercely and eagerly about the Trifles of this World, . . . or to be much pleased with any earthly Accommodations, when the End of all these Things is at hand?" (39). The wider adoption of this otherworldly perspective, he added, would mitigate the resentment occasioned by social and financial inequality. There would be no need for anyone to "Envy . . . the Honors and Grandeurs" of their betters, when he or she would shortly receive a "*Crown of Glory*" in heaven (40). Baptized slaves, he thereby implied, would be much less inclined to agitate for freedom. His rejection of the earthly millennium and the general resurrection made it much safer to preach Christian liberty to them. In a later sermon, Beach noted that "an abused slave" who became a Christian might "in the next world become a glorious king, and be vastly exalted above his cruel master."[144] The slave in question, however, would have to earn this elevation by performing his present "drudgery faithfully" and "in obedience to Christ." This stipulation was entirely in keeping with the SPG's position that the baptism of the enslaved did not necessitate their emancipation. But it may also indicate that Beach still clung to some aspects of the heresy that he had supposedly disavowed by the autumn of 1757.

Where the SPG insisted that Christian conversion was not enough to bring Africans into the secular body politic, *A Modest Enquiry* effectively applied this principle to the afterlife, too. Every believer, from whatever nation, would rise again, the tract insisted, but not to join a millennial community on earth, or to lead any kind of bodily life in heaven. African saints could then be smoothly integrated into the "Congregation of the Righteous" because the black bodies that had marked them out as a political problem in this life would have been definitively discarded.[145] Whether or not Beach still secretly doubted the resurrection of the flesh in 1768, the three soteriological sermons he published that year make very few references to resurrection at all, even as a metaphor for the translation of the soul into heaven. By disconnecting personal salvation from the continuation of the same body into eternity, he suppressed the politically transformative potential of the evangelization of the dispossessed and the enslaved—a particularly important task in the wake of the mid-century revivals, when all sorts of marginalized people began to claim that their future in paradise imbued them with spiritual authority here and now.[146]

Race, Resurrection, and Revivalism

At the turn of the eighteenth century, the African Christian was still a primarily notional concept in the British Atlantic. Though both Anglicans and Nonconformists had been advocating for a more concerted mission for decades, very few enslaved men and women across the Caribbean and North America had been successfully converted. As Protestant authors sought to change this situation, they unsurprisingly argued that winning souls for God must take precedence over any secular reservations about the social, political, and economic implications of their project. In the eternal world, they contended, every soul was worth the same. It was a scandal, therefore, that those who bought and sold human beings as chattel gave so little thought to the fact that they were trading in "reasonable creatures" who were as "equally capable of salvation" as themselves.[147] The equality of all peoples in heaven had no bearing on their relative standing in this life. Christian politics, according to Anglican missionary Morgan Godwyn, was not grounded in "Parity, but [in] Superiority"—it reinforced the rule of "Kings and Magistrates" and "establishe[d] the Authority of Masters, over their Servants and Slaves."[148] This line of argument was deployed by those who insisted, with Godwyn, that there was absolutely no obligation for enslavers to release enslaved men and women who converted.[149] But it was also employed by others, including Richard Baxter, who thought that masters should be encouraged to emancipate Christianized slaves.[150] Even Samuel Sewall, who was uncomfortable with the idea of Christians being held in bondage, stressed what he perceived to be the comparative inferiority of the African people. Though many slaveholders continued to resist any attempt to get them to take the salvation of their captives seriously, the trade-off between dutiful servitude before death and total liberty afterward was a central feature of missionary rhetoric in the period.

The doctrine of resurrection cut across this strict separation of mortal and immortal life. Protestant orthodoxy held that the same individual body that died would rise again. Though that frame would be spiritualized and cleansed of sin, something of its original substance would remain. This article of faith was invoked by Protestant missionaries of all denominations, but it presented them with a problem, too. Across the British Empire, people of color were subject to strict social controls. Even in church, African converts were closely regulated and scrutinized.[151] How, then, could their unruly bodies be admitted into paradise? Protestantism's emphasis on individual conversion provided a practical answer to this question. Anglicans and Nonconformists alike characterized black conversion as a drawn-out process that required close supervision and methodical instruction.[152] Having undergone a lengthy spiritual probation at the hands of white ministers and masters, Africans would be ready for redemption in the world to come. Yet even as Mather and his SPG counterparts were setting out this approach to proselytization, the rise of the plantation model of enslavement threatened to render it obsolete already. Mather's paradigm required a relatively low ratio of black subjects to white instructors, and demanded that converted slaves be treated as part of their enslavers' religious household.[153] As the number of bondsmen and women in New England rose sharply in the first two decades of the eighteenth century, most Africans were forced further toward the margins of society. The situation was even more pronounced in the southern and Caribbean colonies, where more and more slaves toiled in increasingly appalling conditions, and SPG ministers had to struggle ever harder to gain access to them. The fact that during the 1720s enslaved people in Georgia and South Carolina "outnumbered whites by more than two to one" made slaveholders there especially reluctant to contemplate the Christianization that might encourage insubordination among their slaves.[154]

The religious awakening that spread across British North America in the middle decades of the eighteenth century gave white Protestant advocates of black conversion new cause for optimism. But it also amplified their anxieties about the political and social consequences of their mission. Though the Christianization of African Americans and Afro-Caribbeans did not begin in earnest until the last two decades of the eighteenth century, from the 1740s onward increasing numbers of enslaved and free black people were drawn to the new religious culture of revivalistic evangelicalism.[155] In southern New England, 1741 and 1742 also saw a sharp increase in the number of Native Americans affiliating with local Congregationalist churches.[156] Scholars have typically argued that the "egalitarian" style and message of George Whitefield and the other New Lights held a particular appeal for marginalized and oppressed men and women of color.[157] The revivalists' emphasis on experiencing "new birth" imbued the convert with a spiritual, moral, and emotional authority. Early African and Native American evangelicals took advantage of that fact, seeking recognition as full members of existing and newly founded congregations, and even leading religious meetings themselves.[158]

By the 1770s and 1780s, several prominent black writers had emerged. These authors published devotional poetry, religious meditations, and sermons, as well as autobiographical accounts of their enslavement, emancipation, and conversion. As Joanna Brooks has demonstrated, the literary tradition they developed made extensive use of the trope of resurrection. Seeking to escape slavery's world of death and construct new identities and communities for themselves, African Americans and Afro-Britons looked back to the biblical figure of Lazarus, and forward to the saints' triumph over the grave.[159] Though they were inspired by Whitefield's message of spiritual freedom, they also had to reckon with his support for slavery and concomitant reluctance to extend too much liberty to African Christians before the day of resurrection itself.[160]

Many of the first generation of black authors in the Anglophone Atlantic encountered Whitefield at first hand, and several of the most notable (including Phillis Wheatley and John Marrant) received the support of Whitefield's own patron, Selina Hastings, the Countess of Huntingdon.[161] But though evangelicalism's theology, organizational structure, and general religious style were critically important for the growth of the culture of the black Atlantic, African writers found that white revivalists had yet to think through the implications of their spiritual populism for the concept of racial difference.[162] Early evangelicals emphasized spiritual and moral uplift over political or social change and followed the lead of the SPG and Congregationalism in courting the support of slaveholders for their missions.[163] Furthermore, most of them perpetuated the eschatological attitude described in this chapter, whereby the Christianization of Africans was framed as only a partial alleviation of an ethnic identity that the next world would eliminate altogether. Developing a black evangelicalism, as we shall see shortly, would involve producing descriptions of the afterlife that directly asserted that bodies of color belonged in heaven.

Among white evangelicals, the Moravian Church came closest to acknowledging this fact. German Moravian Johann Haidt's frequently reproduced 1747 painting *The First Fruits* depicts specific individuals from a variety of different backgrounds (including African, African American, Native American, Armenian, Persian, and Greenlandic), most of whom "were among the very first [Moravian] converts in their own country or mission field."[164] These men, women, and children clutch palms of victory as they gather around Christ's throne, indicating that they have already received their reward in heaven. In keeping with this vision, Moravian missionaries to the Danish West Indies allowed Africans to serve as lay leaders or "helpers" in their congregations. In that capacity, black men and women led prayer and study groups, gave personal testimonies during services, and served as mentors to candidates for baptism.[165] Although the Moravians sought to work within the framework of the institution of slavery, their encouragement of black religious leadership aroused suspicion among the other clergy and slaveholders of the islands. On St. Thomas, the progressive approach of the missionary Friedrich Martin led to rumors that he was preaching that "come resurrection day [the] Blacks [would] be ruling the [Whites]."[166] When Johannes Borm, the island's Dutch Reformed minister, questioned baptized slaves during an investigation into the potentially seditious aspects of the Moravian mission, a woman denied that Martin had predicted a revolution in the next world. Instead, she affirmed her belief that "after death, we will be with God, and there we will all be equal."

The equality of all souls in the eyes of their creator was indeed a major theme of the ministry of Whitefield, John Wesley, and other prominent evangelicals. Whitefield's letter "To the Inhabitants of Maryland, Virginia, North and South-Carolina," published in 1740 by Benjamin Franklin, sternly criticized slaveholders in those colonies for not "taking Care of your Negroes Souls."[167] This failure, he added, was proof that enslavers were not bound for heaven themselves. The white "Pastors and People" of the South demonstrated just as much "Deadness ... to Divine Things" as the Africans who suffered under their cruelty.[168] Wesley, who unlike Whitefield would become a proponent of abolition, made the same point more forcefully in his *Thoughts upon Slavery* (1774). Buying and selling human beings "who [have] souls [as] immortal as your own," he warned slaveowners, would incur an awful price on the Day of Judgment, when "the Great GOD [will] deal with *you*, as you have dealt with *them*, and require all their blood at your hands."[169] In a few instances—most notoriously the abortive South Carolina rebellion inspired by Hugh Bryan in 1742—white evangelicals convinced enslaved people that the moment of reckoning was closer at hand.[170] Generally speaking, however, they framed the conversion of black men and women as a question of their adaptation to English society.

Whitefield's 1740 letter stressed that "there [was] a vast Difference between civilizing and christianizing" people of color.[171] Baptizing and educating slaves only "imposed outward Restraints" on them. True conversion required a complete interior rebirth—a standard that applied equally to blacks and whites, who were "just as much . . . conceived and born in Sin" as each other. Yet Whitefield also suggested that enslaved adults would require an extra degree of acculturation before they could attain salvation. In this regard, the ordeal of enslavement, "however ill-designed," would "do them good, as to break their Wills, increase the Sense of their natural Misery, and consequently better disposed their Minds to accept the Redemption wrought out for them, by the Death and Obedience of Jesus Christ." Advocating the legalization of slavery in Georgia eleven years later, he told a white colonist there that it would be "by mixing with your people" that Africans would "be brought to JESUS."[172] Whitefield's friend Anne Dutton, meanwhile, noted that it would be the privilege of Europeans and Euro-Americans, "we that were in Christ before *you*," to welcome "*you despised Negroes*" into the body of "our JESUS."[173] Although evangelicals tended not to address the potential transformation of black bodies directly, they still saw the preparation of Africans for heaven as a question of containing disruptive ethnic otherness.

For their part, Protestant authors of color frequently discussed the association of blackness with sin and whiteness with salvation. On a rhetorical level, they often continued to employ the same set of binary oppositions used by white Christians. In his autobiography—the first published by an African in English—James Albert Ukawsaw Gronniosaw described the Devil as a "black man," and noted that in a period of penury as a freedman in England he could still "perceive light . . . through the thickest darkness," thanks to his faith.[174] Jupiter Hammon, the first black author to be published in colonial America, described the salvation of the "Nations" in terms of the transformation of "dark benighted Souls."[175] In a verse addressed to Phillis Wheatley, he counseled his fellow poet to "adore" the divine "wisdom" that had brought her as a slave to Christian America, when she "might[] have been left behind" in the "dark abode" of Africa.[176] Wheatley herself would use this last phrase to describe the ascent of a young girl (presumably of African descent) to heaven ("From dark abodes to fair etherial light / Th' enraptured innocent has wing'd her flight").[177] And in keeping with Hammon's advice, she agreed that it was "mercy" that had "brought [her] from [her] Pagan land," and "Taught [her] benighted soul to understand / That there's a God, that there's a Saviour too."[178] In the same poem, "On Being Brought from Africa to America," Wheatley rejected the notion that the "colour" of her "sable race" was a mark of damnation, "a diabolic die." At the same time, she appeared to countenance the idea that African believers would be resurrected white: "Remember, Christians, Negroes, black as Cain, / May be refin'd, and join th' angelic train."

The ambiguous grammar of this couplet has received a great deal of scholarly attention. The process of refining it describes could be interpreted to apply strictly to saints of color (the "Negroes" of the first line), and therefore assumed to denote the literal bleaching of their bodies. However, if "Christians" *and* "Negroes" are read in apposition to "black," then the latter word describes the internal sinfulness shared by all human beings, rather than Africans' darker complexions.[179] In that case, the lines would seem to argue that all races are equally in need of resurrection's sanctifying improvement. Elsewhere, Wheatley adopted a different, but related, means of arguing for racial equality in religion. "To the University of Cambridge in New England" contrasts her lowly position as a slave only recently transported from "The land of errors" with the "privileges" of Harvard students, whose studies afford them the opportunity "to traverse the ethereal space, / And mark the systems of revolving worlds."[180] Yet the poem ends with a warning that even they, the "blooming plants of human race divine," must guard against "sin, that baneful evil to the soul." In a telling detail, this advice is framed as coming from "An Ethiop." As Sondra O'Neale has observed, this self-description alludes to the Bible's frequent references to Ethiopia as a place of "piety and royalty" (including to Psalm 68:31), and thereby suggests that Wheatley's own faith is part of a rich tradition.[181] In this way, a woman whom some enslavers would have dismissed as a "souless animal[]" asserts the right to guide white men to "life without death, and glory without end."[182]

Jupiter Hammon's writing, with its warning that escaping "bondage to sin and Satan" was of greater urgency than was achieving "temporal freedom,"[183] might seem less contentious than Wheatley's. Yet some scholars, including O'Neale, have identified strong black nationalist themes in his work.[184] By becoming Christians, Hammon suggested, African Americans could demonstrate a "moral autonomy" that would enable them to form their own nation.[185] The discussion of the next life at the close of his last work, *An Address to the Negroes in the State of New-York* (1787), certainly carries a significant political charge. Addressing his fellow enslaved men and women, Hammon claims that "there are no people who ought to attend to the hope of happiness in another world so much as we. Most of us are cut off from comfort and happiness here in this world, and can expect nothing from it."[186] But he also insists on the radical equality of the celestial city: "If we should ever get to Heaven, we shall find nobody to reproach us for being black, or for being slaves."[187] He observes besides that "not many rich, not many noble [people] are called [to salvation]."[188] Instead, "God hath chosen the weak things of this world." The likelihood that the enslaved will outnumber their enslavers in paradise—currently "one of the things that are not"—holds the power "to confound the things that are." While Hammon believed that "liberty in this world" was "nothing" compared to liberty in the next, he also hoped that the rising generation of African American Christians would be "set . . . free."[189] Their spiritual election, he implied, was proof that they also deserved emancipation in the present.

As Hammon's example indicates, the fact that the first generation of black authors in English continued to link blackness and sinfulness should not be construed as a passive or submissive acceptance of Euro-Christian prejudice. Even as they redeployed the trope, they emphasized its limitations, arguing that spiritual darkness was of much greater account than darkness of complexion. Several of them, moreover, directly challenged the soteriological conceit that has formed the subject of this chapter: the idea that black skin was potentially at odds with resurrected life in heaven.

In a collection of correspondence published two years after his death, Afro-British composer Ignatius Sancho (c. 1729–1780) insisted that people of "all countries, colours," and even "faiths" would "mix" together in the "world without end."[190] Where Mede and Staynoe predicted that the final chapter of history on earth would see some members of the pagan nations consigned to hell forever following their failed attempt to overthrow the rule of the saints, Sancho refused to accept that a just God could condemn his creatures to "eternal Damnation."[191] Christ "died for the sins of all," he maintained.[192] That meant that men and women of every religion ("Jew, Turk, Infidel, and Heretic"), as well as every shade of skin ("fair—sallow—brown—tawny—black"), would ultimately enter heaven. In arguing for the universality of salvation, Sancho undermined the association of Christianity with whiteness and made a case for abolition that was rooted in sensibility and cosmopolitanism.[193] While thanking a Philadelphia Quaker for sending him antislavery writings as well as Phillis Wheatley's book of poetry, he noted his respect for the Society of Friends and added that he "hope[d] to see and mix amongst the whole family of Adam in bliss hereafter."[194] Slavery, he wrote elsewhere, was the product of "a total indifference (if not disbelief) of the Christian faith," most especially a reluctance to believe that people of all backgrounds and beliefs could (and would) be saved.[195]

Ottobah Cugoano's *Thoughts and Sentiments on the Evil and Wicked Traffic of the Slavery* (1787), the first extended abolitionist treatise published by an African, also argued that race and color would be irrelevant in the next life. Cugoano (c. 1757–c. 1791) was born in what is now Ghana, enslaved as a child and transported to the Caribbean, and subsequently taken to London and freed. There he worked as a servant for the painters Richard and Maria Cosway.[196] His book proposed that God had allowed Africans to develop darker skin purely so that it could serve as an emblem of the "sinful blackness" of the entire human race, as well as to allow Jeremiah to pose the "instructive question" that underlined the impossibility of Ethiopians altering their appearances. Since no one can "change [his or her own] nature," Cugoano argued, humankind is united in its dependence on God's grace: "All men are like Ethiopians (even God's elect) in a state of nature and unregeneracy, they are black with original sin, and spotted with actual transgression, which they cannot reverse [themselves]." Only "the blood of Jesus" could wash away "the stains and blackest dyes of sin and pollution" so that "the darkest sinner [was] made to shine as the brightest angel in heaven." Despite this symbolic significance, Cugoano insisted, "the external blackness of the Ethiopians, is as innocent and natural, as spots in the leopards."[197] When people die, he continued, "It makes no difference whether [they were] black or white, ... male or female, ... great or small, or ... old or young; none of these differences alter the essentiality of the man, any more than [if] he had wore a black or a white coat and thrown it off for ever." Though this last sentence might seem to imply that Cugoano believed that men and women would cast aside their complexion after death, it must be noted that he stopped short of assuring so directly. Indeed, the logic of his argument could be taken to suggest the opposite: if skin colors were as inconsequential as he claimed, there would be no need to remove them through resurrection.[198]

In North America, abolitionist and founder of black Freemasonry Prince Hall reworked Jeremiah's question to similar effect. "Ethiopeans" might not be able to "change their skin," he observed, "but God can and will change their conditions, and their hearts too."[199] Hall was speaking in 1797, as the ongoing Haitian Revolution seemed poised to deal a major blow to the slaveholding interest. Like Cugoano, he invested the fight against slavery with special eschatological significance. Soon traders would "bewail the loss of the African traffick" just as the "merchants" mentioned in Revelation 18:11 mourned over the fall of Babylon and the destruction of its markets. A millennial era was approaching in which the white world would learn to treat Africans equally, having realized that God "hath no respect of persons."[200] Hall also attacked the assumption that resurrected bodies would be white. At the end of his speech, he quoted an "old poem" he had supposedly "found among some papers" (but had likely composed himself).[201] Only "blind admirers," the poem claimed, admired "handsome faces" or the "red and white" of Caucasian complexions. True "beauty" was spiritual—human beings did not "resemble" God in their "flesh and blood," but by "being pure and holy, just and good." There was therefore no reason to assume that blackness and salvation were mutually exclusive.

By suggesting that resurrected bodies could be black, Hall, Cugoano, and Sancho made a powerful case for African political emancipation. As they realized, mainstream Protestant eschatologies did not present a truly equitable vision of heaven. Most white theologians claimed that ethnic distinctions would not matter in the next life, but still framed heaven as a place where bodies of color would not be welcome. While that vision prevailed, people of African descent would always be seen as junior partners in Christian churches and societies. In the nineteenth century, Pequot minister William Apess would revise the critique that early black authors had mounted against white resurrection theology. Apess insisted that Christ himself was "colored."[202] This simple fact undermined the widespread preconception "that every body [who] is not white" should be "counted as barbarians."[203] A free and equal society would embrace the possibility of resurrected bodies of color. Once that premise was accepted, the exclusion of Native Americans and Africans from the ministry, political office, and other civil privileges would be revealed to be the blasphemy that it was.[204]

"The Heaven of Comparative Freedom": Radical Black Eschatologies

While writers such as Hammon, Hall, and Cugoano saw the universal resurrection of the dead as grounds for political optimism, the men and women of the black Atlantic were also drawn to other eschatological models. Enslaved Africans brought their mortuary practices and beliefs about the afterlife across the ocean with them. These traditional ways continued to shape attitudes toward death on American and Caribbean plantations, right through the eighteenth century and into the nineteenth. Although African beliefs often persisted in combination with Christian faith, they were incompatible with the doctrine of resurrection in several respects. Where Protestants thought that the souls of the dead rested in heaven, awaiting reunification with their bodies, many Africans were convinced that departed spirits lingered around the place where they had died. At the same time, enslaved people also found solace in the notion that their souls returned home to Africa after death.[205]

As late as the 1830s, former enslaved man Charles Ball would note that in his experience African-born slaves were "universally of the opinion... that after death they shall return to their own country, and rejoin their former companions and friends, in some happy region." Ball attributed a different outlook to the "mass" of American-born slaves "on the cotton plantations," who had "borrowed all [their] ideas of present and future happiness, from the opinions and intercourse of white people, and of Christians." Despite accepting the fundamentals of Protestant resurrection theology, these men and women apparently repudiated its universal scope, refusing to countenance "the idea of living in a state of perfect equality, and boundless affection, with the white people." Instead, Ball claimed, they believed that they would be elevated above their former "master[s] and mistress[es]," who would, with only the occasional exception, be damned. As long as slavery persisted, he claimed, African Americans would reject the concept of a universal and equal afterlife. And though he conceded that their vision of heaven was not "in strict accordance with the precepts of the Bible," he noted his own sympathy with the view "that those who have... lived in ease and luxury, at the expense of their fellow men" would "have to be punished" in the next world.[206]

Ball's autobiography demonstrates that the questions that occasioned the eschatological and millennial speculations discussed in this chapter were still very much at issue in the nineteenth century. Both opponents and defenders of slavery were divided among themselves on the sociopolitical and religious futures of Africans in the Americas. Even so, some clearer patterns of thought on the issue had started to take shape. The origin of human diversity continued to be a highly controversial subject. Yet the eighteenth century's stress on environmental and external factors, which led many thinkers to assume that racial characteristics could change over time, was being replaced with a more rigid approach that framed race as an inherited and immutable quality that inevitably determined an individual's biological and psychological attributes.[207] That change, together with the exponential increase in enslaved people across the American South (and concomitant rise in the number of free blacks in the North), contributed to a growing emphasis on various forms of social and political separation between the races.

In the South, the growth of industrial-scale plantations following the invention of the cotton gin led to an intensification of the hierarchy that placed both rich and poor whites above and apart from the enslaved. In the middle and northern states, free black Protestants formed their own separate congregations, many of which would join together to form a breakaway African Methodist Episcopal Church. Some of the leaders of this organization would initially support the black Quaker Paul Cuffe's plan for African American emigration to the recently established British colony of Sierra Leone.[208] The 1816 formation of the American Colonization Society, which included many supporters of slavery among its members, led most free black people to reject the concept of a "return" to Africa. Although they gradually adopted the self-description "Colored" as a result, many black Americans retained a strong sense of a distinctive African identity.[209] In the meantime, a majority of white northerners refused to contemplate a United States in which blacks and whites lived together as equals.[210]

Despite these developments, most white American Protestants continued to believe that racial difference would cease to be of any consequence in heaven. And while some enslaved men and women may have hoped to enact postmortem revenge on their enslavers, black converts to Christianity generally accepted the prospect of equality after death. Nevertheless, the unifying power of the future resurrection of all flesh was not acknowledged by every thinker working within a broadly Protestant framework. For instance, an American Indian "nativist" movement emerged in the second half of the eighteenth century. Nativist prophets encouraged their followers to resist the loss of ancestral cultures and lands, formulating syncretic blends of indigenous teachings and Christian doctrines in the process. They also argued that different races had been created by different gods and would therefore be sent to separate afterlives.[211]

Meanwhile, radical African American authors looked for a political resurrection of enslaved people. In his autobiographies, Frederick Douglass would describe his transformative physical confrontation with the "slavebreaker" Covey as a self-actualized "resurrection." Rather than suffer through the horrors of his enslavement with Christian patience, and in expectation of a reward in the next life, Douglass decides to stage his own ascent from "the dark pestiferous tomb of slavery" to the "heaven of comparative freedom."[212] For Jared Hickman, the qualification of the liberty achieved in this moment in Douglass's second autobiography is crucial. Not only does it indicate his intuition that even as a free man his freedom will always be "partial" and "provisional," but also reflects Douglass's rejection of the conceptual category of "the sublime Absolute" and therefore his rebellion against the idea of an all-powerful Euro-Christian God.[213]

David Walker's *Appeal to the Coloured Citizens of the World* (1828) contested the white Protestant scheme of salvation in a comparable way. American and European Christians, Walker observes, assume that they have "a name to live" (Revelation 3:1)—are destined to go to heaven—and will therefore be spared punishment for the crime of slavery.[214] In fact, their destiny was very much in doubt. They had endeavored to keep enslaved Africans "ignorant of our Maker, so as to make us believe that we were made to be slaves for them and their children" (67). But white Christians had shown a greater ignorance of the true meaning of the gospel. Walker imagined a range of biblical and ancient peoples who had not had the benefit of "the revelation from Jesus Christ"—"those who were burnt up in Sodom and Gomorrah," "the Scribes and Pharisees of Jerusalem," "the whole heathen world of antiquity"—rising up to "condemn" those who had twisted the New Testament to support slavery (66). In contrast to this white complacency, he described the approaching "salvation" of the "whole body" of the African race (35). Indeed, Walker suggested that the entire planet would soon be "Christianized" ... through the means ... of the *Blacks*, who are now held in wretchedness," rather than by white evangelism (21n). However, that millennial hope, alongside the prospect of eternal life itself, is overshadowed by his *Appeal*'s call for righteous violence in pursuit of the immanent redemption of emancipation. Walker warned white Americans that "we must and shall be [as] free and enlightened as you are" (79). "Will you wait," he continued, "until we shall, under God, obtain our liberty by the crushing arm of power?"

Hickman draws on Walker and on Douglass in the course of an extensive exegesis of the literature of the radical black Atlantic. He contends that the interrogation of transcendental redemption by black authors writing against slavery should lead modern scholars to realize that the very concept of the "Absolute" (or the universal) "needs to be historicized and relativized as a racial construct."[215] This argument carries serious and potentially controversial implications for the study of resurrection theology. Is the mere idea of a perfected, immortal, and sinless body inherently racially loaded, even when considered apart from the related subject of the proselytization and salvation of pagan peoples? Early modern Protestants knew that their faith in the resurrection of the flesh could be traced back to the ancient Israelites. They also (mostly) believed that scriptural prophecies dictated that men and women of all nations would need to be counted among the saints brought back in the flesh at the end of time. But as the response of the earliest black writers in English shows, the hardening of racial distinctions in the period led some European and Euro-American Protestants to assume that the untrammeled, unburdened, and elevated body of the resurrected elect must also be free from the mark of color.

4
Thomas Prince and the Resurrection of the World

Prince's Globalism

In his sophomore year at Harvard (1704–1705), Thomas Prince happened across "a Terrestrial Globe" in the room of a classmate. This chance encounter with an "entertaining and instructive Image of the Earth" led him to educate himself in the "1st Principles" of global geography. In March 1730, by now an experienced minister at Boston's Old South Church, he revisited this episode in print. Writing in the *New-England Weekly Journal*, he confessed that he had been "*exceedingly surprized*" by the puzzled response to a passing geographical reference in his funeral sermon for Samuel Sewall, who had died that January.[1] Some "*Gentlemen of Learning*" had objected to Prince's observation that Canaan lay "about *Five thousand five hundred* Miles to the *East-north-eastward*" of Boston, arguing instead that as the Holy Land lay "*near* 10 *Degrees* South" of New England, it would be reached by heading in a southeasterly direction.[2] Their mistake had been to fail to account for the curvature of the planet—their objections would only have been valid "if the Surface of the Earth were a mere Plain, and not Globular." Prince advised all those who still doubted him to study a model globe like the one that had captivated him as a sophomore. It was particularly important, he concluded, that New England's "*rising Gentry*" should have a clear sense of its topographical position, lest they "*run into the most absurd and confused ideas of the scituations of the Places*" on the earth.

Prince understood that learning to orient oneself geographically could help to set one's spiritual journey on the right trajectory. In a further article for the *Weekly Journal* he encouraged Bostonians to visualize the position of Jerusalem on the horizon so that they might arrive at "a clear conception of t[he] admirable Workmanship of the GREAT CREATOR."[3] The following year, he published *Vade Mecum*, a "Companion FOR *Traders* and *Travellers*." This handbook collected geographical and administrative information about

"The BRITISH *Colonies* and *Provinces* on the Shoars of NORTH-AMERICA," as well as tables for calculating interest and currency exchange rates, and guides to the weighing and measuring of certain commodities. Prince also included a list of Boston's churches, together with their locations and dates of founding, as well as a timetable of Quaker and Baptist assemblies in New England and the Middle Colonies. The text's preface signaled its intention to enable "the Flourishing of Liberty and Commerce, universal Charity, good Neighbourhood, and every other Virtue that by the Divine Blessing" would make "the *American Plantations* . . . prosperous and happy."[4] As productive, cosmopolitan citizens of the British Empire, Americans could help to fulfill God's providential plan for the earth.

Prince was always looking for signs that the world was coming together. In 1740 he told the annual convention of Massachusetts ministers that the revivals George Whitefield was then leading in the southern and middle colonies might signal the beginning of the Christianization of the entire planet. In the years ahead, he claimed, "all the southern, western, and north-western parts of this new world . . . will . . . be full of pure and pious churches."[5] Then, he continued, "The gospel will go round and conquer every nation in Japan and China, Tartary, India, Persia, Africa, and Egypt, until it returns to Zion, where it rose." Prince closely associated this proliferation of evangelical Protestantism with the extension of British commercial and military power. In July 1745, he suggested that the recapture of Cape Breton from the French might prove to be "the *dawning Earnest* of our DIVINE REDEEMER'S carrying on his Triumphs thro' the [New World's] *Northern Regions*; 'till He extends his Empire from the *Eastern* to the *Western Sea*, and from the River of *Canada* to the Ends of *America*." This imperial extension of "*British Liberties*," protected by "*a happy Constitution of Civil Government*," would enable the global growth of true religion, long predicted by millenarian readers of Isaiah 24: "THEN from the uttermost Parts of the Earth shall be heard *Songs*, even Glory to the righteous GOD."[6]

Prince was also fascinated by the eschatological destruction of the planet. His 1740 convention sermon observed that after the "whole globe" had been "successively enlightened" by the gospel, the entire earth would be consumed by a "conflagration" that would be succeeded by "a glorious state of universal and abundant light and grace, and peace and blessedness."[7] Prince took an eager interest in the material means by which this transformation would be effected. Though he never published an extended discussion of the science of the process, he would return to it repeatedly in a variety of literary contexts.

In 1719, for instance, he published an account of a strange phenomenon (the aurora borealis) that he had seen three years previously, while living in England. Crimson *"Spears of Light"* in the sky above Stowmarket, Suffolk, had led him to think that "the *Conflagration* . . . was now begun" and "the very *Frame of the World was a Dissolving.*" As he reckoned with that awful prospect, Prince had considered competing explanations of the apocalyptic destruction of the earth by two English physico-theologians. At first, he wondered if "Mr [William] WHISTON's *Hypothesis* was coming to pass, & the Train of a *Burning Comet* was then a seizing on this Terrest[r]ial World."[8] But then, as the scene changed, "& Pillars of Smoak ascended from ev'ry side of the *Horizon,*" he thought instead that Thomas Burnet's theory might be more accurate, and the earth was about to be consumed by *"Subterranean Fires* . . . issuing out of gaping *Caverns* & *Vulcanoes* in the Country round about us."[9] Though he refrained from offering any firm conclusions about the providential significance of the mysterious event, Prince closed his tract with a lengthy quotation of the description of the Conflagration in 2 Peter 3. As the passage suggested, the terrifying immolation of *"the Heavens"* and melting of *"the Elements"* should ultimately be viewed with hope. After that devastation, God had reminded his people to *"Look for New Heavens, & a New Earth, wherein dwelleth Righteousness.*"[10]

Ranging across Prince's career, this chapter will address a subject prominent in much of his work: the relationship between the apocalyptic reconstruction of the planet and mortal attempts to master the earth in the present. Previous chapters have shown how Protestant resurrection theology described the persistence of various entities into the next world: the church, the person, the nation, racial groups. While Prince was certainly invested in most of these continuities, he was especially preoccupied by the problem of the globe itself—how would the fallen, corrupted earth be made worthy of the resurrected and perfected saints of the millennium? In its technical detail, his answer to this question was not particularly innovative (in common with his mentor, Cotton Mather, Prince believed that the Conflagration would totally purify the planet, which would then be populated by immortalized "changed saints" under the government of the resurrected elect [the raised saints]). But the way in which Prince responded to new ecclesiological and social developments makes his eschatology particularly worthy of study.

Many of his peers in the New England ministry (Prince's generation and the one just before) adopted fresh approaches to both church and society. Scholars continue to disagree about the theological beliefs of this "catholick" group, which included Benjamin Colman, Ebenezer Pemberton, and Thomas Foxcroft.[11] However, it is clear that these ministers advocated ecumenical cooperation between Protestant denominations, favored a more inclusive approach to church membership, and stressed the compatibility of Christian faith with human reason and ability. They also encouraged a new attitude toward commercial enterprise. In the seventeenth century, Puritan clergy had criticized and sometimes disciplined parishioners for offering loans at high rates of interest or refusing to forgive debts; these practices were deemed sinful because they jeopardized the integrity of godly community for the sake of personal profit.[12] But Colman, Pemberton, Foxcroft, and their allies insisted that moneymaking could be compatible with religious life: a rational, pious, and polite approach to business could promote social harmony and civility.[13]

Prince was in sympathy with all these attitudes. Nonetheless, his funeral sermons reveal a significant point of difference with the group. As we shall see, Prince placed a much heavier weight on the physical corruption of mortal existence than did Colman, Pemberton, or Foxcroft. This emphasis was indicative of his greater misgiving about the ability of mortal men and women to effect substantial change in the world. With Mather, he thought that a second corporeal life on a regenerated planet would be required to put the endemic sinfulness of the present globe right. For that reason, his pastoral writings for a general audience include some finely drawn accounts of the processes behind the resurrection of the body and the formation of the New Earth. Popularizing the literal, supernaturalist interpretation of the Bible's millennial prophecies, Prince believed, would help to preserve the Puritan ethos of conversion. By linking individual death and salvation to the renovation of the entire terrestrial sphere, he emphasized humanity's total dependency on divine grace.

Although Prince was a prominent supporter of them, the evangelical awakenings of the 1740s posed a serious challenge to this resurrection theology. *Christian History*, the newspaper he produced between 1743 and 1744 in collaboration with his son, Thomas Prince Jr., attempted to demonstrate that revivals across the Atlantic world were revitalizing mainstream Protestant churches. However, the rise of evangelical religion across the American colonies was accompanied by widespread adoption of the kind of radical eschatologies discussed in chapter 1. Like Anne Hutchinson, Samuel Gorton, and the early Quakers, the most extreme "New Lights" boasted that they had been spiritually resurrected. As he set out his own vision of revivalistic Protestantism, Prince not only had to reckon with heretical claims of this kind, but also with the incautious rhetoric of more respectable evangelicals such as George Whitefield and Gilbert Tennent, who also likened conversion to resurrection. In response, he reinforced his position that the material degradation of the fallen earth prevented even regenerated human bodies from expunging their biological "vileness." Though Prince supported Whitefield's and Tennent's efforts to expand the awakening's reach, his wariness of their potentially divisive approach to proselytization led him to echo positions held by Charles Chauncy, prominent critic of the New Lights.

Moderate by inclination, Prince attempted to lead New England Congregationalism down a middle way. He blended "catholick" inclusivity with a determination to preserve Puritan tradition (as evidenced in his collection of an extensive library of Congregationalist books and manuscripts, and authorship of a *Chronological History of New England* [1736]). He also fought to strike a balance between Chauncy's dismissal of the millennial significance of the revivals and radicals who bore witness to an internally accomplished eschaton. In the medium term, these struggles to hold the center ground reflected a fragmentation of New England Congregationalism that accelerated in the 1750s, spurred by the multiplication of separating revivalist sects. This chapter will also take a longer view, considering Prince's endeavors in the light of the connection between globalization and secularization.

If Prince saw the European (and especially the English/British) settlement of the New World as part of a providential scheme to spread the gospel, modern scholars identify the same process as a key contributor to the development of what Charles Taylor terms an "immanent frame" for human endeavor.[14] The hugely complex global economy that emerged from the colonization of the Americas and the Atlantic slave trade produces the sense that material, mundane, and secular considerations are enough to give meaning to our existence. Reality need no longer revolve around a transcendent or divine plane. As José Casanova puts it, in secular modernity "The cosmic order is increasingly defined by . . . science and technology; the social order . . . by the interlocking of 'democratic' states, market economies, and mediate public spheres; and the moral order . . . by the calculations of rights-bearing individual agents, claiming human dignity, liberty, equality, and the pursuit of happiness."[15] Peter Sloterdijk, meanwhile, suggests that this immanent frame was already apparent in models like the one that Prince saw at Harvard. Where ancient maps of creation surrounded the world with a protective "vault," terrestrial globes reveal that the planet "lacks an enclosing edge"—those who live on it dwell on "the threshold" of "nothingness."[16] Sloterdijk stresses the antieschatological and disenchanting implications of this image. Once the enclosing arc of the heavens has been dismantled, the "final boundaries" of sacred history, as well as of cosmology, "are no longer what they once seemed; the support they offered [is revealed to be] an illusion, its authors we ourselves."[17]

For Casanova, however, the primacy of the mundane "does not necessarily entail the disenchantment of consciousness, the decline of religion, or the end of magic" (215). Similarly, Taylor observes that even in the secular contemporary West the immanent frame does not completely close off the transcendent—many people continue to believe that there is something "beyond the 'natural' order [of things]."[18] The sacred retains a power that is much less "localizable" than it used to be, no longer so "clearly marked out in ritual and sacred geography."[19] I would add that the more telling disagreement with the premodern era is not over the existence of a transcendent spiritual plane, but over its *location*. For more than a few of us, heaven is still there. But it is no longer over our heads. It endures instead in an entirely separate sphere, almost another dimension.

Thomas Prince may not have realized that the immanent frame was taking shape, or that Western society was in the process of being secularized. But he was well aware that some of his peers discounted the importance of material, "scientific" accounts of the route between this world and the next (whether describing the transformation of the fallen planet into the millennial New Earth or the resurrection of the individual believer). His "catholick" ministerial colleagues often argued that it was unwise to pry too deeply into eschatological mysteries of that kind. The most radical revivalists thought that paradise could be found within the soul, here and now. Insofar as these positions undermined the materiality of the afterlife, Prince's resistance to them never wavered. In 1757, the year before he died, he published *A Brief Discourse Concerning Futurities*, a millennial tract composed by Massachusetts layman William Torrey seventy years earlier. By issuing this text (previously only circulated in manuscript), Prince was able to publicize his own approach to the chiliad, at a time when the Seven Years' War with France was causing a surge of interest in the end times. Though he did not agree with every particular of Torrey's vision, he certainly approved of *A Brief Discourse*'s emphasis on the corporeal resurrection of the saints at the Second Coming, and the supernatural transformation of the globe to render it suitable for their inhabitation. Just as he had encouraged Bostonians to discover the way to Jerusalem, Prince urged all Christians to learn how they would get to the world to come.

"Perpetual Spring throughout the Earth": Prince and the Millennial Transformation of the Planet

On September 5, 1717, at the weekly Thursday lecture in Boston, Prince preached a sermon on Psalm 107:30, "so he bringeth them to their desired haven." He had chosen this text to give thanks for his own safe return to New England after eight years away. His exposition addressed the conventional theme of God's providential government of the high seas, both through the ordinary operation of the tides and winds, and through special influence over sailors and passengers' decisions to embark on one ship rather than another. This second subject was of personal relevance. As Increase Mather's preface to the published version of the sermon observed, one year previously Prince had almost boarded a ship that was wrecked on its way to Boston, resulting in the death of all its passengers.[20] Mather predicted that Prince would go on to do great things. Travels in England, Europe, and the Caribbean had provided the younger man with a breadth of knowledge and experience that would serve him well in his incipient career as a minister. Furthermore, Mather claimed that "*Eminent deliverances of Providence, are oft-times a sign that the Subjects of them, shall either do or suffer in the cause of* Christ & Truth *that which will be Eminent.*" The following October, Prince would be ordained minister of the Old South Church, where he would work alongside Joseph Sewall for another forty years.[21] Cotton Mather shared his father's sense of Prince's potential, writing in his diary that he now had "a Companion with whom I may unite, more than any one upon Earth in doing services for the Kingdom of GOD."[22]

Notwithstanding Increase's and Cotton's approval, Prince's sermon also had much to recommend it to the "catholick" group of ministers with whom the Mathers did not always agree. As he set out his doctrine ("*it is God the Lord who brings those that pass thro' the dangerous Seas to their desired Haven*"), he considered the reasons why travelers risked the perils of the ocean to settle in a distant land. Some people emigrated to "life in greater Ease and Pleasure, or rise to higher Respect & Dignities, or to do more extensive Good in the World." Some "remove[d] for the Benefit of more plentiful Soils, wholesomer

Airs, healthier Climes, or pleasanter Prospects & Situations." Others were looking "for a Neighbourhood of People more agreeable to their religious or political Tempers & Principles" or seeking "to injoy the Properties, Rights, & Liberties of Human nature in an equalled Degree & in a greater Security." "Finally," others sought "to live unmolested in a quiet & peaceable Exercise of Conscience, a purer Observance of Divine Institution, and a fuller Injoyment of religious Society, the proper Means of Grace & other invaluable Priviledges of *the Gospel of Christ*."[23]

The sequence of this catalog plainly indicated Prince's special approval of the last motivation (his grandfather John Prince had migrated to New England in 1633 to avoid the Laudian persecution of Puritans, and the "religious Society" of his birthplace was no doubt a primary consideration in his own recent decision to return).[24] Yet he nonetheless suggested that the other reasons for relocation were legitimate in their own right. This frank endorsement of the benefits and pleasures of living in a prosperous, genteel, and orderly community revealed Prince's sympathy with the social and economic outlook of ministers such as Colman, Foxcroft, and the recently deceased Pemberton. As Mark Valeri observes, Cotton Mather recognized the moral value of commercial endeavor too. However, as his sermon *Theopolis Americana* indicates, Mather saw the development of New England's economy in fundamentally "apocalyptic" terms, as part of the "looming Armageddon between Protestant states and [Roman] Catholic powers." Like much of the preaching of Colman and his allies, Prince's homily was free from this eschatological "urgency," maintaining that the primary religious significance of mercantile enterprise was its contribution to the "natural social order." "Colman and Prince," Valeri concludes, "gave merchants confidence that they were moral paragons and servants of providence as they obeyed the laws of trade."[25]

The sermon's treatment of the human mind and body points to another point of alignment between Prince and the Boston "catholicks." Prince admires the "Affection" that men and women inevitably feel for the country in which they are "born & educated." The presence of our family and friends, he explains, is "the most powerful ... Attraction" of our hometown, the "most irresistible Incentive[] & Allurement[] of Humane Nature." Just as falling bodies gather speed as they approach their gravitational "Center[]," so "our impatient Longings" for our loved ones "increase, ... the nearer we draw unto them."[26] Similar celebrations of human instincts and desires can be found in the work of Colman and his colleagues. Though these ministers retained a strong sense of the destructive effect of original sin on corporeal existence, they argued that the body and the needs and emotions it displayed could still prove "useful to the soul" in the "spiritual improvement of the individual."[27]

In a series of addresses on the value of the conscience, Benjamin Wadsworth observed that since "GOD has made our *Bodies* and *Souls*, and all the powers they're endow'd with," Christians should employ all their "*Faculties*" and "*Abilities* . . . in conformity to His *Preceptive Will*."[28] Another of his sermons urged Protestants to follow their natural inclination to "live peaceably with *all men.*" The emotional exhaustion that followed passionate debates over doctrine should be heeded. Better to accept that believers would always differ concerning certain issues and apply oneself to "those great weighty & necessary duties, about which . . . all are agreed."[29] For his part, Colman preached several times on the religious uses of "Moderate Mirth." If merriness "*were indecent in all Circumstances,*" he argued, "*Nature had not put this Faculty and Disposition into us, and made it so beautiful in us.*" "Health, Peace, Plenty, Children, [and] Friends" were God's "Fatherly Provision" and "Royal Munificence." How were the faithful to "acknowledge this if [they did] not rejoyce in it?"[30] Colman's defense of Christian laughter and good humor was linked to his belief that the world was steadily becoming more polite, productive, and moral. Prince, as we have seen, shared this view. With God's help, Protestants would lead the nations toward greater piety and civility. "What continual Blessings do these Godly and Faithful spread round about them," he remarked in a 1746 funeral homily, "and how Desireable to live a *long while* on the Earth, which greatly needs them, if not 'till CHRIST Himself appears."[31]

However, Prince's sermons also frequently emphasized the vitiation of the planet's natural environment, discussing the material causes of that degradation in stark detail. In one address of uncertain date, he contrasted the tremendous ages attributed in Genesis 5 to the patriarchs (Methuselah, 969 years, Lamech, 777) with the brief lives of men and women in his own era. "Before the Flood," he explained, the earth's "wholesom Fruits and air" had supported much longer lifespans and therefore a much larger global population. It was "highly Probable," he suggested, "that the Children of men exceedingly increased to Vast many millions more than there are People now on the Face of the Earth." Now nature was so polluted that there was "no Hope" of ending the continual deluge of death "until another universal Flood, not of water, but of Fire, [should] come and turn up the ungodly of all Nations in one dreadful Day together."[32] In a 1727 sermon he considered the reasons for human ephemerality at greater length. So great were the fragility of the body and the dangers of our habitat (the "corruptible and fleeting" nature of our food sources, the "changeable & noxious" quality of our "Air") that God "need only withhold his vital Influence from us" for one second "and we immediately die & sink and return to the Earth to which we are enclin'd, and from whence we came."[33]

While Prince never produced a long-form physico-theological or eschatological treatise, he would discuss the postdiluvian corruption of the world in funeral sermons delivered and published throughout his career. Though he argued elsewhere that British imperialism and Protestant evangelism were gradually unifying humankind, these texts set a hard limit to that process of integration, suggesting that it would always be frustrated by the planet's biological putrefaction. The entropic effect of the earth's polluted atmosphere thwarted the ambitions of the most powerful and Christian nobles. It even hindered learned attempts to develop a science of mortality. Prince's special emphasis on the debilitating impact of the fallen world on mortal men and women set him apart from most of his contemporaries, especially Boston's "catholick" ministers.

Consider, for example, Prince's treatment of the shocking death of Frederick, Prince of Wales, in the spring of 1751. The sudden loss of the heir to the English, Scottish, and Irish thrones was an event of worldwide proportions. The "*British* Nations," Prince wrote, were united "in universal Sorrow" at the loss of their next king; British possessions in "*Asia, Africk, Europe* and *America*" had seen their "*principal Hope*" destroyed.[34] The last Prince of Wales to die before being crowned king had been James I's oldest son, Henry, who succumbed to typhoid fever in 1612. Henry's demise, Prince reminded his congregation, had "made way for his younger, arbitrary Brother to ascend the Throne by the Name of Charles I, in 1625" (19). That unhappy contingency had allowed the "*Popish* Branch" of the Stuart family to torment the country "for a Course of *Sixty-three Years*," until the glorious year of 1688. For the moment, the Protestant succession still seemed to rest secure in the house of Hanover, but the precedent of the loss of Henry gave Prince pause. The "Liberties of *Europe* and *North-America*, and the Protestant Religion in *all the Earth*" rested on "the perpetual Succession" of that "Royal Line, under God" (20). Now, with a king in his late sixties and a teenaged heir apparent, Britain and her empire faced the threat of another period of instability and conflict. The death of Frederick, then, underlined "the utter Uncertainty of all earthly Friends, Enjoyments, Hopes and Glories" (29). As the collapse of

Israel and the fall of Byzantium demonstrated, no worldly nation, not even those favored by God, was ever safe from destruction.

Warnings like this were the usual ministerial response to the loss of a prominent figure in the Protestant world: both Jonathan Mayhew and Samuel Mather used the same occasion to admonish their own Boston congregations in similar ways.[35] But Prince's sermon also adopts another, less common, approach to the subject at hand. Its opening acknowledgment of Britain's bereavement gives way to a lengthy consideration of the relationship between human mortality and the environmental noxiousness of the world. Frederick's death, Prince suggests, should remind us of the planet's material, as well as political, instability. The sermon's text—"Thou *destroyest the Hope of Man!*" (Job 14:19)—is obviously intended to refer to both these vicissitudes. But Prince quotes the wider context of this verse in order to address the physico-theological angle first. Job's lament on the death of his children contrasts the irreplaceability of individual men and women with natural cycles of regeneration: "here is Hope of a Tree, if it be cut down, that it will sprout again.... Thô the Root thereof wax old in the Earth, and the Stock therefore die in the Ground; yet thrô the Scent of Water it will budd, and bring forth Boughs like a Plant: But Man dieth and wasteth away; yea Man giveth up the Ghost, and where is he!" (2). Following the Geneva Bible's exegesis, Prince assumes that Job's answer to his own question ("Man lieth down, and riseth not 'till the Heavens be no more") alluded to the fulfillment of 2 Peter 3's prophecy that the "Aerial *Heavens* about the Earth" would be "*dissolved*" and would "*pass away with a great Noise.*" Only when the Conflagration had made the earth new would the curse of death be lifted.

Prince linked his commentary on Job to a scientific consideration of the ways in which the present world is inimical to human existence. Our bodies, he explained, are constitutionally sensitive and vulnerable: "The Vessels and Membranes" of the "Parts... needful to preserve our Lives, are so exquisitely fine and tender... that a very small Degree of Force either without or within us" may have fatal consequences (7).[36] The "various *Elements*" moving through the atmosphere are the other primary source of danger: by entering the pores of our skin, or passing into our lungs, bowels, or blood, they "produce Obstructions and Impostumes, Consumptions, Putrefactions, Fevers, Appoplexies, or other effectual Causes of our Dissolution" (8). Prince noted that the first of these threats, the weakness of the human frame, was caused by the Fall. Before their sin, Adam and Eve had likely been under the protection of "beneficent *Angels*" who would have "continually repair[ed]" the "wasting

Substance" of their bodies (6). Once this shield was "justly withdrawn," the "*first Parents*" and all "their Offspring" were rendered "frail and mortal."[37] The second danger, atmospheric pollution, was the direct result of the "general *Deluge* in the year of the World 1657" (6). During the Noahic Flood, vast caches of water previously hidden near the planet's core ("the Fountains of the great Deep") had broken through the earth's crust, bringing pestilential vapors with them. The "Course of the Earth" was also altered (perhaps by "Means of a *Comet*" passing close by), making "the Seasons extreamly unequal." From that moment, "the Elements we live and breath[e] in became so variable, disordered, poysonous and pernicious, as exceedingly to weaken our Constitutions and shorten our Lives."[38]

Despite this disruption, God was still in total, continuous control of the planet. His supervision of gravity, for instance, meant that "the *whole Globe* of the Earth, Air and Water, . . . even *every Atom* in them to the Center, acts as if it perfectly knew how much material Substance there is in *the Moon*, and how exactly both her Distance & her Motion are and alter" (10). The degeneration of the atmosphere, and the millions of deaths that it caused, were very much part of his plan. Prince extracted the standard Christian moral from this fact—believers must accept the "utter *Uncertainty* of *humane Life*" and make "ready for every Providence" as well as "Death and Eternity" (16). But the sad occasion of his sermon also led him to consider another implication.

Frederick was the most cosmopolitan, globally connected royal imaginable. Chancellor of the University of Dublin, he was exceptionally knowledgeable about even "the most distant Colonies" of the British Empire, and "a great Encourager of their Manufacture, Fishery, Trade, Virtue, Ingenuity, Arts and Sciences" (24). He had taken special interest in New England's retaking of Cape Breton and had even offered to fund the colonies' "attempts to christianise the *Houssantonick* & *Mohawk Indians*" from "his own Revenue." As king, he would have been ideally equipped to extend British influence even further across the earth. But now, a rather smaller sphere had laid him low. In accordance with the then prevalent assumption, Prince claimed that an "accidental Blow" of a tennis or cricket ball two years earlier had been responsible for Frederick's demise (26). As a result of this impact, "Some tender Vessels were pressed and bruised, some Fluids obstructed in their Circulations, and thence ferment[ed] to a Putrefaction." Eventually, "The Vessel relax[ed] [and] enlarge[d] . . . till they suddenly burst, and he falls back and dies!" Prince warned, as convention demanded, that a death of this magnitude showed that God was angry with the British people and might seek to punish them further (27–28). Yet his focus on the medical details of Frederick's fatal complaint highlighted his sermon's distinctive message: the very fabric of the world strained against the global aspirations that the heir to the throne had embodied. Human vulnerability and environmental toxicity would always frustrate aspirations toward terrestrial supremacy.

In another of his learned funeral addresses (a 1736 sermon on the death of Mary, wife of Massachusetts governor Jonathan Belcher), Prince made the same point in a different way. The demographics of mortality, he observed, were extremely difficult to comprehend. "What a horrid World would this appear," he noted, "if we cou'd but have a universal View of the Multitudes at this Instant labouring under [death's] destroying Power!"[39] In a postscript to a treatise on the level of population growth that the city of London was theoretically able to support, the seventeenth-century economist and scientist Sir William Petty (1623–1687) had nonetheless attempted to estimate the number of people who died since the "Beginning of the World."[40] Drawing on the work of Petty, his collaborator John Graunt, and other scholars, Prince proposed that "about a *Thirtieth Part*" of the "near *Thousand Million* People on the Face of the Globe" must die each year.[41] On any given day, therefore, "there must be near a *Hundred Thousand* . . . a Dying." Most of those fatalities, moreover, took place in "the meer Course of Nature." Once the multitudes "murthered, executed, drowned, or kill'd by Plagues or Battles" were accounted for, the extent of death's power over the world became almost impossible to comprehend.

Petty and Graunt had been more sanguine about the possibility of deriving useful information from the study of death on a large scale. Their pioneering research in demographics began in 1662 with a comparative study of London's bills of mortality across the previous seventy years. By observing the number of people who had succumbed to particular diseases, studying the citizens' sex ratio, and comparing London's birth and death rates with those of the surrounding counties, they aimed to give the newly restored Charles II a more scientific understanding of the population at his command, and with it the opportunity to construct a more efficient and productive national economy.[42] Petty would later attempt to coordinate this statistical method with the biblical narrative of human history, estimating the total population of the world in the lifetimes of Moses, David, and Christ, as well as calculating the year—3682—in which the "whole World will be fully peopled."[43]

Prince no doubt approved of the underlying political objective of Petty's thought: giving Britain a competitive advantage over her rivals by rationalizing population growth at home and in her Irish, Caribbean, and North American colonies.[44] Yet his sermon seemed to question one of the demographer's basic methodological principles (extrapolating from historical records of epidemics). While Prince provided rough mortality statistics for some of the most deadly contagions, earthquakes, and fires in the past (including the Plague of Cyprian in third-century Rome, the medieval Black Death, and the 1693 Sicilian earthquake), he concluded that "the universal and continual Destruction of the innumerable Multitudes of Men" across the generations is too vast and too distressing for the human mind to come to terms with.[45] "The Mind of Man," he wrote, "is unable to comprehend the wide and dismal Prospect, to conceive it without Horror, and the full View would be too terrible to bear" (34). A truly comprehensive enumeration of the humanity would therefore not be possible until mortality was abolished. Only at the resurrection of the just would God's chosen ones be able to perceive the full extent of death's devastation of their kind. Then, "their *bodily dust*" would "be sublimated into a *spirituous Substance*, pure and fine as Æther, bright and quick as Light, or rather like the more perfect Substances in the heavenly world" (32). This transformation would leave them "free from the Laws of Gravity, . . . Incorruptible, Immutable, [and] Immortal." Through God they would possess "perfect Life and Strength, . . . Vision, Knowledge, Joy and Blessedness." Until that time, human understanding must remain partial, as both our powers of perception and our moral sensibilities are fitted to the "disordered" state of the present world (11).

How did Prince's approach to this subject compare with that of his "catholick" Boston colleagues? As a rule, Colman's, Foxcroft's, and Pemberton's memorial sermons were more likely to dwell on the moral degeneracy of the world than on its material corruption. In an address on the death of a young man in a duel, Colman observed that "the same Pains & Torments rend and tear Persons of the most different Characters. . . . And the same noisome Diseases corrupt the Bodies, and destroy the Lives of Saints and Sinners."[46] Rather than discuss the material causes of this dysfunction, he focused on the analogous way in which humanity's moral failings disrupt the "beauteous & useful" regularity of God's "*Creation*."[47] Indeed, Colman even suggested that ethical "*Disorder* and Confusion" might be considered "worse than Death" and physical decay for their aggregate impact on this life and the life to come.[48] Foxcroft's *Death the Destroyer* (1726), a homily on the same verse (Job 14:19) that Prince would later discuss in his sermon for Prince Frederick, does briefly discuss the "Vicissitudes,... Decays, and Desolations" of the world.[49] If the earth's "very *Mountains & Rocks*... may be unfixed from their places, ... removed & broken to pieces," Foxcroft wrote, then it was "no marvel" that "frail Mankind" was in such "a wasting condition." As this sample indicates, the sermon presents only very general observations about the planet's material instability, without discussing its causes. Meanwhile, Pemberton's funeral sermon for Councilor John Walley concentrated instead on the disjuncture between the "Putrefaction" of the corpse in the grave and the "*Incorruption* . . . of the Resurrection Body"—a common trope in Protestant memorialization.[50] His sermon for Samuel Willard presented an equally conventional contrast between heaven and "this World of Sin and Darkness," without touching on the corruptions of nature.[51]

This comparative lack of concern with the biological degeneration of the earth registers the "catholick" ministers' eschatological disagreement with Prince. The former group were certainly not opposed to millennialism. Even though Colman was not "inclined toward extensive apocalyptic speculations," he continued to find millennial significance in Britain's wars against her Roman Catholic enemies.[52] In his preface to a 1741 soteriological treatise by New Jersey Presbyterian Jonathan Dickinson, Foxcroft suggested that the current revivals were a sign that the "Day of CHRIST" was at hand.[53] However, the "catholicks" did not share Prince's conviction that there would be a corporal resurrection of the dead elect at the beginning of the eschaton. They saw the millennium as a time of extraordinary spiritual blessings and religious change (Foxcroft anticipated the "*triumphant Progress of the* [Protestant] *Gospel of Peace, in its Purity and Power, into the Spanish* AMERICA"), but not as a sudden break with mortal life.[54] It was Prince's belief that all saints, living and dead, would live together in a world without sin or death that occasioned his interest in the degradation and regeneration of the planet.

How would that transformation take place? Prince's sermons were more specific about the means by which the earth had been disfigured in the first place, but they did offer some clues about its reconstruction after the Conflagration. For example, his memorial address for Mary Belcher proposed that "*before the Flood*, the *Sun* and *Moon* [had been] always in the *Equinoctial*."[55] While the text does not say so directly, it is reasonable to assume that Prince believed that the millennial globe would be returned to that equilibrium. Once the planet's axial tilt had been corrected, there would again be "a *perpetual Spring* throughout the Earth." The "Soils, Airs, and Fruits," which were now unhealthy and infertile in so many latitudes, would be restored to their primitive fecundity. In his funeral sermon for his only son, Thomas Jr. (who died in 1748 at the age of twenty-seven), Prince viewed the rebuilding of the world from a microscopic perspective. Taking Philippians 3:21 ("The Lord Jesus Christ: who shall change our vile body . . .") as his text, he considered the original perfection of Adam's and Eve's constitutions, as well as the "vileness" that was seeded in their bloodline by the Fall. The corruption of the human body, he insisted, is not inherent to the matter from which it is formed. Instead, "It is only the particular accidental form of the [microscopic] connections" between individual "particle[s] of material substance" that "render[s] . . . them . . . excellent at one time, or vile at another." The same could "be said of the earth we live on."[56] The terrestrial sphere was not intrinsically toxic, but it would need to be thoroughly decontaminated before it could support the changed saints who would inhabit it during the millennium.

The inclusion of this kind of physico-theological detail in a sermon reflected Prince's opinion that Christians should be knowledgeable, sophisticated, and cosmopolitan. But it also betrayed his belief that both human self-improvement and the ongoing Protestant civilization of the world were seriously compromised by the present state of the natural environment. His memorial for his son imagined a situation in which mortal men and women were granted almost totally perfect health. Even then, he argued, the "innumerable . . . worms and putrid substances" in "the elements we breathe in" and "the food we live on" would inevitably recorrupt "every vessel" of the body.[57] Only after the purification of the planet would an optimal circulatory system be possible. For the time being, the networks of trade that encircled the globe were similarly flawed. With Boston's "catholick" ministers, Prince told the city's growing merchant class that they were doing God's work. Unlike these colleagues, he also highlighted the challenging prospect that it was not until the earth had been destroyed and remade that it could be properly integrated. As he saw it, maintaining awareness of this difficult truth could offset the risk that the irenic and polite Christianity he favored might become too preoccupied with God's secular blessings of prosperity and social order. During the mid-century awakening he worked so hard to promote, Prince had to contend with worldliness of a different order, when a new breed of radicals revived the old idea that resurrection could take place before death.

Revivalism and Immortalism

In early 1742, Boston printers Daniel Fowle and Gamaliel Rogers issued an anonymous text that spoke to the growing controversy around the colonial revivals. *The Wonderful Narrative* furnished readers with an extensive account of the "French Prophets"—a group of radical Huguenots who had scandalized London in the first decade of the eighteenth century. The Prophets' visions, ecstasies, and purported miracles, the author argued, were typical of the enthusiasts of ages past. To underline this claim, he included sketches of historical religious frauds, from the "MAGICIANS in Egypt" who attempted to match the of miracles Moses and Aaron, through Simon Magus, Montanus, and "MAHOMET," to latter-day figures such as Anne Hutchinson, George Fox, and assorted American Quakers.[58] The suggestion was that many of the revivalists then roaming across New England belonged in the same category. An appendix to the main text, signed "Anti-Enthusiasticus," made this point very plainly. Precedent showed that the subjects of "VISIONS" and "TRANCES" had always been "the *weak* and *ignorant*, or those who are naturally of a *warm Imagination*."[59] Respectable, pious Christians, by contrast, had never made such "Pretences" to be moved by the Holy Spirit "in an extraordinary manner." Anti-Enthusiasticus was particularly concerned about "Those TRANCES . . . wherein the Subjects of them have a clear and distinct View of *Heaven* and *Hell*; of the *Process of the last Judgment*; of the *Book of Life*, with the Names of particular Persons wrote there."[60] He had good cause to be. Since the autumn of 1741, a startling number of new converts in the colonies, mostly young people, had attested to undergoing a vision of this sort.[61]

The central section of *The Wonderful Narrative* itself described an even more dramatic attempt to transgress the boundary between life and death. In early December 1707, Dr. Thomas Eames, an English member of the French Prophet circle in London, had taken seriously ill. Several of his associates, including the group's leader, John Lacy, suggested that if Eames died, he would soon rise again.[62] Eames succumbed to his sickness on December 22, and was buried in Bunhill Fields on Christmas Day. A week later, John Potter prophesied the precise date of Eames's resurrection: May 25, 1708. On the appointed day a huge crowd gathered around Eames's grave. Only one of the Prophets was present, as the others had already accepted that their prediction would not come to pass.[63] "There are some Persons now living in *New-England*," *The Wonderful Narrative* observes, "who appeared with the Multitude at *Bunhillfields*, . . . [and] can testify, that nothing remarkable then happened."[64] Dr. Eames, the tract notes, still lies at rest, "and will do so, 'till the *Voice of the Arch-Angel* shall, at the *last Day*, awake the Dead, and summon them to Judgment."

For the anonymous author, the failure of the Prophets' prediction was a rebuke to any group who were inclined to boast that their ministry would spread "OVER ALL THE WORLD, in a *short space of Time*," bringing about the coming of Christ's kingdom.[65] Accordingly, he closed his history with a warning taken from a tract by Edmund Calamy, a London Presbyterian minister who had preached against the French Prophets in John Lacy's presence: "If we don't learn to be afraid of any Thing that *borders* upon *Enthusiasm*, either in our selves or others; we shew that we are not to be instructed by the Experience of other Men, but are of the Number of those, that can only be taught by Feeling the Danger of making *Divisions in Religion*, and of taking the Spirit of *Error and Delusion* for the Spirit of *Truth and Soberness*."[66]

A little over a year after the publication of *The Wonderful Narrative*, Thomas Prince decided he needed to counteract the fearful message that it and other critical texts, such as Charles Chauncy's *Letter from a Gentleman in Boston*, had spread about the revivals. In a circular letter sent to his ministerial colleagues across the colonies, Prince asked for "*cautious and exact*" delineations of "the Rise, Progress, and Effects" of the recent awakenings in their towns.[67] The proposed outline for his correspondents' narratives called for specific details about "the *most Remarkable Instances* of the Power and Grace of GOD" in *convincing* and *converting* Sinners" in their local areas. But it also stipulated that the ministers should set out the improvement in the "Knowledge, Faith, Holiness," and moral behavior of these recent converts. Together with his son, Prince planned to publish the work he received in their newspaper, *Christian History*. By balancing descriptions of the extraordinary religious affections occasioned by the awakening with accounts of the longer-term improvement of the religious life of New England, the journal would contest the charge that the rise of revivalist Christianity had merely fostered enthusiasm and social instability. Over the course of its two-year run, the *Christian History* struggled to fulfill this mission. It proved more difficult than expected to gather narratives of recent revivals, and many of those that were received featured more extreme religious affections too prominently.[68]

Prince always insisted that the awakenings of the early 1740s had been a genuine work of God that had strengthened international Protestantism and brought the total unity of the church during the millennium closer. But the closure of *Christian History* in February 1745 reflected wider problems with the moderate revivalism that the paper had sought to champion. New England had been bitterly divided since autumn 1740, when star preacher George Whitefield had first visited the region. In towns whose ministers were opposed to the awakening, or even too lukewarm in their support of it, separate revivalist congregations had formed. On the northern fringes of the colonies, groups as radical as the French Prophets themselves had started to emerge. Some of these extremists would declare that they had been miraculously resurrected without dying, appearing to support the *Wonderful Narrative* and Anti-Enthusiasticus's contention that the cultivation of spectacular conversion experiences was always likely to lead to heretical excess.

Immortalism was of course anathema to Prince, who insisted that the resurrection of the world was an essential condition of perfect human life on earth. In his capacity as a leading promoter of revivalism in Boston and across the Anglophone world, he attempted to minimize the significance of the more enthusiastic aspects of the awakening whenever possible. But this task involved collaborating with itinerants whose evangelical approach was more extreme than his was. Whitefield and the New Jersey Presbyterian Gilbert Tennent were central to the growth of New England revivalism in the early 1740s. Prince opened his pulpit at the Old South Church to both men, noting that the former "awakened the Consciences of many" and that the latter's "*searching*" preaching had led "*many Hundreds*" of Bostonians to repent of their sinfulness.[69] Other authors published in *Christian History* praised them in similar terms. The paper also printed a series of accounts of Whitefield's exploits in the colonies before his first arrival in Boston, as well as Tennent's own descriptions of his involvement in revivals at New Brunswick and Philadelphia.[70]

Like Prince, Whitefield and Tennent saw the awakening as a worldwide event that would revitalize Protestant churches and prepare the way for the kingdom of Christ. They also shared his view that affective preaching was a powerful means of bringing about lasting change in the spiritual lives of previously lukewarm believers. However, Whitefield and Tennent's close association of individual conversion with bodily resurrection constituted an important difference between their revival sermons and Prince's. While they denied that Christians could become entirely perfect (or preemptively resurrected) in this life, the eschatological tenor of their accounts of personal awakening encouraged some of their followers to believe this was possible. Although their popular appeal impressed Prince, he was careful to distinguish his moderate revivalism from both their bolder approach and the enthusiastic extremists it inspired (whose beliefs echoed those of the seventeenth-century radicals discussed in chapter 1).

Whitefield's and Tennent's sermons consistently described the unconverted as dead men and women, and conversion as a kind of resurrection. There was plenty of precedent for this approach in Protestant homiletic tradition—William Perkins, Richard Baxter, John Cotton, and Cotton Mather, among many others, all employed this figure.[71] Even so, the intensity of the two revivalists' rhetoric was striking. In a much-reprinted sermon first delivered at Moorfields in London in 1739, Whitefield warned his hearers that "we have no more Power to let in Christ, than a dead Man has to raise himself to life."[72] He expanded on this image two years later, preaching south of the Thames in Blackheath:

> As to spirituals [he argued,] we are quite dead, and have no more Power to turn to God of ourselves, than *Lazarus* had to raise himself, after he had lien stinking in the Grave four Days. If thou canst go, Oh Man, and breathe upon all the dry Bones that lye in the Grave and bid them live; if thou canst take they Mantle and divide yonder River, as *Elijah* did the River *Jordan*, then will we believe thou hast a Power to turn to God of thyself. But as thou must despair of the one, so thou must despair of the other, without Christ's preventing and quickening Grace.[73]

Tennent, too, alluded to Ezekiel's vision of the valley of bones (37:1-14). In a 1735 tract, he warned his readers: "Thou can'st no more change thy self, than a dead Man can raise himself out of his Grave."[74] In this respect, they were "like the dry Bones the Prophet speaks of.... Could these bones put Sinews and Flesh upon themselves? No, it was God only, that by his Word and Spirit could put a Shaking among them, and Breath into them." Mere intellectual faith in the future triumph over the grave was not enough—prospective saints had to undergo a spiritual resurrection right now. Another of Whitefield's most popular sermons used the story of Lazarus to underline this point. The congregation were urged to meditate on the time when "that same Jesus, *who cried with a loud Voice Lazarus come forth*," would summon them from their graves.[75] Whitefield's closing prayer compared his own voice to Christ's, asking God "that all who hear me at this Day may be then enabled to lift up their Heads and rejoice, that the Day of their compleat Redemption is indeed full come." The moment in which saints heard him speak and the time of their resurrection were specially linked.

As this example demonstrates, the most popular New Light evangelists suggested that their preaching and ministry provided a quick and direct route to salvation. Skilled at self-promotion, they employed various means to perpetuate this impression. In an account of his career published in *Christian History* in November 1744, Tennent attributed his efficacy as a gospel minister to a symbolic death and resurrection he had undergone a few years previously. The beginning of his ministry at New Brunswick, New Jersey, had not been particularly successful, earning no new converts for Christ. After he had been there for around six months, however, he had been struck down with a sickness serious enough to bring him to "affecting Views of Eternity."[76] "The secure State of the World," he explained, then "appeared to me in a very affecting Light; and one Thing among others pressed me sore; viz. that I had spent much Time in conversing about Trifles, which might have been spent in examining People's States towards GOD, and perswading them to turn unto him." After asking for just "one *half Year* more" of life, Tennent was "rais'd up to Health" and was immediately able to help bring about "the *Conviction* and *Conversion* of a considerable Number of Persons . . . in that Part of the Country."[77] Tennent's brothers John and William had comparable experiences. In Jon Butler's words, by "manifesting supernatural power in their own bodies," the family "set [themselves] apart as holy men," rather than "mere expositors of God's written word."[78]

Whitefield, meanwhile, infused his preaching appearances with high eschatological drama. In a 1739 sermon on the parable of the ten virgins, he spoke as if the end times and Last Judgment were immediately at hand: "Perhaps to Day, perhaps this next Midnight, the Cry may be made."[79] It was time for all Christians "to put themselves in a Posture to meet [their] Bridegroom" (15). For the moment, opponents of the revivals could dismiss Whitefield and his devotees as "Enthusiasts and Mad-men" (15) aiming "to turn the World upside down" (16). Any day now, these critics would be exposed as "Heart-Hypocrites" and "Whited Sepulchres" who "had only the Form of Godliness" and "contented [themselves] with desiring to be good" (16). Though Whitefield was still only "a Child," he had been "sent" by God to warn his listeners to "*watch and pray*" for that approaching hour (38–39).

While a significant segment of the New England clerical establishment supported the revivals, Whitefield's and Tennent's claims to special spiritual power held the potential to undermine ministerial authority. Whitefield warned that it was "absolutely necessary, before a Minister undertakes to preach the Gospel, that he should have an experimental Acquaintance with the *Lord Jesus Christ*," since "a dead Clergy will make a dead People."[80] Tennent's *The Danger of an Unconverted Ministry* (1740), one of the most controversial sermons preached during the awakening, urged those among his hearers "who live[d] under Ministry of dead Men" to "repair to the Living, where they may be edified."[81] There was nothing to be gained from "keep[ing] within the Parish-line" if one's appointed preacher was not spiritually resurrected.[82] In the early 1740s, James Davenport and Andrew Croswell intensified these criticisms of unconverted clergy. As well as urging students at Yale to rebel against their instructors, Davenport outrageously declared that the "greatest part of . . . the Ministers of the Gospel" in New England "knew nothing of Jesus Christ" and "were leading their People blindfold down to Hell."[83] On occasion, he would single out particular clerics (including Benjamin Colman and Prince's colleague Joseph Sewall) as spiritually dead.[84] Croswell defended Davenport's provocations, arguing that those moderate defenders of the revival who attacked his colleague had betrayed the cause.[85] He also preached the doctrine of particular faith, which held that in order for a saint to "*pass*[] *from Death to Life*" it was necessary for him to believe that Christ was "*his* Saviour" whose death and resurrection had taken place for his own individual sake.[86] This intensely personal conception of salvation and sanctification implied that each and every believer had the competency to act as a religious teacher and leader.

By 1744 Davenport and Croswell had both distanced themselves from these extreme attitudes.[87] Whitefield returned to Boston that year. Dining with Prince, Joseph Sewall, Colman, and Foxcroft, he reassured his hosts that he would not "promote or encourage separations" from Congregationalism.[88] He added that he did not consider it "absolutely impossible" for a spiritually "Dead" minister to "beget a living Child," but only "highly improbable." Nevertheless, the provocative soteriological message that he and his fellow itinerants had carried around the colonies would inspire some men and women to claim that conversion and resurrection were literally the same process. Richard Woodbury, an illiterate layman from Rowley, Massachusetts, was among the most notorious of these heretics. Together with Nicholas Gilman, minister of Durham, New Hampshire, he led revivals across northeastern Massachusetts in the summer of 1744. During these travels, Woodbury claimed to be able to channel God's power directly. Not only did he boast that he was personally sinless and immortal ("the same to day, yesterday, and for ever"), but he also suggested that he was able to bring others into this pseudo-resurrected state, or else to damn them if he so preferred.[89] Writing in the *Boston Gazette*, citizens of Ipswich, Massachusetts, complained that Woodbury had told one "Person at whom he was enrag'd, that he should be dead, dead, and in Hell, in the Space of an Hour or two."[90] Another resident, John Fowler, was released from the "Power of the Devil" and "declared [to be] ... truly blessed," with "his Name ... written in the Book of Life."

Other notable New England immortalists included Sarah Prentice, wife of Solomon Prentice, minister of Grafton, Massachusetts. In 1753, Prentice informed the Baptist revivalist Isaac Backus that she had "passed thro' a change in her Body equalent [sic] to Death, so that She had been intirely free from any disorder in her Body or Corruption in her Soul ever Since."[91] As a result, she believed that "that her Body would never see Corruption, but would Live here 'till Christs personal coming." Prentice was a known associate of other men and women who claimed the same blessing, among them Nat Smith of nearby Hopkinton, who declared that he was "the Most High God & wore a Cap with the Word GOD inscribed on its front."[92] Both Smith and Prentice were connected to Shadrach Ireland, a tradesman from Charlestown near Boston, who left his wife and children to preach his brand of perfectionism in Grafton, Hopkinton, and further afield. Ireland would later establish a secretive communal society in Harvard, Massachusetts, maintaining his hold over his followers through the promise that he would never die.[93] Through the middle decades of the eighteenth century, other circles of immortalists emerged on the borders of Massachusetts and Rhode Island around Cumberland, as well as in the separatist churches in Norwich (present-day Lisbon) and Canterbury in eastern Connecticut. For Douglas Winiarski, the personal links and theological similarities between immortalist groups demonstrate that these were not "isolated ... incidents of religious extremism."[94] He shows that "shadowy network of perfectionists . . . spread across the northern New England frontier" and accompanied the emigration of New Englanders to Nova Scotia.[95]

Unsurprisingly, Prince's writings on the revivals make little overt reference to these enthusiastic excesses. *Christian History* reprinted James Davenport's apology for his criticisms of ministers and other disorderly conduct, included only a couple of passing references to Croswell's ministry, and altogether ignored the antics of Woodbury and other immortalists.[96] Prince also chose not to respond directly to the harshest local critic of the awakening, Thomas

Fleet, editor of the *Boston Evening Post*.[97] Instead, he preferred to model a moderate revivalism oriented around social and religious reform, rather than disruption. This approach, which was closely informed by Prince's resurrection theology, had three key elements: a disinclination to describe conversion as a resurrection, an insistence that it was a long-form process, and an emphasis on its inability to remedy the material vileness that suffused the fallen earth.

The final six issues of *Christian History* (spanning January to February 1744) were devoted to Prince's own account of the revival in Boston. This narrative described converts undergoing a process of "renovation" or "awakening" rather than resurrection.[98] Prince had adopted this practice at the height of revivalistic excitement in the city. A series of four sermons preached sometime between 1742 and 1743 in support of the awakening broke conversion down into several parts, beginning with a "conviction" of one's sinfulness, followed by the "regeneration, or renovation of the heart," the "illumination" of the soul (as to the utter worthlessness of worldly things compared to Christ), and, finally, the "work of actual conversion" itself.[99] Underlining the "supernatural" and vital quality of this procedure, in the face of "the Socinian spirit" of the times, Prince presented it as a means of "convincing, renewing," and "enlightening" men and women, but not of raising them from the dead, even figuratively.[100] He was still using very similar language several years later, when he preached a sermon to the youth of Boston, at the "dying Desire of a Near, and dear young Relative" (almost certainly his daughter Mercy, who died in 1752).[101] There he explained that those who "are found [to be] reconciled to Christ" at the end of their lives become "Spirits," now "Perfect in Power and Holiness," carried up to heaven by angels.[102] Then, on the "Great Day of [Jesus's] Second Appearance," these souls would be reunited with "Bodies" raised in "Perfect Purity and Holiness, Beauty, Strength and Glory" (87). Prince observed that conversion, or "Renovation" was an essential prerequisite for receiving these privileges (88). But he avoided connecting it with resurrection too closely. Instead, he presented conversion as one aspect of preparation for salvation, alongside "a Right understanding and Belief of the main Truths of Divine Revelation" and "Hearty Desires, Resolutions, Prayers and Labours after an intire Conformity to [God] both in Heart and Life" (88–89).

The sermon closed with an urgent appeal typical of revivalistic preaching. Prince warned his young hearers to "*hearken unto to me now*, at the Present moment, without one moments more Delay" (136). Yet he also advised them that conversion was a drawn-out, even lifelong affair, necessitating solicitous observation of their "continual Sins and Failings," "the Constant Exercise of Some Grace, Suitable to [their individual] Circumstances," and the desire "to grow to further measures of Knowledge of Divine truths and Objects" (125). In another address inspired by the death of one of his offspring he set out the time frame of a model conversion. Prince's eldest daughter, Deborah, had been brought "to a more earnest Labour after vital Piety and the Power of Godliness" after hearing Whitefield preach in the autumn of 1740. But this development was a continuation of an earlier effort, inspired by the "Ministry" of Joseph Sewall, his colleague at the South Church.[103] What is more, Deborah had not received actual conviction of her justification until December 13, 1740 (23). Even that happy day had not concluded her striving. Prince noted that right up until her death (in the summer of 1744) his daughter continued to examine herself for evidence of "*sanctifying Grace*," "grow[ing] dead to the present world" as she endeavored "to *make* her *Calling and Election sure*" (24). While the "searching Preaching" of Gilbert Tennent proved "useful" (and challenging) in this respect, Deborah was also drawn to classic Puritan works of "Experimental" piety by Thomas Shepard, William Guthrie, John Flavel, Matthew Mead, Solomon Stoddard, and Samuel Mather (23–24).

Shepard was a frequent point of reference for Prince during and after the revivals. His narrative of the Boston awakening observed that hearing Whitefield and Tennent speak "seem'd" to have given the citizens "a renewed Taste for . . . *old* pious and experimental Writers," including Shepard.[104] Likewise, Prince's series of sermons defending the revivals noted that people crying out in church was nothing new, since it had frequently occurred during Shepard's preaching.[105] As this assertion implied, the Cambridge minister had strong revivalistic credentials, having always insisted on the critical importance of regeneration through grace. But Shepard was also New England Puritanism's archpreparationist, an advocate of the idea that conversion was an arduous, multistage procedure, requiring endurance, discipline, and rigorous self-analysis. In 1747, Prince published two of Shepard's theological tracts, together with selections from his diaries, in order to underline the relevance of this perspective in the age of awakening. Revivalist and missionary David Brainerd, who died shortly before the book was published, contributed a preface to the diary excerpts. Brainerd praised Shepard's tireless private exercises and meditations as ideal remedies to the recent tendency to place too much stock in brief, spectacular expressions of religious affection.

The "*deep unfeigned* Self-Abasement *in these Experiences*," the "Sense of great Unfruitfulness, Selfishness, [and] exceeding Vileness of Heart," highlighted the foolishness of those "*poor deluded Souls*" who assume they are saved because they experience "*a sudden Suggestion . . . that* Christ is theirs, *that* God loves them, *and the like.*"[106]

Vileness—of body, soul, and heart—bring us to the third aspect of Prince's revivalistic program. For Whitefield, Tennent, and the more extreme exhorters they inspired, dwelling on the natural human corruption was a powerful means of urging the necessity of conversion. Whitefield prayed with the crowds who came to see him that God would "make them . . . see their own Vileness" and thereby make them realize "how lost and undone" they would remain "without true Repentance."[107] More inclined to visceral language, Tennent warned the unconverted that they lay "polluted in [their] Blood and Gore, in a helpless and loathsome State" in which they "must lie and perish eternally."[108] Extrapolating from this kind of discourse, enthusiasts such as Sarah Prentice, Shadrach Ireland, and Richard Woodbury were convinced that spiritual regeneration would render their flesh incorruptible and incapable of sin (this belief was often accompanied by new attitudes toward sexuality: Woodbury maintained that it was better for believers to be celibate, free from sexual impurity; Ireland, like many other immortalists, thought that converts should only be sexually intimate with other converts).[109] More orthodox New Lights were also inclined to interpret changes in their physical demeanor as signs of the inward presence of saving grace—one Connecticut women noted that her conversion made it "seem[] as if [she] had a new soul and body."[110] Prince himself was not entirely averse to this kind of hyperbole. In a December 1741 letter to Whitefield (which was published as an appendix to the latter's defense of his ministry in New England), he celebrated the alteration of "some who were like *incarnate* Devils . . . into eminent Saints, full of Divine Adoration, Love, and Joy unspeakable and full of Glory."[111]

Yet Prince also reminded his fellow revivalists that conversion could not entirely ameliorate humanity's endemic fallibility and weakness. His account of the Boston revivals bemoaned the "*spiritual Pride*" that had led some new converts to judge other too harshly: "Every Soul *renewed* has *Remains* of the *same Corruptions* (tho' not reigning) *as before*; they mix with all our Graces; Unbelief with Faith, Pride with Humility, precipitant Zeal or Passion with Wisdom, rash Judging of others with condemning ourselves."[112] Most people regenerated during the awakening, however, had retained a sense of their "*remaining Vileness*" and had "generally grown more humble & jealous of themselves."[113] Where Whitefield and the Tennents placed their rhetorical emphasis on conversion's transformation of the believer into a purified "new creature,"[114] Prince tended to stress that the "natural power, constitutions, tempers, and infirmities" of "renewed" men and women "remain the same in some degree."[115] Until "the present state of nature" was overturned and "the time of the new earth ... arrive[d]," even the most "wonderful work[s] of God," would be accompanied by both "human ... errors" and "satanic influence[s]."[116]

Revivalistic rhetoric that suggested otherwise threatened to compromise the respectable image that Prince and other moderates attempted to create for the awakening. It was straightforward enough to repudiate the most egregious instances of enthusiasm. Prince joined most of his fellow Boston ministers in signing a declaration condemning Davenport's predilection for "judging the spiritual state of Pastors and People ... too positively," and when a radical member of the Old South Church who made a "bold Pretence to Inspiration" baptized some women in Boston Harbor, Prince and Sewall censured him for acting like a minister "without any regular Call or due Qualifications."[117] Whitefield and Tennent presented a more complex problem. Prince's claim that the awakening was a transformative, international movement depended in large part upon Whitefield's accomplishments. When Charles Chauncy of Boston's First Church suggested that leading revivalists, including the Englishman, had popularized the "*Quakerish* Notion" of "*sinless Perfection*" before death and thereby caused the same kind of religious and social disorder as the French Prophets had, Prince mounted a strong defense.[118] Recalling Whitefield's first appearance at the Second Church for the readers of *Christian History*, he conceded that the young preacher had now and then "dropped some Expressions that were not so accurate and guarded as we should expect from aged and long studied Ministers."[119] Nonetheless, Whitefield's "Doctrine was plainly that of the *Reformers*," balancing the maintenance of "*good Works*" against the "absolute Necessity of Regeneration by the HOLY GHOST," and allowing for the possibility that some of those "who think themselves renewed" may be "deceive[d]." Despite this support for Whitefield, Prince sought to correct the perception that the itinerant was the primary catalyst of the awakening in New England. His history of revivalism in Boston traced the beginning of the phenomenon back to the earthquake of 1727 and highlighted the importance of the awakenings that had swept through western Massachusetts and Connecticut in the mid-1730s.[120] This narrative complemented his ongoing attempt to counterbalance the more radical aspects of Whitefield's theology.

Long after his own church's revivalistic fervor had cooled, Prince was still hopeful that a wider-scale awakening would take place. In 1748, he was one of the signatories to the preface of *An Humble Attempt*, a tract in which Jonathan Edwards advocated an ecumenical and international concert of prayer for a revival that would ensure "the advancement of the universal and happy reign of Christ on the earth."[121] Yet Prince was often reminded that one of the chief legacies of the last awakening was the proliferation of religious separatism and resentment of credentialed ministers. In the same year, he and Sewall declined an invitation to Andrew Croswell's inauguration of a new church of New Lights gathered from Boston's established congregations. Among the reasons they provided for their refusal to attend was Croswell's prior claim that they and other moderates placed too much trust in "Sanctification" as a sign of probable election, and therefore risked "damning many Thousands of Souls."[122] As Winiarski's research shows, similar events unfolded many times across New England in the 1740s and 1750s. Laypeople who had adopted Whitefield's definition of conversion as "an instantaneous event" clashed with ministers who clung to the older Puritan expectation that it usually took many years.[123] Many dissatisfied New Lights formed separate churches. In the same period, a considerable number of antirevivalist Congregationalists, including Prince's brothers Joseph and Nathan, turned to Anglicanism.[124] The old Puritan consensus was breaking apart.

As Prince struggled against its disintegration, he frequently returned to one of his favorite themes: the fulfillment of the millennial prophecies. Though most separating radicals fell some way short of immortalism, they tended to attribute much greater spiritual capacity and autonomy to the converted believer than mainstream Congregationalists did. For Prince, the prospect of the immolation and resurrection of the earth was a powerful corrective to this hubris (as well as to the temptation to devote too much attention to economic acquisition). In 1757, the year before his death, he would make one of his strongest public statements of his eschatological literalism.

The Resurrection of Other Worlds: Prince and William Torrey's *Brief Discourse*

Although Prince had always taken a keen interest in antiquarian work, the last few years of his life were particularly productive. In 1755, he published three supplementary pamphlets to his unfinished *Chronological History of*

New England, covering late September 1630 to August 1633. Between 1755 and 1758 he worked on a revised edition of *The Bay Psalm Book*, which had been first published in 1640 and last updated in 1650.[125] In the preface to his version, Prince noted his intention "to preserve the *Substance*" of its predecessors, while rendering the verse more appealing to the "refined Taste and Judgment" of his own day.[126] His will, issued shortly before his death in October 1758, bequeathed two separate collections of books to the Old South Church. The volumes "in Latin, Greek, & . . . the Oriental Languages" were termed the "Public" or "South-Church-Library," while the "New England Library" comprised "Books, Pamphlets, Maps, Papers in Print, & Manuscript[s], either published in New England, or pertaining to its History, & Public Affairs."[127] Prince hoped that his donation would remind future generations of New England scholars of their Puritan patrimony.

The 1757 publication of Captain William's Torrey's *A Brief Discourse Concerning Futurities* can be seen of part of this effort to secure Congregationalism's legacy. Torrey (1608–1690) had written the text in 1687 and circulated it in manuscript. His preface acknowledged that he was a "Stranger" to "human Learning," and that he had only been able to study his subject in "short *Interims* pincht out of . . . other Occasions."[128] Yet it also noted that the line of inquiry it followed had been "too little . . . trodden by others." The "*first Resurrection,*" the "*new Heaven,*" and the "*new Earth,*" as well as "*the burning of the Old,*" deserved to be "better credited in the World by them that are wise."[129] Prince agreed. His own introduction to the text praised the author's "*great and accurate Acquaintance with the Scriptures*" and noted that Torrey's work provided "*a lively Instance of what* eminent Men *of the* civil Order *came over* hither *and adorned our* New-England Churches" during the Great Migration.[130] As this chapter has shown, Prince was always attempting to get laymen and women to take greater interest in the technical details of the millennium, and Torrey was exemplary in that regard—well versed in the relevant scriptures, aware of the limitations of his knowledge, and, most of all, completely committed to the literalist exegetical approach that Prince himself supported.

The decision to reissue Torrey's book was a timely one. The 1750s had witnessed a surge in eschatological sentiment in New England, largely due to the Seven Years' War with France. In the North American theater, the early years of this global conflict had been characterized by ineffectual leadership among colonial governors and British officers, allowing the enemy to register significant victories at Oswego (August 1756) and Fort William Henry on Lake George (August 1757). Protestant ministers across the colonies warned that the Roman Catholic Antichrist was now ready to sweep the true faith away from American shores.[131] Furthermore, in November 1755 the Atlantic basin had been hit by a series of earthquakes that had devastated Lisbon and caused considerable infrastructural damage to Boston. Both pro- and antirevivalist clergy warned that the shocks might carry an apocalyptic meaning. For Gilbert Tennent, the quakes suggested that "some extraordinary Revolutions" might be "near at Hand."[132] And although Jonathan Mayhew declined to speculate whether the end times were imminent, he did note that "there has probably been no age or period of the world" more conformable to the "prophetic description[s]" of the onset of the millennium.[133]

Most of the sermons inspired by the earthquakes and the ongoing conflict were too preoccupied with the tumultuous events that would attend the end of secular history to concern themselves with the nature of the millennium itself.[134] Through Torrey's tract, Prince was able to correct that oversight. Those who rejected the prospect of an earthly millennium often cited Jesus's words to Pilate in the Gospel of John: "My kingdom is not of this world" (18:36). But Torrey explained that "there are more Worlds then [sic] one."[135] The "*present* evil World" succeeded the antediluvian world, which "was drowned, . . . tho' not universally destroyed," by the Flood. In time, a second earth would replace the current one, as the Conflagration consumed, but not utterly incinerated, the planet. This regenerated globe would be put into "total Subjection to Christ" (38). Like Prince and Cotton Mather, Torrey thought that the saints raised in the First Resurrection would govern this New Earth on God's behalf. Under their regime there would be "no more Apostacy, or Backsliding in Holiness" (22). Creaturely life would also be transformed. Although Torrey did not believe that the living saints who survived the Conflagration would be immortal or sinless, he suggested that they would enjoy "*long Life*" and "*a Fulness of other temporal Blessings*" (23), including plentiful harvests, and an end to "*violent Death*" (22). Moreover, he was particularly exercised by the fate of the "Birds and Beasts of all kinds" (41). Just as Noah's ark had prevented the extinction of animals following the Flood, so some means would be found to preserve them from the apocalyptic inferno. In the millennium that followed they would be delivered from the abuse they had suffered due to the "Vanity" of fallen humanity.[136] "The Enmity of the Creatures amongst themselves, and against Man," would "be taken away" (46). Isaiah (11:6) had prophesied that "*the Wolf shall dwell with the Lamb, and the Leopard lie down with the Kid, and the Calf and the young Lion, and a little Child* [shall] *lead them.*" Torrey insisted that the literal meaning of eschatological scriptures should be preserved wherever possible—why "make *Allegorie* or *Metaphors* where God makes none?"

That sentiment encapsulates the appeal of Torrey's tract for Prince. Publishing *A Brief Discourse Concerning Futurities* was a means of contesting the eschatological scheme that his fellow revivalist Jonathan Edwards had been publicizing since the late 1730s.[137] The ethos of Edwards's *History of the Work of Redemption* sermon cycle was very much in sympathy with Prince's millennialism. Edwards sought to demonstrate that human history could only be properly understood as an expression of God's soteriological plan for the world.[138] There was also a strong global dimension to his eschatology. Edwards argued that the invention of "the mariner's compass, . . . whereby men are enabled to sail over the widest oceans," was a providential intervention intended to facilitate the transplantation of the true faith to heathen lands remote "from those parts of the world that are already Christianized."[139] Yet Edwards read Revelation's account of the millennial reign of the saints allegorically. In his account, the First Resurrection was a spiritual revitalization of the church "after it had been long . . . dead in the times of Antichrist."[140] During the millennium, he noted, "true religion" would eventually achieve "absolute universality" across "the habitable world."[141] "Vital piety" would "take possession of thrones and palaces," the "common business of daily life" would be "dedicated to God," and humankind's formerly "abusive" relationship to nature would be reformed.[142] For Prince, Torrey's vision of a world in which the resurrected dead and the living dwelt alongside each other in a "holy and heavenly Correspondency" was a helpful corrective to Edwards's argument that the millennium would inaugurate a new phase in history rather than regenerate the planet completely.

Prince disagreed with both Edwards and Torrey about the fate of the terrestrial sphere at the end of the millennium. Citing Revelation 20:11, Torrey predicted that "during the Time of the general Judgment . . . the Earth & Heavens" as we knew them would cease to exist: they would "fly away from the Face of him that sits on the Throne," and "no Place [would be] found for them."[143] Edwards maintained that once the chiliad was concluded, "the mountains [would be] carried unto the depth of the sea . . . , and this lower world [would] all be dissolved."[144] The "new earth" described in Revelation was therefore none other than heaven itself.[145] The "globe we now dwell upon," he explained, "is not to be refined to be the place of God's everlasting abode [or the home of the saints], because 'tis a moveable globe, and must continue moving always if the laws of nature are upheld." It was "not seemly," for "God's eternal glorious abide, and fixed and everlasting throne," to be "a moveable part of the universe."

In Prince's account, the last members of the human race would ascend into the heavenly realm at the end of the millennium (which he assumed would last for "*three hundred and sixty thousand years*").[146] But the renovated earth (as Ecclesiastes 1:4 suggested) would "endure[] for ever," conserved as "an ever lasting theatre" of God's love and mercy. "Another sort or series of inhabitants" would witness "another scene of wondrous dispensations[,]" as Christ's "government increase[d]" eternally, "even in this lower world."[147] This conjecture about posthuman earthlings was linked to Prince's belief that other planets were also likely to be home to intelligent life. God's kingdom was spatially, as well as temporally, infinite. "All the globes about us," Prince suggested, "are so many worlds of perpetual probation, from whence innumerable companies have been, are, and will be constantly ascending to the heavenly world around them."[148] If this was indeed the case, "The glorified regions of ... celestial space" would need to expand "proportionally ... for ever." Prince even argued that it might be possible to view that zone of the universe from earth. His 1738 funeral sermon for Nathanael Williams, master of the Boston Latin School, noted that on a "clear Night[,] by the Help of Glasses," it was possible to observe "several wonderous *Openings* in the Heavens over us; where immeasurable *Spaces of Light* appear, underived from any visible Bodies," and apparently "beyond the starry Regions."[149] Could "the *Light* appearing in those amazing *Chasms* ... be the distant Rays of the heavenly Glory?" At the moment of death, Prince speculated, the spirits of believers would be granted a much clearer sight of that faraway place, before speeding there to await their reunion with their bodies.[150]

Cotton Mather was also invested in these cosmological matters. He, too, was fascinated by the likelihood that there were "other worlds" where God was known and worshiped.[151] But Prince carried this line of thought further. *The Endless Increase of Christ's Government* (his sermon to the 1740 convention of Massachusetts clergy) raised the possibility of a kind of resurrection that had no relation to sin, mortality, or environmental degradation. The new race of rational creatures who would populate the "refined earth" would presumably know nothing of these afflictions.[152] Nonetheless, "endless" numbers of them would be "raised up" into "the world of glory," alongside their peers from extraterrestrial planets. Transition from earthly to heavenly life was therefore not only a means of arriving at the redemptive telos of the fallen earth's history. It was also an eternal process—the governing principle of the entire universe.

The sermon's concluding section offered a "brief [practical] *improvement*" of this cosmic perspective. The realization that resurrection was foundational to all of creation, Prince argued, should lead believers to center their devotions on their "divine Redeemer."[153] The "boundless and enlarging empire" of the New Jerusalem, "all these numberless and grown multitudes of happy saints through eternity," were the "fruits" of his "purchase," his incarnation, death, and victory over the grave. By encouraging ordinary saints to consider the kind of question that other ministers reserved for eschatological specialists (How would the regeneration of the earth take place? Were there beings on other planets who would also be redeemed?) Prince was broadening their understanding of and love for Christ. His address also urged its audience to consider the relationship between current events and the endless series of resurrections it described. In 1740, Prince speculated that the colonial revivals were hastening the Christianization of the globe and inaugurating the next phase in the salvation of creation. When he preached the sermon again in 1756, he added a reference to the "present war" with France, suggesting (somewhat hopefully) that it might "open[] a way to enlighten the utmost regions of America."[154] His own congregation was flourishing that year (in 1756 the Old South admitted fifty-two new members, the highest annual rate for many decades to come), but the divisive broader impact of Whitefieldarian evangelism was readily apparent.[155] In those unsettled times, contemplation of the millennium's universal scope was particularly reassuring: though the progress of God's cause was not always easy to track through secular history, the eventual redemption of all things was certain.

Thomas Prince died in October 1758. In the years that followed, most eschatological speculation in America continued to center around the potentially apocalyptic outcome of the war with France. Yet as the relationship with the metropole deteriorated through the 1760s, the struggle to protect colonial liberty and religious freedom from imperial overreach began to take on a millennial significance. By the eve of the Revolutionary War, patriotic Congregationalist, Presbyterian, and Baptist ministers framed the struggle against Britain as part of the fight against the Antichrist. While some predicted that an independent America would realize the glories of the kingdom of Christ on earth, others made the even bolder claim that the young country would lead the entire world into a new age, spreading

Christianity across the planet and converting the Jewish people.[156] Exceptionalist millennialism remained a powerful force in the United States' religious culture throughout the nineteenth century, when it became conceptually intertwined with the nation's manifest destiny to master the entire North American continent.[157] Though republicanism had replaced monarchism as providence's political vehicle, this narrative was an outgrowth of the imperialist and globalizing rhetoric of the Protestant Interest promoted by Prince and his contemporaries.

But what of Prince's other millennial focus, the resurrection of the world? The early national and antebellum eras bore witness to a plethora of apocalyptic visions of the transformation of the planet. In the 1790s, Baptist-turned-Universalist Elhanan Winchester predicted that the Conflagration would take place at the end of the millennium, when it would transform the earth into a "liquid mass" of fire where the wicked would be punished for refusing the gift of salvation.[158] In the 1840s, Joseph Smith claimed that the "sanctified and immortal" earth of the next age would be "made like unto crystal," thereby resembling the scrying stones that he had used to decipher the gold plates on which the Book of Mormon had supposedly been transcribed.[159] The Church of Latter Day Saints would develop a complex and expansive eschatology from his teachings. At the end of time, the Mormon faithful would be physically transported to the heavenly sphere, where the social and familial relationships they had constructed in life would form "the framework in which they would live eternally."[160] Last, Irish Anglican John Nelson Darby, whose works would prove extremely influential in the United States, predicted a premillennial "tribulation" during which the planet would be ransacked by the rule of an incarnate Antichrist and Satan's party would enjoy "Complete power."[161] True Christians (drawn from across the Protestant denominations) would be secretly raptured into heaven immediately before this dark period began, and would return with Christ at the beginning of the earthly millennium.[162]

At root, each of these schemes was motivated by the same conviction as Prince's was: even the conversion of the world's entire population, and the moral and political reform of all its nations, could not create an terrestrial environment worthy of hosting the kingdom of God. But their authors were not as closely concerned with the material particulars of the earth's regeneration. As I have shown, Prince was committed to understanding (as far as was possible) the scientific processes by which the regeneration of the world would take place (the adjustment of the earth's orbit, the purification of its atmosphere). He also sought to bring this line of inquiry to the attention of a wider audience. Later millennialists of a literalist persuasion were as a rule more likely to accept the transformation of the planet as a mysterious manifestation of divine power. Darby, for instance, simply noted that the coming of Christ would "change the whole state of the world," while Smith prophesied that "the Earth shall pass away . . . by fire" and then be "rolled back into the presence of God and crowned with celestial glory."[163] Some scholars have suggested that an optimistic, anthropocentric millennialism dominated the United States in the nineteenth century. Certainly, many Protestants looked for the coming of the kingdom in human endeavor ("moral reform," missionary outreach, national prosperity).[164] And as my next chapter will demonstrate, post-Christian authors adapted eschatological tropes to describe a purely secular progress. Nevertheless, Winchester, Smith, and Darby speak to the persistence of more supernaturalist perspectives. The most significant difference between Prince and most of the millennialists who came after him was not over the timing of the Second Coming or the degree of human agency in it, but about the extent to which the transition from our world to the next needed to, or could be, explained.

One reason for this development was declining belief in the corporeality of resurrection. Natural science contended that the material continuity of the mortal and risen bodies was improbable; theologians, under the influence of Locke's theory of mind, suggested that the persistence of the soul or consciousness was more important anyway.[165] As a result, the idea of a physical link between the old and new earths became even more difficult to sustain. In the longer term, the secularization that accompanied economic globalization also contributed to the dematerialization of life after death. For Peter Sloterdijk, one of the essential features of capitalism's globalized world is the "horizontal" and decentered orientation of the thought and practice it fosters. Both political progress and economic enterprise are figured as multilateral, collaborative, and diffuse.[166] The world is all "surface," with no imperial hub, and no heavenly city above it—"On the last orb," he concludes, "there will be no sphere of all spheres[,] . . . [no] power-holding centre of all centres."[167] Contemporary attitudes toward eternal life support this claim that there is no place for collective symbols and narratives of transcendence on the globalized earth. Although faith in human immortality endures, the difficulty of believing in corporeal resurrection has significantly altered the character of this "vertical" trajectory of transcendent meaning. The concomitant weakening of causal and spatial links between our planet and the ethereal locations occupied by the dead (whether a celestial paradise or the New Earth) makes it harder to conceive of material, political, and ecclesiastical connections between mortal and immortal existence.[168] People still believe in heaven, but (unlike Thomas Prince) cannot explain how they will reach it. How one imagines eternity is therefore a matter of personal preference, rather than of universal consequence. The prospect of the earth being remade (or of the saints being reunited) may still be invoked, but the survival of the self is paramount. In this way, an afterworld becomes an afterlife.

5
Secular Resurrections

Reworking and Rejecting Protestant Eschatology

In the early 1770s, while living in London, Benjamin Franklin collaborated with Sir Francis Dashwood on a new version of the Anglican Book of Common Prayer. This much-shortened version, published anonymously in 1773, removed the Creed's references to Christ's resurrection and the future resurrection of the dead (while retaining its invocations of "The Forgiveness of Sins; And the Life everlasting").[1] The catechism for candidates for confirmation was also substantially altered. The Creed, the Ten Commandments, and descriptions of the two sacraments recognized by the Church of England were all excised (all that remained were the Lord's Prayer and descriptions of the Christian's duties toward God and his or her neighbor).[2] Around fifty years later, Thomas Jefferson produced an abridgment of the Gospels, which he titled "The Life and Morals of Jesus of Nazareth." Using scissors and glue, Jefferson cannibalized Greek, Latin, French, and English Bibles to create four parallel columns of text. The parallel texts he constructed cast the story of Christ as that of a moral instructor by removing what Jefferson elsewhere called the "artificial systems" that the church had erected around it: "the immaculate conception of Jesus, his deification, the creation of the world by him, his miraculous powers, his resurrection and visible ascension, his corporeal presence in the Eucharist, the Trinity, original sin, atonement, regeneration, election, orders of Hierarchy, &c."[3]

The *Jefferson Bible*, as it is now sometimes known, was not published in his lifetime, and most likely was never intended to be circulated outside of a small group of the former president's friends.[4] During the rancorous election of 1800, supporters of his Federalist opponents had argued that as an apparent atheist Jefferson was unfit to assume the presidency.[5] He was therefore reluctant to reveal publicly the full extent of his skepticism toward Christian soteriology and eschatology. Tom Paine did not share this circumspection. In the first part of *The Age of Reason* (1794), his deist attack on "Christian Mythology," Paine boldly asserted that "the story" of Christ's resurrection "has every mark of fraud and imposition stamped upon the face of it."[6] In the second part, published the following year, he took aim at the very possibility of a corporeal afterlife. Though Paine did not question the truth of human immortality,[7] he argued that the doctrine of resurrection presented in Paul's epistles was logically self-contradictory: "For if I have already died in this body, and am raised again in the same body in which I have died, it is presumptive evidence that I shall die again. That resurrection no more secures me against the repetition of dying, than an ague-fit, when past, secures me against another."[8] Nature, not fraudulent revelation, provided the best evidence for the reality of the life after death. "The belief of a future state is a rational belief," Paine insisted, "founded upon facts visible in the creation: for it is not more difficult to believe that we shall exist hereafter in a better state and form than at present, than that a worm should become a butterfly, and quit the dunghill for the atmosphere." While Paul's concept of a "celestial" body was "nothing better than the jargon of the conjuror," it was plausible to presume that the human mind (which produced "immortal" thoughts and was "of a nature different from every thing else that we know of") would live on into eternity.[9]

There were main three reasons why Franklin, Jefferson, Paine, and others on the radical wing of the American Revolution were averse to the orthodox Protestant resurrection theology I have explored through this book. First, as this last example from *The Age of Reason* demonstrates, they rejected the idea of divine revelation through scripture, preferring to believe that religious and ethical principles could be rationally induced from the observation of nature. Second, they were determined to break what they saw as the oppressive political power of the clergy. As a result, they were disgusted by the idea of an eschatological day of judgment that would divide humanity between those who professed the right set of beliefs and those who did not. Eighteen months before his death, Thomas Jefferson wrote to the Dutch-American revolutionary François van der Kemp, expressing his excitement at the work of the French physiologist Jean Pierre Flourens, whose experiments on animals appeared to have proved that "the cerebrum is the organ of thought, & possesses alone the faculty of thinking."[10] After removing a large portion of a chicken's brain, the scientist had been able to keep the animal alive for almost a year, despite having "deprived" it "of perception[,] intelligence, memory[,] and thought." Flourens's discovery, Jefferson predicted, would be "a terrible tub" to Trinitarian Christians, who "must tell us whether the soul remains in the body in this state, . . . or does it leave the body, as in death?" He added that it would "be incumbent on them to answer otherwise than by the dogma that every one who believeth not with them without doubt shall perish everlastingly." Finally, though radicals were skeptical of the supernatural regeneration of the body through resurrection, they believed that a worldly equivalent was entirely possible. Democratic government and republican ethics would gradually transform American (and then global) society. As injustice, inequality, and superstition were eradicated, men and women would lead healthier, happier, and longer lives. Scientific progress would accelerate, and the natural environment would be ameliorated.

Should that process be seen as a secular equivalent of resurrection? In answering that question, Hans Blumenberg's critique of the secularization thesis must be reckoned with. Blumenberg attacks the school of thought (emerging from the work of Carl Schmidt) that casts modern political positions and social movements as disguised reiterations of sacred principles or forms. Though he acknowledges that there are continuities between the religious and secular periods of Western history, Blumenberg contends that the modern age is characterized by a new form of human "self-assertion." Modern men and women recognize that they are responsible for the adversities that confront them, but no longer connect that liability to original sin.[11] Instead, they accept that they are accountable for the "reality surrounding [them]" because they have the capability to reshape that reality themselves.[12] Although the narrative of human progress that emerges from this change is influenced by the Christian eschatology of the premodern era, Blumenberg insists that the two models are fundamentally distinct, insofar as the latter describes "an event breaking into history," while the former looks toward "a future that is immanent in history."[13]

With this caveat in mind, it is important to acknowledge that the political revolutions of the late eighteenth century brought with them their own, immanent models of human perfectibility—such as the French concept of *régénération*, which described the process of reform by which the nation's diverse and disputatious inhabitants would be shaped into a unified body of citizens.[14] Nonetheless, the early national authors I turn to now continued to engage with the doctrine of resurrection in three distinct but sometimes overlapping ways. In the first place, they employed the term *metaphorically*, to denote the resurgence of a statesman's, a faction's, or a nation's political fortunes. In the second, they invoked it *metonymically*, in describing the ways in which political or philosophical reforms would increase individual happiness and longevity (while some presented this secular progress as a replacement for Christian eschatology, others insisted that the two were complementary). In the third, they discussed traditional beliefs about resurrection *literally*, arguing variously that they ought to be abandoned, reformed, or conserved for the benefit of American society. Though Protestant theologians produced conventional exegeses of the eschatological scriptures throughout the period (and beyond), the survey that follows will focus on texts in which resurrection and the millennium appear in new guises or roles.

The chapter's final section will address further adaptations and critiques of conventional resurrection theology in the later antebellum era and the immediate aftermath of the Civil War (c. 1830–1870). This period saw several significant changes in American attitudes toward death and the afterlife. While some more orthodox evangelical denominations (especially Methodists and Baptists) flourished, an array of post-Christian religions emerged or were revitalized. Echoing the rhetoric of seventeenth-century sectaries, some of these groups claimed that their members had already been resurrected. At the same time, a new form of religious skepticism gained ground. Questioning the truth of biblical revelation, rejecting Christ's divinity, and disavowing Christian eschatology were no longer largely the preserve of a highly educated class of elite radicals: newspapers published in major cities across the country sought to foster deism and skepticism in the working classes.[15] The growth of the American publishing industry also reinforced the appeal of the sentimental cult of the dead that had been developing since the turn of the nineteenth century. American women were especially attracted to its portrayal of heaven as home and its suggestion that the souls of the departed might return as guardian angels to watch over their families. Spiritualist theologians later developed more systematic explorations of these ideas.

Scholars have often characterized the domestic turn in antebellum attitudes toward immortality as a break with conventional Protestant theology, which supposedly emphasized the divide between the living and the dead and took a theocentric view of the celestial sphere. However, Erik Seeman has shown that the nineteenth-century "cult of the dead" was actually an evolution of seventeenth- and eighteenth-century Protestant forms of intimacy with the departed.[16] Building on his work, I uncover parallels between Puritan resurrection theology and the eschatological speculations of three mid-nineteenth-century authors: sentimental novelist Elizabeth Stuart

Phelps, influential Spiritualist Andrew Jackson Davis, and health reformer William Alcott. I then turn to literary writing that resisted the domestication of death and the afterlife—texts by Edgar Allan Poe, Henry David Thoreau, and George Lippard that center around the experience of dying and the materiality of the corpse. Although Thoreau was highly critical of mourning and memorialization practices that sought to prettify the hard natural facts of death and decay, his own materialist thanatology partook of the sentimental universalism of the popular cult of the dead. Poe and Lippard, meanwhile, depicted gothic perversions of resurrection: men and women entombed alive, cadavers that can move and speak, living bodies degenerated into unthinking automatons. In their writings, the (actual or apparent) return of the dead is more obviously representative of the uncertainty and impurity of the material world than of hope or redemption.

Resurrection as Metaphor

In their private correspondence, the statesmen of the early national era often spoke of resurrection in a metaphorically broad sense. Two years after winning the presidency, Thomas Jefferson hoped that he could heal the factional divisions that the election of 1800 had exacerbated. He informed his attorney general, Levi Lincoln, that he was confident that "such of the body of the people as thought themselves federalists, would find that they were in truth republicans, and would come over to us by degrees."[17] However, the "leaders" of that party (who included his one-time friend John Adams) were beyond redemption. Jefferson noted that he would "take no other revenge than by a steady pursuit of economy, and peace, and by the establishment of republican principles in substance and in form, to sink federalism into an abyss from which there shall be no resurrection for it." Fourteen years later, following their reconciliation, Adams wrote to Jefferson to observe that he did "not like the late Resurrection of the Jesuits" who he believed were then "more numerous" in the United States than was commonly suspected.[18] "If ever any Congregation of Men could merit... eternal Perdition on Earth and in Hell," he continued, "it is this Company of Loiola." In 1823, Adams informed the same correspondent that he had recently read George Bethune English's account of his travels up the Nile to Sudan with the army of Ibrahim Pasha, the son of the Wāli of Egypt.[19] Enthused by English's adventure, Adams imagined the "Stone Cutters" of his hometown of Quincy, Massachusetts, making the river "as navigable as our Hudson[,] Potomac[,] or Missis[s]ippi."[20] Such a project would create a "free communication" between Europe, India, and even West Africa, thereby effecting the "resurrection from the dead of those vast and ancient Countries of Abyssinia and Etheopia."[21]

These passing references touched on eschatological beliefs in a loose and general way. But other deployments of resurrection as a political metaphor engaged much more specifically with relevant biblical passages and exegetical traditions. In the 1790s, James Winthrop, former Harvard librarian and third great-grandson of John Winthrop, the first governor of the Massachusetts Bay Colony, published two detailed interpretations of the apocalyptic scriptures. The first of these works sought to translate the "*hieroglyphical*" and mystical language of the book of Revelation into plainer speech, thereby uncovering its applicability to recent political events. In a prefatory glossary, Winthrop defined the millennium as a "thousand years of tranquillity . . . when the governments shall be defensive" (i.e., nonoppressive) and "regulated by the principles of religion and justice."[22] The First Resurrection, accordingly, referred to "the revival of the principles of religion, and their being made by compact the basis of government." Winthrop was convinced that the American and French Revolutions had fulfilled that prophecy and argued that those "states" that had opposed those events would "remain in heathen darkness" (under repressive regimes) "till after the Millennium is expired."

There were plenty of precedents in the Protestant exegetical tradition for reading Revelation in an allegorical way. As we saw in chapter 1, John Cotton, among others, believed that the vision of St. John described the organizational and disciplinary purification of Protestant churches as well as the decline of papal and Ottoman power. Winthrop took this line of interpretation in a much more political direction, however. Like Cotton, he suggested that the millennial prophecies were partially accomplished within each of the faithful, as well as through global history. But while the seventeenth-century minister identified spiritual rebirth as the means by which any individual could participate in the millennium (even if they died before the period began in earnest), Winthrop instead underlined the eschatological significance of republican virtue. "Christ's kingdom," he argued, was realized through the soul's "steady love of virtue . . . produc[ing] its effect in outward conduct."[23] Those who belonged to it would refrain from "invad[ing] the rights" of their fellows and recognize their responsibility to perform "all those acts of benevolence, which serve to promote public and private happiness."[24]

Winthrop even went so far as to allegorize Revelation's description of the Last Judgment. He claimed that the book's depiction of "the dead, small and great, stand[ing] before" God's "great white throne" (20:11–12) pertained to a political reckoning at the end of the millennium.[25] These verses did not refer to the physical resurrection and spiritual judgment of the departed, but rather to the impact of future revolutions on every living individual, even "those in the most obscure and retired situations"—people who were politically dead. According to Winthrop, the culmination of sacred history outlined in Revelation's last two chapters should also be understood metaphorically. The "new heavens and new earth" (21:1) described there represented a new republican world order, in which noncoercive governments would be established in every country.[26]

Although Winthrop read Revelation entirely allegorically, he was not prepared to reduce every soteriological and eschatological passage in the Bible to a political metaphor. While resurrection was "*figurative*" in the Apocalypse, in the Gospels it was "*historical, as it respects Christ.*"[27] "*In the reasonings of St. Paul,*" he added, the word "*must be understood literally, as it relates to believers in general, or his argument will lose it whole force.*" Indeed, Winthrop hoped that his secularization of the concept of the millennium would help to preserve faith in individual immortality. He welcomed the fact that he lived "in a free country, where every question is open to every body," and claimed to respect the "opinion" of those who used that freedom to attempt "to discredit the Bible."[28] Nonetheless, he was personally convinced "that the dead shall live again."[29] Disproving what he saw as the more outlandish, supernaturalist interpretations of the eschatological scriptures (which claimed that the dead and the living would coexist during the millennium) would make Christianity's "primary" and "fundamental" claims about the next world seem more plausible.

Another notable secularizer of millennialism seems to have intended the opposite. In his epic poem *The Vision of Columbus* (1787) and its later expansion *The Columbiad* (1807), Joel Barlow presented a mythologized account of America's past and a prophetic description of her future. Both texts begin in 1500, during the during the six-week period when Christopher Columbus was imprisoned for his misgovernment of the Spanish Indies. The mariner despairs that rather than being settled under the auspices of freedom and peace, the New World is now threatened by the "murderous reign" of exploitative European "tyrants."[30] His complaint is interrupted by the appearance of a radiant angelic figure, named Hesper in *The Columbiad*, but simply "the

Seraph" in the earlier poem. This visitor conjures Columbus's chains and cell away, leading him through a dream of significant events that had already transpired or were yet to come. In the longer *Columbiad* these episodes include the rise of the noble Incan empire, its destruction by the conquistadors and their clerical allies, the growth of a supposedly superior English colonialism in North America, the Seven Years' War, the American Revolution, the growth of a progressive US republic, and, finally, the global victory of democracy and science over the forces of superstition and oppression. At each work's conclusion, Columbus's celestial guide enjoins him to endure his present ordeal with patience—his discovery has prepared the way for a new epoch of human history, in which a global confederacy will "bind all regions in the leagues of peace."[31]

Having grown up a Congregationalist, Barlow was more than familiar with the tropes of chiliastic prophecy and exegesis. The last few books of each poem outline the spread of democratic republicanism across the globe in terms that self-consciously echo Protestant descriptions of the millennium. As in the accounts of Thomas Brightman, John Cotton, and many other millennialists, the fall of the Ottoman Empire creates the possibility for a unified, peaceful world ("The Turk's dim Crescent, like a day-struck star . . . Shrinks from insulted Europe, who divide / The shatter'd empire to the Pontic tide").[32] But where Protestant theologians pictured a planet joined together by reformed religion, Barlow imagined that the earth would be transformed by commercial integration, political emancipation, and the triumph of rational inquiry over superstitious "mystery."[33] Eventually, the poems suggest, an international "general congress" will be founded, from whence "the legates of all empires" would wield a federal authority over "each realm."[34] Barlow's description of this global capital—its "Four blazing fronts, with gates unfolding high," and "glittering spires" rising from "golden roofs"—is clearly intended to parallel John's vision of the golden and "foursquare" New Jerusalem, which descends from the sky in Revelation 21. To underline the resemblance, he directly compares the journey of "the gathering throng" of representatives to the world assembly with that of angels ("the guardian guides of heaven") to the celestial "mount of God . . . in mid universe," where they might gather to "exchange their counsels and their works compare."[35]

In an explanatory note to the ninth and final book of *The Vision of Columbus*, Barlow appears to take Winthrop's position, by presenting the political new world order as the fulfillment of the eschatological scriptures—"It has long been the opinion of the Author," he observed, "that such a state of peace and happiness as is foretold in scripture and commonly called the millennial period, may be rationally expected to be introduced without a miracle."[36] This claim was likely meant to propitiate some of his friends—the Federalist circles he moved in in the 1780s included conventional Protestants such as Timothy Dwight, future president of Yale. However, both poems contain more than a few gestures toward Barlow's doubts about orthodox teaching on the millennium and the afterlife.

For example, *The Vision of Columbus* features a brief depiction of Christ's ministry, passion, resurrection, and ascension: "See nature's laws suspended by his power! / Unclosing graves their slumbering death restore.... He dies, he conquers death, ascends on high, / And rising saints attend him thro' the sky" (234). Although this epitome alludes to Jesus's power to bring others back to life, it is not really concerned with salvation and individual immortality at all. Christ's purpose is not to reveal the one true path to heaven, but rather to embody "the great moral Sense" (234) that "all [genuine] religion[s]" preach (235). His message is therefore political and cosmopolitan, rather than spiritual and sectarian; he seeks to end war and tyranny, not to save humankind from hell:

> To teach how pain and death and endless woes,
> From wayward strife, and breach of order, rose;
> How each discordant wish, the soul that swells,
> 'Gainst human bliss and heavenly power rebels,
> Weakens the chain of love, subverts the plan,
> While nature drives the vengeance back on man. (235)

The account of the global congress in *The Columbiad* makes a comparable point in a more obviously iconoclastic manner. There the courtyard of the "sacred mansion" in which the delegates meet is said to be home to a statue of "earth's ... Genius," holding "truth's mighty mirror ... in his hands."[37] We read that "each envoy" casts "some old idol from his native land" beneath the feet of the image. Among the symbols of monarchy ("sceptres, mitres, crowns") and false religion ("a pagod," "a crescent") discarded there, "a cross" is set down "to sleep." For the sake of peace and progress, Barlow suggests, this icon of sin, sacrifice, and resurrection must be rejected.

The most striking critique of Christianity in both poems arises from the Seraph's/Hesper's refusal to grant Columbus a *supernatural* vision. The Genovese asks his interlocutor for a preview of the Second Coming:

> Command, celestial Guide, from each far pole,
> John's vision'd morn to open on my soul,
> And raise the scenes, by his reflected light,
> Living and glorious to my longing sight.
> Let heaven unfolding show the eternal throne,
> And all the concave flame in one clear sun;
> On clouds of fire, with angels at his side,
> The Prince of Peace, the King of Salem ride,
> With smiles of love to free the bridal earth,
> Call slumbering ages to a second birth,
> With all his white-robed millions fill the train,
> And here commence the interminable reign![38]

The spirit replies:

> Such views . . . for sense too bright,
> Would seal thy vision in eternal night;
> Men cannot face nor seraph power display
> The mystic beams of such an awful day.
> Enough for thee, that thy delighted mind
> Should trace the temporal actions of thy kind.

This exchange offered Barlow a degree of plausible deniability. He could argue that he did not mean to deny the Last Judgment, Second Coming, or other features of the Christian apocalypse, but only to warn against potentially divisive speculation into them. However, the strong implication is that the secularized outline of the millennium that followed should be seen to supersede the biblical account. While it was understandable for Columbus himself to cling to these superstitions, a late eighteenth- or early nineteenth-century audience ought to know better.

Notwithstanding Barlow's thinly disguised skepticism toward the literal truth of the doctrine, the two poems suggest that Protestant resurrection theology continued to influence his imagination. In book 1 of both works, the author compares Columbus's first visionary sight of the North American continent to the perspective of a resurrected believer ascending into heaven:

> As when some saint first gains his bright abode,
> Vaults o'er the spheres and views the works of God,

> Sees earth, his kindred orb, beneath him roll,
> Here glow the centre, and there point the pole;
> O'er land and sea his eyes delighted rove,
> And human thoughts his heavenly joys improve;
> With equal scope the raptured Hero's sight
> Ranged the low vale, or climb'd the cloudy height,
> As, fit in ardent look, his opening mind,
> Explored the realms that here invite mankind.[39]

Seeking to justify the selection of a Catholic Italian who never set foot in North America as the protagonist of his epic, cosmopolitan, and creole framing of United States history,[40] Barlow looked back to the Puritan millennialism and soteriology he had all but renounced.[41] Since he could not claim a genetic or cultural connection between Columbus and American citizens, he adopted a quasi-spiritual model of affiliation comparable to the allegorical interpretation of the First Resurrection favored by John Cotton, Jonathan Edwards, Samuel Hopkins, and Ezra Stiles, president of Yale in Barlow's last two years at the college.[42] Hopkins, for instance, claimed that the saints and martyrs who had died before the beginning of the millennium would not be literally "raised to life," but would instead "live again and reign with Christ in the revival, prosperity, and . . . triumph of that cause and interest in which they had lived"—the propagation of the gospel.[43] The central premise of *The Vision of Columbus* and *The Columbiad* is that their eponymous hero enjoyed a similar relationship to the people of the United States.

Through the course of both poems, Barlow repeatedly draws a direct link between Columbus and the various collectives, individuals, and institutions who would bring freedom, progress, and wealth to the Americas in the seventeenth and eighteenth centuries. So it is that the Genovese sailor is described as the "Patriarch" of the English settlers at Jamestown, of Braddock's and Washington's doomed expedition to Fort Duquesne in the Seven Years' War, of the Patriot cause in the American Revolution, and, most of all, of the new historical era inaugurated by the European colonization of the Americas. And while Columbus as colonist is depicted as the preeminent forebear of modern American democracy, the indigenous Incan emperor Manco Cápac is also singled out as an important ancestor of those who favor enlightened, tolerant government.[44] The bond that each of these men share with those who come after them is ecumenical and (figuratively) spiritual. Like John Cotton's departed saints, they live again through successors who share their ethos.

Beginning and ending his narratives with allusions to heaven helped Barlow to reinforce his secular and republican message. The most important transgenerational connections were those that transcended ethnic, national, and sectarian distinctions, just as political resurrection was supposed to.[45] In the poems, the imprisoned Columbus is reassured that his will be proved to be an unprecedented contribution to global history. Though he is personally trapped in an age of fanatical priests, tyrannical monarchs, and "courts insidious," his "example" will inspire those who establish "freedom's first empire" in the New World.[46] Barlow offers his readers the same consolation, urging them to look beyond the controversies and crises of the present (the framing of the Constitution in 1787; national debt, Republican-Federalist factionalism, and the Napoleonic Wars in 1807) toward a gloriously global republican future. As citizens of a democracy, they live in circumstances far preferable to those of Columbus, who is depicted as a liberal republican born before his time. Yet both texts admit that the new world of peace is still some way off. The forces of tyranny, nationalism, and superstition, the spirits note, are extremely persistent enemies, often reestablishing themselves when they seem to have been definitively defeated. Although American republicanism was destined to be imitated by the rest of the planet, the men and women of Barlow's generation would die long before this was accomplished. He therefore asks them to make an imaginative leap. In common with Columbus, they need not think of themselves as sacrificing their lives in the struggle to secure the secular millennium. Instead, they must realize that they will be resurrected in the world citizens whose integrated, cosmopolitan planet they will help to create. For Barlow, then, exchanging Protestantism for secular republicanism did not mean forsaking, but rather repurposing, humanity's need to believe in a personal afterlife.

Natural and Social Resurrection

Barlow's epics also engage with resurrection metonymically, depicting natural, political, and social equivalents of the process. The poems claim that as more and more countries adopt the democratic republicanism pioneered in the United States, the natural environment and the humanity will be reciprocally transfigured. Free trade and the fairer distribution of land will yield a "tenfold" increase in agricultural productivity, which will cause the "renovating [human] race" to "multiply in every land."[47] That growth in population will increase productivity, lightening the burden of labor, improving physical health, and expanding mental proficiency ("And while she [nature] rears them with a statelier frame / Their soul she kindles with a diviner flame, / Leads their bright intellect with fervid glow / Thro all the mass of things that still remains to know"). The resulting scientific advances will carry the transformation of humankind even further, increasing life spans and invigorating old age ("With long wrought life to teach the race to glow, / And vigorous nerves to grace the locks of snow").[48] This biological refinement, finally, will help to generate a global political harmony. Living longer without any need to compete for resources with other nations, Barlow implies, will enable people to move beyond the "narrow" chauvinism of former ages.[49]

Instead of plotting to profit at the expense of "neighboring lands," men and women will "work[] with enlighten'd zeal, to see combined / The strength and happiness of humankind." This new internationalism, both poems suggest, will unfold in opposition to the myth of Babel. The book of Genesis claims that the multiplicity of languages on earth is a punishment for a hubristic attempt to emulate the Creator. But in the new republican age, people will develop godlike capabilities without any fear of divine reprisal. The next phase of human development will witness a "blend[ing]" of "the tongues of nations," until "one pure language" is spoken by all.[50] Global monolingualism, Barlow explains, will make it easier to transmit scientific and philosophical truths, and harder for "dark authorities" (sophists and priests) to entrance the vulnerable with arcane mysteries.[51]

As this reversal of the Babel story suggests, Barlow viewed the remaking of human nature and the reformation of the natural world as replacements for the Christian concepts of resurrection and the millennium. Other radical republicans shared this perspective. In 1784, poet Philip Freneau predicted that the westward expansion of the United States would offer immigrants fleeing the corruption of the Old World the chance to start again:

> From Europe's proud, despotic shores
> Hither the stranger takes his way,
> And in our new found world explores
> A happier soil, a milder sway,
> . . . .
> While virtue warms the generous breast,
> There heaven-born freedom shall reside,

> Nor shall the voice of war molest,
> Nor Europe's all-aspiring pride—
> There Reason shall new laws devise,
> And order from confusion rise.[52]

The "genius" of American democracy would bring about ways of life ("happier systems") that surpassed the paradisal fantasies of "all the eastern sages."[53] It was even possible, Freneau suggested, that this groundbreaking society would find a way to triumph "over death" itself.

In 1780, Benjamin Franklin expressed a similar sentiment in a letter to the English chemist and Unitarian Joseph Priestly. "The rapid Progress" of "true Science" in recent years, Franklin observed, made him regret "being born so soon."[54] It was "impossible to imagine" the "Height" that "the Power of Man over Matter" would attain over the next "1000 Years." He predicted that "agriculture may diminish its Labour & double its Produce. All Diseases may by sure means be prevented or cured, not excepting that even of Old Age, and our Lives lengthened at pleasure even beyond the antediluvian Standard."[55] A few years earlier he had jokingly outlined a method by which the dead might be brought back to life. Writing to the French scientist Jacques Barbeu-Duborg, Franklin reported that he had witnessed the apparent resurrection of two "mouches noyées" (drowned fleas), which had been preserved in a bottle of Madeira sent from Virginia to a friend of his in London.[56] Having been strained out of the wine and exposed to the sun for a little while, they had eventually revived and flown away, finding themselves in England, without understanding how they had arrived there ("et s'envolerent à la fin, se trouvant dans l'ancienne Angleterre sans sçavoir comment elles y étoient venues"). Franklin encouraged his friend to develop a similar method for the preservation and resuscitation of human beings. He noted that rather than experience an ordinary death, he would prefer to be entombed with several of his friends in a cask of wine, and then (having been transported back to America) returned to life by the heat of the sun of his beloved homeland ("je préférerois à une mort ordinaire d'être entonné avec quelques amis dans des muids de Madere . . . pour être alors rendu à la vie par la chaleur du soleil de ma chere patrie"). This unusual fate, Franklin observed, would allow him to satisfy his great curiosity about the advanced state of America one hundred years in the future ("ayant une extrême envie de voir et de reconnoître l'état de l'Amérique dans cent ans d'ici").

Thomas Jefferson's vision for the future of the United States was grounded in a comparable confidence in science's potential to transform humanity. He was convinced that people were "perfectible to a degree of which we cannot as yet form any conception," and believed that America offered the ideal testing ground for that endeavor.[57] Counterrevolutionaries and "despots" promulgated the opposite position ("that it is not probable that any thing better will be discovered than what was known to our fathers"), yet Jefferson thought the "American mind . . . already much too opened, to listen to these impostures." The abundance of fertile land on the continent would help to preserve freedom of thought. In *Notes on the State of Virginia*, his survey of the natural, economic, and political potential of his home state, Jefferson argued that the progressive momentum of the United States could be maintained by ensuring that farmers formed the majority of the American population. Because "their subsistance" depended on "their own soil and industry," rather than the "caprice of customers," they were more likely to preserve their honesty, independence, and virtue than were those who manufactured commercial goods.[58] The same text proposed that young people should not be permitted to read "the Bible and Testament" until they were "sufficiently matured for religious inquiries." As someone who held that "*the earth belongs . . . to the living*," Jefferson resented the idea that rising generations should be bound by the religious beliefs of the past.[59] His now famous remark (made in an 1822 letter to Benjamin Waterhouse, cofounder of Harvard's medical school) that "there is not a young man living in the US. who will not die a Unitarian" also reflected this position.[60] To worry too much about the nature of life after death and other "formulas of creed" was to "give up morals for mysteries." Young Americans should therefore fight to stop old dogmas from reasserting themselves: "For as long as we may think as we will, & speak as we think, the condition of man will proceed in improvement."[61]

But it was not only religious skeptics who predicted that the United States would change the terms of secular life forever. Some of those who shared Jefferson's enthusiasm for the scientific regeneration of the world also held quite conventional eschatological beliefs. Benjamin Rush (1746–1813), Philadelphia physician and social reformer, was prominent among this group. As a medical student in Edinburgh, Rush was drawn to the empirical rationalism of the Scottish Enlightenment.[62] While spending a year in London after graduation, he joined an intellectual circle of radical Whigs who promoted republican politics.[63] Yet Rush also retained the strong religious faith he had developed in his youth, when he had been taught by the evangelical Presbyterians Gilbert Tennent and Samuel Finley.[64]

All three of these influences are legible in *An Enquiry Into the Influence of Physical Causes upon the Moral Faculty*, an address he delivered to the American Philosophical Society in 1786. There Rush argued that an individual's ethical character was shaped by environmental causes (atmospheric and chemical), as well as educational background. The foundation of the United States, he suggested, had presented scientists and philosophers with the perfect moral laboratory. The nation was situated in the Northern Hemisphere's "middle latitudes," which were liable to "produc[e] gentleness and benevolence" in their inhabitants.[65] Its democratic and republican politics both facilitated and depended on the cultivation of morally independent and judicious citizens ("VIRTUE is the living principle of a republic") (40). To capitalize on this opportunity, Rush recommended two practical courses of action to the government of Pennsylvania. First, legislators should fund public schools across the state (and, by extension the nation). Planting "the seeds of virtue and knowledge" in the populace would be more productive than passing repressive "laws for the suppression of vice and immorality." Second, educators should approach the shaping of young minds more holistically, regulating the "diet" and physical "exercise" of their charges, as well as imparting "moral precept[s]" (36).

These measures carried far-reaching potential. Rush noted that he was "not so sanguine as to suppose, that it is possible for man to acquire so much perfection from science, religion, liberty, and good government, as to cease to be mortal" (37). Yet he maintained that a course of therapy that systematically treated "the reason, the moral faculty, the passions, the senses, the brain, the nerves, the blood and the heart" could "produce such a change in the moral character of man, as shall raise him to a resemblance of angels—nay more, to the likeness of GOD himself." As this religious rhetoric suggests, Rush did not see this man-made process of perfection as a substitute for conversion and resurrection. Elsewhere in his address he claimed that in instances "where bad men are suddenly reformed," God might choose to circumvent the "physical—moral—or rational causes" of good behavior and make a direct intervention (27). To try to explain these "extraordinary cases," he advanced a hypothesis reminiscent of Cotton Mather's theory of the Nishmath-Chajim. When a formerly wicked individual saw the light, "The organization of those parts of body, which form the link that binds it to the soul, undergoes a physical change; and hence the expressions of a 'new creature,' which are made use of in the scriptures to denote this change, are proper in a literal, as well as a figurative sense" (28). In keeping with Puritan and evangelical tradition, he suggested that such conversions were "only the beginning" of the "perfect renovation of the human body," which (as the apostle Paul put it) would not be complete until the "VILE BODIES" of mortal men and women were "fashioned according to ... [the] glorious body" of Christ.[66]

Toward the end of his speech, Rush conceded that his call for a "SCIENCE of MORALS" might seem to make Christian eschatology redundant. By expanding their influence over "the monarchs and rulers of the world," natural philosophers could "extirpate war—slavery—and capital punishments," thereby establishing a millennium grounded in "human reason" (38–39). Yet he also noted that "truths, upon all subjects, mutually support each other" (39). Any apparent opposition between science and faith must be ascribed to "our imperfect knowledge of the phaenomena, and laws of nature." As human knowledge expanded, the rivalry between "reason and religion" would end. Then, "The divine and the philosopher" would "unite their labors, for the reformation and happiness of mankind!"

By the late 1790s, however, many American Protestants were beginning to doubt that radical political change was a friend to the cause of Christianity. The continuing instability of Revolutionary France, growing division and unrest at home, and the apparent proliferation of deist sentiments led them to fear for the future.[67] Rush was no exception. In 1799, he told Granville Sharp, a longtime English correspondent of his, that he was relieved that the French Revolution was faltering: "Had [France] . . . succeeded in establishing a pure and peaceable government under the influence of their present deistical and atheistical principles, they would have rendered the coming of Jesus Christ in the flesh, and all that he has done and suffered for the human race of no effect."[68] The failure of the Jacobin project gave him hope that antireligious radicals would soon accept the power of "the Gospel . . . to restrain evil, and . . . promote general happiness." The only perfect polity that would ever be established on earth would not be a republic, but rather the millennial monarchy that would be "ministered in person by our Saviour." Two years later, Rush made a variation on this claim in another letter to Sharp. Before the millennium, he predicted, the "world will . . . be enlightened by the prevalence of universal liberty."[69] Amid that freedom, people would realize that they were still in a state of "moral, physical and political misery," and would look to the only "deliverer" able to "save them from *themselves*."

In the meantime, the struggle to preserve America's Protestant heritage continued. On that note, Rush informed his friend that the recently inaugurated President Jefferson was not "unfriendly to religion," despite the claims of his Federalist opponents. "I am satisfied," he continued, "that [Jefferson] has no hostility to Christianity, that he believes in the divine mission of our Saviour, in the resurrection of the body by his power, and in a future state of rewards and punishments."[70] Rush's confidence in Jefferson was misplaced as far as the doctrine of resurrection was concerned. While scholars continue to debate whether Jefferson believed in some form of life after death,[71] it is clear that he rejected resurrection entirely. Before his turn away from radicalism, Rush believed that social reform would revitalize American Christianity; for all his admiration for Christ as a moral philosopher, Jefferson anticipated the opposite.

Rush and Jefferson also disagreed on the future of African Americans in the United States. Though he advocated for the abolition of slavery, Jefferson could not accept the idea of free black citizens participating in American public life. In *Notes on the State of Virginia*, he speculated that Africans were either "originally a distinct race" (i.e., species) or alternatively had been rendered "inferior to the whites" by "time and circumstances."[72] For that reason (among others),[73] he argued that emancipated slaves should be educated up until the age of their majority, and then "colonized" to a territory where they could live as "a free and independent people" beyond the borders of the United States.[74] Rush, by contrast, did think it theoretically possible for African Americans to be "assimilated" into the citizenry of the nation.[75] In another lecture delivered before the American Philosophical Society (this time in 1792), Rush outlined one way in which that process might unfold. The "black color" of African skin, he argued, was originally caused by leprosy.[76] The contingency of this cause undermined "all the claims of superiority of the whites over the blacks, on account of their color."[77] It also suggested that physicians might find a "remedy" for the darker African complexion. In closing, Rush called on his colleagues in the Society to support this endeavor. Curing "this disease of the skin" would "destroy one of the arguments in favor of enslaving" people of color, as their skin tone had been "supposed by the ignorant to mark them as objects of divine judgments, and by the learned to qualify them for labor in hot, and unwholsome climates."[78] It would also "add weight to the Christian" revelation by providing tangible proof for the biblical claim that "the whole human race" was "descended from one pair." Last, it would "remove a material obstacle" to treating Africans as full equals—worthy recipients of the "universal benevolence" owing to the children of God, and, by extension, of the political rights afforded citizens of a democratic republic.

This final example of a discourse metonymically related to resurrection recalls the earlier eighteenth-century speculations into the relationship of black bodies to the afterlife I discussed in chapter 3. While Rush believed that scientists should be charged with discovering a reliable treatment for blackness, he also cited recent evidence that "Nature" had "spontaneous[ly] cure[d]" the "disease" in "several black people."[79] In 1796, he and many other prominent Philadelphian doctors had made close physical examinations of Henry Moss, an African American man whose skin appeared to be turning white in patches.[80] The fact that this and other similar cases had transpired "in this country" was highly significant for Rush. His student Benjamin Barton, who had also studied Moss at first hand, proposed that the freedman's change in complexion might be attributed to the fact that he had spent much of his life as an independent farmer. That possibility suggested that following the ideal American way of life—for Republicans, that of the self-sufficient cultivator of the land—could whiten the appearance of people of color.[81] Princeton professor Stanhope Smith had advanced a comparable argument in a 1787 tract. Though Smith doubted that the darker complexion of African Americans could ever be altered,[82] he predicted that if enslaved people "were admitted to a liberal participation of the society, rank and privileges of their masters" their facial features would come to resemble those of Europeans.[83] Furthermore, he asserted that living in "the same state of society, united with the same climate, would make the Anglo-American and the [American] Indian countenance very nearly approximate."[84]

In the same year that Smith published his book, Barlow's *The Vision of Columbus* expressed an identical sentiment in poetic form:

> The countless swarms that tread these dank abodes,
> Who glean spontaneous fruits and range the woods,
> Fix'd here for ages, in in their swarthy face,
> Display the wild complexion of the place.
> Yet when the tribes to happy nations rise,
> And earth by culture warms the genial skies,
> A fairer tint and more majestic grace

> Shall flush their features and exalt the race;
> While milder arts, with social joys refined,
> Inspire new beauties in the growing mind.[85]

Barlow believed that the refinement of Native American culture would involve the rejection of revealed religion; Rush was sure that the whitetification of African Americans depended on their conversion to Christianity. Despite this important difference, their models of racial integration in republican America were both shaped by Protestant eschatological thought. Cotton Mather, Samuel Sewall, and John Beach had insisted that Africans could and would be saved, but had implied that black bodies would not be admitted to heaven. Barlow, Rush, and the other proponents of racial transformation theory employed an analogous discourse of assimilation as they imagined a United States that admitted a degree of ethnic diversity but was fundamentally uniform. They also suggested (in another echo of earlier rhetoric) that if people of color attempted to be more like whites, their aspirations would be providentially, or naturally, rewarded.

One notable early national writer questioned the narratives of racial, natural, and social resurrection that proliferated in the period. In his 1798 novel *Wieland*, Charles Brockden Brown portrayed a German American family attempting, and failing, to free itself from a legacy of religious fanaticism. In the rural "temple" where their father had conducted secret rites, Theodore and Catherine Wieland preside over intellectual discussions and musical and poetic recitations. But this idyll is destroyed by the arrival of Carwin, a mysterious stranger who can project and disguise his voice so that it seems to issue from another person or a supernatural being. Carwin's manipulations (apparently unintentionally) lead Theodore to murder his wife, children, and servant, believing that God has demanded this sacrifice of him. Although the novel is set before the Revolution, *Wieland* suggests that the United States may struggle to contain the forces of religious enthusiasm (Theodore), political radicalism (Carwin), and ethnic difference. Under the right circumstances, even the most enlightened citizens can become dangerous, divisive zealots.

In *Edgar Huntly* (1799), Brown presented another vision of social entropy. As the titular protagonist, a lapsed Quaker turned rationalist deist, investigates the murder of his friend Waldegrave, he becomes obsessed with Clithero Edny, an Irish farm laborer whom he suspects has something to do with the crime. Edgar develops a pitying sympathy for the troubled Clithero, whose somnambulism registers his distress at a killing he has accidentally perpetrated in Dublin. Halfway through the book, Edgar awakens in a remote cave on the Pennsylvania frontier, having sleepwalked there himself. To escape the wilderness, he must shed his pacifism and inflict brutal violence on the Lenni Lenape Indians who stand in his way. Although he thereby avenges Waldegrave (who he discovers was likely murdered by one of the Lenni Lenape he has killed), Edgar's troubles are not over. His misguided conviction that Clithero can be rehabilitated results in the miscarriage of his mentor Sarsefield's wife's child as well as Clithero's own suicide. At the end of the novel, Edgar renounces his attempt to extend a republican solidarity to the Irishman and submits himself to Sarsefield's authority, which carries echoes of Federalist authoritarianism and British imperialism.[86]

Both novels delineate the instability of American society through a series of corporeal and mental discontinuities. Catherine, *Wieland*'s primary narrator, is liable to faint when confronted by traumatic events (she also swings between disgust and fascination with the enigmatic Carwin). Edgar's sleepwalking carries him from his bed to a deep pit. When he awakes, he fears that he has "fallen into a seeming death" and been "buried alive" in a "tomb, from which a resurrection [is] impossible."[87] In fact, he is able to break out, but only by allowing a new "soul" (one that is "vengeful, unrelenting, and ferocious") to take control of his actions.[88] Theodore Wieland is also transformed into a killing machine—in his case, after hearkening to what he thinks is the voice of God. Following his eventual capture, Theodore breaks his fetters and escapes confinement more than once, as if after his "conversion" he now inhabits a spiritual or resurrected body.

By exploring these inconsistencies of character and being, Brown contested the then-prevalent expectation that republican politics would substantially ameliorate human nature. While sin, as such, had no place in his worldview, he was too certain of mortal fragility and fallibility to suppose that democratic equality would inevitably generate a better breed of men and women. *Wieland* and *Edgar Huntly* also call Rush's and Smith's theory of "civilizing" racial transformation into question. In his struggle against the Lenni Lenape, Edgar adopts Native American garb, weaponry, and methods of warfare. Catherine describes her brother's violence against his family as both "inhuman" and "worthy of savages trained to murder."[89] The American environment, in Brown's eyes, is perhaps more likely to cause the cultural degeneration of white people than it is the secular resurrection of people of color.[90]

Debating Literal Belief in Resurrection

In addition to offering secular alternatives to resurrection, some radical republicans directly attacked the doctrine, arguing that it was incompatible with democratic politics. In 1784, Vermont revolutionary Ethan Allen published *Reason the Only Oracle of Man*, a deistic assault on revealed religion that he had first drafted with physician Thomas Young in the 1760s. Allen was determined to "exalt the reason of mankind, above the tricks and impostures of Priests, and bring them back to the religion of nature and truth."[91] Reforming beliefs about the afterlife was critical to achieving this objective. Like most eighteenth-century deists, Allen accepted that it was rational to expect reward or punishment after death for one's comportment on earth: the prevalence of the concept across different cultures suggested that it was an "intuition of nature" rather than "mere tradition" (120). Yet he could not accept that a just and benevolent God would eternally damn fallible mortals for committing transgressions of a limited duration. All wise leaders understood that the purpose of correction was "reformation and repentance," so why would the ruler of the universe be any different (118)? If unending perdition was illogical and unfair, then so was everlasting salvation. Furthermore, the very idea of a perfected, resurrected body was absurd: only God could exist in a "confirmed and perpetual state of blessedness" (124). It was no more possible for men and women ("finite cogitative beings") to be unceasingly happy than it was for them to maintain an enduring "moral rectitude." Though it was impossible to draw firm conclusions about "the manner of our future existence," Allen was convinced that its ethical framework would be familiar (159). Though "unembodied" (157), individuals would still be "capable of moral action" for which they would be held accountable (123); people would still experience alternating periods of "happiness" and "misery" in recompense for their behavior (126).

This critique of conventional eschatology had clear political overtones. Allen claimed that it was "impossible, that there should be a particular day of judgment, in which mankind, or any . . . of them, shall receive their eternal sentence of happiness or misery" (128). Such an event would rob people of the moral "agency" they would require to carry on living as discrete individuals in the world to come. "Absolute power," he explained, could "inflict physical evils" on earth, but that capability would have no meaning in the spirit realm (126). The afterlife's judicial system would therefore not operate through "mere positive injunction," but would instead require its subjects to recognize that they would be "happy or miserable on the basis of their own [behavior]." That arrangement would eventually lead to a preponderance of happiness among immortal humans: extrapolating from "the wisdom and goodness of God, Allen concluded "that moral goodness and happiness will ultimately be victorious over sin and misery" (133). The suggestion that postmortem existence would witness gradual improvement was not new—many Protestant theologians, including Cotton Mather, speculated that the saints in heaven would be granted ever richer spiritual blessings and ever greater intellectual understanding.[92] But in Allen's eschatological model, eternal progression is more a product of human growth than of expanding revelation. By emphasizing that distinction, he also underlined the value of liberty in secular politics. In the United States, as in the afterlife, men and women must be given the freedom to develop into good citizens on their own initiative.

Elihu Palmer, president of the Deistical Society of New York, adopted an even more radical position than Allen did. In a series of tracts and lectures composed around the turn of the nineteenth century, this former Presbyterian minister insisted that the notion of any kind of world beyond death was unrepublican and should therefore be forsaken. Having "renovated" the "civil condition" of humanity, the American revolution should now reform its "moral relations," establishing ethical principles based solely on "nature and her laws," with no admixture of supernaturalist "fanaticism."[93] This would not only involve renouncing faith in the ridiculous notion of corporeal resurrection,[94] but also moving beyond belief in "a spiritual, immaterial, and indestructible soul."[95] In their stead, Palmer hoped to popularize his conviction that "nothing is immortal but matter" (331). All living organisms, like every other kind of substance, were part of an unending "rotation" of change, decay, and rebirth. After death, the individual human body would be broken down and reconstituted into "an infinite diversity" of forms. "Personal" identity (and therefore self-consciousness) would not survive this transition. But the corpse's particles would be integrated into other "structures of animal existence," and thereby regain "the capacity of enjoying pleasure, or suffering pain." Palmer conceded that this was "not the [individual] immortality to which man is so strongly attached" (332). Yet he urged his readers to embrace the egalitarianism of his scheme. The prospect of their remains combining with those of others to produce new life provided "instructive lessons of sympathy, justice, and universal benevolence."[96]

This theory of "philosophical immortality" carried profound political implications. Palmer insisted that the promulgation of the truth about postmortem existence would disseminate "a sentiment of equality" across the planet, that would be "terrifying to every species of spiritual or political aristocracy" (332). The realization that all humans shared the same fate after death would prevent the church and state from threatening heretics and dissidents with eternal damnation. Furthermore, the definitive rejection of old fables about the afterlife would inaugurate the final victory of reason and liberty over superstition and tyranny:

> A new age, the true millennium, will then commence; the standard of truth and of science, will then be erected among the nations of the world; and man, the unlimited proprietor of his own person, may applaud himself in the result of his energies, and contemplate with indescribable satisfaction, the universal improvement and happiness of the human race. (334)

In this inversion of the common Protestant narrative, the growing global unity of the millennial age is a consequence of renouncing Christian soteriology. Palmer addressed his audience as if he were still a preacher, only he urged them to turn away from heaven, rather than toward it. Though it was understandable for men and women to "wish to continue their li[ves] here forever," they must sacrifice this vain hope for the sake of the republic and the wider world (332). Accepting reality would bring individuals "the highest intellectual joy" and lead them to "practice . . . an exaulted [*sic*] virtue" (334). Moreover, it would help to establish "the immortal . . . felicity of the intelligent world," by generating a progressive momentum that "all the powers of superstition c[ould] never arrest." For Palmer, then, the resurrection of the United States and of the world would be achieved by the mass repudiation of personal resurrection.

Some of Philip Freneau's poems also suggested that Americans would be better off if they relinquished their faith in resurrection. "The Jamaica Funeral" (1776), composed during a nearly four-year stay in the Caribbean, describes the obsequies for "Alcander," a wealthy slave owner. Freneau satirizes the excesses of the presiding Anglican cleric, who is more interested in drinking the wine that has been laid on for the wake than in fulfilling his solemn duty. When he finally rises to deliver a drunken sermon, he advises the dead man's friends to disregard "the senseless clay" that is about to be committed to the tomb and mourn instead for the "plenteous board" that the deceased kept, as well as the "splendid balls" he used to throw.[97] Although the priest acknowledges that Alcander's soul may be feasting in "heaven" or "wander[ing]" the infernal "coasts below" (129), he insists that the living should "be jovial while [they] can," since they are only granted "a few short years" on the earth (131). The subversive implication is that even professional ministers do not really place much stock in Christian soteriology: they have used the doctrines of heaven and hell and resurrection of the dead to swindle comfortable livings out of the superstitious and ignorant.

In "The House of Night" (1779, revised 1786), Freneau explored human mortality by means of a dream vision. Wandering through a dreary American landscape, the dreamer stumbles across a "noble dome" in which a personified Death lies dying (103). The advertisement that accompanied the first publication of the poem in Hugh Henry Brackenridge's *United States Magazine* claimed that Freneau's composition was "founded upon the authority of Scripture, inasmuch as these sacred books assert, that *the last enemy that shall be conquered is Death* [1 Corinthians 15:26]" (101). Nevertheless, the poet fully exploited the anticlerical potential of his conceit. The cursed burial ground in which Death is interred is home to a church "rais'd by sinners' hands, in ages fled" (121). Spurning the "shivering, naked stranger[s]" who begged them for alms, and declining "to aid the helpless orphan," these wicked men instead used their wealth to erect "this building tall and fair." Their hypocritical piety, however, was of no account: "With pride they preach'd, and pride was in their prayer, / With pride they were deceiv'd, and so to hell they went." The inference, of course, is that this self-deception was typical of many who considered themselves Christians. Similarly, the inverted platitudes mouthed by "Death's Chaplain," who "comfort[s]" the funeral procession with idle talk "of *Satan*, and the land of woe," suggest that the reassurances that Christian ministers offer mourners are equally empty (122).

At the end of the 1786 version of the poem, Freneau appears to endorse a broadly conventional account of the immortality of the human soul:

> When Nature bids thee from the world retire,
> With joy thy lodging leave, a fated guest;
> In Paradise, the land of thy desire,
> Existing always, always to be blest. (123)

Yet as David Shields observes, "The House of Night" pointedly ignores the "event in which death dies for Christians, the resurrection."[98] Moreover, it also advances "the Lucretian [materialist] principle" that "death is no more than one unceasing change" in which "new forms arise, while other forms decay."[99] If death really were to die in America, Freneau implies, it would be because the people had learned to conquer their irrational anxiety about the eternal fate of their bodies and souls. It was "Fancy[']s . . . power" of delusion that led men and women to make bold pronouncements about "immortality," to "depict new heavens, or draw the scenes of hell."[100]

Conversely, Americans of a more conservative disposition were convinced that the happiness and security of their young nation demanded that faith in Christian eschatology be preserved or remolded. The symbolic significance of the presidency, for instance, meant that the soteriological views of the chief executive were a matter of considerable public interest. George Washington's Farewell Address, delivered in 1796 at the end of his second term, claimed that despite "slight shades of difference," Americans shared "the same religion, manners, habits, and political principles."[101] The speech also warned that "national morality" could not "be maintained without religion."[102]

Following Washington's death in 1799, memorial works of art combined symbols of classical heroism with emblems of Christian resurrection such as "a willow or an evergreen."[103] John James Barralet's famous engraving *The Apotheosis of George Washington* (1802) depicted the president "dressed in grave clothes, being raised from his tomb by Immortality and . . . Father Time," who are poised to lead him to heaven.[104] Though the image was obviously allegorical, representing the president's ascension to the pantheon of American heroes, its structural imitation of paintings of Christ's resurrection and the assumption of the Virgin Mary endorsed the view that Washington would literally rise again one day.[105] In 1797, an elderly admirer from North Carolina wrote to Washington to express his wish to be present on that happy occasion. Enclosed with his letter he included clippings of his hair, which he asked should be used "to help to fill [a] Pillow" that would be placed under the president's head in his coffin.[106] This measure, the author claimed, would mean that he and Washington would "have a Joyfull resurrection" together on the last day. Washington's annotation of the letter described it as "singular." The author himself conceded that his long military service had impacted his "mind" as well as his "Estate" and "Body." Nonetheless, his unusual request is representative of how invested many Americans were in the salvation of their political leaders.[107]

Correspondence received by Thomas Jefferson following his presidential tenure reveals that some of his political supporters were concerned by his rumored apostasy. In August 1814, a Methodist preacher named Miles

King wrote a lengthy letter recounting his own personal spiritual history and asking for details of Jefferson's own religious opinions. King argued that the ongoing War of 1812 was a punishment for American "impiety," and maintained that "nothing short of National reformation" would save the nation.[108] It was "not sufficient," he claimed, "that our rulers . . . merely tolerate religion: they must themselves become religious—thier [sic] Light must shine to the Glory of God! & the illuminating of others." To further convince Jefferson of the need to repent, King asked him to imagine the resurrection of a group he termed the "illuminati." These deist and skeptical thinkers (he named Voltaire, D'Alembert, Diderot, and Condorcet, alongside Xavier von Zwack and Adolph Freiherr Knigge of the radical Bavarian society that called itself the Illuminati) would find that "all thier learning" would count for nothing on Judgment Day. Indeed, it would only serve to confirm their damnation, since it had been employed to attack rather than defend religion. As a republican, King insisted, Jefferson ought to embrace the egalitarian message of the "religion of Jesus," in whose "Blessings" the "most simple and illiterate," as well as "the Learned and great, may participate . . . without distinction."

Letters sent by Presbyterian ministers Abraham Stansbury (in 1815) and William Wisner (in 1823) registered a similar concern at Jefferson's apparent unorthodoxy. Stansbury urged him to reconsider his assumption that "Christianity [was] no more than the morality of Jesus."[109] As the Gospels attested, Christ laid claim to powers that were far beyond those of any merely human teacher, "declaring that the time should come when all that were in their graves should hear his voice and come forth." Wisner, meanwhile, noted his anxiety about the world-weary posture Jefferson had struck in a letter sent to John Adams in 1822 and recently published "in one of the new York papers."[110] It was deeply distressing, Wisner confessed, to read a respected statesman "profess a contempt for life" and articulate "a desire to die without the most distant allusion to the *Hope of Israel.*" Since Jefferson had shown such "prudence" in every other aspect of his life, it would be particularly senseless for him to "venture down into the 'dark valley of the shadow of death' without an interest in him who is 'the resurrection and the life.'"

Other correspondents with less conventional views encouraged Jefferson to accept a modified form of Christian eschatology. In 1816, an anonymous advocate of abolition confessed that the evils of slavery, the "Crueties [sic]" of the French Revolution, and human suffering in general had "convince[d] him of [the truth of] the Christian System," despite "some of the Absurdities [that had been] mixed with it."[111] "The Doctrines promulgated by Jesus

Christ" were the only "Medicines" that could "cure" the political and moral "disorders" caused by "the Evil propensitys of our Nature." Although he still doubted Christ's miracles and even his divinity, the author underlined his conviction that "the Mind of Jesus . . . was . . . raized" from the dead and "Sanctified." Faith in this truth, he added, would "cast out & destroy every evil disposition" within the convert, and ultimately allow him or her to "transmigrate from this State of Being" to a better place. Around two months later, François van der Kemp wrote to Jefferson asking for clarifications about the opinions expressed in his "Syllabus"—a brief sketch comparing Christ's moral teachings to those of classical philosophers and the ancient Israelites.[112] Even if Van der Kemp believed, as Jefferson did, that "Jezus [sic] was a man . . . in every respect," he was simultaneously convinced of the truth of the resurrection. The prospect of an eternal reward for good behavior, a feature of Christian philosophy of which the "Syllabus" had approved, depended on the fact that the founder of the religion really had been "restored again to life" after his death.[113]

Though these letter writers disagreed on the nature of Christ's triumph over the grave, as well as on the nature of life after death, they understood the political significance of beliefs about resurrection. At root, they all thought that promoting faith in some form of the doctrine would promote ethical and social responsibility. While he remained a "Church going Animal" throughout his life, John Adams came to doubt the wisdom of this view. During his presidency, he had declared days of national fasting and prayer as relations between the United States and Revolutionary France deteriorated. These solemnities were intended to foster unity but proved highly divisive. In proclaiming the second of them (observed in April 1799), Adams suggested that Jefferson and his allies were motivated by radical French "principles" that were "subversive of the foundations of all religious, moral, and social obligations."[114] By the 1810s, his private correspondence was striking a different tone. Adams still believed that there was an unbreakable connection between the "general Principles of Christianity" and the "Principles of Liberty" that had propelled the American Revolution.[115] Yet he was increasingly wearied by religious "controversies, between Calvinists and Arminians, Trinitarians and Unitarians, Deists and Christians,"[116] and was more willing to search for a middle ground between his questioning faith and Jefferson's searching skepticism.[117]

Adams was reconciled with Jefferson in 1812, through the efforts of Benjamin Rush.[118] From then on, he regularly wrote to his old friend on religious matters, updating him on his developing views. In 1813 the pair exchanged a series of letters in which they complained of Christian intolerance. "Even the most liberal" professors, Adams observed, issued "Comminations" (or threats of divine vengeance) against those "who disbelieved or doubted the Resurrection of Jesus or the Miracles of the New Testament."[119] Joseph Priestly, who did not accept that Christ was God, "would denounce the man who should deny" the Bible's key eschatological texts—"The Apocalyps" [sic] and "the Prophecies of Daniel." Attitudes like these, which sought to delimit the way in which salvation was understood, were obstructing humanity's pursuit of "Perfection" in this life.

Although his opponents had accused him of being a religious bigot himself, Adams protested that he could never "deal damnation round the land on all I judge the Foes of God or Man."[120] He presented an even more ecumenical view in an 1820 letter to his grandson George Washington Adams:

> All men [are] happy in their own religion, whatever it may be—the Mahometan is confident that he shall go to paradise,—the Hindoo to Brahma,—the Hebrew to Abrahams bosom,—the Calvinist is sure that he is one of the elect,—the churchman, has a sure and certain hope of a resurrection to life eternal; the North American Indian expects to go to a level country without Swamps or mountains—where grand & beautiful rivers meander thro' vast prairies & lofty forest abounding with deer elk & buffaloe, indian corn—kidney beans, pumpions & squashes, growing spontaneously—[121]

Adams concluded that this diversity of opinion was "all as it should be." He now felt that the historical evidence for Jesus's return to life was shaky,[122] and was satisfied that Christian teachings about resurrection were just as fictive as was the Native American mythology of the Happy Hunting Ground. When in December 1813 he warned Jefferson of the danger of "believing . . . too much," eschatological dreams like these had been on his mind.[123]

In the same letter, Adams also cautioned his friend against "believing too little." Though he disliked what he saw as the narrow sectarianism of Calvinist theology, he was proud of his Puritan heritage, confiding in one correspondent that the Calvinists in his family were the best people he had ever known.[124] He believed that materialism led to fatalism and anarchism, and was therefore convinced, as his Congregationalist ancestors had been, that there was "a better World" in store for the righteous. However, Adams had a very different understanding of the relationship between this life and the next, as the following story he recounted to Jefferson demonstrates. If this "Anecdote" were "true," he observed, there was "no Philosopher, or Moralist[,] ancient or modern[,] more profound [and] more infallible than [George] Whitefield."[125] In the pulpit one day, the preacher had "gracefully" turned his "hands and Eyes . . . to the Heavens" as if to interrogate one of the biblical patriarchs who resided there:

> "Father Abraham," "who have you there with you?" "have you Catholicks[?]" No. "Have you Protestants[?]" No. "Have you Churchmen[?]" No. "Have you Dissenters[?]" No. "Have you Presbyterians[?]" No. "Quakers"? No. "Anabaptists"? No. "Who have you then? Are you alone"? No. My Brethren,! you have the Answer to all these questions in the Words of my Text, He who feareth God and worketh Righteousness, Shall be accepted of him.

Adams obviously approved of the irenicism his anecdote attributed to Whitefield. He himself, of course, favored an even more reconciliatory perspective, affording salvation to "all good Men in all Nations."[126] But the story is less notable for what it includes than for what it elides: the key tenet of Whitefield's evangelical soteriology, which held that only those who undergo a life-changing spiritual and emotional transformation are bound for heaven.

Adams, who valued practical virtue over affective experience and rejected the concept of innate depravity, saw no need for such an alteration.[127] By extension, he denied that the dead would need to exchange mortal vileness for resurrected glory to be worthy of eternal life. Instead, he imagined the afterlife as a "social State," in which friends would resume the philosophical discussions death had interrupted, and people would continue to practice the same virtues they had exhibited on earth.[128] Though far more sympathetic to the traditional Christian vision of heaven than either Allen or Palmer was, Adams in his own way was just as convinced that faith in resurrection was at odds with republican citizenship. Any democracy worthy of the name would be home to many men and women who would not be out of place if they were immediately translated to paradise as they were.

Spiritualism, Sentimentalism, and Materialism

Intellectual debates about the social and national political significance of resurrection and its secular equivalents continued into the mid-nineteenth century. Skeptics and religious apologists debated the truth and social value of Christian eschatology on stage and in print.[129] In the *Free Enquirer* (1828–1835), the widely circulated deist newspaper he founded with Frances Wright, Robert Dale Owen criticized the socially divisive and destructive impact of the idea "*that true belief is a virtue, to be rewarded with heaven; and untrue belief* (however sincere) *a vice, to be punished with hell.*"[130] Amos Gilbert, Wright's and Owen's successor as editor, proposed that establishing an entirely secular education system that offered every individual (including African Americans) equal opportunity would produce a "perfection" of morality and happiness "of which we can form no adequate conception."[131] On the other hand, Charles Grandison Finney, the most influential evangelist of the time, claimed that Americans could only bring about significant social change by embracing revivalism. Following Jonathan Edwards's lead, he anticipated that the coming millennium would be a "temporal" (i.e., secular-historical) period in which the prophecy of the First Resurrection would be fulfilled allegorically by "the majority of men" becoming God's "obedient subjects."[132] Religious radicals argued instead that true believers participated in a kind of resurrection in this life. John Humphrey Noyes maintained that converts were spiritually risen from the grave and free from sin.[133] His community of perfect Christians at Oneida, New York had therefore transcended conventional sexual morality (every woman was married to every man) and would eventually lead the United States and the world into a new age of peace. The resurgent Shakers also linked spiritual resurrection with a change in sexual practice. In their account, those who entered a "state of grace" must thenceforth be celibate, to signify their renunciation of the flesh.[134] During the years Shakers dubbed "the Era of Manifestations" (1837–c. 1860), many of those who had undergone this alteration received visions and direction from the dead.[135]

The antebellum period also witnessed a new development in the American religious scene. Thanks to the development of cheaper printing and publishing, lay speculation about the mysteries of the next life flourished. American women, in particular, wrote fiction, poetry, diaries, and autobiography that romanticized mourning and explored the world beyond. A parallel material culture of memorialization commemorated the departed through embroidery, portraits, daguerreotypes, and jewelry. Popular health literature addressed the subject of mortality from another angle, arguing that self-discipline and temperance could greatly extend one's life span. These texts and practices prepared the way for the Spiritualist churches that sprang up in the 1850s, following the national sensation around the "spirit rapping" supposedly experienced by the Fox sisters of New York State. Spiritualism would attract some deists (such as Robert Dale Owen) who continued to believe in the immortality of the soul despite their disdain for Christian soteriology.[136]

This commercialized culture of death and mourning differed in several ways from the seventeenth- and eighteenth-century Protestant eschatologies discussed in this book. Female perspectives on the life to come were afforded a greater prominence and respect. Vernacular texts were more exercised by reunion with friends and family in heaven than they were by the triumph of the church. The material dimension of resurrection was de-emphasized in favor of spiritual transcendence of bodily existence. Health reformers suggested that godliness would be rewarded with physical well-being in this life as well as the salvation of the soul. But the new antebellum deathways did not constitute a complete break with older Protestant beliefs. Although nineteenth-century authors painted the afterlife in a more domestic and sentimental light than their forebears had, their accounts of the spirit world and its proximity to the land of the living paralleled earlier resurrection theologies in surprising ways.

Elizabeth Stuart Phelps's *The Gates Ajar*, one of the most popular products of this new culture, takes the inadequacy of most conventional Protestant accounts of the afterlife as its main theme. Mary Cabot, the novel's narrator, has lost her brother Royal ("Roy") to the Civil War. Searching for consolation through discussion of heaven, she chafes against the pious but unfeeling sermonizing of the minister and deacon of her Congregationalist church. Deacon Quirk advises Mary that it is her "duty, as a Christian and a church-member, to be resigned" to Roy's death.[137] If her brother has been saved, he will be too caught up with the eternal task of "worshipping before the great White Throne" to spare a thought for "this miser'ble earthly spere [sic]" (19). A half-remembered homily of Dr. Bland's makes similar claims in a higher intellectual register, arguing that "an infinite mind must of necessity be eternally an object of study to a finite mind." Although the minister accepts that the saints would likely "recognize [their] friends in heaven," he maintains that there will be no "special selfish affections" among them. Mary's aunt Winifred offers her a much more compelling vision of the next world. Winifred promises her grieving niece that her departed brother "will love you and wait for you and be very glad to see you, as he used to love and wait and be glad when you came home from a journey on a cold winter night" (53). Human relationships will be perfected, rather than transcended, in heaven. People will "talk and laugh and joke and play" with their family and friends (82). Talents for painting, sculpture, writing, and music that were frustrated on earth will find their full expression through eternity. While she acknowledges that the eighteenth-century Swedish mystic Emmanuel Swedenborg has influenced these ideas of hers, Winifred insists that they are supported by the Bible (169–70).

Much of Winifred's dissatisfaction with mainstream Protestant eschatology revolves around resurrection. On the one hand, she critiques the "abstraction" of Dr. Bland's theocentric heaven (109), which she characterizes as an overcorrection "from the materialism of the Romish Church" (110). On the other, she mocks Deacon Quirk's expectation that he will "rise in his own entire, original body, after it has lain the First Church cemetery a proper number of years, under a black slate headstone" (114). The total reconstruction of the mortal form, she explains, involves too many "physiological impossibilities" (in a racist aside, she raises the old problem of the resurrection of cannibals: "Imagine, for instance, the resurrection of two Hottentots, one of whom has happened to make a dinner of the other some fine day. A little complication there!"). Instead, Winifred imagines a resurrected body that is both spiritual and in some sense material, though not of "flesh and blood." The solidity of the immortal frame is crucial to her vision of heaven as a place of long-awaited reunion. "What would be the use of having a body that you can't see and touch?" she asks Mary (117). "Why should you not, having seen Roy's old smile and heard his own voice, clasp his hand again, and feel his kiss on your happy lips?"

Though Phelps contrasts this eschatology with traditional teachings about the next life, Winifred's theories mirror seventeenth- and eighteenth-century resurrection theology in two key respects. First, her hypothesis about a material connection between the corpse and the resurrected body closely conforms to Cotton Mather's views on the subject. In an echo of his concept of the Nishmath-Chajim, she suggests that a "deathless frame" or "spiritual body" that occupies the physical body during life will become the vehicle for the soul through eternity (116). More broadly, her assurance that resurrected people will recognize and converse with each other corresponds to his belief that saints would remember and rejoice in their friends in the world to come. There are certainly important differences between Winifred's eschatology and Mather's. He would have been horrified by her suggestion that angels were not a separate kind of being but the resurrected and spiritualized "Christian dead" (90). He would also have been concerned by the lack of any reference to the eschatological purification of the church as a corporate body. Last, both he and Thomas Prince would have scorned her claim that "it is a waste of time to speculate" over the physical process by which God would resurrect the body (116). But while many nineteenth-century ministers attacked Phelps's novel for its innovations, *The Gates Ajar* was an evolution of previous Protestant teachings about the intimacy of this world and the next.

While Phelps was still recognizably Christian in her theology, prominent Spiritualist Andrew Jackson Davis rejected the Bible's authority as the revealed word of God. Davis disavowed the divinity of Christ and the existence of the Devil as well as the prospect of Judgment Day and the damnation of sinners. He argued, moreover, that the "general resurrection" of the dead was a "mythological" trope that was not actually treated as an actual event in either the Old or New Testaments—Paul's assertion that "we are sown in a natural body, and raised in a spiritual body" (1 Corinthians 15:44) described "the external phenomenon of death, and the elevation of the real, or internal man, to a higher sphere."[138] It was therefore distinctly embarrassing that theologians still took the idea of corporeal resurrection seriously. Christ himself had "labored for a moral resurrection" (435). The religion that had been built around his memory had perpetuated a worthless literalization of that metaphor. Davis urged believers to move beyond the church's teachings about resurrection and heaven and hell, noting that it would be a sign of Western society's "mental resurrection from ignorance and superstition" if they were to do so (576). In place of Christian cosmography, he developed a complex spiritual topography that divided the universe into seven concentric spheres. After death, every human soul left the first sphere (where the earth was located) and journeyed upward, living for a time in each of the others (which, like the soul itself, were composed of a rarefied matter).[139]

Davis's account of the second of these spheres, supposedly gleaned from conversation with the dead, underlined how difficult it could be to leave inherited doctrines behind. At the beginning of their afterlives, some souls were so "ashamed" of their former faith in "the literal resurrection of the material body" that they "str[o]ve to hide their memory of it from the perception of [their peers]" (658). Others, still in thrall to falsehood, attempted to "harmonize" their experience with Christian eschatology. After a little while, they would accept their mistake and continue their "ascending progress" toward the higher planes of the spiritual world. Like many of his contemporaries, Davis claimed that familial affections would be strengthened in the next life. In the lower planes of postmortem existence, the souls of the dead continued to resemble their earthly bodies and were particularly drawn to those they had known and loved in mortal life (658–61). As they moved on through the spheres toward "the Divine Mind," ever wiser and purer souls would grow so attached to every other spirit around them that it would become increasingly difficult "to make a distinction between them" (663). The glories of the seventh and final sphere, Davis noted, could not be described or comprehended. He hinted nevertheless that the souls who reached it entered into a union with God (672–74).

For all his contempt for the doctrine, Davis's system was comparable in certain respects to Thomas Prince's resurrection theology. Just as Prince envisioned an unending series of resurrected beings rising to heaven from numberless planets across the universe,[140] Davis imagined that souls from "various earths" would continually move upward through the seven spheres of creation. He also predicted his own equivalent of the earthly millennium that Prince anticipated. Rather than a sudden alteration of the globe through the Conflagration, Davis looked for humanity's gradual "realization" of "the nearness of the Spiritual World to the Natural world" as well as the possibility of direct conversation with the departed.[141] These transformations would lead to "the reorganization of society," which he described as "a commencing of the kingdom of heaven on earth." Although he denied that the resurrection of Christ held a central place in sacred history, Davis was happy to draw on Christian eschatology when it suited him. He might have balked at the physical resurrection of individual believers, but he still foresaw the continual "refinement" of human souls, civilization, and even the material substance of the universe itself into more spiritual forms.[142]

Moral reformer and physician William Alcott also adapted Christian resurrection theology to his own ends. As a young man, Alcott had entirely rejected Christian teachings (though he accepted the existence of God). His investment in improving American medicine and education meant that he was particularly disturbed by the doctrine of original sin, preferring to believe instead in humanity's capacity to perfect itself and in the individual's ability to maintain bodily health through behavioral and mental discipline. By the early 1830s, Alcott had come to accept the truth of Christian revelation.[143] The hugely influential advice literature he produced over the rest of his career counseled Americans that living well was part of their duty to God (especially since he had blessed them with residence in the "happiest [country] below the sun").[144] In *The Laws of Health* (1856) he underlined the importance of following both God's "*moral*" and "*physical*" laws, through ethical conduct and bodily care respectively.[145] This compliance would lead to a long and healthy life. Some Christians, Alcott observed, thought that by "finding fault with this life—calling it a mean and unworthy existence"—they increased "the value of the life that is to come" (10). In fact, the faithful would be compensated for their diligence immediately, as well as eternally: "The moment we enter the path of obedience," he argued, "we receive a reward, leaving all the future out of consideration" (15). True holiness and healthiness would enable modern men and women to live as long as the biblical patriarchs had. That argument, Alcott acknowledged, also raised the possibility of "immortality on the earth" (17). Although he insisted that he had no "settled opinion" on that question, he hinted that humans might learn how to live forever corporeally without undergoing death and resurrection. This was impossible "under the present constitution of things," but who knew what science, medicine, and religion might achieve in combination?

Despite their differences, Alcott's, Phelps's, and Davis's approaches toward mortality and the afterlife shared an underlying optimism. Like those who explored secular forms of resurrection in the early national era, they offered their readers ways of taming the fear of death (healthy living, the prospect of reunion with departed loved ones, and intellectual understanding of the land of spirits, respectively). Other mid-nineteenth-century writers were less sanguine. Cynical, gothic, and sensationalist texts presented the dead body as an object of horror, disgust, fascination, and despair. This perspective would become more prevalent following the carnage of the Civil War.[146] Nevertheless, antebellum authors such as Edgar Allan Poe and George Lippard issued widely popular texts that framed death in this way (working in a very different mode, Henry David Thoreau attempted to read a hopeful message into the macabre dimension of mortality). According to Gary Laderman, the death-fixated sensationalist writing of antebellum America reflected the declining influence of Protestant tradition, as well as medical professionals' more assertive insistence that the cadaver should be seen "as an instrument for improving anatomical knowledge and medical care."[147] Uncertainty about corporeal resurrection also informed this new literature. Spiritualist and sentimentalist works obviated the issue by stressing the spiritual nature of the world to come. Materialist and gothic texts could not allow the scandal of the unredeemed corpse to be resolved so easily. A body that was destined to decay without hope of resurrection was an obvious emblem of religious doubt. Alternatively, bodies that refused to lie quietly in the grave could symbolize the return of political evils thought to be long dead.

Some of Edgar Allan Poe's most famous stories—"The Fall of the House of Usher," "The Cask of Amontillado," "The Black Cat," and "The Pit and the Pendulum"—are concerned with the entombment of living people. He also addressed the subject in "Berenice," "Ligeia," and "The Premature Burial." While burial alive was a useful vehicle for exploring a range of difficult subjects, including mental illness, emotional repression, and illicit desire, Poe's frequent return to the trope also spoke of his fascination with death and his skepticism toward Christian teachings about the afterlife. Several of these stories feature grotesque parodies of resurrection. Seven or eight days after her interment, Madeline Usher breaks out of the family vault, killing her brother through fright in the same moment that she finally dies. The narrator of "Berenice" realizes to his horror that in a stupor he has opened the grave of his recently buried wife and extracted all of her teeth. In fact, she is not dead at all—the household staff discover her "disfigured[,] ... enshrouded, yet still breathing" body after hearing her screams.[148] At the climax of "Ligeia" a man spends the night watching over the corpse of his second bride. Toward dawn, "The thing that was enshrouded" stirs and "advance[s] bodily and palpably into the middle of the apartment" (1:201). As the figure's "ghastly cerements" fall away, the features (and black hair) of his dead first wife—the eponymous Ligeia—are revealed (1:202). The implication is that Ligeia's spirit has somehow found a way to possess, transform, and revivify her replacement's cadaver. In each of these tales, the female body that returns from the tomb has little in common with the perfected form of the resurrected Christian saint. Poe depicts a temporary escape from death propelled by violent human emotion (revenge, pain, fear of death) rather than the power of God.

In "The Facts in the Case of M. Valdemar," Poe addressed corporeal afterlife from a different viewpoint. The narrator, a mesmerist, secures the permission of a man dying of tuberculosis to place him in a trance just before he expires. Shortly after he has been mesmerized, Valdemar dies: his eyes roll back in his head, his mouth gapes open, and he ceases to breathe. However, his "swollen and blackened tongue" begins to vibrate, and an inhuman voice issues from his "distended and motionless jaws" (2:330–31). Speaking as if "from a vast distance, or from some deep cavern within the earth," Valdemar informs the narrator and the attendant medical professionals that he is dead. He remains in this state of living death for a period of "*nearly seven months*," after which the mesmerist attempts to awaken him (2:333). Just before he leaves the trance, Valdemar reiterates that he is dead and begs for total annihilation. The narrator, however, resolves to return him to full consciousness.

The last stage of the experiment fails spectacularly. Bringing Valdemar out of his reverie causes his body to liquefy into a "mass of loathsome . . . putridity" (2:334). While the cruel detachment with which the narrator treats the unfortunate Valdemar certainly register misgivings about medical experimentation on human bodies,[149] the story can also be read as a materialist critique of the doctrine of resurrection. Although Poe considered the possibility of a disembodied afterlife in other writings, "The Facts in the Case of M. Valdemar" suggests that he viewed the dissolution of the corpse as final.[150] Valdemar's ordeal—being reduced to nothing more than a semiconscious and decayed body for months on end—exposes the absurdity of longing to perpetuate our somatic existence after death.

While his writings have nothing of the gothic about them, Henry David Thoreau was just as intrigued as Poe was by death as a material phenomenon. His naturalist's eye was drawn to the decaying corpses of animals and humans alike. When encountered in nature, mortal remains were an invigorating and morally clarifying sight. Although he found the stench of horse carcass near his cabin at Walden repulsive, he was "cheered" by the thought that other creatures would be sustained by the carrion: "I love to see that Nature is so rife with life that myriads can be afforded to be sacrificed and suffered to prey on another; that tender organizations can be so serenely squashed out of existence like pulp."[151] When a powder mill on the outskirts of Concord exploded, Thoreau rushed to the scene of the accident, hitching a lift in another man's wagon. His journal described the human impact of the incident in fascinated, dispassionate detail, picking out the dismembered, "naked[,] and black" forms of the victims, "some limbs and bowels here and there, and a head at a distance from its trunk."[152] At the beginning of a trip to Cape Cod, he took a detour to Cohasset to view the aftermath of the wreck of a ship carrying Irish emigrants from Galway. In the posthumously published account of his journey, Thoreau provocatively claimed that the "beauty of the shore . . . was enhanced" by the corpses that washed up on it.[153] His description of the scene lingered over the "livid, swollen, and mangled body of a drowned girl, . . . who [had] probably . . . intended to go out to service in some American family," but was now "the coiled-up wreck of a human hulk, gashed by the rocks or fishes, so that the bone and muscle were exposed."[154]

As he concluded his account of the wreck at Cohasset, Thoreau made his feelings about human remains plain. "Why care for these dead bodies?" he asked. "They really have no friends but the worms or the fishes."[155] When he reached Cape Cod itself, he found that it too was "a vast *morgue*, where . . . [t]he carcasses of men and beasts together lie stately . . . , rotting and bleaching in the sun and waves."[156] The brutal but "inhumanly sincere" conditions of the Cape scorned the Christian belief that the corpses of saints were precious because they would one day rise again.[157] Since he rejected the prospect of corporeal resurrection, Thoreau found graveyards and elaborate tombs distasteful and absurd: why construct "a monument to the body" or put up "a stone to a bone?"[158] In "Autumnal Tints" (1862), another posthumously published work, Thoreau appears to flirt with the possibility of natural burial—interring human bodies directly into the soil of wild places (leaves that are "resigned to lie and decay" on the ground, "afford[ing] nourishment to new generations of their kind . . . teach us how to die").[159] This was less of a serious proposal and more of a jab at fashionable rural cemeteries such as Boston's Mount Auburn and Baltimore's Greenwood. The sanitized, sentimental culture of mourning that they represented disturbed him almost as much as traditional Protestant eschatology did. In "Economy," *Walden*'s opening chapter, he had mounted a similar attack on the domestication and commercialization of death. "We have built for this world a family mansion, and for the next a family tomb," Thoreau complained.[160] "The best works of art," he continued, "are the expression of man's struggle to free himself from this condition." As well as possessing intellectual self-sufficiency, living well meant confronting the difficult fact of one's mortality directly.[161]

Yet there were still certain confluences between Thoreau's attitude to death and the sentimental culture that he dismissed. Following the loss of his father, he drew comfort from the thought that the departed were materially (though not spiritually) close at hand ("How enduring are our bodies, after all! The forms of our brothers and sisters, our parents and children and wives, lie still in the hill and field round about us").[162] Amid the human flotsam of Cohasset, he even invoked the consolation of a spiritual afterlife. The drowned Irish immigrants were not so unlucky as they appeared, as they had arrived at "a newer world than even Columbus dreamed of," by way of "the safest port in Heaven."[163] Whether or not Thoreau really believed that this was true, his philosophy of mortality mirrored the universalism of the popular eschatologies of the day. In common with Phelps, Davis, and many other Spiritualists,[164] Thoreau had little time for the judgment and division of the dead foretold by Christian scripture. Although he was usually reticent (and perhaps undecided) on the subject of conscious immortality, he consistently underscored death's democratic trajectory. Though some people might die more bravely and honestly than others, every human body would return to the earth, fortifying the soil and sustaining new life.

George Lippard's sprawling serial novel *The Quaker City; or, The Monks of Monk Hall* (1844–1845) blends Thoreau's democratic materialism with Poe's dark Romanticism. In so doing, this exuberant, salacious, and acerbic book travesties traditional beliefs about resurrection, the secular equivalents of the process described by social reformers, and the sentimentalism and Spiritualism of the antebellum era. *The Quaker City* was Lippard's contribution to the "city-mysteries" genre, a sensationalist form of fiction that purported to expose the hidden corruption of the world's expanding metropolises. It recounts a series of complexly interwoven intrigues centering around the titular edifice—a crumbling colonial mansion that is the headquarters of a secret society dedicated to excessive consumption and moral turpitude. Resurrection and gravedigging are the novel's leitmotifs. Its heroes, villains, and distressed damsels are forever recovering from apparent death or escaping from burial alive. Characters who have undergone deep psychological traumas are said to resemble corpses or the risen dead.[165] A sinister doctor keeps a collection of "dead men in fragments, in great pieces and little, in all shapes and every form" (179). Devil-Bug, the hulking and hunch-backed caretaker of Monk Hall, is accompanied wherever he goes by the bloody ghosts of his murder victims. In the novel's preface (which is "INSCRIBED TO THE MEMORY OF CHARLES BROCKDEN BROWN" [3]) a dying man urges the narrator to "lift the cover from the Whited Sepulchre" that is Philadelphia, exposing "the festering corruption that rankles in its depths" (4). These symbols, metaphors, and tropes prepare the way for two dramatic set-pieces toward the end of the novel, in which resurrection is addressed more directly.

The second of these sees Ravoni, a fraudulent mystic, scientist, and mesmerist who claims to have lived for over two hundred years, raise a woman from the dead before an audience of his acolytes. The miracle is a fake—the subject has been placed into a temporary drug-induced coma that simulates the signs of death. Her "resurrection" is to bring international fame to a new religion that will render all others obsolete. Despite the occult trappings of his order, Ravoni is an atheist who worships only the supreme power of the human will. By exploiting superstition and credulity, he plans, paradoxically, to rid the world of "priestcraft" and inaugurate a new age of reason, "built in the name of MAN for the good of MAN!" (380). While its emphasis on marriage links Ravoni's creed with Mormonism, his rational religion also evokes the secular resurrection of society discussed by Jefferson, Adams, Franklin, and Rush. As if to underline this connection, Ravoni claims to have been present when their "immortal Signatures" endorsed the Declaration of Independence in Philadelphia. Though apparently sympathetic with the Founders' goals, he boastfully contrasts his "deathless career" with their mortality (358). "Where is Washington now?" he asks. "And where is La Fayette and Adams and Jefferson and Hamilton? Ask the dust of annihilation to give back its dead?" In fact, Ravoni's mesmeric influence over his American followers is a sign that well-intentioned republicanism remains vulnerable to manipulation by a continually shapeshifting oligarchy. Before he succumbs to a wound inflicted by Devil-Bug, Ravoni reassures his disciples that after his body is burned, "a New Being will arise" from his ashes (428).

The first set-piece also warns of a threat to American democracy. In a dream, Devil-Bug witnesses the apocalyptic destruction of Philadelphia in the year 1950. Guided by a ghost, he wanders around a city transformed into the seat of a repressive monarchy: Independence Hall has been replaced with "a royal mansion"; a huge jail has been erected in Washington Square; "a proud and insolent" nobility ride through the streets (316); "the Holy Ministers of God" preside over a gallows of "blackened timbers" (317). With Devil-Bug watching on, "From every grave-yard . . . [rise] the shrouded dead," "mingling" unseen with "throngs of laughing citizens" (319) who are celebrating "the anniversary of the death of Freedom" (325). These mournful souls have returned to "warn" their family and friends of "their coming doom," but their message goes unheeded (319). At last, the veil is lifted. As America's king leads a glorious procession (including the priests of an established church and manacled slaves, "white and black" [328]) he suddenly sees the "ghastly corpse" walking beside him (330). Too late, the rest of the crowd realize that the dead have risen, and the "Last Day" is upon them. Bolts of red lightning strike them down, and a massive earthquake levels the marble palaces and churches of the kingdom.

In these scenes, the dead returning to life signals the disintegration of the body politic, whether by means of human conspiracy or merciless divine judgment. *The Quaker City* thereby contests the various narratives of secular resurrection discussed in this chapter. In Lippard's dark vision of the present and future, republican liberty fails to improve the moral and material conditions of the American people. Elitism, slaveholding, and superstition prove to be less easily vanquished than Jefferson and others had suggested they would be. The strong sectarian charge of the Protestant eschatological tradition turns out to be difficult to dissipate too (the revivalist F. A. T. Pyne, a secret debauchee and member of Monk Hall, makes a fortune from his hateful invectives against "Pagan Rome" [226]; the procession of royalists in Devil-Bug's dream includes "a pure old fashioned orthodox mob" that threatens "eternal death in the next world, for every soul that disbelieves in our creed" [328]). And while the novel's most nefarious villains are eventually punished with death or disgrace, the narrative holds out little hope that a systematic regeneration of American life and society is likely.

Might a return to conventional belief in bodily resurrection be the remedy for political pessimism? Although the novel is highly critical of Christianity as it was practiced in nineteenth-century America, scholars generally agree that Lippard (who was raised as Methodist) did not seek to encourage his readers to forsake their faith.[166] Sure enough, a clarificatory note accompanying the text's first mention of the scandalous Reverend Pyne emphasizes the author's "fixed love and reverential awe" for the true "religion of Jesus Christ, our Savior and Intercessor" (170n). However, the redemptive potential of Christian soteriology and eschatology is little in evidence. Saving faith is difficult to come by in *The Quaker City*, even in extremis. As the atheist Ravoni lies dying, he hears "a Voice within him" ask if "there is another world" beyond death. All the sorcerer can see, however, is "vacant space, darkness, nothingness!" (457). Recoiling from this prospect, he reflects that even "the terrors of hell, the gnawing of eternal torture" would be preferable. Sympathizing with Devil-Bug despite his crimes, the narrator notes that there "had never been a church, a Bible, or a God!" in his life (189). America's elite, by contrast, have been "sunned in the light of religion as [they] grew toward manhood," but have squandered this inheritance, "spurn[ing] [God's] laws," and staining their "very lives, with the foul pollution of libertinism and lust." Devil-Bug's vision of Philadelphia's devastation suggests that these hypocrites will be punished in the end. Yet Lippard's rewriting of the book of Revelation excises the triumphant conclusion of its prophecies. In his account, resurrection is but a prelude to annihilation. The risen dead fail to pass on their warning to their loved ones. At first, the living simply look past them; once they are revealed, the resurrected elicit only fear and disgust. When the city falls, the living and the dead are destroyed together.

The abortive resurrection witnessed in Devil-Bug's dream epitomizes corporeality in *The Quaker City*: its bodies are fragile yet strangely indestructible, repulsive yet dangerously beautiful, animalistic yet angelic, tenacious yet easily drugged or hypnotized into submission.[167] This antithetical aesthetic speaks to the novel's ultimate ambivalence on the politics of death and immortality. Lippard could not accept material resurrection as a solution to the finitude and other deficiencies of the human form. But his obsessive circling around the subject suggests that he was not yet ready to denude the body of all its sacredness. If nothing else, the sheer length of his parodies of secular and eschatological resurrection hints at a nostalgia for the political cohesion and psychological wholeness that could be fostered by those ideas. Like his friend Poe, Lippard was caught between Protestant tradition and secular modernity on the question of the relationship between the body and the self. Though they were not Christians, these authors did not fully accept the modern principle that the brain is the seat of selfhood. The decaying and unquiet corpses that haunt their works represent a faith in resurrection that was, for them and many others, ailing but not quite dead.

Coda

Resurrection Hereafter

Thomas Jefferson was convinced that the world belonged to the living. He first made this claim in a famous letter to James Madison, written in Paris in September 1789. "The dead," he insisted, "have neither power nor rights over [the earth]." Since laws governing the inheritance of private property operated according to that principle, why should the public sphere not follow suit? Jefferson proposed that "every constitution" and "every law" should be abrogated at the end of each generation (which he calculated to last for nineteen years).[1] He returned to this theme several times in the years that followed but articulated it most powerfully in an 1824 letter to the English democratic reformer John Cartwright. Even as he professed his pride in the US governmental system, Jefferson affirmed that it should be subject to regular alteration. Despite the tremendous achievements of the founding generation, it had no right to "bind" its successors "for ever." "Rights and powers," Jefferson argued, "can only belong to persons, not to things, not to mere matter, unendowed with will." Indeed, he added, "the dead are not even things." Their "matter" was dispersed through "the bodies of other animals, vegetables, [and] minerals of a thousand forms." It was absurd not to question "laws and institutions" contrived by men who were now dust (or would soon be).

Jefferson's radical plan for the generational redrafting of the Constitution came to nothing. But his argument about the relationship of the dead to the public square anticipated the modern consensus on the subject. As Thomas Laqueur observes, the "dead still do work for the living . . . in public."[2] Mourning for fallen soldiers, commemorating victims of terrorism or police violence, and grieving for deceased celebrities give political and social communities definition and purpose. Yet the dead in general are less present than they used to be. At the beginning of the 1980s, Philippe Ariès observed that the twentieth century had rendered death "invisible" in the West. The dying were now generally taken to hospital, where treatment and sedation extended and therefore softened their transition out of life.[3] No longer governed by an elaborate social code, mourning now took place in private, with overly demonstrative grieving viewed as evidence of psychological instability.[4] In the 2000s, Charles Taylor claimed that secularization distances people from death intellectually and culturally. Convinced that religious teachings about postmortem existence are "childish" and delusional, but aware of a "void" in their feelings about mortality, secular moderns "ignore [death] as much ... as possible" and "concentrate on life."[5] As the twenty-first century progresses, the occlusion of the dead in public life seems set to intensify. The high cost of burial, increasing popularity of cremation, and the rise of the practice of scattering ashes point toward the decline of the cemetery as a space of memorialization.[6] At the same time, technological and pharmaceutical innovations raise the prospect of extending the life spans of the living, perhaps indefinitely. Immortalists hoping to overcome death through cryogenics or the digitization of consciousness now wield "major influence in Silicon Valley" and pursue research taken seriously by the wider scientific community.[7] The secular eternity that they seek would establish a permanent disconnection between those already dead or bound to die and the privileged few destined to live forever or be revived after death.

In response to these developments, some contemporary Christian thinkers have argued for a return to serious intellectual engagement with resurrection. Theologians associated with the Radical Orthodoxy movement contend that restoring faith in the doctrine can help to redress what they see as the nihilistic materialism of secular culture. In life, they argue, a "bourgeois ... obsession with fitness, cooking, sex, and bodily fluids ... commodifies ... [and] dehumanizes" the body.[8] Meanwhile, moderns view death as the only "truly permanent reality," the "nullity at the heart of things."[9] For Graham Ward, those who believe (and therefore participate) in the resurrection of Christ thereby imbue their corporeal lives with meaning. Though they will continue to be "a Greek, a Jew, a male, a female, a slave, or a freeborn," they will no longer be solely defined by their cultural background, political status, or economic consumption.[10] As members, with the righteous dead, of the body of Christ, they are not only offered eternal salvation, but also a new, more ethically satisfying way of participating in the things of this world.[11] In a similar vein, John Milbank argues that ethical action is in fact impossible without hope of resurrection. Where Jefferson dreamed of a moral sphere defined by the living, and freed from any sense of obligation to the departed, Milbank claims that an ethics purely focused on the present, secular moment will always be "contaminate[d]" by death, through our "experience of loss."[12] Fallible humans tend to recognize their obligation to the other too late, once she reveals her irreplaceability by dying, or else they overlook the value of "the present loved one," failing to realize how ephemeral his presence is.[13] The promise of resurrection redeems these flaws, foretelling a time in which our benevolence will be reciprocated and lost others found. This eschatological triumph over death reveals the intrinsic "cruel[ty]" of visions of secular progress (such as those emerging from the American and French Revolutions) that demand that individual interests yield to those of "*an abstract* [and always receding] *space*."[14] When "*every* generation" is told in turn that their self-sacrifice will guarantee the prosperity of the nation, then "consummation is forever postponed, and . . . morality itself is *defined* as perpetual postponement."

The work of Catholic philosopher Emmanuel Falque takes a different approach to making resurrection relevant in a secular age. Where Radical Orthodoxy contends that faith in the doctrine necessarily posits the reality of a transcendent world where the resurrected will live again, Falque's Christian phenomenology frames resurrection as a kind of conversion that should be primarily understood in terms of its impact on earthly existence (our "experience [of] finitude").[15] First, he seeks to disassociate the prospect of rising again from what he calls "the fiction of the other world" that frames heaven as a place (95). Second, he rejects the notion (common to almost all the Protestant thinkers discussed in this book) that resurrection changes "human nature . . . itself" (105). Instead, he describes the process as something that offers the believer "a new way of being" (109). Though it takes place during life on earth, resurrection is not an earthly event: rather than a "transformation *in* the world," it constitutes a "transformation *of* the world" for the individual concerned (5). If we accept this gift, a "horizontal" transcendence unfolds—our subjectivity is intertwined with God and other people, whom we now no longer treat as objects but as brothers and sisters (110). Eternal life, therefore, is not a "reward" or compensation for mortal suffering that awaits us after death (111). On the contrary, it begins here and now. As we live through the time allotted us on earth, we are already part of the unending communion of saints, together with the departed (112–26).

But does a re-engagement with resurrection have anything to offer non-Christians, or society at large? Although contemporary immortalism is often considered to be antithetical to Christianity (and other mainstream religions), a comparison with beliefs about resurrection may help to illuminate some of the ethical issues around "artificial" immortality. Researchers in cryonics, the earliest form of modern immortalism, speculate that it may be possible one day to reanimate corpses stored at ultra-low temperatures. As Abou Farman observes, the practice of freezing cadavers against that eventuality generates a very particular form of "secular eschatology," as "cryopreserved" persons (potentially) exceed the limits of a normal life span, existing on "alongside other living beings in time," "coeval" with, but remote from, a succession of generations.[16] Deliberation about the ontological and historical status of these frozen people, who may be resuscitated many thousands of years after they died, recalls early modern debates about the status and whereabouts of departed souls awaiting resurrection. Meanwhile, immortalist neuroscience, which is working toward the transference of consciousness from the brain to digital forms of storage, revives the old question of the relationship of personhood to the material body.

More broadly, the long history of resurrection theology can be used to stage a political critique of immortalist transhumanism. Several of the Protestant thinkers discussed in this book attempted to understand the science of corporeal immortality (as far as was possible). But they were also concerned with the collective nature of resurrected life, with the persistence and perfection of corporate bodies in the next life. Can the same be said of their transhumanist counterparts? Farman's anthropological study identifies a pronounced libertarian tendency among contemporary American immortalists. Their expensive projects, he argues, are implicitly ordered after the central hypothesis of what Foucault called biopolitics: some lives are more worth saving than others are (297–99). Their claim that they are working to preserve human civilization cannot disguise the truth that they see that civilization as "white and Western" (315). Some immortalists, moreover, have explicitly stated that the ultimate telos of their transhumanism is the colonization of the universe (305).

Early American Protestants, as we have seen, sometimes imagined resurrected life on the millennial earth along colonial or imperial lines. Some of them were also inclined to assume that resurrected bodies could not be black. Nevertheless, their theologies of resurrection were grounded in justice. They believed that God had entirely equitable reasons for choosing those who would rise again in glory with the saints and those who would rise to be damned. Even if we may no longer agree with seventeenth- and eighteenth-century criteria for how a just final judgment of each individual could be made, we can still appreciate the universal scope of Protestant eschatology.

By envisioning a future in which a select few are able to transcend mortality, American immortalism undoes the unity of the human race.[17] Against this ontological elitism, the doctrine of resurrection affirms that death must come to all. Resurrection's promise of an embodied life beyond the grave also raises questions about the different kinds of postmortal existence envisioned by transhumanists. Would uploading memories and personalities into a cybernetic frame really be enough to preserve personhood, as some immortalists claim? Would such a life be a blessing or a curse? One theologian warns that pursuing artificial immortality in that form would cultivate "a Manichaean disdain" for the "material body" and by extension the natural world.[18]

Given its insistence on the embodied nature of human life, might the eschatological doctrine of future resurrection help us to reckon with the environmental apocalypse confronting us here and now? To the contrary, several influential ecological philosophers and historians have suggested that Christian soteriology has contributed to the climate crisis. Carolyn Merchant claims that Protestant Christianity played an important part in what she has identified as the "death of nature" in the seventeenth century. As the scientific revolution popularized a mechanistic view of the universe, redefining the earth as "dead, inert, and exploitable," Protestantism declared that the individual was "responsible for his or her own salvation," thereby reinforcing the "egocentric" attitude that the natural world was to be put to use in pursuit of that goal.[19] Bron Taylor advances a similar argument, proposing that "Christianity in general, and Puritanism in particular" directed "European settlers" in North America to see "land . . . as a resource to be exploited."[20] Where Native American animism cultivated "reverence" for particular landscapes, animals, and foodstuffs, the otherworldliness of their God (and of his heaven) led Christians to subordinate the natural world to the spiritual. While he acknowledges that there have been attempts to "green" Christianity, Taylor suggests that the success of the environmentalist cause may depend upon the decline of Christian influence around the world.[21]

Taking an even longer view, Timothy Morton links the emergence of monotheistic religion in the Middle East's Fertile Crescent in the Axial Age (circa 800 to 200 BCE) to the development of "agrilogistics"—a human behavioral algorithm governing agriculture, economics, and politics that has been running for twelve thousand years.[22] The story of Eden in Genesis (in common with a passage on a lost golden age in the Ramayana) narrates the adoption of agriculture as a Fall into a more knowledgeable, but sinful, kind of being (38). But Morton also draws an implicit link between the three "axioms" of agrilogistics and the Christian soteriological scheme. The axioms are as follows:

(1) The Law of Noncontradiction is inviolable.
(2) Existing means being constantly present.
(3) Existing is always better than any quality of existing. (47)

These three principles map neatly onto conventional Christian beliefs about immortality. The first dictates that only humans (not animals) can be granted eternal life, the second that once one is born, one is constantly present (on earth, heaven, or hell) through eternity, the third that suffering in this life is nothing besides the joys of heaven (and therefore should be endured without complaint). According to Morton, our desire for eternal life, like our desire for more food, more money, and more sex has been coded into us by agrilogistics. Since all these appetites are destructive of the environment that sustains us, they are also expressive of what Freud called humanity's death drive (52–53, 97). Thinking ecologically means breaking this disruptive loop, renouncing our appetite for more, accepting that the universe is not human scaled, learning to living interdependently with, or even as, nonhumans, and letting the dream of immortality die (124, 150, 71).

Yet resurrection's rich and complex history suggests that we should not be too quick to dismiss the ecological potential of Christian soteriology. Although the doctrine promises eternal life, it also emphasizes the vulnerability, materiality, and finitude of human existence, by insisting that life cannot be understood without reference to corporeal form. The prospect of eschatological re-embodiment also encourages believers to see themselves as living in two time frames: an uncertain present and a settled hereafter that in certain senses has already begun. Resurrection can therefore serve as an imaginative resource in the struggle against climate change, providing a conceptual alternative or complement to the "deep time" model favored by environmental philosophers.

Many scholars have called for human history to be viewed from the perspective of the prehistoric geological and evolutionary processes that continue to shape the present. Others argue that the contemporary Anthropocene must be studied through the lens of the disquieting future it has created—by recognizing, for instance, that we are living alongside "new immortals," human-made materials such as plastics and nuclear waste that will "circulate through air, water, rock, and flesh for untold millions of years."[23] Morton, meanwhile, claims that sensitivity to "inhumanly large timescales" will elicit "solidarity with nonhumans," as the borders between our world and theirs are revealed to be "permeable."[24] Seen through deep time, rocks are agents like us, "coming and going, moving, shifting, melting."[25] This realization, Morton suggests, should lead us to be kind to them, by considering their and other nonhuman needs "in our social designs."[26] But strengthening our imaginative relationships with people of different eras could be just as beneficial and significantly easier to comprehend than Morton's somewhat abstruse account of coexistence with nonhumans. What if we knew we would be judged at the end of time, made to answer for our stewardship of the world in the presence of those who came before and those who will come after us? Would we be better global citizens if we lived as if we were going to return to the earth one day? Even if we may struggle to believe in a literal resurrection from the dead, the faith of a former age may still have something to teach us.

Notes

Introduction

1. Seeman, *Death in the New World*, 78–105, 143–78.
2. Vincent Brown observes that largely thanks to yellow fever and malaria, most white immigrants to Jamaica in the middle of the eighteenth century died before they had been on the island for thirteen years. Those whites who were born in the colony and reached adulthood "were likely to die before they reached the age of forty" (*The Reaper's Garden*, 17).
3. Bradford, *Bradford's History*, 91–92, 92.
4. *The Book of Common-Prayer*, n.p. Edward Bond notes that "many Anglicans in colonial Virginia testified to the importance of religion in their wills by mentioning forgiveness of sins, a sure and certain hope of the resurrection, or an explicit request for Christian burial" ("Anglican Theology and Devotion," 315 n. 4).
5. Seeman, *Death in the New World*, 97–98.
6. Seeman, *Speaking with the Dead*, 54. In the late seventeenth century, it was increasingly common for sermons to be preached on the day of the burial itself (Stannard, *Puritan Way of Death*, 115–16).
7. The Savoy Conference of 1661, at which Charles II's new bishops debated liturgical questions with Puritan and Presbyterian clerics, resolved to remove the words "sure and certain" from the Anglican Book of Common Prayer. See Stannard, *Puritan Way of Death*, 72–73.
8. Hariot, *Briefe and True Report*, [38]–[39].
9. Williams, *Key into the Language of America*, 5.
10. Ligon, *True and Exact History*, 51.
11. Caroline Walker Bynum's *The Resurrection of the Body in Western Christianity* surveys a wide range of beliefs about resurrection between the third and fourteenth centuries.
12. Hill, *World Turned Upside Down*, 16–17.
13. Proponents of the former view included Henry Layton, William Coward (who each continued to believe in the resurrection of the body), John Toland, and Julien de La Mettrie, while Denis Diderot, David Hume, Jeremy Bentham, and Percy Shelley were advocates for the latter. For a helpful overview, see Thomson, *Bodies of Thought*, 97–134 and 175–215.
14. For a summary of these scientific (or physico-theological) accounts of resurrection, see Vidal, "Brains, Bodies, Selves," 950–65.
15. Rivett, *Science of the Soul*, 223–70.
16. See, for instance, McDannell and Lang, *Heaven*, 178–80.

17. The great distance between heavenly and worldly life was a particularly common theme in Puritan writing. Even though he encouraged believers to "meditate" on the blessings of heaven, "as if th[ey] were all the while beholding them," Richard Baxter stressed that these things were "beyond our conceiving," and disparaged "Papists" for pictorially and ritually representing them (*Saints Everlasting Rest*, 760, 328, 760). Boston minister Samuel Willard explained that "our present Condition" precluded us from "Conceiving or Crediting" the "Felicity" of the saints in the celestial city: until the "happy day" on which he or she died, the "poor Believer" would remain the "field" of a "War" between his or her sanctified soul and earthbound body (*Compleat Body of Divinity*, 556, 503). Increase Mather, for his part, emphasized that the "Blessed Fellowship" the elect would enter into "with the Son of God" would reveal the comparative inadequacy of the rest of creation. "In Heaven[,]" he affirmed, "God will be instead of all." There would be "no need of any thing else to make us Happy" (*Meditations on the Glory*, 234, 240). Puritan poets often dwelt on this and other comparable themes. Anne Bradstreet's lines "Upon the Burning of Our House" set the loss of her family's abode against her "permanent" home "on high," which she portrayed as "a Prise so vast as is unknown" (*Works*, 41–42). Edward Taylor, meanwhile, wondered that his corrupted flesh—"a jumble of gross Elements," "A snaile Horn where an Evill spirit tents," "a Ball of dirt"—could ever be clothed in "More glorious robes, than glorious Angells bare" (*Gods Determinations*, 197).
18. Marshall, *Invisible Worlds*, 17–33, and Laqueur, *Work of the Dead*, 99–102.
19. See Seeman, *Speaking with the Dead*, 42–129.
20. Weber, *Protestant Ethic*, 61. Weber's influence is apparent in Carlos Eire's account of Reformed religion's contribution to the changing relationship between the living and the dead. See *Reformations*, 753–54.
21. Weber, *Protestant Ethic*, 61–62, 62.
22. Taylor, *A Secular Age*, 38, 41, 542.
23. Laqueur, *Work of the Dead*, 537.
24. Vidal, "Brains, Bodies, Selves," 936.

Chapter 1

1. The clearest summary of this change in Protestant eschatology can be found in Gribben, *The Puritan Millennium*, 26–56.
2. For the lasting influence of Augustine's eschatology, see Gribben, *The Puritan Millennium*, 33–40.
3. In *The City of God*, Augustine notes that the "first resurrection . . . is not the resurrection of the body, but of the soul," adding that it takes place "now," rather than at the end of secular history (975).
4. Brightman, *Revelation of the Apocalyps*, 654.
5. Alsted, *The Beloved City*, 17–19; Mede, *Works*, 604–5. Mede changed his mind on whether the saints raised in the First Resurrection would reign in heaven or earth.

Though he originally favored the former interpretation (604), he had changed his mind by 1629, when he noted that he "agree[d] with *Alstedius*, That the Saints of the First Resurrection should reign on Earth during the *Millennium*, and not in Heaven" (772).

6. Como, "Print, Censorship," 822.
7. Capp, "Political Dimension," 112, 114–17; Rogers, *The Fifth Monarchy Men*.
8. Gribben, *The Puritan Millennium*, 105–26.
9. Nye and Goodwin, "To the Reader," n.p.
10. Baillie, *Dissuasive from the Errours*, 112.
11. Baillie, *Dissuasive from the Errours*, n.p.
12. Gribben, *The Puritan Millennium*, 54–55.
13. Baillie, *Dissuasive from the Errours*, 58.
14. For example, the influential English Puritan theologian William Ames described the spiritual sanctification that attended conversion as a resurrection accomplished by "the Spirit of God, which raised Christ from the dead" (*Marrow of Sacred Divinity*, 144). High Church Anglicans such as Anthony Farindon and Henry Hammond presented similar pictures. Farindon noted that "our conversion may . . . be stiled a Rising for many reasons," most of all because it raised the soul of the believer up from the "Grave" of worldly things (*LXXX Sermons*, 998). For his part, Hammond noted that it was particularly apt to label the conversion of a hardened, or "customary" sinner as "a kind of death, and resurrection," since it involved the "new Creation of another nature" (*Sermons*, 267).
15. Gribben, *The Puritan Millennium*, 181–82.
16. Weber, *Protestant Ethic*, 35, 61.
17. Eire, *Reformations*, 317, 753.
18. Eire, *Reformations*, 317.
19. Taylor, *A Secular Age*, 209.
20. As both David Stannard and Erik Seeman have pointed out, Puritans were just as concerned when a dying person expressed too much confidence in his or her redemption as they were when he or she exhibited excessive fear of death and judgment. See Stannard, *Puritan Way of Death*, 83–84; Seeman, *Death in the New World*, 180–81, and *Pious Persuasions*, 64–65.
21. Baillie, *Dissuasive from the Errours*, 62.
22. For a discussion of competing lay and clerical claims to religious authority in New England up to the Hutchinson affair, see Bremer, *Lay Empowerment*, 69–104.
23. For an overview of this interpretive tradition, see Traister, *Female Piety*, 64–68.
24. See, respectively, Caldwell, "The Antinomian Language Controversy"; Westerkamp, "Anne Hutchinson"; Burnham, *Folded Selves*, 95–114.
25. J. F. Maclear's "Anne Hutchinson and the Mortalist Heresy," published in 1981, remains the most notable treatment of the significance of beliefs about resurrection and the afterlife in Hutchinson's case.
26. Hall, *The Antinomian Controversy*, 351.
27. Philip Gura points out that the "Antinomian Controversy . . . must not be seen as a stubborn defense of long-held principles" against the assault of "heretical

invaders from outside the colony," but rather as part of the long process of defining Massachusetts's "ecclesiastical system." Those who broadly accepted Hutchinson's soteriology, he notes, constituted "a significant minority" in the early years of the Bay Colony (*Glimpse of Sion's Glory*, 239).
28. While the subject of the sabbath was not raised directly in either of Hutchinson's trials, John Winthrop's journal for January 1638 bemoans the proliferation of heretical opinions in Boston. These included the beliefs "That the Sabbath is but as other days. That the soul is mortal, till it be united to Christ, and then it is annihilated, and the body also, and a new given by Christ. [And] That there is no resurrection of the body" (*Winthrop's Journal*, 1:259).
29. Bulkeley, Davenport, and Winthrop all made this connection in the course of an exchange on the first day of the hearing (Hall, *The Antinomian Controversy*, 362–63). Cotton repeated the point shortly afterward, during his admonition of Hutchinson (372).
30. Hutchinson's prevaricating claim that she had not "altered" her "Judgment," but only her "Expression" of it, strongly suggests that she had not actually rejected her unconventional beliefs (Hall, *The Antinomian Controversy*, 378).
31. Westerkamp, "Anne Hutchinson," 496; Battis, *Saint and Sectaries*, 286.
32. Burnham, *Folded Selves*, 105.
33. Traister, *Female Piety*, 35.
34. Traister notes that "nearly every history of the United States at least mentions [the Antinomian Controversy], and most discuss it and Hutchinson in some detail (*Female Piety*, 61–62). Typically, Hutchinson's radical theology has been assigned an almost entirely secular "legacy"—the supposedly quintessentially American "freedom to dissent and to be free from state suppression" (68).
35. The term "monstrous birth" is John Winthrop's. See *Winthrop's Journal*, 1:277.
36. Gura, *Glimpse of Sion's Glory*, 245–47.
37. Johnson, *History of New-England*, 95–96.
38. Taylor, *A Secular Age*, 209, 38.
39. Taylor, *A Secular Age*, 37–39.
40. Taylor notes that the distinction between buffered and porous selves must be understood as relating to "*experience*" rather than to "'theory' or 'belief'" (*A Secular Age*, 39). At the same time, he observes that the ability of the buffered self to disengage from the world outside and "[give] its own autonomous order to its life" (38–39) nonetheless "removes a tremendous obstacle to unbelief" (41).
41. Field, "Antinomian Controversy," 449, 452–56. For more on the epidemiological rhetoric employed by Winthrop, see Silva, *Miraculous Plagues*, 75–94.
42. See Maclear, "Anne Hutchinson," 98–100. As Maclear notes, Thomas Shepard's lengthy sermon series *Theses Sabbaticæ*, which he delivered in the 1640s, reflected his perception that some people in the Bay Colony were still inclined to "allegorize" eschatology and resurrection, as well as the commandment to keep the sabbath. I discuss *Theses Sabbaticæ* below.
43. Winship, *Making Heretics*, 198.
44. Hall, *The Antinomian Controversy*, 353.

45. For the text of the conference's proceedings, which was published in London in 1646, see Hall, *The Antinomian Controversy*, 173–98.
46. For attempts to do so, see Winship, *Making Heretics*, 237–28, and Ziff, *Career of John Cotton*, 261–68.
47. Cotton, *Gods Free Grace*, 27, 30, 31–32.
48. Cotton, *The Churches Resurrection*, 26, 9–10.
49. Cotton, *Thirteenth Chapter*, 93.
50. Cotton, *The Churches Resurrection*, 6.
51. Cotton, *The Churches Resurrection*, 20.
52. Cotton, *The Churches Resurrection*, 21.
53. As Jan Stievermann points out, "In the 1640s," Cotton "hoped that the Puritans could create something like an exemplary anticipation of the millennial church in the colonies" ("Reading Canticles," 219). However, "He never assumed that New England . . . would occupy any special place in Christ's coming kingdom."
54. Cotton, *The Churches Resurrection*, 20–21, 25.
55. Cotton, *Congregational Churches Cleared*, 1:103, 21–22.
56. Cotton, *The Churches Resurrection*, 26.
57. Cotton, *The Churches Resurrection*, 9.
58. Cotton, *The Churches Resurrection*, 30.
59. Shepard, *Parable of Ten Virgins*, 2:2.
60. Since it twice cites John Saltmarsh's 1647 tract *Sparkles of Glory*, we can be reasonably confident that *Theses Sabbaticæ* was first preached in that same year at the earliest. For the citations, see *Theses Sabbaticæ*, 1:66, 73.
61. Reiner Smolinski ("Apocalypticism," 45–46) emphasizes the similarities between Cotton's and Shepard's view of the millennium, though he does point out that unlike his colleague the latter expected a period of religious persecution and spiritual decline to take place before the chiliad began. These events were supposedly predicted by Revelation's prophecies of the murder of the two witnesses (11:7–14) and the slaughter of martyrs (6:9–11).
62. When explaining his understanding of the millennium at the beginning of *The Parable of the Ten Virgins*, Shepard claimed that even "in those daies . . . wherein the Churches of Christ, and Professors of the Gospel shall grow Virgin-Churches" whose "Members [all] seem to be espoused to Christ, yet there will be found desperate folly in some, and in time great security will fall upon all" (1:10).
63. Shepard, *The Sincere Convert*, 48.
64. Shepard, *The Sincere Convert*, 48, 49. The 1640 first edition of Shepard's tract has several errors in paging. After page 48 (cited here and in the note earlier), the page numbers return to 47 (so that the relevant pages are numbered 48, 47, 48, 49).
65. Shepard had already drawn a connection between the problem of spiritual hypocrisy and the parable of the ten virgins in a sermon series preached during his ministry in England. Published in London in 1640 (apparently without his consent [Neumann, *Jeremiah's Scribes*, 36]), *The Sincere Convert* would go on to become his "most popular work," appearing in at least twenty-one editions by 1812 (McGiffert, "Thomas Shepard"). For references to the parable, see *The Sincere Convert*, 70, 134, 138.

66. Shepard, *Wine for Gospel Wantons*, 15; *Parable of Ten Virgins*, 1:44. For more on the "renewability of conversion" in Shepard's soteriology, see McGiffert, *God's Plot*, 26.
67. Shepard, *Parable of Ten Virgins*, 2:61–62.
68. The part of the parable of the ten virgins that was relevant to this point was the refusal of the wise virgins to give any oil to the foolish virgins (Matthew 25:8–9). Shepard explained that the oil represented grace. It was "not in the power" of the elect to "convey" saving grace to the reprobate (*Parable of Ten Virgins*, 2:89). Yet just as the wise virgins in the parable took pity on the foolish, urging them to visit those who sold oil, the elect ought to be compassionate toward hypocrites, by encouraging them to seek the help of ministers (2:95–96). It was always of benefit for Christians to hear the Gospel from trained clergy as part of a godly congregation, even if pastoral guidance and "the fellowship of God's people" would not produce a saving effect in all believers. Shepard employed one of his favored medical analogies to explain this principle: "It is not in the people of God as it is in salves, that there is an inherent virtue abiding alway to heal, and that in any man which is cureable; but there is only an adherent virtue which doth not alway abide; and when it is there, works not upon all, but only at the pleasure of the principal Agent the Lord Jesus" (2:90).
69. Saltmarsh, *Sparkles of Glory*, 278, 276, 265, 267.
70. Shepard, *Theses Sabbaticæ*, 1:87.
71. Shepard, *Theses Sabbaticæ*, 2:91.
72. Shepard, *Theses Sabbaticæ*, n.p.
73. Saltmarsh, *Sparkles of Glory*, 204.
74. Shepard, *Theses Sabbaticæ* 1:65, 74, 78.
75. Shepard, *Theses Sabbaticæ*, 2:93.
76. Shepard, *Theses Sabbaticæ* 2:[95]. Here Shepard was alluding to the *Book of Sports*, a declaration issued nationally by James I in 1618, and reissued by his son Charles I in 1633. The *Book of Sports* proclaimed that some recreational activities, including "archery, other exercises, dancing (including Morris dances), maypoles, and church ales," could be enjoyed on Sundays (Hall, *The Puritans*, 210). Taking a more hardline approach than his father had, Charles insisted that this attack on the Puritan attitude toward the sabbath should be read out by every parish priest.
77. Shepard, *Theses Sabbaticæ*, 2:[96].
78. Shepard, *Theses Sabbaticæ*, 2:[98].
79. Shepard, *Theses Sabbaticæ*, 2:89–90.
80. Shepard linked the right of secular authorities to require Sunday worship to their responsibility to prevent the spread of heresy. "Lunactick and Phrantick men," he observed, "are in best case when they are well fettered and bound" (*Theses Sabbaticæ*, 2:90).
81. Shepard, *Theses Sabbaticæ*, 2:85.
82. Shepard, *Treatise of Liturgies*, 180.
83. Shepard, *Subjection to Christ*, 185.
84. Shepard, *Subjection to Christ*, 181.
85. Fessenden, *Culture and Redemption*, 16.
86. Gillis, "Memory and Identity," 18, qtd. in Fessenden, *Culture and Redemption*, 15.

87. Gorton, *Antidote*, 287.
88. Gorton, *Antidote*, 286.
89. Gorton, *Incorruptible Key*, 73.
90. Gorton, *Simplicities Defence*, 72, 68, 72.
91. Gorton's stay in Aquidneck ended with his being banished by the governor, Antinomian Samuel Coddington. Along with Hutchinson and her husband, Gorton had rebelled against Coddington's attempt to increase his executive power. Between 1639 and 1640 their faction managed to establish a more democratic government over the settlement, before Coddington reestablished control. See Donoghue, *Fire under the Ashes*, 130–33.
92. Burnham, "Samuel Gorton's Leveller Aesthetics," 447–54.
93. Burnham, "Samuel Gorton's Leveller Aesthetics," 454.
94. Field, *Errands into the Metropolis*, 65, 69, 65.
95. According to Robert Baillie, while the Hutchinsons were living on Aquidneck, Anne "did perswade her husband to lay down the office of the Magistrate, as that which was unlawfull for Christians to bear" (*Anabaptism*, 79, qtd. in Gura, *Glimpse of Sion's Glory*, 76).
96. Gorton, *Saltmarsh Returned*, 152.
97. Gorton, *Saltmarsh Returned*, 152, 32.
98. Gorton, *Antidote*, 171.
99. Austin, *Genealogical Dictionary*, 304.
100. Gorton, *Simplicities Defence*, 21.
101. Gorton, *Simplicities Defence*, 96.
102. Gorton, *Simplicities Defence*, 21.
103. Gorton explained this difficult point as follows: "For if we make the death of Christ according to the true mystery of it, wherein salvation doth consist, to be of lesse continuance then eternity; wee shall annihilate Christ, and make salvation it selfe of no longer continuance; for if Christ once dye unto the flesh in the godly, he never lives unto it any more" (*Saltmarsh Returned*, 190).
104. Gorton, *Simplicities Defence*, 21.
105. Gorton, *Saltmarsh Returned*, 76.
106. Gorton, *Antidote*, 42.
107. Gorton, *Saltmarsh Returned*, 40.
108. Gorton, *Antidote*, 254, 132.
109. Asad, *Formations of the Secular*, 107, 149.
110. Asad, *Genealogies of Religion*, 46.
111. Asad, *Genealogies of Religion*, 46, 47.
112. Gorton, *Saltmarsh Returned*, 179.
113. Taylor concedes that "it is doubtful that humans could ever live exclusively" in "'homogenous, empty time'" (*A Secular Age*, 174). Contemporary lives, he maintains, continue to be structured in part by temporal cycles of various kinds: professional, commemorative, and revolutionary (714–15).
114. Taylor, *A Secular Age*, 55.
115. Gorton, *Antidote*, 165.

116. In his account of the trouble Gorton had caused Massachusetts, Edward Winslow, the colony's agent in London, complained that he and his followers made a mockery of "the being of Christ in the flesh, making him no other than such an one as actually suffered from the beginning of the world, and shall doe to the end of it" (*Hypocrisie Unmasked*, 49).

117. On this issue, Gorton observed that "if we say . . . that [we] must be made better by our endeavours and use of means, . . . then we divide our selves from Christ, making his condition one, and our own another" (*Antidote*, 157).

118. Gorton, *Antidote*, 163.

119. As Taylor puts it, in the secular age, the old "routines" of access to higher time "are still there, but they fail to unite our life across their repeatable instances. They cannot give unity to the whole span of a life, much less unite our lives with those of our ancestors and successors" (*A Secular Age*, 718–19).

120. Mackie, "Samuel Gorton," 380, 381.

121. Haefeli notes that "the most significant figure" in the development of an official policy of toleration in colonial Rhode Island was Robert Rich, Earl of Warwick, who would become "patron" to Roger Williams as well as Gorton ("Toleration and Empire," 117). As chair of Parliament's Committee on Foreign Plantations, Warwick not only issued the Rhode Island charter of 1643, but "was also influential in securing the first general proclamation of religious toleration in in America"—the 1645 act "for the establishment of freedom of worship in the American Plantations and especially in Bermuda" (117–18). Following the Restoration, Charles II reapproved the Rhode Island charter and sought to establish an even broader degree of toleration across England's empire (123).

122. For Gorton's probable influence in this matter, see Gura, "Radical Ideology," 98–99; for details of Quaker influence over the government of Rhode Island in the seventeenth century, see Weddle, *Walking*, 99–103.

123. Gorton, *Antidote*, 286, 292, 291.

124. Morton, *New Englands Memoriall*, 108.

125. Morton, *New Englands Memoriall*, 138.

126. Gorton, "Letter to Nathaniel Morton," 4.

127. Gorton, "Letter to Nathaniel Morton," 6.

128. The full title of the tract, *Saltmarsh Returned from the Dead, in Amico Philalethe*, may also have referred to Robert Bacon, another radical English minister who, like Saltmarsh, was connected to Giles Calvert's London bookshop at the Black-Spread-Eagle. As Mario Caricchio explains, "Philalethe" may have been Bacon's "nickname" within this circle ("Giles Calvert," 81). For more on Bacon, who was still alive when Gorton's book was published, see Birrell, "English Catholic Mystics," 66–69.

129. Using language comparable to that which Gorton would later employ, Saltmarsh described a Christian as "one . . . who is in fellowship and conformity with Jesus Christ in his crucifyings, death, and resurrection, in whom the flesh, and life of the flesh must dye, as it did in him" (*Sparkles of Glory*, 103–4). For more on the similarities between Gorton and Saltmarsh, see Gura, *Glimpse of Sion's Glory*, 293–95.

130. Pooley, "Saltmarsh, John," n.p.
131. Gorton, *Saltmarsh Returned*, n.p.
132. Gura, *Glimpse of Sion's Glory*, 144–48; Winship, *Making Heretics*, 241.
133. Winship, *Making Heretics*, 241.
134. Mackie, "Samuel Gorton," 381.
135. Fox, *A Journal*, 211.
136. Fox, *A Journal*, 242.
137. Morton, *New-Englands Memoriall*, 157.
138. On Fox's "belief in the outward Cross of Jesus in history" and his criticisms of radical Quakers who questioned the need for such a faith, see Gwyn, "Seventeenth-Century Context," 23. Fox affirmed his trust in the historical Christ in his reply to Roger Williams's attack on his theology: "We own God, who is over all, and in us all, as well without us, as within us" (*New-England-Fire-Brand*, 162–63).
139. Gwyn, "Quakers, Eschatology, and Time," 204–5.
140. Allen, "Restoration Quakerism," 35.
141. See Gwyn, "Quakers, Eschatology, and Time," 207–8.
142. Fox, *Works*, 7:66, qtd. in Gwyn, "Quakers, Eschatology, and Time," 204.
143. Fox, *Works*, 7:160.
144. Fox, *A Journal*, 558.
145. Penn, *Rise and Progress*, 98.
146. Fox, *An Encouragement for All*, 12; Penn, *Rise and Progress*, 50, qtd. in O'Donnell, "This Side of the Grave," 47.
147. See, for instance, Bailey, *New Light*, and Tarter, "Quaking in the Light," 148.
148. Frost, "Unlikely Controversialists," 26. Melvin Endy, too, notes that it is risky to assume that Fox had a "fixed position" on the subject, due to the "inherently ambiguous and metaphorical" nature of the "doctrine of inhabitation by the glorified heavenly flesh of Christ that is incorporeal and yet intangible" ("George Fox," 33).
149. Fox, *Collection of Several Books*, 196.
150. Bishop, *New England Judged*, 36, 29, 36.
151. Martindell, *Relation of the Labour*, 43.
152. Fox, "For the Governor," 66, 67, 70.
153. Penn, *Frame of Government*, xlvii.
154. Penn, *Frame of Government*, lxiii.
155. Murphy, *Political Thought*, 141.
156. Penn, *Frame of Government*, lxii.
157. See, Endy, "William Penn," 211–21, and "Some Contributions," 466.
158. Penn, *Quakerism*, 243. Penn also consistently argued against too much speculation into the abstruse theological details of Christ's incarnation and resurrection, or into the related question of "what Bodies we shall have" in the next world (*Address to Protestants*, 75). Bringing too much "*Philosophy*" into theology occluded the essential "*Simplicity*" of the *Gospel*" (73), and created sectarian conflict by making contrasting human "*Judgment*[s] . . . the *Rule* of *Christian Faith* and *Canons* of *Christ's Church* (76). See also *Quakerism*, 202.

159. Penn, *Invalidity*, 369. Penn also stressed that resurrection would involve an "Exchange" of bodies. The "Spiritual" form the saints would be granted would not be "the same Numerical Body, that was the Natural; for so the Natural and Spiritual Body would be one and the same."
160. Penn, *Invalidity*, 381.
161. Penn, *Perswasive to Moderation*, 46.
162. Contesting Richard Bailey's claim that Penn's writings deliberately concealed the radicalism of Fox's thought (especially on the issue of the divinity of the light within), Melvin Endy argues convincingly that both men were aware of the need to present moderated versions of Quaker doctrine to outsiders. The political survival of the movement "required the partial submergence" of aspects of their resurrection theology ("George Fox," 28). Fox's response to the Anglicans of Barbados, Endy observes, "does not represent the essence of early Quaker or Fox's thought."
163. Keith, *Testimony*, 10.
164. See Calvert, *Quaker Constitutionalism*, 124.
165. Nash, *Quakers and Politics*, 160, qtd. in Murphy, *Political Thought*, 210. For more on the political and theological stakes of the Keithian schism, see Smolenski, *Friends and Strangers*, 149–77.
166. Butler, "Into Pennsylvania's Spiritual Abyss," 166.
167. McClure, "Hell and Anxiety."
168. See Harrison, "Science and Secularization" and *Territories*.
169. See Israel, *Radical Enlightenment*, and Jacob, *The Secular Enlightenment*.
170. See Taylor, *A Secular Age*; Eire, *Reformations*; and Gregory, *Unintended Reformation*.
171. See Erdozain, "A Heavenly Poise" and *The Soul of Doubt*.
172. Bryce Traister's *Female Piety and the Invention of American Puritanism*, the most sophisticated recent account of the relationship between Puritanism and secularism, advances a comparable argument. Traister shows how a variety of "female" forms of religious expression (including Hutchinsonian "Antinomianism" and Quakerism) "helped [to] produce an incipient secular liberalism" by means of a critique of patriarchal and textual religious authority (1). He also notes that histories of the modernization and secularization of the United States have retrospectively minimized these movements' religious orientation or marginalized them on the basis of their female spirituality (1, 205–7).

Chapter 2

1. Tillotson, *Works*, 1:411.
2. Rogers, *Sermon Preached*, 29.
3. Willard, *Reformation the Great Duty*, 20, 7–8.
4. Stoughton, *New-Englands True Interest*, 10.
5. Miller, *New England Mind: The Seventeenth Century*, 479–84.
6. Abram Van Engen provides a helpful overview of Miller's claims about the Puritan contribution to US history. See *City on a Hill*, 241–55.

7. Rivett and Van Engen, "Postexceptionalist Puritanism," 680.
8. Miller, *New England Mind: The Seventeenth Century*, 479.
9. Winship, *Godly Republicanism*, 8, 233, 248–49.
10. Goodman, *The Puritan Cosmopolis*, 80.
11. Mather, *Triparadisus*, 263.
12. Smolinski, "Caveat Emptor," 161.
13. For more on this scientifically informed literalism and its relationship to another form of literalist exegesis that developed out of the Protestant belief in the supremacy of scripture over other religious authorities, see Harrison, *Bible, Protestantism*, 121–60.
14. See Almond, *Heaven and Hell*, 138–40. More read scriptural texts apparently referring to a future resurrection of the body metaphorically, arguing "that the same men that die and are buried, shall as truly appear in their own persons at the day of judgment, *as if* those bodies that were interred should be presently actuated by their souls again and should start out of their graves" ("Grand Mystery of Godliness," 224, qtd. in Almond, 138. My emphasis).
15. For a useful summary of Spinoza's influence on Toland, Blount, and other English and Irish radicals see Israel, *Radical Enlightenment*, 599–627. For the intellectual similarities between Bayle and Spinoza, despite the former's public criticism of the latter's philosophy, see 331–41.
16. Fernando Vidal explains that by the end of the eighteenth century Locke's separation of the self from the body had led to the widespread perception that it was "the resurrection *of the (same) body*" that was "implausible," rather than resurrection *tout court* ("Brains, Bodies, Selves," 970). This rejection of traditional resurrection theology then led in the nineteenth century to the adoption of "metempsychosis" as the prevalent model of afterlife existence in the West.
17. Mather, *Cœlestinus*, 2:39.
18. Mather, *Magnalia Christi Americana*, n.p.
19. One notable example of a biography framed around this trope is *Abel Being Dead Yet Speaketh* (1658), John Norton's life of John Cotton.
20. Mather, *Magnalia Christi Americana*, 2:37.
21. Mather, *Biblia Americana*, 5:855.
22. Mather, *Magnalia Christi Americana*, 4:192.
23. See Loveman, "*Strange Finding Out*," 273–74.
24. Clearly enjoying the numerical coincidence, Mather here was quoting Job 14:14 ("If a man die, shall he live *again*? all the days of my appointed time will I wait, till my change come").
25. In describing Walley's acceptance of a literal reading of the prophecy, Mather quoted Mede's description of his own journey to that conclusion in a 1634 letter to the Dutch scholar and minister Ludovicus de Dieu: *Postquam alia omnia frustra tentassem, tandem Dei ipsius Claritudine perstrictus, paradoxo Succubui* (Mede, *Works*, 571)— "After all the other approaches I had tried in error, I was at last struck by an insight from God himself and yielded to the mystery."
26. The classic articulation of the *Magnalia* as a declension narrative and jeremiad remains Perry Miller's *The New England Mind: From Colony to Province* (see especially

47 and 189). In the 1990s, Michael Winship modified Miller's reading in presenting the text as the "last great document" in the Puritan tradition of the interpretation of providential signs and wonders (*Seers of God*, 74). More recently, Reiner Smolinski, Paul Giles, and Jan Stievermann have contested the idea that Mather's book describes or embodies the waning of Puritan orthodoxy, respectively emphasizing instead its irenicism, Augustan exploration of the limits of human reason, and valorization of the newness of American religious experience ("Seeing Things Their Way," 38–45; *Global Remapping*, 44–55; "Quandry of *Copia*").

27. See Mather, *Magnalia Christi Americana*, 2:30, 3:31–32, and 3:68, respectively.
28. For an overview of Mede's claims about the eschatological fate of the New World, see Smolinski, "Israel Redivivus," 369–71.
29. The quotation from Turrettini also celebrates the blow that the leaders of the Reformation have given to the kingdom of the Antichrist ("*Antichristi Regnum Concusserunt*"), thereby calling attention to the eschatological context of Mather's catalog of notable New England saints.
30. Mather memorably compared his attempt to fit so many lives into his book to engraving "above an *Hundred Portraitures*" on a "*Cherry-stone*." He noted that the French medic Charles Patin (1633–1693) had seen such an artifact at "a certain *Musæum* at *Vienna*" (*Magnalia Christi Americana*, 3:213).
31. My argument that the *Magnalia*'s structural and rhetorical ungainliness is part of its method is influenced by Paul Giles's and Jan Stievermann's compelling readings of the text. Giles highlights the tension between Mather's search for typological parallels and his interest in idiosyncratic unruliness of individual human bodies. Through this opposition, he argues, the book dramatizes reason's inability to impose total order on the fallen natural world (*Global Remapping*, 43–55). Stievermann, meanwhile, interrogates the *Magnalia*'s aggregation of other authorial voices. Mather's many quotations and allusions, he notes, are intended to support the argument that the short history of Reformed Protestantism in the New World casts a fresh light on earlier theological and historical texts ("Quandry of *Copia*," 265–72). However, Stievermann also acknowledges Mather's anxiety that this compendiousness will degenerate into an "incoherent verbosity" (277) and/or an imitative "compilation of textual fragments" (278).
32. Bercovitch, *Puritan Origins*, 89.
33. Stievermann, "Quandry of *Copia*," 265.
34. Stievermann, "Reading Canticles," 222.
35. Erwin, *Millennialism of Cotton Mather*, 58.
36. Mather, *Problema Theologicum*, 406.
37. Lovelace, *American Pietism*, 243–49.
38. Silverman, *Life and Times*, 414–15.
39. Stievermann, *Prophecy*, 340–51; Komline, "Controversy," 454–55.
40. Mather, *Reason Satisfied*, 11, 28–29.
41. Rivett, *Science of the Soul*, 261.
42. Grainger, "Vital Nature," 869.
43. Thomson, *Bodies of Thought*, 74–75; Thiel, "Personal Identity," 881–84.

44. Stievermann, *Prophecy*, 182–83.
45. Rivett, *Science of the Soul*, 254–63.
46. These tracts included *The Spirit of Life* (1707) and *Coheleth* (1720).
47. Warner "Minister's Medical Role," 279, 294.
48. Breen, "Angelical Ministry," 352.
49. Silva, *Miraculous Plagues*, 147, 153–56.
50. Almond, *Heaven and Hell*, 47–54.
51. Young, "Politics and Heresy," 64–65, 79–80.
52. Thomson, *Bodies of Thought*, 97–133.
53. Locke, *Essay Concerning Human Understanding*, 181.
54. Locke's anonymous treatise *The Reasonableness of Christianity* (1695) confirmed that he recognized and approved of the mortalist implications of his model of personal identity. There he argued that each individual ceased to exist at death, only to be restored to life "again at the Resurrection" (10). Following judgment, people would either be granted a new "Spiritual" and "Immortal" body (203), or else have their consciousness definitively annihilated (rather than undergoing "endless torment in Hell-fire" [4]). For more discussion of Locke's theory of identity, and of the arguments of some of his critics, see Thiel, "Personal Identity," 888–902. Liam Dempsey, meanwhile, argues that Locke's "deflation of the importance of an immaterial soul with respect to persons, [and] personal immortality" is indicative of a private skepticism about the very existence of souls altogether ("John Locke, 'Hobbist'").
55. Thomson, *Bodies of Thought*, 126.
56. Mather, *Coheleth*, 7–8.
57. Mather, *A Midnight Cry*, 9–10.
58. Mather, *Triparadisus*, 114.
59. Mather, *Triparadisus*, 113.
60. Mather, *Triparadisus*, 117.
61. Mather, *Comfortable Chambers*, 12.
62. Mather, *Awakening Thoughts*, 13.
63. Mather, *Angel of Bethesda*, 34.
64. Paul's account of his experience is ambivalent about whether he was "in the body, or out of the body" when it happened (2 Corinthians 12:3).
65. Mather, *Comfortable Chambers*, 12.
66. Mather, *Cœlestinus*, 2:39.
67. Mather, *Angel of Bethesda*, 30.
68. In a passage that appears in both *The Angel of Bethesda* and *Triparadisus*, Mather employs and translates a Greek phrase. "Many of the Ancients," he claims, were of the "Opinion that there is Διαφορα κατα τας μορφας *A Distinction* (and so a Resemblance,) *of men as to their Shapes after Death* (*Angel of Bethesda*, 31; *Triparadisus*, 124). Reiner Smolinski notes that Mather's use of Greek here "alludes to the recognizable shapes of departed heroes, in Homer's *Iliad* 23 and *Odyssey* 11" (*Triparadisus* 371 n. 49).
69. Mather, *Angel of Bethesda*, 31–32; *Triparadisus*, 124.
70. Mather, *Angel of Bethesda*, 34.

71. Mather, *Triparadisus*, 30. Mather speculated that this "Operation" was analogous to the development of the fetus in the maternal womb. He also described the filling up of the body with "*Ethereal Matter*" in *Coheleth* (20).
72. Mather, *Triparadisus*, 255.
73. Mather, *Triparadisus*, 264–65, 255; *Comfortable Chambers*, 10.
74. Mather, *Comfortable Chambers*, 10.
75. Mather, *Triparadisus*, 249.
76. Mather, *Triparadisus*, 249; *Coheleth*, 22.
77. Mather, *Coheleth*, 22–23.
78. Mather, *Triparadisus*, 149, 128.
79. Mather, *Hades Look'd Into*, 13.
80. Mather, *Cœlestinus*, 2:44.
81. Stievermann, *Prophecy*, 387.
82. Mather, *Bonifacius*, 29.
83. Mather, *Triparadisus*, 126, 121.
84. Mather explained that Christ would be "enthroned" in the "*New Heavens*," but would sometimes "*Visibly* exhibit Himself" to the changed saints on the New Earth (*Triparadisus*, 287, 288).
85. At a conference held at London's Salters' Hall in 1719, it had become apparent that the city's Dissenting clergy were more or less evenly divided over whether ministers should be required to subscribe to the doctrine of the Trinity. David Komline notes that in "at least three" letters and diary entries Mather explicitly connected the outbreak of Arianism among English Dissenters to a global "spiritual decline" that heralded the end of days ("Controversy of the Present Time," 455). In January 1726, for example, he told his junior colleague Thomas Prince that the apparent willingness of many their English "Brethren" to embrace the heresy had "a deep share in preparing the world" for the "*Catastrophe*" of the Conflagration (Mather, *Diary*, 2:817, qtd. in Komline, "Controversy of the Present Time," 456).
86. Mather, *India Christiana*, 47.
87. Mather reinforced this point in two sermons inspired by the Boston earthquake of October 1727. See *Terror of the Lord*, 28–29, and *Boanerges*, 43–45.
88. Mather, *Manuductio*, 1, 116, 124, 125, 124, 127.
89. Mather, "Latin Preface," 83.
90. By putting Glasgow first, Mather not only expressed his gratitude for the honorary doctorate of divinity it had awarded him in 1710 but also his continuing resentment at being overlooked for Harvard's presidency in 1724. See Silverman, *Life and Times*, 403.
91. Mather, "Latin Preface," 125.
92. Mather, *Manuductio*, 116.
93. With this in mind, Mather recommend that the young ministers' preaching should concentrate on the three "MAXIMS of the *Everlasting Gospel*" (*Manuductio*, 116) on which all true Christians ought to agree: (1) total "*submission*" to "The ONE most High GOD," (2) complete reliance on Christ's "great *Sacrifice*" as the only source of salvation, and (3) treating other people as one would expect to be treated oneself (118).

94. Mather, *Manuductio*, 145.
95. Mather, *Manuductio*, 145, 119.
96. Mather, *Christian Loyalty*, 16, 18, 20, 24.
97. Mather, *Triparadisus*, 237.
98. Mather, *Problema Theologicum*, 422.
99. Reiner Smolinski dates the shift in Mather's eschatology to 1724, the year in which he read *Good Things to Come*, a tract by English Fifth Monarchist Praisegod Barebones, which had been published anonymously in 1675. Barebones's distinction between the saints raised from the dead at the First Resurrection and the living saints saved from the Conflagration by the Rapture and then rendered immortal helped Mather to understand how the inferno predicted in the Epistle of Peter could consume the entire globe (Smolinski, "Introduction," 33–34). However, Jan Stievermann argues convincingly that Mather had already been working toward this position for several years, with the help of William Lowth's 1714 commentary on Isaiah (*Prophecy*, 334–40).
100. Mather, *Triparadisus*, 289.
101. Mather, *Theopolis Americana*, 43.
102. Bercovitch, *Puritan Origins*, 107–8.
103. Mather, *Theopolis Americana*, 48.
104. Mather, *Theopolis Americana*, 49.
105. Mather, *Diary*, 2:15.
106. See Middlekauff, *The Mathers*, 325–29; Stievermann, "Reading Canticles," 233–34; Kennedy, *The First American Evangelical*, 139. Quotation is from Middlekauff, 325.
107. Mather made this claim again in a 1720 letter to Englishman Daniel Neal, who had authored a history of New England sympathetic to the Congregationalist cause. There, Mather noted that his "poor Country was never famous for Gratitude unto its Benefactors" (*Diary*, 2:598). Those who "serve[d] N.E." would most likely not receive any "Recompense" until "the Resurrection of the Just" (2:599).
108. Mather, *Theopolis Americana*, 50.
109. Mather, *Theopolis Americana*, 5.
110. Mather, *Theopolis Americana*, 39.
111. While Mather did not condemn slavery outright, he did quote the critique of the slave trade in Richard Baxter's casuistic tract *Christian Directory*, where the English Presbyterian attacked those who would "use [Africans] as *Beasts*, for their meer Commodity" (*Theopolis Americana*, 42, qtg. Baxter, *Christian Directory*, 559).
112. Mather, *Theopolis Americana*, 32, 148.
113. Silverman, *Life and Times*, 148; Kennedy, *The First American Evangelical*, 84.
114. [Mather], *A Collection*, 6.
115. Silverman, *Life and Times*, 155–56.
116. Colman, *Holy Walk*, 13.
117. Colman, *Holy Walk*, 11.
118. Colman, *Holy Walk*, 10.
119. See also Colman, *Ten Virgins*, 334, *Devout and Humble Inquiry*, 24, and *The Master Taken Up*, 4.

120. Colman, *Ten Virgins*, 417.
121. Colman, *Holy Walk*, 13.
122. Colman, *Glory of God*, 15, 20.
123. Colman, *Ten Virgins*, 416. Quoting Matthew 24:36, Colman claimed that "*of that day and hour knoweth no man, no not the Angels of Heaven, but the Father only.*"
124. See Adams, "Benjamin Colman," 331–32, and Kidd, *The Protestant Interest*, 143–46.
125. For Colman and the Indian missions, see Kidd, *The Protestant Interest*, 42–50. For his involvement in the conversion of Judah Monis, the Harvard teacher, see 152–54, as well as Hoberman, *New England / New Israel*, 99–109. For his hope that the New England awakenings marked a millennial regeneration of the church, see Kidd, *The Protestant Interest*, 29–30, 50.
126. Kidd, *The Protestant Interest*, 42.
127. Colman, *Brief Enquiry*, 32.
128. Colman, *Holy Walk*, 26.
129. Colman, *Death and the Grave*, 11. This sermon was occasioned by the death of a young Bostonian in a duel.
130. Colman, *Death and the Grave*, 13, 14.
131. Colman, *Ten Virgins*, 229.
132. Colman, *Death and the Grave*, 13.
133. Colman, *Ten Virgins*, 419.
134. *Brief Enquiry*, 421.
135. See, for instance, *Triparadisus*, 342, and *A Midnight Cry*.
136. Mather, *Triparadisus*, 347, 343.
137. Mather, *Triparadisus*, 273. Mather was not sure whether the changed saints would be taken up to the celestial world "Successively[,] . . . as they may Ripen for it," or "*all at once*" at a certain time.
138. Mather, *Triparadisus*, 276.
139. Mather, *Terra Beata*, 33.
140. Mather and Mather, *Three Letters*, 25.
141. Colman, *Ossa Josephi*, 26.
142. In his 1729 tract *The Credibility of the Christian Doctrine of the Resurrection*, Colman offered an explanation of the process that was similar to Mather's. Like his senior colleague, he compared the formation of the resurrected body from fragmentary remains to the creation of the individual form from tiny "Seeds or *Stamina*" in the maternal womb (7).

Chapter 3

1. Williams, *Key into the Language*, 196–97; Hariot, *Briefe and True Report*, 26; Ogilby, *Africa*, 93. Rebecca Goetz observes that early English colonists saw Native American beliefs about postmortem existence as evidence that the Indians would be amenable to accepting Christian eschatology (*Baptism of Early Virginia*, 45).
2. Kidd, *The Forging of Races*, 61–62.

3. For the hostile response to La Peyrère, see Kidd, *The Forging of Races*, 64–66, and Smith, *Nature, Human Nature*, 103–5. José de Acosta, Joannes de Laet, Thomas Gage, and Samuel Purchas proposed that Native Americans were descended from Tartars (Rubiés, "Hugo Grotius's Dissertation," 224–25; Cogley, "Ancestry of American Indians," 313). Hugo Grotius, meanwhile, suggested that American Indians from different parts of the Americas, North and South, were of varying ancestries, including Norse, African, and Chinese (Rubiés, 228–34).
4. Thorowgood, *Iewes in America*, 13. For more on Thorowgood's presentation of the Jewish origins theory and the debates it occasioned, see Cogley, "Ancestry of the American Indians" and "Peopling of Ancient America." Cogley notes that Thorowgood convinced Thomas Gage to abandon his original position and accept the lost tribes thesis ("Ancestry of American Indians," 326).
5. Stillingfleet, *Origines Sacræ*, 534, qtd. in Kidd, *The Forging of Races*, 65.
6. Godwyn, *Negro's & Indians Advocate*, 157, 165, 157.
7. Godwyn, *Negro's & Indians Advocate*, 71.
8. Mayhew, *Indian Converts*, 11.
9. [Dutton], *Letter to the Negroes*, 6.
10. Brown, *Reaper's Garden*, 204.
11. Sweet, *Bodies Politic*, 143.
12. See, for instance, Goetz, *Baptism of Early Virginia*, 6; Glasson, *Mastering Christianity*, 133; Kopelson, *Faithful Bodies*, 76, 99; Kidd, *Great Awakening*, 233.
13. As Kristina Bross observes, English imperialism in the Americas and Asia was framed as a vehicle of millennial progress from the very beginning. See *Future History*, 8–10, 28–36, 73–74, 93–99.
14. Hening, *Statutes at Large*, 450.
15. Barbados had already passed an act in 1697 that explicitly defined the island's freeholders as white (Gerbner, *Christian Slavery*, 74).
16. Greene, *Negro in Colonial New England*, 179.
17. Sweet, *Bodies Politic*, 62.
18. Sweet, *Bodies Politic*, 63.
19. Jordan, *White over Black*, 132.
20. Kopelson, *Faithful Bodies*, 191.
21. Shoemaker, *Strange Likeness*, 141–42.
22. Shoemaker, "How Indians Got Red," 627.
23. Block, *Colonial Complexions*, 2.
24. Stevens, *The Poor Indians*, 26.
25. Ira Berlin's *Generations of Captivity* provides tabular summaries of the expansion of slavery in colonial America and the United States (272–79).
26. Davis, *The Problem of Slavery*, 330.
27. Kopelson, *Faithful Bodies*, 7; Goetz, *Baptism of Early Virginia*, 139.
28. Gerbner, *Christian Slavery*, 3, 74–90. As Gerbner observes, Moravian churches in the Danish West Indies permitted African converts a greater degree of freedom, allowing them to serve as religious leaders, for instance (175–78). I discuss the Moravians' attitude to racial equality further below.
29. Glasson, *Mastering Christianity*, 75–110.

30. Jernegan, "Slavery and Conversion," 506.
31. Kopelson, *Faithful Bodies*, 122.
32. For an overview of the development of this theme in Protestant eschatology, see Crome, *Restoration of the Jews*. As Crome explains, those Puritans who looked for a national conversion of the people of Israel before the millennium were particularly closely influenced by the posthumously published biblical commentaries of the Anglican cleric Thomas Brightman (1562–1607).
33. Matar, *Islam in Britain*, 155–67.
34. As Richard Cogley notes, "by October 1656" Eliot would reject the theory (*John Eliot's Mission*, 96). For the impact of Sewall's acceptance of the Jewish origins thesis on his millennialism, see Smolinski, "Israel Redivivus," 378–80.
35. Mather, *The Negro Christianized*, 3. At the same time, Mather often bemoaned the cruelties of slave trafficking. See *Theopolis Americana*, 21–23, *Compassions Called for*, 22, and *India Christiana*, 47.
36. Curran, *The Anatomy of Blackness*, 224.
37. Mbembe, *Critique of Black Reason*, 53, 54.
38. Goetz outlines the development of this perspective in Virginia in the midst of the conflict between Jamestown and the Powhatan Confederacy in the 1620s (*Baptizing Early Virginia*, 70–74). Doubts about the possibility of truly converting Indians also proliferated in New England following King Philip's War (1675–1678). See Bross, *Dry Bones*, 146–85).
39. Cogley, *John Eliot's Mission*, 6–7.
40. Mather, *India Christiana*, 27, 29.
41. Brooks, *American Lazarus*, 59.
42. Goetz, *Baptism of Early Virginia*, 22.
43. Sewall, *Diary of Samuel Sewall*, 2:305.
44. *Boston News Letter* April 4, 1723. Qtd in Hutchins, "Sewall's Secret," n.p.
45. *Boston News Letter* April 15, 1723. Qtd in Hutchins, "Sewall's Secret," n.p.
46. Hutchins, "Sewall's Secret," n.p.
47. For this view, see Jordan, *White over Black*, 195–97, and Greene, *Negro in Colonial New England*, 50–51. More recently, Wendy Warren, Maurice Jackson, and Richard A. Bailey have characterized the text as a critique of slavery in general (*New England Bound*, 8; *Let This Voice Be Heard*, 44–45; *Race and Redemption*, 140–41).
48. Stievermann, "Genealogy of Races," 554 n. 64.
49. John Saffin, Adam's owner, would make exactly this point in his reply to Sewall ("Brief and Candid Answer," 254).
50. Sewall, *Selling of Joseph*, 3.
51. *Athenian Oracle*, 2.
52. See, for instance, Kopelson, *Faithful Bodies*, 110–11; Peterson, "The Selling of Joseph," 8; Stievermann, "Genealogy of Races," 564 n. 84; and Davis, *The Problem of Slavery*, 344–45.
53. Kopelson, *Faithful Bodies*, 110.
54. This conviction that the Americas would be central to the eschaton also led Sewall to be sympathetic to the theory that the lost tribes of Israel could be found among the continents' indigenous peoples (*Phaenomena*, 36, 41, 43). Yet he also proposed that

a significant number of the first Iberian settlers of the New World may have been Jewish conversos (41). The *Phaenomena* also takes particular interest in the existence of Jewish communities in Barbados, Jamaica, New York, and Brazil. It was likely, Sewall suggested, that those "*Jews*" would be "converted, before any great Numbers of the *Indians*" would "be brought in" (43).
55. Sewall, *Phaenomena*, 28.
56. For example, Sewall was excited to hear of the formation of the Company of Scotland, which planned to trade in the Americas, Africa, and India (*Letter-Book*, 1:227). Writing in 1700 to the Presbyterian ministers stationed at the short-lived colony of New Caledonia on the Isthmus of Panama, he noted that he now believed that the "Scots Company" would prove to be the "Angel" that poured the sixth of the seven vials mentioned in Revelation 15–16, the one that would dry up the Catholic Euphrates. Furthermore, he was struck by the prophetic significance of the "Synchronisme" between the founding of the Company in 1696 (of which he had then been unaware), and his own "Meditation" in that year on the subject of the prophecy of the sixth vial, which had led him to write the *Phaenomena*.
57. Sewall, *Letter-Book*, 1:325.
58. Sewall, *Letter-Book*, 2:80.
59. Sewall, *Phaenomena*, 2.
60. Zachary Hutchins notes that Sewall consistently approached the question of slavery by way of the international warfare that led to its proliferation. Only by examining the particulars of each relevant conflict and "the idiosyncratic circumstances" of associated enslavements could the Christian purchaser determine whether his investment was legal and ethical ("Sewall's Secret," n.p.).
61. Sewall, *Letter-Book*, 2:39. Qtd. in Hutchins, "Sewall's Secret," n.p.
62. Sewall, "Appendix," 14.
63. Sewall's conception of the relative importance of London over New England during the millennium comes across most clearly in the course of his argument that "*Englishmen* would meet with no Inconvenience" if the New Jerusalem were to be built in the Americas (*Phaenomena*, 49). All along their route, he explains, the denizens of English colonies would be "ready to meet them with a Welcom to the New World." If these pilgrims should care to take a brief side trip on their way back home, Sewall added, "our *New-English Tirzah*" would be eager to welcome them (50). For more on the comparatively peripheral position and role of New England in Sewall's millennium, see Sweet, "Local and Global," 215–16, 230–32.
64. Sewall, *Phaenomena*, 38.
65. Whiston, *A Supplement*, 121.
66. Sewall, *Selling of Joseph*, 3.
67. Sewall, *Diary of Samuel Sewall*, 2:329.
68. Sewall, *Diary of Samuel Sewall*, 2:143.
69. Sewall, *Diary of Samuel Sewall*, 2:143 n. 1.
70. On March 24, 1704, for instance, Sewall mourned the accidental death of "Arthur Mason's Negro" as a great loss, due to the man's "being faithfull and in his full strength" (*Diary of Samuel Sewall*, 2:96). On Christmas Day the following year, he noted the burial of Captain Belchar's "Coachman, a very good Servant" (2:150).

71. Sewall, *Diary of Samuel Sewall*, 3:394.
72. *New England Weekly Journal*, February 24, 1729, 2.
73. See, for instance, *Diary of Samuel Sewall*, 1:311, 379, 2:142, 333, 359. In these cases, Africans had been found guilty of serious crimes (or else killed themselves, as in the last example). Sewall also recorded acts of violence against black servants and slaves. See 3:32, for example.
74. Hutchins, "Sewall's Secret."
75. Sewall, *Phaenomena*, 69.
76. Sewall, *Phaenomena*, 49.
77. Sewall, *Diary of Samuel Sewall*, 2:44.
78. Sewall, *Diary of Samuel Sewall*, 2:43.
79. Sewall, as we have seen, interpreted most of Revelation's prophecies allegorically, or politically.
80. Mather, *The Negro Christianized*, 15–16.
81. Mather, *The Negro Christianized*, 16.
82. For a helpful summary of Mather's complex position on slavery, which recognized its contravention of natural law but ultimately affirmed that the enslavement of non-Christians was permitted by the Bible, see Stievermann, "Genealogy of Races," 551–54.
83. Mather observed that in large households, where the paterfamilias might not have time to teach his slaves himself, the task could be entrusted to his sons and daughters (*Negro Christianized*, 29).
84. Mather, *Negro Christianized*, 26–28. As Stievermann notes, Sewall tied himself to the contrary position (that Christian slaves were a legal contradiction in terms) by republishing the *Athenian Oracle* article on the subject ("Genealogy of Races," 557–58).
85. Mather, *Negro Christianized*, 20. For a discussion of the treatment of mastery and servitude in the text, see Ceppi, *Invisible Masters*, 147–54. Ceppi criticizes the "instrumental hypocrisy" of the tract's appeal to white masters (152). As she notes, Mather makes it clear that their efforts to instill Christian discipline in their black servants will be rewarded both spiritually and materially, regardless of whether the servants' soul are actually saved.
86. Mather, *Diary of Cotton Mather*, 1:564–65, 570.
87. Mather, *Diary of Cotton Mather*, 1:571, 570.
88. Mather, *India Christiana*, 47, 48.
89. Noyes, "To Rev. Cotton Mather," 484.
90. Noyes, "To Rev. Cotton Mather," 485.
91. Noyes, *New-Englands Duty*, 64.
92. Mather, *Negro Christianized*, 24–25. Calling for more attention to the spiritual lives of Boston's African servants in *Advice from the Watch Tower* (1713), Mather referenced Jeremiah 13:23. By accepting Christ as their "Saviour," the town's "*Ethiopians*" would experience "a *Change of Soul*, which is much better than a *Change of Skin*" (29). See also *Biblia Americana*, 1:697–99.

93. Mather, *Negro Christianized*, 24. In discussing how Native Americans first came to the New World themselves, Mather's *India Christiana* makes the related observation that "the *Biggest Part of Mankind*" have an "Olive *Complexion*" (22).
94. See *Brethren*, 7; *Coheleth*, 21; *Baptismal Piety*, 16; *Agricola*, 150; and *Triparadisus*, 221.
95. Mather, *Triparadisus*, 136.
96. Mather, *Biblia Americana*, 1:375.
97. For Stievermann's claim, see "Genealogy of Races," 515. Lorenzo Greene (*Negro in Colonial New England*, 285–86) and Winthrop Jordan (*White over Black*, 200–201) have been the most influential of the scholars he mentions. Dana D. Nelson, whom Stievermann does not cite, provides a nuanced view of the question of Mather's possible prejudice in *Word in Black and White*, 24–29.
98. Stievermann, "Genealogy of Races," 568, 532.
99. Stievermann, "Genealogy of Races," 564, 565.
100. Stievermann, "Genealogy of Races," 567.
101. Mather, *Triparadisus*, 313. Mather made this point in the course of an explanation as to why (to Samuel Sewall's chagrin) he had abandoned his former view that there would be a collective conversion of the Jewish people to Christianity before the millennium commenced. Now, he saw that any special relationship between God and Israel was defunct. "The Carnal *Children of Israelites*," he explained, "are to our *Holy One of Israel*, no better than *Children of Ethiopians*." As Reiner Smolinski points out, around a year after Mather's death, Sewall wrote to the latter's son Samuel, expressing his disappointment that Mather had changed his mind on the "general Calling or convertion of the Jews" (*Letter-Book*, 2:263, qtd. in Smolinski, "Introduction," 36).
102. Stievermann, "Genealogy of Races," 566.
103. Stievermann, "Genealogy of Races, 567, 566 n. 86.
104. Mather, *India Christiana*, 18–19.
105. Mather, *Terra Beata*, 35.
106. Mather, *Biblia Americana*, 5:96. Stievermann cites this passage in his study of Mather's Old Testament exegesis in the *Biblia Americana* (*Prophecy*, 339–40).
107. Mather, *Triparadisus*, 265.
108. Mather, *Triparadisus*, 274.
109. Mather, *Triparadisus*, 287.
110. Mather, *Problema Theologicum*, 422.
111. Mather, *Triparadisus*, 294. For Staynoe's claims see *A Short Inquiry*.
112. Mather's preferred theory was that Satan would summon "a Vast Number" of the "*Ghosts*" of the damned to form his army (*Triparadisus*, 294).
113. Mather, *A Faithful Man*, 23. Nearly twenty years later Mather made a comparable claim following the death of a sixteen-year-old member of his church, Rebekah Burnel: "MY Friends, There are Methods of PIETY to be taken, which if they be taken, Our *many days of darkneß*, will be Days wherein we shall see a *Marvellous Light*.... Our *days of darkneß*, will be all Spent, [and *never Spent*!] in the *Inheritance of the Saints in Light*" (*Light in Darkness*, 11–12).
114. Mather, *A Good Master*, 54.
115. Mather, *Negro Christianized*, 2–3.

116. Mather, *Negro Christianized*, 25. Though a proverb about the futility of attempting to wash off a dark complexion has been associated with Aesop ever since an attribution made by Erasmus in 1515, it is first attested in the work of Lucian, the second-century Syrian satirist (Massing, "Greek Proverb," 182–83). The earliest example of a full story illustrating the saying can be found in the fourth-century Aesopian fables of Aphthonius of Antioch, where we read of a man who believes that the black skin of the Ethiopian slave he has just purchased is not permanent, but is rather the result of the neglect of the slave's former master (183). The moral of the story was that it is extremely difficult to alter ingrained qualities or habits. Mather was likely also thinking of Jeremiah 13:23, which was "often cited in connection" with the Greek proverb (181): "Can the Ethiopian change his skin, or the leopard his spots? Then may ye also do good that are accustomed to do evil." Samuel Sewall quoted the first part of this verse in *The Selling of Joseph* (2).
117. Mather, *Advice*, 29.
118. Mather, *Small Offers*, 58.
119. Mather also described the decline of white saints from the high standard expected of them in terms of a metaphorical blackening of their souls (*Advice*, 8).
120. Mather, *Brethren*, 9.
121. Mather, *Brethren*, 10; *Negro Christianized*, 31.
122. See, for example, John Wynne in 1724 (Wynne, *A Sermon*, 9–10), Henry Egerton in 1728 (Egerton, *A Sermon*, 25), and John Thomas in 1746 (Thomas, *A Sermon*, 5).
123. Fleetwood, *A Sermon*, 15–16.
124. Glasson, *Mastering Christianity*, 130–31; Wilson, *Essay towards an Instruction*, xxii.
125. Wilson, *Essay towards an Instruction*, xxii.
126. Wilson, *Essay towards an Instruction*, 119.
127. Wilson, *Essay towards an Instruction*, 123.
128. Klingberg, *The Carolina Chronicle*, 102. The belief that slaves would occupy an inferior place in heaven (and would even be expected to labor there) was widely held among the enslavers of the nineteenth-century South. See Smith, *Heaven*, 89.
129. Klingberg, *The Carolina Chronicle*, 70.
130. Qtd. in Lambert, "Slave Readings," 15.
131. Glasson, *Mastering Christianity*, 112–13.
132. Glasson, *Mastering Christianity*, 119–21.
133. Dexter, *Biographical Sketches*, 1:240.
134. Mather, *Selected Letters*, 186.
135. Hawks and Perry, *Documentary History*, 1:253.
136. Hawks and Perry, *Documentary History*, 2:134.
137. Young, "The Soul-Sleeping System," 73.
138. Young, "The Soul-Sleeping System," 78, 79.
139. In the same year that Beach published *A Modest Enquiry*, noted mortalist Edmund Law (later bishop of Carlisle) presented the case for the doctrine "in two appendixes to the third edition of his *Considerations on the theory of religion*" (Young, "The Soul-Sleeping System," 74). Attempting to excuse his tract eight years after its publication, Beach claimed that his intention had been merely to prevent "the notion of the

soul's sleeping, or insensibility after death" from spreading in America (*A Friendly Expostulation*, 36).
140. Beach, *A Modest Enquiry*, 2, 35.
141. See Mather, *Triparadisus*, 227, 221.
142. Beach, *A Modest Enquiry*, 24.
143. Mappen, "Anglican Heresy," 470.
144. Beach, *Three Discourses*, 18.
145. Beach, *Three Discourses*, 11.
146. For Beach's opposition to revivalism, see Mappen, "Anglican Heresy," 467.
147. Baxter, *Christian Directory*, 3:557.
148. Godwyn, *Negro's & Indians Advocate*, 129, 128.
149. Godwyn, *Negro's & Indians Advocate*, 139–43.
150. Baxter, *Christian Directory*, 3:559.
151. Sweet, *Bodies Politic*, 111–12.
152. Jordan, *White over Black*, 211–12.
153. Stievermann, "Genealogy of Races," 561.
154. Berlin, *Generations of Captivity*, 68.
155. Kidd, *Great Awakening*, 214.
156. Fisher, *The Indian Great Awakening*, 84–106. Fisher explains that the number of affiliations declined rapidly from 1743, perhaps because converts "realized that their newfound association with Christianity did little to increase the respect of their Anglo neighbors [for them]" or "to halt the continual land loss" to white settlers (105).
157. See Kidd, *Great Awakening*, 213; Frey and Wood, *Come Shouting to Zion*, 80–117; and Simmons, "Great Awakening," 31–32. Katherine Gerbner broadly concurs, but also notes that scholars have tended to overemphasize "the significance of emotive worship" for black converts, and have consequently overlooked "the powerful draw of literacy that was associated with Protestant conversion both before and after the Great Awakening" (*Christian Slavery*, 11). Moreover, John Wood Sweet notes that in the wake of the revivals, Africans in New England "were also attracted in large numbers to even the most hierarchical and staid Anglican, Congregational, and Presbyterian congregations" (*Bodies Politic*, 123). While Linford Fisher does not rule out the attraction of evangelical "emotionalism" for Native Americans, he also notes that "Indians expected affiliation with Christianity to *do* something for them, whether spiritually, politically, or materially" (*The Indian Great Awakening*, 101). He therefore concludes that "Native affiliation" in the 1740s was "less . . . a momentous point of religious and cultural disjuncture for Indian communities" than it was "one more step in the ongoing, decades-old engagement with Christian ideas and Euroamerican culture, all with an eye toward community and cultural survival and revitalization."
158. See Winiarski, *Darkness Falls*, 184–86, and Seeman, "Justise," 395.
159. Brooks, *American Lazarus*, 8–9.
160. Brooks claims that one of the key tasks that this black resurrection theology had to accomplish was convincing white revivalists to live up to a Protestant "ideal" of

God's colorblindness (*American Lazarus*, 31). White evangelicals, she claims, were "more concerned with ecclesiastical expansion than [with] theologian introspection," and therefore "reiterated" the "negative valuation of race" they had inherited from the Reformed tradition. Like the established Protestant churches, they believed that race "did *not* signify salvation or damnation," and therefore did "*not* matter to God." This chapter, however, has shown that some eighteenth-century Protestants stopped short of such a position. While they held that Africans and other pagan peoples could and would be saved, they also wondered if that process might necessitate the transfiguration of the black body. George Whitefield's outreach to Africans, as I explain below, was informed by this question.

161. Brooks, *American Lazarus*, 26–27.
162. Brooks, *American Lazarus*, 30–32.
163. Kidd, *Great Awakening*, 228; Brooks, *American Lazarus*, 30.
164. Sensbach, *Rebecca's Revival*, 189.
165. Sensbach, *Rebecca's Revival*, 92–100.
166. Qtd. in Sensbach, *Rebecca's Revival*, 125.
167. Whitefield, "Inhabitants of Maryland," 15–16.
168. Whitefield, "Inhabitants of Maryland," 16.
169. Wesley, *Thoughts upon Slavery*, 51, 52.
170. In a letter sent to the South Carolina government, Bryan warned that "an Angel of Light" had told him of the imminent destruction of Charleston by slaves (qtd. in Schmidt, "The Grand Prophet," 243). Although Bryan repented of his radicalism shortly afterward, opponents of the revivals were quick to seize on the episode as evidence of their politically dangerous nature. See Schmidt, "The Grand Prophet," 244–45, and Kidd, *Great Awakening*, 218–19.
171. Whitefield, "Inhabitants of Maryland," 15.
172. Whitefield, *Works*, 2:204. For more on Whitefield's changing attitudes toward slavery, see Parr, *Inventing George Whitefield*, 61–80.
173. [Dutton], *Letter to the Negroes*, 6, 9.
174. Gronniosaw, *Narrative of the Life*, 17, 41.
175. Hammon, *Collected Works*, 46.
176. Hammon, *Collected Works*, 41.
177. Wheatley, *Poems on Various Subjects*, 13.
178. Wheatley, *Poems on Various Subjects*, 10.
179. See Schieck, "Phillis Wheatley's Appropriation," 135–36, also Shields, *Poetics of Liberation*, 107; O'Neale, "A Slave's Subtle War," 150; and Balkun, "Construction of Otherness," 129–30.
180. Wheatley, *Poems on Various Subjects*, 9.
181. O'Neale, "A Slave's Subtle War," 154.
182. O'Neale, "A Slave's Subtle War," 154; Wheatley, *Poems on Various Subjects*, 9.
183. Hammon, *Collected Works*, 117, 101.
184. See O'Neale, *Biblical Beginnings*; Richards, "Nationalist Themes"; and Guruswamy, "Jupiter Hammon's Regards."
185. Richards, "Nationalist Themes," 133.

186. Hammon, *Collected Works*, 116.
187. Hammon, *Collected Works*, 117.
188. Hammon, *Collected Works*, 116.
189. Hammon, *Collected Works*, 113, 112.
190. Sancho, *Letters*, 112.
191. Sancho, *Letters*, 125.
192. Sancho, *Letters*, 126.
193. For more on Sancho's cultivation of sensibility, as well as the influence of his correspondence with Laurence Sterne on his writing, see Ellis, "Ignatius Sancho's Letters."
194. Sancho, *Letters*, 159.
195. Sancho, *Letters*, 124. English and Euro-American proponents of universal salvation, by contrast, tended to oppose abolitionism, linking the eventual redemption of all sinners after death to *gradual* social reform in the present. See Bressler, *Universalist Movement in America*, 85–88.
196. Caretta, "Cugoano, Ottobah," n.p.
197. Cugoano, *Thoughts and Sentiments*, 45–47.
198. This latter interpretation is supported by Cugoano's criticism of "slave-holders, in the West-Indies" who argue that an African should not be baptized "without giving him a Christian name" (147). "Christianity," Cugoano insisted, "does not require that we should be deprived of our own personal name, or the name of our ancestors."
199. Hall, *A Charge*, 5.
200. Hall, *A Charge*, 5. Cugoano, meanwhile, predicted that if Britain were to abolish the slave trade and free all the enslaved people in its overseas colonies, it would profit handsomely from a "very considerable ... trade" with Africa (*Thoughts and Sentiments*, 133). He described this prospective future in quasi-millennial terms, predicting "blessing and plenty in abundance" for a British Empire without slavery (138). But if Britons chose otherwise, they would face providential punishment: "loss of territory and destructive wars, earthquakes and dreadful thunders, storms and hurricanes, blasting and destructive insects, inclement and unfruitful seasons, national debt and oppressions, poverty and distresses of individuals" (101–2).
201. Hall, *A Charge*, 18.
202. Apess, *Five Christian Indians*, 60.
203. Apess, *Five Christian Indians*, 58.
204. While Apess understandably focusses on issues confronting him and other Native people in New England (resistance to Indian ministers, laws against the marriage of Natives and whites ["An Indian's Looking Glass," 58–59]), he also condemns the enslavement of Africans (56), as well as all prejudice based on skin color. "If black or red skins, or any other skin of color is disgraceful to God," Apess notes, "it appears that he has disgraced himself a great deal—for he has made fifteen colored people to one white, and placed them here upon this earth" (55).
205. Seeman, *Death in the New World*, 188.
206. Ball, *Slavery*, 219–22.
207. Katy Chiles provides a useful summary of this difference in racial thinking between the centuries: "If we have understood nineteenth-century and later racial logic to be

'white is white because it is not black,' we should understand the eighteenth-century racial logic to run closer along the lines of 'white is white for now because it is no longer nor not yet black'" (*Transformable Race*, 26).
208. Sidbury, *Becoming African in America*, 178.
209. Sidbury, *Becoming African in America*, 201–2.
210. Not only did northern states deny African Americans their political and legal rights (Berlin, *Generations of Captivity*, 231–32), but they also ensured that their black inhabitants "lived apart from most white people ... in the least desirable areas" (233).
211. Gin Lum, *Damned Nation*, 127–35.
212. Douglass, *My Bondage*, 286.
213. Hickman, *Black Prometheus*, 160. In *Narrative of the Life*, his first autobiography, Douglass describes his triumph over Covey in very similar, but less equivocal terms: "It was a glorious resurrection, from the tomb of slavery, to the heaven of freedom" (65).
214. Walker, *Appeal*, 83.
215. Hickman, *Black Prometheus*, 68.

Chapter 4

1. *New-England Weekly Journal*, March 2, 1730, [2].
2. *New-England Weekly Journal*, March 2, 1730, [2]; Prince, *Death of Samuel Sewall*, 12.
3. *New-England Weekly Journal*, March 9, 1730, [2].
4. Prince, *Vade Mecum*, iv.
5. Prince, *Six Sermons*, 27.
6. Prince, *Extraordinary Events*, 35, 34, 35.
7. Prince, *Six Sermons*, 28.
8. Prince, *Strange Appearance*, 6, 11.
9. Prince, *Strange Appearance*, 11–12. For Whiston's cometary explanation of the Conflagration, see *New Theory*, 442–52. Burnet advances his volcanic theory in *Theory of the Earth*, 2:52–65.
10. Prince, *Strange Appearance*, 13.
11. This term is taken from *The Prism of Piety*, John Corrigan's study of Colman and his allies. Corrigan argues that this group was essentially liberal and strongly influenced by Anglican latitudinarians John Tillotson and Edward Stillingfleet (17–23). Thomas Kidd, however, casts the ministers as irenic, orthodox evangelicals ("From Puritan to Evangelical," 52–59). While they may have been "less inclined toward extensive apocalyptic speculations" than the Mathers and other traditionalists (*The Protestant Interest*, 145), they continued to find millennial significance in Britain's wars against her Roman Catholic enemies (142–46). Mark Valeri, meanwhile, steers closer to Corrigan's characterization, noting the new generation's opposition to the "sacramental orthodoxy of [Samuel] Willard and Cotton Mather," and emphasizing their "progressive, tolerant, and ecumenical practices, including liberal access to the Lord's Supper" (*Heavenly Merchandize*, 200).
12. Valeri, *Heavenly Merchandize*, 57–73.

13. Valeri, *Heavenly Merchandize*, 217–19.
14. Taylor, *A Secular Age*, 539–93.
15. Casanova, "Religion," 214.
16. Sloterdijk, *World Interior of Capital*, 29, 31.
17. Sloterdijk, *World Interior of Capital*, 29.
18. Taylor, *A Secular Age*, 553.
19. Following Weber, Taylor links this "excarnation" of Christianity to the Protestant Calvinist tradition (*A Secular Age*, 554). This argument overlooks the transcendent power attributed to the sabbath in Puritan culture (see my discussion of Thomas Shepard's soteriology above, pp. 33–38).
20. Mather, "To the Reader," i–ii.
21. Hill, *Old South Church*, 1:394–95.
22. Mather, *Diary of Cotton Mather*, 2:505.
23. Prince, *God Brings to Haven*, 7, 8.
24. Prince, *Elder John Prince*, 3.
25. Valeri, *Heavenly Merchandize*, 220, 223.
26. Prince, *God Brings to Haven*, 9, 8, 10, 11.
27. Corrigan, *Prism of Piety*, 66.
28. Wadsworth, *Benefits of Good Conscience*, 34.
29. Wadsworth, *Mutual Love and Peace*, 2, 22.
30. Colman, *Government & Improvement*, 22, 27–28.
31. Prince, *Pious Cry*, 16.
32. Prince, *Three Sermons*, 3, 8.
33. Prince, *Morning Health*, 7, 8.
34. Prince, *God Destroyeth*, 1, 19.
35. See Mayhew, *Sermon Preached at Boston*, 17–20, and Mather, *Funeral Discourse*, 9.
36. Here Prince likely had the manner of Frederick's untimely death in mind. Medical consensus at the time held that the royal heir (a keen sportsman) had died due to complications arising from the impact of a tennis or cricket ball.
37. Prince, *God Destroyeth*, 6, 5.
38. Here Prince was primarily drawing on Thomas Burnet's explanation of the Flood. See Burnet, *Theory of the Earth*, 127–38.
39. Prince, *Christ Abolishing Death*, 11–12.
40. Petty, *Several Essays*, 42.
41. Prince, *Christ Abolishing Death*, 12.
42. See Graunt, *Natural and Political Observations*, 66–70.
43. Petty, *Several Essays*, 25, 41.
44. See Lewis, "William Petty's Anthropology," 284–87.
45. Prince, *Christ Abolishing Death*, 33, 34.
46. Colman, *Death and the Grave*, 3, 5.
47. Colman, *Death and the Grave*, 9.
48. Colman, *Death and the Grave*, 10.
49. Foxcroft, *Death the Destroyer*, 2.
50. Pemberton, *True Servant*, 19, 20.
51. Pemberton, *Funeral Sermon*, 77.

52. Kidd, *The Protestant Interest*, 145.
53. Foxcroft, "To the Reader," ii. Foxcroft went on to suggest that a passage from Cotton Mather's *Theopolis Americana*, published over thirty years previously, had predicted the revivals: "Ye, the DAY IS AT HAND, when that Voice will be heard, *Put on thy beautiful Garments*, O America, *the holy City!*" (ii, quoting Mather, *Theopolis Americana*, 46).
54. Foxcroft, "To the Reader," iv.
55. Prince, *Christ Abolishing Death*, 8n.
56. Prince, *Six Sermons*, 140, 141, 140.
57. Prince, *Six Sermons*, 142.
58. *The Wonderful Narrative*, 59–90.
59. *The Wonderful Narrative*, 97. Edwin Gaustad argues that Charles Chauncy, minister of Boston's First Church, was the author of this appendix, which, he claims, "manifests the same style, vocabulary, [and] most of all the same over-cautious self-justification that characterise Chauncy in this period" ("Charles Chauncy," 127).
60. *The Wonderful Narrative*, 97.
61. Winiarski, *Darkness Falls*, 248–60. The letter to a Boston gentleman that comprises the main section of *The Wonderful Narrative* was sent from New Haven in January 1742. This means that it is possible that the author may have witnessed an incident that had taken place there the previous November, when two women had collapsed and "continued in a Sort of Extasie" for almost a week (Chauncy, *Seasonable Thoughts*, 129). When they returned to full consciousness, the women attested that they "*had been to Heaven,* [and] *had seen the Book of Life,* [with] *the Names of many Persons of their Acquaintance wrote in it.*"
62. *The Wonderful Narrative*, 52–53; Schwartz, *The French Prophets*, 113.
63. See Schwartz, *The French Prophets*, 120–23.
64. *The Wonderful Narrative*, 59.
65. *The Wonderful Narrative*, 51.
66. *The Wonderful Narrative*, 91–92.
67. Prince, "It Being Earnestly Desired," n.p.
68. Timothy Gloege argues that Prince's efforts to present "a broad evangelical unity" through the magazine led him to print more and more of these radical narratives over time ("Trouble with *Christian History*," 164). Despite its moderate remit, therefore, *Christian History* "reported a revival whose later turn was characterized by enthusiasm and excess" (162).
69. *Christian History*, 2:387, 390.
70. *Christian History*, 2:358–74, 285–98. The journal followed Tennent's narrative with a summary of the revival of religion at Freehold, New Jersey, written by his brother William (2:298–310).
71. See Perkins, *Golden Chaine*, 599; Baxter, *Call to the Unconverted*, 128; Cotton, *The Churches Resurrection*, 28–29; Mather, *The Widow of Naim*, 23.
72. Whitefield, *Exhortation*, 7.
73. Whitefield, *The Marriage of Cana*, 23–24.
74. Tennent, *Solemn Warning*, 144. In Ezekiel's vision, God commands the prophet to give life to a valley full of bones. God then explains that the bones represent the people of Israel, and their resurrection the Israelites' arrival in the promised land.

75. Whitefield, *Five Sermons*, 135.
76. *Christian History*, 2:293.
77. *Christian History*, 2:293, 294.
78. Butler, *Awash in a Sea*, 183, 185.
79. Whitefield, *Wise and Foolish Virgins*, 29.
80. Whitefield, *Duty of Gospel Minister*, 6.
81. Tennent, *Danger of Unconverted Ministry*, 30.
82. Tennent, *Danger of Unconverted Ministry*, 22.
83. *Boston Evening-Post*, September 6, 1742, [1].
84. Kidd, *The Great Awakening*, 146.
85. Kidd, *The Great Awakening*, 144.
86. Croswell, *What Is Christ*, 31.
87. Kidd, *The Great Awakening*, 164–67.
88. Whitefield, "Unpublished Journal," 317.
89. Bridenbaugh, *Itinerarium*, 120. Hamilton, a Scottish-born doctor from Maryland, traveled through New England, New York, and the Middle Colonies in 1744. He learned of Woodbury in Salem through Justice Stephen Sewall, nephew of Samuel Sewall.
90. *Boston Gazette*, July 24, 1744.
91. Backus, *Diary of Isaac Backus*, 1:294, qtd. in Winiarski, *Darkness Falls*, 405.
92. Stiles, *Extracts from the Itineraries*, 418.
93. Walett, "Shadrack Ireland," 548.
94. Winiarski, *Darkness Falls*, 426.
95. Erik Seeman sees the "uniformity of beliefs among Immortalist groups separated by dozens of miles" as evidence of organized "proselytization" (*Pious Persuasions*, 141). For him, Prentice and Ireland "were [the] likely leaders" of this effort.
96. Prince's account of the revival in Boston also downplayed the prevalence of biblical "*Impulses*"—episodes in which a scriptural passage suddenly came to a believer's mind, supposedly through the direct intervention of the Holy Spirit (*Christian History*, 2:413).
97. Gloege, "Trouble with *Christian History*," 138–39.
98. See, for instance, *Christian History*, 2:378, 384, 386, 391, 395, 396.
99. Prince, *Six Sermons*, 70, 69–79.
100. Prince, *Six Sermons*, 84, 85.
101. The sermon, on Proverbs 8:32, appears in an octavo volume of three fair-copy manuscript tracts on death and dying, held by the American Antiquarian Society in the Prince Family Papers collection. Prince was predeceased by three of his four daughters: Grace, the youngest, died in 1742, after living only a week; Deborah died at the age of twenty in July 1744, Mercy in 1752 at twenty-six. The sermon was most likely occasioned by this last death. Prince had already published another address on Deborah's passing, in which he sketches her religious life in some detail, outlining her conversion in December 1740, a few months after seeing George Whitefield preach for the first time (*Sovereign God*, 22–23). Moreover, the fact that the second sermon in the volume concerns the death of Prince's brother Nathan in 1749 suggests that 1752 is the more likely date of composition for this, the third text.

102. Prince, *Three Sermons*, [86].
103. Prince, *Sovereign God*, 23, 21.
104. *Christian History*, 2:392.
105. Prince, *Six Sermons*, 60.
106. Brainerd, "Preface," v, vi. Jonathan Edwards would later quote much of this preface, including this portion, in an appendix to his *Life of David Brainerd*, published in 1749.
107. Whitefield, *A New Heart*, 34.
108. Tennent, *Solemn Warning*, 144.
109. Seeman, *Pious Persuasions*, 134; Wallet, "Shadrack Ireland," 548. Seeman notes that although Sarah Prentice was suspected of using the concept of spiritual fraternity as a cover for free love, in fact she seems to have "opt[ed] for celibacy as a way to gain purity" (140).
110. Barbara Lacey, *The World of Hannah Heaton*, 10, qtd. in Winiarski, *Darkness Falls*, 237.
111. Whitefield, *Some Remarks*, 29.
112. *Christian History*, 2:405.
113. *Christian History*, 2:406.
114. See, for instance, Whitefield, *Nature and Necessity*; Tennent and Tennent, *Nature of Regeneration Opened*, 29–47. These tracts both note that conversion is a spiritual change and does not involve either the physical transfiguration of believers or the alteration of their soul's "essence" (Whitefield, 6–7; Tennent and Tennent, 30–31). Ireland, Woodbury, Prentice, and other immortalists would later insist that true regeneration did in fact necessitate material transformation of this order.
115. Prince, *Six Sermons*, 88.
116. Prince, *Six Sermons*, 91.
117. Bushman, *The Great Awakening*, 50–51; Hill, *Old South Church*, 1:539, 540. For more on Nathaniel Wardell Jr., the man in question, see Winiarski, *Darkness Falls*, 323–24. Wardell would be finally excommunicated from the Old South in 1748.
118. Chauncy, *Seasonable Thoughts*, 354, 371–76.
119. *Christian History*, 2:380.
120. *Christian History*, 2:377–80. See Gloege, "Trouble with *Christian History*," 143.
121. Edwards, *Apocalyptic Writings*, 309. In January 1743, religious societies in Edinburgh had proposed a similar endeavor. Their plan was printed in the *Christian History* issue for May 14, 1743, alongside a letter to Benjamin Colman from minister John Wilson, describing the progress of the revivals in Scotland. See *Christian History*, 1:86–87.
122. Qtd. in Hill, *Old South Church*, 1:593.
123. Winiarski, *Darkness Falls*, 16.
124. Winiarski estimates that around "one hundred New England congregations fractured into competing factions between 1742 and 1760" (*Darkness Falls*, 377). By the 1770s, meanwhile, there were "as many as twenty-five thousand" Anglicans, "organized into seventy-four congregations administered by approximatively fifty [Society for the Propagation of the Gospel] missionaries" (449). For Prince's brothers, see *Darkness Falls*, 452.

125. Hill, *Old South Church*, 2:32–40.
126. Prince, *Psalms*, iii, ii.
127. Qtd. in Winsor, *The Prince Library*, ix.
128. Torrey, *Brief Discourse*, iii.
129. Torrey, *Brief Discourse*, i, ii.
130. Prince, "Preface," iv.
131. See Davidson, *Logic of Millennial Thought*, 196–97.
132. Tennent, *The Good Mans Character*, 23.
133. Mayhew, *Practical Discourses*, 370.
134. Bloch, *Visionary Republic*, 22–50.
135. Torrey, *Brief Discourse*, 37.
136. Romans 8:18.
137. Edwards, *Work of Redemption*, 5–6.
138. Zakai, *Edwards's Philosophy of History*, 224–25.
139. Edwards, *Work of Redemption*, 435. Edwards also speculated that America had only been populated following the "wonderful success of the gospel that was the first hundred years after Christ" (434). The devil, "seeing the gospel spread so fast, and fearing that his heathen kingdom would be wholly overthrown through the world, led a people from the other continent into America, that they might be quite out of the reach of the gospel that here he might quietly possess them and reign over them as their god."
140. Edwards, *Work of Redemption*, 352.
141. Edwards, *Apocalyptic Writings*, 332.
142. Edwards, *Apocalyptic Writings*, 339, 338, 345.
143. Torrey, *Brief Discourse Concerning Futurities*, 47.
144. Edwards, *Work of Redemption*, 527.
145. Edwards, *The "Miscellanies," 501-832*, 382.
146. Prince, *Six Sermons*, 28. Prince arrived at this figure by following the common eschatological principle that each year mentioned in biblical prophecies actually stood for 360 years (there were 360 days in the ancient year).
147. Prince, *Six Sermons*, 29.
148. Prince, *Six Sermons*, 34.
149. Prince, *Funeral Sermon*, 14.
150. Prince, *Funeral Sermon*, 14–15. In *Christ Abolishing Death* (1736), Prince had pointed to certain biblical passages that suggested that the light of heaven could sometimes be rendered more clearly visible to mortal earth. The apostles Stephen and Paul, and John of Patmos had all seen visions of celestial light (30).
151. Mather, *Cœlestinus*, 2:146.
152. Prince, *Six Sermons*, 33.
153. Prince, *Six Sermons*, 35.
154. Prince, *Six Sermons*, 27.
155. This figure includes four people admitted on December 28, 1755. It is possible that the surge in applications was connected to the earthquake that hit Boston November 1755. See Hill, *Old South Church*, 2:28–29.
156. Bloch, *Visionary Republic*, 77–87.

157. This nationalist millennialism found its classic expression in the preaching of Presbyterian evangelical Lyman Beecher (1775–1863). In *A Plea for the West* (1835), Beecher urged Americans to recognize their nation's "high calling"—its providential destiny "to lead the way in the moral and political emancipation of the world" (11), and thereby bring about the millennium (9–10). To fulfill this potential, he argued, the United States needed to secure the west for Protestantism through establishing churches and seminaries on the frontier (18–35) and prevent further immigration by superstitious Catholics who were unacquainted "with the principles of our government" (115). For more on Beecher's anti-Catholic rhetoric and its relationship to the Texas Revolution of 1835 to 1836 and the Mexican-American War of 1846 to 1848, see Pinheiro, *The Missionaries of Republicanism*, 15–35.
158. Winchester, *Prophecies That Remain*, 158, 189–207.
159. *Doctrine and Covenants*, 130:9. For more on the role of scrying stones in early Mormonism, see Brown, *In Heaven*, 81–83.
160. Francaviglia, "Geography and Mormon Identity," 427.
161. Darby, *Seven Lectures*, 26.
162. Darby believed that the First Resurrection of deceased saints would take place at the same time as this Rapture. Both the living and the dead would "go to meet the Lord in the air" before the tribulation began (*Seven Lectures*, 27).
163. Darby, *Seven Lectures*, 14; Smith, "Revelation Book 1," 70; "Discourse, 5 January 1841," [1].
164. Bloch, *Visionary Republic*, 230. James Moorhead, on the other hand, argues that after the Civil War, reform-oriented "postmillennialism" underwent a precipitous decline, as a supernaturalist "premillennialism," which held that Christ would return suddenly and in person at the beginning of the thousand years, emerged as the standard model of American millennialism ("Erosion of Postmillennialism"). Crawford Gribben's history of transatlantic evangelical millennialism, meanwhile, claims that "a new system of premillennial thinking" began "to dominate the evangelical imagination" from "the 1830s onwards" (*Evangelical Millennialism*, 72).
165. For more on changing attitudes toward resurrection in nineteenth-century America, see Brown, *In Heaven*, 56–59, and Laderman, *Sacred Remains*, 51–55 and 172–73.
166. Sloterdijk, *World Interior of Capital*, 148.
167. Sloterdijk, *World Interior of Capital*, 147–48.
168. It should be noted that Mormonism is an important exception in this respect. Joseph Smith divided heaven into three levels, the terrestrial, telestial, and celestial. This last, highest, plane, would be reserved for those who were members of the Mormon church, or else had been posthumously "adopted" into it through the ritual of baptism for the dead (Brown, *In Heaven*, 219–28). Samuel Brown characterizes this aspect of Smith's thought as a return to Puritanism's covenantal soteriology in an era when most Protestants "focused less on covenant or election and more on the individual experience of conversion" (210).

Chapter 5

1. [Franklin], and [Dashwood], *An Abridgement*, n.p.
2. In a 1785 letter to his London friend Granville Sharp, Franklin recalled that editing the catechism and the Psalms was his contribution to the project. Benjamin Franklin to Granville Sharp, July 5, 1785.
3. Thomas Jefferson to William Short, October 31, 1819, 391 n. 3.
4. Jefferson had hoped to publish his first attempt to edit the Gospels—a pamphlet he completed in 1804 titled "The Philosophy of Jesus of Nazareth extracted from the account of his life and doctrines as given by Mathew [sic], Mark, Luke, & John." See Bryan, "Jefferson's Scissor Edit," 19–20.
5. For attacks on Jefferson's assumed lack of faith before, during, and after the 1800 election, see Schulz, "Jefferson's Religion."
6. Paine, *The Age of Reason*, 6.
7. Paine also clarified this point at the beginning of the first part of *The Age of Reason*, where he professed his "hope for happiness beyond this life," as well as his belief in "one God, and no more" (8).
8. Paine, *The Age of Reason: Part the Second*, 79.
9. Paine, *The Age of Reason: Part the Second*, 81–82.
10. Thomas Jefferson to François Van der Kemp, January 11, 1825.
11. Blumenberg, *Legitimacy*, 137.
12. Blumenberg, *Legitimacy*, 138.
13. Blumenberg, *Legitimacy*, 30.
14. Alyssa Sepinwall notes that until the middle of the eighteenth century in France *régénération* had been a "relatively rare word" associated with God's transformation of the believer through baptism and resurrection (*Abbé Grégoire*, 57). Then, under the influence of d'Alembert's employment of the term in the preface to the *Encyclopédie* (58), and Charles Bonnet's adaption of it in his naturalist writings (59), political philosophers started to use *régénération* to refer to humanity's ability to remake the social and natural worlds in its own image. Unsurprisingly, this usage of the word proved popular during the French Revolution, when many radicals invested it with an "anti-Christian" significance (110).
15. Schlereth, *An Age of Infidels*, 8; Grasso, *Skepticism and American Faith*, 14–15.
16. Seeman, *Speaking with the Dead*, 189–228.
17. Thomas Jefferson to Levi Lincoln, October 25, 1802.
18. John Adams to Thomas Jefferson, May 6, 1816.
19. English himself had in 1813 published a book that cast doubt on Christ's resurrection. The "written testimony" of the four Gospels on the matter, he argued, was so "contradictory" that it "would not be received in a modern court of Justice to settle *the fact about a debt of five dollars*" (*Grounds of Christianity Examined*, 148–49).
20. John Adams to Thomas Jefferson, March 10, 1823.
21. In the same letter, Adams jokingly wished that Jefferson, then recovering from a broken arm, would continue to thrive until he felt inclined to complain of his longevity, as Calvin had ("Mon dieu Jusque au quand Lord how long!"). Jefferson's reply

reiterated his contempt for the Swiss Reformer (of which the more religious Adams was well aware): "The wishes expressed, in your last favor, that I may continue in life and health until I become a Calvinist, at least in his exclamation of 'mon Dieu! jusque à quand'! would make me immortal. I can never join Calvin in addressing his god. he was indeed an Atheist, which I can never be; or rather his religion was Dæmonism. if ever man worshipped a false god, he did." It was better "to believe in no god at all," he added, than to suppose as Calvinists did that "without a revelation, there would not be sufficient proof of the being of a god." That opinion gave "a great handle to Atheism" insofar as it overlooked natural proofs of the universe's intelligent design, and condemned the great majority of humanity who did not accept the Christian revelation to hell. There would come a time, Jefferson claimed, when the doctrines of that revelation, including "the mystical generation of Jesus, by the supreme being as his father in the womb of a virgin," would "be classed with the fable of the generation of Minerva in the brain of Jupiter."

22. Winthrop, *Attempt to Translate*, 13.
23. Winthrop, *Systematic Arrangement*, 10.
24. Winthrop, *Systematic Arrangement*, 11.
25. Winthrop, *Attempt to Translate*, 70.
26. Winthrop, *Attempt to Translate*, 71–79.
27. Winthrop, *Attempt to Translate*, 5.
28. Winthrop, *Systematic Arrangement*, 43.
29. Winthrop, *Systematic Arrangement*, 16.
30. Barlow, *The Columbiad*, 26.
31. Barlow, *The Vision of Columbus*, 257; *The Columbiad*, 381.
32. Barlow, *The Columbiad*, 355. Richard Cogley provides a helpful overview of this tradition in Protestant exegesis and its relationship to the anticipated conversion of the Jewish people ("Fall of Ottoman Empire").
33. Barlow, *The Columbiad*, 348.
34. Barlow, *The Columbiad*, 378, 381. Compare *The Vision of Columbus*, 256–58.
35. Barlow, *The Columbiad*, 379. Compare *The Vision of Columbus*, 256.
36. Barlow, *The Vision of Columbus*, 242n.
37. Barlow, *The Columbiad*, 380.
38. Barlow, *The Columbiad*, 376. Compare *The Vision of Columbus*, 254.
39. Barlow, *The Columbiad*, 35–36. Compare *The Vision of Columbus*, 33–34.
40. For more on how Barlow's blending of Anglo- and Latin American perspectives challenged Old World conceptions of history, see Bauer, "Colonial Discourse."
41. The question of Barlow's personal faith (or lack of it) became a matter of public debate in the controversy that followed the publication of *The Columbiad* in 1809. In late summer, American newspapers printed a letter from the French Catholic revolutionary Henri Grégoire that criticized the illustration that depicted the scene of delegates to the imagined world congress throwing the cross at the feet of the statue of humanity's genius (Buel, *Joel Barlow*, 296). In his reply, Barlow claimed that having been born in New England, he "adhere[d]" to "the sect of the puritans" (*Letter to Henry Gregoire*, 4) which forbade the use of religious "emblems" (5). For

this reason, he claimed, he had not realized how much offense the concept of casting down the cross would cause to Roman Catholics (6). In response, Theodore Dwight, the brother of Barlow's former friend, Yale theologian Timothy Dwight, mocked the poet's lukewarm profession of Protestant identity: "If Mr. Barlow has nothing more of the Christian to boast of, than that he was *born among the puritans*, and still *adheres* to them, his title ... is hardly worth the trouble of renunciation" (qtd. in Buel, *Joel Barlow*, 299).

42. For details of Hopkins's framing of the millennium, see Bloch, *Visionary Republic*, 101–2.
43. Hopkins, *Treatise on the Millennium*, 260.
44. See Barlow, *The Columbiad*, 80–132; *The Vision of Columbus*, 65–126.
45. At the same time, Barlow suggested that Anglo-American culture was particularly well suited to producing free, secular, and republican citizens. In an endnote to book 5 of *The Columbiad* (which discusses the mustering of the Continental Congress), he insisted that he should "not be suspected of laying any stress on the mere circumstance of lineage of birth, as relating either to families or nations" (418). Yet he also observed the "undeniable act" that "under a parity of circumstances, such as climate, soil and productions," England's colonies had "flourished far better" than those of her European rivals. He credited that success to the "civil, political and religious institutions" of the mother country. The English had enjoyed "liberty of the press" and "trial by jury in open court." They expected "accountability" from "public agents" and had "some voice in the election of legislators." Consequently, "Their minds [were] prepared to open and expand themselves as occasion [might] offer." Having been "transplanted" to "an unlimited and unoccupied country," this flexibility could now produce a new, more democratic and equal way of living.
46. Barlow, *The Columbiad*, 382, 44, 43. Compare *The Vision of Columbus*, 258, 38.
47. Barlow, *The Columbiad*, 364.
48. Barlow, *The Columbiad*, 366. Compare *The Vision of Columbus*, 247.
49. Barlow, *The Columbiad*, 368.
50. Barlow, *The Columbiad*, 370. Compare *The Vision of Columbus*, 250.
51. Barlow, *The Columbiad*, 374; *The Vision of Columbus*, 252.
52. Freneau, *Poems of Philip Freneau*, 378–79.
53. *The Rising Glory of America*, a poem Freneau composed with Hugh Henry Brackenridge for the Princeton commencement of September 1771, anticipates this suggestion that American reality will outstrip the eschatological fantasies of the Old World. Freneau and Brackenridge provide their audience with a description of the "Millennium," when "a new Jerusalem" will be "sent down from heaven" and Christ and his saints will "live and reign on earth" (25). However, this comparatively brief account of John's vision in Revelation is overshadowed by the much longer description of the commercial, scientific, and political progress of the Anglo-American people, which is characterized as a secular millennium—"The world at peace, and all her tumults o'er, / The blissful prelude to Emanuel's reign."
54. Franklin to Joseph Priestly, February 8, 1780.

55. Eight years later, Franklin made the same prediction to Boston minister John Lathrop. By 1788, however, he was apparently more optimistic about the speed of scientific discovery, hypothesizing that it would take only "two or three Centuries" for humanity to enjoy the same lifespans as "the Patriarchs in Genesis" (Franklin to John Lathrop, May 31, 1788).
56. Franklin to Jacques Barbeu-Dubourg [end of April 1773?].
57. Jefferson to William G. Munford, June 18, 1799.
58. Jefferson, *Notes*, 175.
59. Jefferson to James Madison, September 6, 1789.
60. Jefferson to Benjamin Waterhouse, June 26, 1822.
61. Jefferson to William G. Munford, June 18, 1799. As Ari Helo points out, Jefferson did not have a fixed conception of the end point of human progress, nor did he think that his own philosophy would be universally adopted in future. Instead, he was primarily motivated by "the achievement and maintenance of free government, resting on enlightened majority opinion," which he believed would allow the future "to retain its open-mindedness" (*Morality of a Slaveholder*, 39).
62. D'Elia, "Philosopher," 20–35.
63. D'Elia, "Philosopher," 35–51.
64. D'Elia, "Philosopher," 9–20.
65. Rush, *Enquiry into the Influence*, 17.
66. Philippians 3:21.
67. See Bloch, *Visionary Republic*, 202–13; Israel, *The Expanding Blaze*, 321–60.
68. Woods, "Correspondence," 32.
69. Woods, "Correspondence," 35.
70. Woods, "Correspondence," 35.
71. Arthur Scherr, for example, claims that Jefferson was "an Epicurean deistic pagan, whose only concept of 'afterlife' was the end of life: death" ("Jefferson versus the Historians," 108). Ari Helo, on the other hand, argues that Jefferson did believe in life after death, even if he did not think that "human happiness entails such a belief" (*Morality of a Slaveholder*, 31).
72. Jefferson, *Notes*, 153.
73. Jefferson was also concerned that an attempt to incorporate formerly enslaved African Americans into the body politic would be hampered by the "deep rooted prejudices" of "the whites" and "ten thousand recollections, by the blacks, of the injuries they have sustained" (*Notes*, 147).
74. Jefferson, *Notes*, 147.
75. Herschthal, "Antislavery Science," 285.
76. Rush, "Observations," 291.
77. Rush, "Observations," 295.
78. Rush, "Observations," 297.
79. Rush, "Observations," 295.
80. John Wood Sweet provides a detailed account a detailed account of American physicians' interest in Moss, and the scientific, political, philosophical conclusions they drew from his case (*Bodies Politic*, 272–86).

81. Eric Herschthal argues that Rush's thought strongly influenced Barton's conclusion. See "Antislavery Science," 299–300.
82. Smith, *Essay on the Causes*, 60n. Unlike Rush and Barton, Smith thought that the darker shade of African skin was primarily caused by the sunny climate of the continent: "Growing up perfectly naked, and exposed to the constant action of the sun and weather, amidst all the hardships of a savage state, their colour becomes very deep" (60n). "The effect" of this climatic condition was heightened as it passed "from one generation to another," until it "assume[d] a permanent form and bec[a]me the character of ... the nation" (87).
83. Smith, *Essay on the Causes*, 59n.
84. Smith, *Essay on the Causes*, 60–61.
85. Barlow, *The Vision of Columbus*, 54. Compare *The Columbiad*, 66.
86. Paul Downes argues that Sarsefield stands for the "persistence of a feudal or monarchic logic" in the postrevolutionary order ("Sleepwalking," 240). Although a proponent of rational enlightenment, Sarsefield resorts to brute strength to subdue Clithero, whom he finds is able "to outreason" him (Brown, *Edgar Huntly*, 3:192). For Downes, Sarsefield's violent turn typifies how democratic judgments must exert an extralegal force that always threatens to exceed their legitimization by the will of the people ("Sleepwalking," 426).
87. Brown, *Edgar Huntly*, 2:131.
88. Brown, *Edgar Huntly*, 2:204.
89. Brown, *Wieland*, 212.
90. Jared Gardner claims that *Edgar Huntly* uses violence perpetrated against and by Native Americans as means of addressing anxiety occasioned by the immigration of non-English Europeans to the United States at the turn of the eighteenth century. In the novel's conceit, these aliens (such as Clithero) were likely to prove just as foreign to Anglo-American culture as Indians were seen to be ("Edgar Huntly's Savage Awakening").
91. Allen, *Reason the Only Oracle*, 456.
92. See above, pp. 89–90.
93. Palmer, *Enquiry*, 26, 31.
94. On the treatment of that topic in the New Testament, Palmer noted that "it is very easy to make naked and unsupported assertions, but unless the reason and evidence of the things accompany these assertions, they are good for nothing.—Paul speaking of the human body and of the resurrection of the dead, says, *it is sown a natural body and it is raised a spiritual body*, by what kind of chemical process it is, that matter is to become spirit, must be left to Paul and other spiritual chemists to determine" (*Principles of Nature*, 329).
95. Palmer, *Principles of Nature*, 330.
96. For more on Palmer's conception of material immortality, and its relationship to the European Enlightenment doctrine of vitalism, which held that all matter was animated by a living force, see Fischer, "Vitalism in America."
97. Freneau, *Poems of Philip Freneau*, 130.
98. Shields, "Mental Nocturnes," 256.

99. Shields, "Mental Nocturnes," 256; Freneau, *Poems of Philip Freneau*, 122.
100. Freneau, *Poems of Philip Freneau*, 102.
101. Washington, *Address of George Washington*, 7.
102. Washington, *Address of George Washington*, 14.
103. Laderman, *Sacred Remains*, 17.
104. Jacobs, "John James Barralet," 115.
105. For details of Barralet's invocation of Christian artistic tradition, see Jacobs, "John James Barralet," 125–26.
106. Thomas Dockery to George Washington, May 25, 1797.
107. A 1791 letter to Washington from Universalist theologian Elhanan Winchester furnishes us with another example. In addition to sending the president a copy of his eschatological work *The Prophecies That Remain to Be Fulfilled*, Winchester expressed his desire that Washington would "have the Approbation of the Great Judge of all, and in the bright and blooming morning of the resurrection be raised in the likeness of [Christ]" (Elhanan Winchester to George Washington, August 15, 1791).
108. Miles King to Thomas Jefferson, August 20, 1814.
109. Abraham O. Stansbury to Thomas Jefferson, January 7, 1815.
110. William Wisner to Thomas Jefferson, July 7, 1823.
111. Anonymous to Thomas Jefferson, May 26, 1816.
112. Later in 1816, Van der Kemp arranged for the anonymous publication of the "Syllabus" in the London Unitarian journal *Monthly Repository of Theology and General Literature*. See Jackson, *Scholar in the Wilderness*, 244–55.
113. Shortly after the publication of the "Syllabus," Van der Kemp produced an outline for a book "respecting the person and doctrine of J. C.," which he sent to John Adams ("Synopsis"). There he underlined his conviction that Christ's body only "became immortal" through "its resurrection," adding that "the reality of his human nature was not altered" in the process, since "our Salvation and resurrection were depend[ent] on the reality of [that] body."
114. Adams, *Works of John Adams*, 172. For more on Adams's fast days and the polarized reaction to them, see Dickson, "Jeremiads."
115. John Adams to Thomas Jefferson, June 28, 1813.
116. John Adams to Thomas Jefferson, July 18, 1813.
117. For more on the evolution of Adams's religious views, see Georgini, *Household Gods*, 17–63.
118. For details of how Rush brought about the detente between the two former presidents, see Wood, *Friends Divided*, 356–64.
119. John Adams to Thomas Jefferson, June 28, 1813.
120. In an 1810 letter to Benjamin Rush, Adams made the same point in a different way. The physician's foregoing missive had quoted John 5:29—"They only who have done good Shall come forth to the Resurrection unto Life." In reply, Adams claimed that "all my Theology is Summed up in your Sentence" (John Adams to Benjamin Rush, February 11, 1810).
121. John Adams to George Washington Adams, January 12, 1820.

122. To Jefferson in 1813, Adams lamented the death of Joseph Priestly nearly a decade before. If only the philosopher "could live again," he might be able to determine whether there were any "Witness[es] of the Existence" of the Gospels "in the first Century" (John Adams to Thomas Jefferson, December 3, 1813).
123. John Adams to Thomas Jefferson, December 3, 1813.
124. John Adams to Samuel Miller, July 7, 1820.
125. John Adams to Thomas Jefferson, December 3, 1813.
126. John Adams to Samuel Miller, July 7, 1820. Adams also told his correspondent, Presbyterian theologian and Princeton professor Samuel Miller, that he viewed "all good Men" as "Christians," regardless of their backgrounds and beliefs.
127. Writing to François Van der Kemp in 1806, Adams noted that he had "read many of the Calvinist . . . Treatises on original sin, and they [had] not convinced [him] of the total Depravity of human Nature" (John Adams to François Adriaan Van der Kemp, March 9, 1806). In the same letter he asked: "Can any Man read Sterne's Tristram Shandy and still doubt whether there is simple benevolence in human Nature?"
128. John Adams to Samuel Miller, July 7, 1820.
129. Schlereth, *An Age of Infidels*, 142–201.
130. Owen claimed that "reason" teaches us that "belief is involuntary; a moral phenomenon similar to the sensation of warmth or of chill over the physical frame; coming to us unsought, and deserting us unrequested" (Bacheler and Owen, *Existence of God*, 44–45). He therefore concluded that the Bible's insistence that belief is the foundation of righteousness had led to bloody exegetical disputes and was "evidence sufficient" that the scriptures were "not of divine origin (45)."
131. Gilbert, "An Address," 36.
132. *Oberlin Evangelist*, December 6, 1843, 195.
133. Noyes wrote that "salvation from sin is effected by the Spiritual application of the death and resurrection of Christ" (*The Berean*, 157). Through conversion, believers discover that "Christ's death [is] their death, and his resurrection their resurrection. Thus they die to sin and live to God." Though they attained "perfect [spiritual] holiness" through this imputation (180), their bodies were still flawed and subject to pain and suffering. Saints therefore still lived in hope of a corporeal resurrection. "It is evident," Noyes concluded, "that there is an important distinction between the initial attainment of eternal life, and the final completed resurrection. The former is an operation on the interior of the person; the latter, on the exterior (138)."
134. Bates, *Divine Book*, 97.
135. Seeman, *Speaking with the Dead*, 170–80.
136. Grasso, *Skepticism and American Faith*, 484–85.
137. Phelps, *The Gates Ajar*, 15.
138. Davis, *Principles of Nature*, 542–43.
139. For a detailed discussion of Davis's spiritual materialism, see Albanese, "Matter of Spirit."
140. See above, pp. 174–75.
141. Davis, *The Great Harmonia*, 1:211.

142. In the second volume of *The Great Harmonia*, Davis explained that "all the matter composing our earth" as well as "all the matter which we can see in the form of suns and planets in the boundless firmament" would eventually be "converted into spirit" (247). But when that final transformation took place, an immeasurable volume of invisible matter, "*millions* of times *lower* than the earth in the scale of progress and refinement," would remain. This material would be melted down in an "ocean of liquid fire," and used to construct another physical universe. In that "new creation" a fresh progress toward spiritualization would begin, culminating in another deconstruction of excess matter (248). This cycle would continue forever. For more on these claims, see Messamore, "Spiritualism," 102–3.

143. Grasso, *Skepticism and American Faith*, 301–4.

144. Alcott, *Young Man's Guide*, 24.

145. [Alcott], *The Laws of Health*, 11.

146. Drew Gilpin Faust connects the unprecedented bloodiness of the Civil War to a rise in American religious skepticism (as well as the emergence of new religious visions of the afterlife) (*This Republic of Suffering*, 171–210). Gary Laderman notes that many soldiers, doctors, nurses, and government officials were obliged to develop an "imaginative and emotional disengagement" from dead bodies in order to fulfill their duties. This "pragmatic" approach, was "one expression" of a broader "tendency to deflate theological readings of the corpse" (*Sacred Remains*, 137).

147. Laderman, *Sacred Remains*, 78.

148. Poe, *Works*, 1:167.

149. Murray, *Liminal Whiteness*, 111–13. Murray also argues that Valdemar's reduction to "a medical specimen" articulates white male anxiety at the possibility of being as socially and politically disempowered as African Americans, whose bodies were more usually subject to medical experimentation in the nineteenth century (113).

150. See, for instance, "The Colloquy of Monos and Una" (1841), *Works*, 1:215–27. Kenneth Hovey and Allan Emery claim that Poe believed in an afterlife despite also insisting that the universe was entirely comprised of matter (see "Poe's Materialist Metaphysics" and "Poe on the Process"). Emery argues that Poe anticipated an "entirely nonspiritual process" of transcendence taking place after death, as individuals learned to recalibrate their thoughts and perceptions as their bodies decayed ("Poe on the Process," 38).

151. Thoreau, *Walden*, 339, 340.

152. Thoreau, *Writings*, 10:455.

153. Thoreau, *Cape Cod*, 9.

154. Thoreau, *Cape Cod*, 4.

155. Thoreau, *Cape Cod*, 9.

156. Thoreau, *Cape Cod*, 173.

157. In the course of a brief history of the ministers of Eastham, Thoreau suggests that their theology was out of place on the Cape by mischievously comparing their "remarkable disputations on doctrinal points" to those of the Middle Eastern "Yezidis, or Worshippers of the Devil" (*Cape Cod*, 48).

158. Thoreau, *Week on the Concord*, 175.

159. Thoreau, "Autumnal Tints," 299.

160. Thoreau, *Walden*, 42.
161. As a famous passage from *Walden* indicates, Thoreau believed that learning how to live morally and learning how to die were one and the same. "If you stand right fronting and face to face to a fact," he writes, "you will see the sun glimmer on both its surfaces, as if it were a cimeter, and feel its sweet edge dividing you through the heart and marrow, and so you will happily conclude your mortal career. Be it life or death, we crave only reality" (106).
162. Thoreau, *Journal*, 11:435.
163. Thoreau, *Cape Cod*, 10.
164. Kathryn Gin Lum describes a growing rebellion against the concepts of hell and damnation among a diverse range of antebellum Americans, including Spiritualists, Swedenborgians, Native American prophets, and religious skeptics (*Damned Nation*, 126–63).
165. See, for instance, Lippard, *The Quaker City*, 64, 96, 116, 123.
166. See Reynolds, "Deformance, Performativity, Posthumanism," 52 n. 21 and Moore, "Religion, Secularization," 223–24.
167. David S. Reynolds argues that the novel's repeated equivalences between "humans, animals, and things" stage a quasi-Marxist critique of social alienation under capitalism ("Deformance, Performativity, Posthumanism," 51). The working-class characters are portrayed as "dehumanized," while the corrupt "elite" are "inhuman" (52).

Coda

1. Jefferson to James Madison, September 1789.
2. Jefferson to John Cartwright, June 5, 1824.
3. Ariès, "Invisible Death," 111–13.
4. Ariès, "Invisible Death, 109–11.
5. Taylor, *A Secular Age*, 721, 723.
6. According to a 2019 report by the National Funeral Directors Association (NFDA), in 2040 "the cremation rate in the U.S. is projected to be 78.7% while the burial rate is predicted to be just 15.7%" ("Cremation"). The NFDA also predicts that "non-burial options for cremated remains" will "gain popularity as well."
7. Farman, *On Not Dying*, 1.
8. Ward, "Metaphysics of the Body," 229.
9. Milbank, "What Is Radical Orthodoxy?," [2].
10. Ward, "Metaphysics of the Body," 248.
11. Ward, "Metaphysics of the Body," 247–50.
12. Milbank, "The Midwinter Sacrifice," 117.
13. Milbank, "The Midwinter Sacrifice," 113, 115.
14. Milbank, "The Midwinter Sacrifice," 126.
15. Falque, *The Metamorphosis of Finitude*, 16.
16. Farman, *On Not Dying*, 167, 170.

17. By way of contrast, Anya Bernstein's study of immortalism in contemporary Russia emphasizes the ongoing influence of Russian Orthodox thinker Nikolai Fedorov (1829–1903), who argued that science should be seeking to find a way not only to "overcome death" but also "resurrect everyone who has already died" (*The Future of Immortality*, 60).
18. Waters, "Whose Salvation?," 171.
19. Merchant, *Anthropocene*, 91; *Radical Ecology*, 65. Merchant also concedes that "established religions have the institutional capacity to promote ethics and responsibilities by grounding people in nature's rhythms and ecological relations" (*Radical Ecology*, 94). With reference to Christianity in particular, she notes that "worship ceremonies within Sunday services can awaken people to the needs and methods to preserve God's earth and personal salvation, and social activities beyond church walls can promote climate justice, peace, and ecological integrity."
20. Taylor, *Dark Green Religion*, 86.
21. Taylor, *Dark Green Religion*, 341.
22. Morton, *Dark Ecology*, 38–40.
23. Bastian and Van Doren, "'The New Immortals," 1.
24. Morton, *Humankind*, 187, 189, 14.
25. Morton, *Humankind*, 187.
26. Morton, *Humankind*, 143.

Works Cited

Adams, Howard C. "Benjamin Colman: A Critical Biography." PhD dissertation, Pennsylvania State University, 1976.
Adams, John. "Letter to Benjamin Rush." February 11, 1810. *Founders Online*. https://founders.archives.gov/documents/Adams/99-02-02-5512.
Adams, John. "Letter to François Van Der Kemp." March 9, 1806. *Founders Online*. https://founders.archives.gov/documents/Adams/99-02-02-7369.
Adams, John. "Letter to George Washington Adams." January 12, 1820. *Founders Online*. https://founders.archives.gov/documents/Adams/99-03-02-3749.
Adams, John. "Letter to Samuel Miller." July 7, 1820. *Founders Online*. https://founders.archives.gov/documents/Adams/99-02-02-7369.
Adams, John. "Letter to Thomas Jefferson." June 28, 1813. *Founders Online*. https://founders.archives.gov/documents/Jefferson/03-06-02-0208.
Adams, John. "Letter to Thomas Jefferson." July 18, 1813. https://founders.archives.gov/documents/Jefferson/03-06-02-0250.
Adams, John. "Letter to Thomas Jefferson." December 3, 1813. *Founders Online*. https://founders.archives.gov/documents/Jefferson/03-07-02-0008.
Adams, John. "Letter to Thomas Jefferson." May 6, 1816. *Founders Online*. https://founders.archives.gov/documents/Adams/99-02-02-6595.
Adams, John. "Letter to Thomas Jefferson." March 10, 1823. *Founders Online*. https://founders.archives.gov/documents/Adams/99-02-02-7788.
Adams, John. *The Works of John Adams*. Edited by Charles Francis Adams. Vol. 9. Boston, 1854.
Albanese, Catherine L. "On the Matter of Spirit: Andrew Jackson and the Marriage of God and Nature." *Journal of the American Academy of Religion* 60, no. 1 (1992): 1–17.
[Alcott, William A.]. *The Laws of Health*. Boston: John P. Jewett, 1857.
Alcott, William A. *The Young Man's Guide*. Boston: Lilly, Wait, Colman, & Holden, 1833.
Allen, Ethan. *Reason the Only Oracle of Man*. Bennington, VT, 1784.
Allen, Richard C. "Restoration Quakerism, 1660–1691." In *The Oxford Handbook of Quaker Studies*, edited by Stephen W. Angell and Ben Pink Dandelion, 29–46. New York: Oxford University Press, 2013.
Almond, Philip C. *Heaven and Hell in Enlightenment England*. Cambridge: Cambridge University Press, 1994.
Alsted, Johann Heinrich. *The Beloved City*. London, 1643.
Ames, William. *The Marrow of Sacred Divinity*. London, 1642.
Anonymous. "Letter to Thomas Jefferson. May 26, 1816. *Founders Online*. https://founders.archives.gov/documents/Jefferson/03-10-02-0049.
Apess, William. *The Experiences of Five Christian Indians of the Pequod Tribe*. Boston, 1833.
Apess, William. "An Indian's Looking Glass for the White Man." In *The Experiences of Five Christian Indians of the Pequod Tribe*, edited by William Apess, 51–60. Boston: James B. Dow, 1833.

Ariès, Philippe. "Invisible Death." *Wilson Quarterly* 5, no. 1 (1981): 105–15.
Asad, Talal. *Formations of the Secular: Christianity, Islam, Modernity. Cultural Memory in the Present*. Stanford, CA: Stanford University Press, 2003.
Asad, Talal. *Genealogies of Religion: Discipline and Reasons of Power in Christianity and Islam*. Baltimore: Johns Hopkins University Press, 1993.
The Athenian Oracle, the Second Edition, Printed at London, 1704. Boston, 1705.
Augustine. *The City of God against the Pagans*. Edited by R. W. Dyson. Cambridge: Cambridge University Press, 1998.
Austin, John Osborne. *Genealogical Dictionary of Rhode Island before 1690*. Baltimore: Genealogical Pub. Co, 1978.
Bacheler, Origen, and Robert Dale Owen. *Discussion on the Existence of God, and the Authenticity of the Bible*. London: J. Watson, 1840.
Backus, Isaac. *The Diary of Isaac Backus*. Edited by William Gerald McLoughlin. 3 vols. Providence, RI: Brown University Press, 1979.
Bailey, Richard A. *New Light on George Fox and Early Quakerism: The Making and Unmaking of a God*. San Francisco: Mellen Research University Press, 1992.
Bailey, Richard A. *Race and Redemption in Puritan New England*. New York: Oxford University Press, 2014.
Baillie, Robert. *Anabaptism, the True Fountaine of Independency*. London, 1647.
Baillie, Robert. *A Dissuasive from the Errours of the Time*. London, 1645.
Balkun, Mary McAleer. "Phillis Wheatley's Construction of Otherness and the Rhetoric of Performed Ideology." *African American Review* 36, no. 1 (2002): 121–35.
Ball, Charles. *Slavery in the United States: A Narrative of the Life and Adventures of Charles Ball*. New York, 1837.
Barlow, Joel. *The Columbiad: A Poem*. Philadelphia, 1807.
Barlow, Joel. *Letter to Henry Gregoire*. Washington City, 1809.
Barlow, Joel. *The Vision of Columbus*. 2nd ed. Hartford, 1787.
Bastian, Michelle, and Thom van Dooren. "Editorial Preface: The New Immortals: Immortality and Infinitude in the Anthropocene." *Environmental Philosophy* 14, no. 1 (2017): 1–19.
Bates, Paulina, et al. *The Divine Book of Holy and Eternal Wisdom*. 2 volumes in 1. New Lebanon, NY, 1849.
Battis, Emery. *Saints and Sectaries*. Chapel Hill: University of North Carolina Press, 2017.
Bauer, Ralph. "Colonial Discourse and Early American Literary History: Ercilla, the Inca Garcilaso, and Joel Barlow's Conception of a New World Epic." *Early American Literature* 30, no. 3 (1995): 203–32.
Baxter, Richard. *A Call to the Unconverted*. London, 1658.
Baxter, Richard. *A Christian Directory*. London, 1673.
Baxter, Richard. *The Saints Everlasting Rest*. London, 1650.
Beach, John. *A Friendly Expostulation*. New York, 1763.
Beach, John. *A Modest Enquiry into the State of the Dead*. New London, CT, 1755.
Beach, John. *Three Discourses, Casuistical and Practical*. Boston, 1768.
Beecher, Lyman. *A Plea for the West*. 2nd ed. Cincinnati, 1835.
Bercovitch, Sacvan. *The American Jeremiad*. Madison: University of Wisconsin Press, 2012.
Bercovitch, Sacvan. *The Puritan Origins of the American Self*. New Haven, CT: Yale University Press, 2011 (1975).
Berlin, Ira. *Generations of Captivity: A History of African-American Slaves*. Cambridge, MA: Belknap Press of Harvard University Press, 2003.

Bernstein, Anya. *The Future of Immortality: Remaking Life and Death in Contemporary Russia*. Princeton, NJ: Princeton University Press, 2019.

Birrell, T. A. "English Catholic Mystics in Non-Catholic Circles I." *Downside Review* 94 (1976): 60–81.

Bishop, George, *New England Judged*. London, 1661.

Bloch, Ruth H. *Visionary Republic: Millennial Themes in American Thought, 1756–1800.*. Cambridge: Cambridge University Press, 1994.

Block, Sharon. *Colonial Complexions: Race and Bodies in Eighteenth-Century America*. Philadelphia: University of Pennsylvania Press, 2018.

Blumenberg, Hans. *The Legitimacy of the Modern Age*. Cambridge, MA: MIT Press, 1985.

Bond, Edward L. "Anglican Theology and Devotion in James Blair's Virginia, 1685–1743: Private Piety in the Public Church." *Virginia Magazine of History and Biography* 104, no. 3 (1996): 313–40.

The Book of Common-Prayer. London, 1662.

Boston Gazette. July 24, 1744.

Boston News Letter. April 4, 1723.

Boston News Letter. April 15, 1723.

Bradford, William. *Bradford's History of Plymouth Plantation: 1606–1646*. Edited by William T. Davis. New York: Barnes & Noble, 1946.

Bradstreet, Anne. *The Works of Anne Bradstreet in Prose and Verse*. Edited by John Harvard Ellis. Charlestown: Abram E. Cutter, 1867.

[Brainerd, David]. "Preface to Meditations and Spiritual Experiences of Mr. Thomas Shepard." In *Three Valuable Pieces*, by Thomas Shepard, edited by Thomas Prince. Boston, 1747.

Breen, Louise A. "Cotton Mather, the 'Angelical Ministry,' and Inoculation." *Journal of the History of Medicine and Allied Sciences* 46, no. 3 (1991): 333–57.

Bremer, Francis J. *Lay Empowerment and the Development of Puritanism*. Basingstoke: Palgrave Macmillan, 2015.

Bressler, Ann Lee. *The Universalist Movement in America, 1770–1880*. New York: Oxford University Press, 2001.

Bridenbaugh, Carl, ed. *Gentleman's Progress: The Itinerarium of Dr. Alexander Hamilton, 1744*. Chapel Hill: University of North Carolina Press, 1948.

Brightman, Thomas. *A Revelation of the Apocalyps*. Amsterdam, 1611.

Brooks, Joanna. *American Lazarus: Religion and the Rise of African-American and Native American Literatures*. Oxford: Oxford University Press, 2003.

Bross, Kristina. *Dry Bones and Indian Sermons: Praying Indians in Colonial America*. Ithaca, NY: Cornell University Press, 2004.

Bross, Kristina. *Future History: Global Fantasies in Seventeenth-Century American and British Writings*. New York: Oxford University Press, 2017.

Brown, Charles Brockden. *Edgar Huntly; or, Memoirs of a Sleep-Walker*. Philadelphia, 1803.

Brown, Charles Brockden. *Wieland; or The Transformation. An American Tale*. New York, 1798.

Brown, Samuel Morris. *In Heaven as It Is on Earth: Joseph Smith and the Early Mormon Conquest of Death*. Oxford: Oxford University Press, 2012.

Brown, Vincent. *The Reaper's Garden: Death and Power in the World of Atlantic Slavery*. Cambridge, MA: Harvard University Press, 2008.

Bryan, Susan. "Reauthorizing the Text: Jefferson's Scissor Edit of the Gospels." *Early American Literature* 22, no. 1 (1987): 19–42.

Buel, Richard. *Joel Barlow: American Citizen in a Revolutionary World*. Baltimore: Johns Hopkins University Press, 2011.

Burnet, Thomas. *The Theory of the Earth*. London, 1697.

Burnham, Michelle. *Folded Selves: Colonial New England Writing in the World System*. Lebanon: Dartmouth College Press, 2014.

Burnham, Michelle. "Samuel Gorton's Leveller Aesthetics and the Economics of Colonial Dissent." *William and Mary Quarterly* 67, no. 3 (2010): 433–58.

Bushman, Richard L., ed. *The Great Awakening: Documents on the Revival of Religion, 1740-1745*. Chapel Hill: University of North Carolina Press, 2004.

Butler, Jon. *Awash in a Sea of Faith: Christianizing the American People*. Cambridge, MA: Harvard University Press, 1990.

Butler, Jon. "Into Pennsylvania's Spiritual Abyss: The Rise and Fall of the Later Keithians, 1693-1703." *Pennsylvania Magazine of History and Biography* 101, no. 2 (1977): 151–70.

Bynum, Caroline Walker. *The Resurrection of the Body in Western Christianity, 200-1336*. New York: Columbia University Press, 1995.

Caldwell, Patricia. "The Antinomian Language Controversy." *Harvard Theological Review* 69, nos. 3–4 (1976): 345–67.

Calvert, Jane E. *Quaker Constitutionalism and the Political Thought of John Dickinson*. Cambridge: Cambridge University Press, 2009.

Capp, Bernard. "The Political Dimension of Apocalyptic Thought." In *The Apocalypse in English Renaissance Thought and Literature*, edited by C. A. Patrides and Joseph Wittreich, 165–89. Manchester: Manchester University Press, 1984.

Caretta, Vincent. "Cugoano, Ottobah [John Stuart]." In *The Oxford Dictionary of National Biography*, edited by H. C. G. Matthew and B. Harrison. Oxford: Oxford University Press, 2004.

Caricchio, Mario. "News from the New Jerusalem: Giles Calvert and the Radical Experience." In *Varieties of Seventeenth- and Early Eighteenth-Century English Radicalism in Context*, edited by Ariel Hessayon and David Finnegan, 69–86. Farnham: Ashgate, 2016.

Casanova, José. "Religion, the Axial Age, and Secular Modernity in Bellah's Theory of Religious Evolution." In *The Axial Age and Its Consequences*, edited by Robert N. Bellah and Hans Joas, 191–221. Cambridge, MA: Harvard University Press, 2012.

Ceppi, Elisabeth. *Invisible Masters: Gender, Race, and the Economy of Service in Early New England*. Hanover, NH: Dartmouth College Press, 2018.

Chauncy, Charles. *Seasonable Thoughts on the State of Religion*. Boston, 1743.

Chiles, Katy L. *Transformable Race: Surprising Metamorphoses in the Literature of Early America*. Oxford: Oxford University Press, 2014.

The Christian History. 2 vols. Boston, 1744.

Cogley, Richard W. "The Ancestry of the American Indians: Thomas Thorowgood's *Iewes in America* (1650) and *Jews in America* (1660)." *English Literary Renaissance* 35, no. 2 (March 2005): 304–30.

Cogley, Richard W. "The Fall of the Ottoman Empire and the Restoration of Israel in the 'Judeo-Centric' Strand of Puritan Millenarianism." *Church History* 72, no. 2 (2003): 304–32.

Cogley, Richard W. *John Eliot's Mission to the Indians before King Philip's War*. Cambridge, MA: Harvard University Press, 1999.

Cogley, Richard W. "'Some Other Kinde of Being and Condition': The Controversy in Mid-Seventeenth-Century England over the Peopling of Ancient America." *Journal of the History of Ideas* 68, no. 1 (January 2007): 35–56.

Colman, Benjamin. *A Brief Enquiry into the Reasons Why the People of God Have Been Wont to Bring into Their Penitential Confessions, the Sins of Their Fathers and Ancestors, in Times Long since Past*. Boston, 1716.

Colman, Benjamin. *The Credibility of the Christian Doctrine of the Resurrection*. Boston, 1729.

Colman, Benjamin. *Death and the Grave without Any Order*. Boston, 1728.

Colman, Benjamin. *A Devout and Humble Enquiry*. Boston, 1715.

Colman, Benjamin. *The Glory of God in the Firmament of His Power*. Boston, 1742.

Colman, Benjamin. *The Government & Improvement of Mirth according to the Laws of Christianity*. Boston, 1707.

Colman, Benjamin. *The Holy Walk and Glorious Translation of Blessed Enoch*. Boston, 1728.

Colman, Benjamin. *The Master Taken up from the Sons of the Prophets*. Boston, 1724.

Colman, Benjamin. *Ossa Josephi; or, The Bones of Joseph*. Boston, 1720.

Colman, Benjamin. *Practical Discourses on the Parable of the Ten Virgins*. Boston, 1747.

Como, David R. "Print, Censorship, and Ideological Escalation in the English Civil War." *Journal of British Studies* 51, no. 4 (2012): 820–57.

Corrigan, John. *The Prism of Piety: Catholick Congregational Clergy at the Beginning of the Enlightenment*. New York: Oxford University Press, 1991.

Cotton, John. *The Churches Resurrection*. London, 1642.

Cotton, John. *The Covenant of Gods Free Grace*. London, 1645.

Cotton, John. *An Exposition upon the Thirteenth Chapter of the Revelation*. London, 1656.

Cotton, John. *The Way of Congregational Churches Cleared in Two Treatises*. London, 1648.

Crome, Andrew. *The Restoration of the Jews: Early Modern Hermeneutics, Eschatology, and National Identity in the Works of Thomas Brightman*. Springer: Cham, 2014.

Croswell, Andrew. *What Is Christ to Me, If He Is Not Mine?* Boston, 1745.

Cudworth, Ralph. *The True Intellectual System of the Universe: The First Part*. [London], 1743.

Cugoano, Ottobah. *Thoughts and Sentiments on the Evil and Wicked Traffic of the Slavery and Commerce of the Human Species*. London, 1787.

Curran, Andrew S. *The Anatomy of Blackness: Science & Slavery in an Age of Enlightenment*. Baltimore: Johns Hopkins University Press, 2011.

Darby, John Nelson. *Seven Lectures on the Second Coming of the Lord*. Toronto, 1863.

Davidson, James West. *The Logic of Millennial Thought: Eighteenth-Century New England*. New Haven, CT: Yale University Press, 1977.

Davis, Andrew Jackson. *The Great Harmonia; a Philosophical Revelation of the Natural, Spiritual and Celestial Universe*. 5 vols. Boston, 1866.

Davis, Andrew Jackson. *The Principles of Nature, Her Divine Relations, and a Voice to Mankind*. New York, 1847.

Davis, David Brion. *The Problem of Slavery in Western Culture*. New York: Oxford University Press, 1988.

D'Elia, Donald J. "Benjamin Rush: Philosopher of the American Revolution." *Transactions of the American Philosophical Society* 64, no. 5 (1974): 1–113.

Dempsey, Liam P. "John Locke, 'Hobbist': Of Sleeping Souls and Thinking Matter." *Canadian Journal of Philosophy* 47, no. 4 (July 4, 2017): 454–76.

Dexter, Franklin Bowditch. *Biographical Sketches of the Graduates of Yale College, with Annals of the College History*. Vol. 1. New York, 1885.

Dickson, Charles Ellis. "Jeremiads in the New American Republic: The Case of National Fasts in the John Adams Administration." *New England Quarterly* 60, no. 2 (1987): 187–207.

Dockery, Thomas. "Letter to George Washington." May 25, 1797. *Founders Online.* https://founders.archives.gov/documents/Washington/06-01-02-0124.

The Doctrine and Covenants of the Church of Jesus Christ of Latter-Day Saints. Salt Lake City, UT, 2013. https://www.churchofjesuschrist.org/study/scriptures/dc-testament?lang=eng.

Donoghue, John. *Fire under the Ashes: An Atlantic History of the English Revolution.* Chicago: University of Chicago Press, 2013.

Douglass, Frederick. *My Bondage and My Freedom.* New York, 1855.

Douglass, Frederick. *Narrative of the Life of Frederick Douglass, an American Slave.* Boston, 1845.

Downes, Paul. "Sleep-Walking out of the Revolution: Brown's 'Edgar Huntly.'" *Eighteenth-Century Studies* 29, no. 4 (1996): 413–31.

[Dutton, Anne]. *A Letter to the Negroes Lately Converted to Christ in America.* London, 1743.

Edwards, Jonathan. *Apocalyptic Writings.* Edited by Stephen J. Stein. The Works of Jonathan Edwards, vol. 5. New Haven, CT: Yale University Press, 1977.

Edwards, Jonathan. *A History of the Work of Redemption.* Edited by John Frederick Wilson. The Works of Jonathan Edwards, vol. 9. New Haven, CT: Yale University Press, 1989.

Edwards, Jonathan. *The Life of David Brainerd.* The Works of Jonathan Edwards, vol. 7. New Haven, CT: Yale University Press, 1985.

Edwards, Jonathan. *The "Miscellanies," 501-832.* Edited by Eva Chamberlain. Works of Jonathan Edwards, vol. 18. New Haven, CT: Yale University Press, 2000.

Egerton, Henry. *A Sermon Preached before the Incorporated Society for the Propagation of the Gospel in Foreign Parts.* London, 1729.

Eire, Carlos M. N. *Reformations: The Early Modern World, 1450–1650.* New Haven, CT: Yale University Press, 2016.

Ellis, Markman. "Ignatius Sancho's Letters: Sentimental Libertinism and the Politics of Form." In *Genius in Bondage: Literature of the Early Black Atlantic,* edited by Vincent Carretta, 199–217. Lexington: University Press of Kentucky, 2001.

Emery, Allan. "Evading the Pit and the Pendulum: Poe on the Process of Transcendence." *Poe Studies / Dark Romanticism* 38 (2005): 29–42.

Endy, Melvin. "George Fox and William Penn: Their Relationship and Their Roles within the Quaker Movement." *Quaker History* 93, no. 1 (2004): 1–39.

Endy, Melvin. "Theology in a Religiously Plural World: Some Contributions of William Penn." *Pennsylvania Magazine of History and Biography* 105, no. 4 (1981): 453–68.

Endy, Melvin. "William Penn and Early Quakerism: A Theological Study." PhD dissertation, Yale University, 1969.

English, George Bethune. *The Grounds of Christianity Examined.* Boston, 1813.

Erdozain, Dominic. "A Heavenly Poise: Radical Religion and the Making of the Enlightenment." *Intellectual History Review* 27, no. 1 (January 2, 2017): 71–96.

Erdozain, Dominic. *The Soul of Doubt: The Religious Roots of Unbelief from Luther to Marx.* Oxford: Oxford University Press, 2016.

Erwin, John Stuart. *The Millennialism of Cotton Mather.* Lampeter: Mellen, 1990.

Falque, Emmanuel. *The Metamorphosis of Finitude.* Edited by John D. Caputo. Translated by George Hughes. New York: Fordham University Press, 2012.

Farindon, Anthony. *LXXX Sermons Preached at the Parish-Church of St. Mary Magdalene Milk-Street, London.* London, 1672.
Farman, Abou. *On Not Dying: Secular Immortality in the Age of Technoscience.* Minneapolis: University of Minnesota Press, 2020.
Faust, Drew Gilpin. *This Republic of Suffering: Death and the American Civil War.* New York: Vintage, 2009.
Fessenden, Tracy. *Culture and Redemption: Religion, the Secular, and American Literature.* Princeton, NJ: Princeton University Press, 2007.
Field, Jonathan Beecher. "The Antinomian Controversy Did Not Take Place." *Early American Studies* 6, no. 2 (2008): 448–63.
Field, Jonathan Beecher. *Errands into the Metropolis: New England Dissidents in Revolutionary London.* Hanover, NH: Dartmouth College Press, 2009.
Fischer, Kirsten. "Vitalism in America: Elihu Palmer's Radical Religion in the Early Republic." *William and Mary Quarterly* 73, no. 3 (2016): 501–13.
Fisher, Linford D. *The Indian Great Awakening: Religion and the Shaping of Native Cultures in Early America.* New York: Oxford University Press, 2012.
Fleetwood, William. *A Sermon Preached before the Society for the Propagation of the Gospel in Foreign Parts.* London, 1711.
Fox, George. *A Collection of the Several Books and Writings Given Forth by That Faithful Servant of God and His People, George Fox, the Younger.* 2nd ed. London, 1665.
Fox, George. *An Encouragement for All to Trust in the Lord.* London, 1682.
Fox, George. "For the Governour, and His Council & Assembly, and All Others in Power, Both Civil and Military in This Island; from the People Called Quakers." In *To the Ministers, Teachers, and Priests (so Called and so Stileing Your Selves) in Barbadoes.* [London], 1672.
Fox, George. *A Journal.* London, 1694.
Fox, George. *A New-England-Fire-Brand Quenched.* London, 1678.
Fox, George. *The Works of George Fox.* 8 vols. Philadelphia, 1831.
Foxcroft, Thomas. *Death the Destroyer of Earthly and False Hopes.* Boston, 1726.
Foxcroft, Thomas. "To the Reader." In *The True Scripture Doctrine*, by Jonathan Dickinson, ii–xiii. Boston: S. Eliot, 1741.
Francaviglia, Richard V. *Geography and Mormon Identity.* Edited by Terryl L. Givens and Philip L. Barlow. New York: Oxford University Press, 2015.
Franklin, Benjamin. "Letter to Granville Sharp." July 5, 1785. *Franklin Papers.* https://franklinpapers.org/framedVolumes.jsp?vol=21&page=453b.
Franklin, Benjamin. "Letter to Jacques Barbeu-Duborg." 1773. *Founders Online.* https://founders.archives.gov/documents/Franklin/01-20-02-0109.
Franklin, Benjamin. "Letter to John Lathrop." May 31, 1788. *Franklin Papers.* franklinpapers.org.
Franklin, Benjamin. "Letter to Joseph Priestly." February 8, 1780. *Founders Online.* https://founders.archives.gov/documents/Franklin/01-31-02-0325.
Franklin, Benjamin, and Francis Dashwood. *Abridgement of the Book of Common Prayer.* London, 1773.
Free Enquirer. November 26, 1831.
Freneau, Philip. *The Poems of Philip Freneau: Written Chiefly during the Late War.* Philadelphia, 1786.
[Freneau, Philip], and [Hugh Henry Brackenridge]. *A Poem on the Rising Glory of America.* Philadelphia, 1772.

Frey, Sylvia R., and, Betty Wood. *Come Shouting to Zion: African American Protestantism in the American South and British Caribbean to 1830*. Chapel Hill: University of North Carolina Press, 1998.

Frost, J. William. "Unlikely Controversialists: Caleb Pusey and George Keith." *Quaker History* 64, no. 1 (1975): 16–36.

Gardner, Jared. "Alien Nation: Edgar Huntly's Savage Awakening." *American Literature* 66, no. 3 (1994): 429–61.

Gaustad, Edwin S. "Charles Chauncy and the Great Awakening: A Survey and Bibliography." *The Papers of the Bibliographical Society of America* 45, no. 2 (1951): 125–35.

Georgini, Sara. *Household Gods: The Religious Lives of the Adams Family*. New York: Oxford University Press, 2019.

Gerbner, Katharine. *Christian Slavery: Conversion and Race in the Protestant Atlantic World*. Philadelphia: University of Pennsylvania Press, 2018.

Gilbert, Amos. "An Address Delivered by Amos Gilbert, at the Hall of Science, in September, 1831." *The Free Enquirer* 4, no. 1 (November 26, 1831): 33–36.

Giles, Paul. *The Global Remapping of American Literature*. Princeton, NJ: Princeton University Press, 2011.

Gillis, John R. "Introduction: Memory and Identity." In *Commemorations: The Politics of National Identity*, edited by John R. Gillis, 3–24. Princeton, NJ: Princeton University Press, 1994.

Gin Lum, Kathryn. *Damned Nation: Hell in America from the Revolution to Reconstruction*. New York: Oxford University Press, 2017.

Glasson, Travis. *Mastering Christianity: Missionary Anglicanism and Slavery in the Atlantic World*. New York: Oxford University Press, 2012.

Gloege, Timothy E. W. "The Trouble with Christian History: Thomas Prince's 'Great Awakening.'" *Church History* 82, no. 1 (March 2013): 125–65.

Godwyn, Morgan. *The Negro's & Indians Advocate*. London, 1680.

Goetz, Rebecca Anne. *The Baptism of Early Virginia: How Christianity Created Race*. Baltimore: Johns Hopkins University Press, 2012.

Goodman, Nan. *The Puritan Cosmopolis: The Law of Nations and the Early American Imagination*. New York: Oxford University Press, 2018.

Gorton, Samuel. *An Antidote against the Common Plague of the World*. London, 1657.

Gorton, Samuel. *An Incorruptible Key*. London, 1647.

Gorton, Samuel. *Saltmarsh Returned from the Dead, in Amico Philalethe*. London, 1655.

Gorton, Samuel. "Samuel Gorton's Letter to Nathaniel Morton." In *Tracts and Other Papers, Relating Principally to the Origin, Settlement, and Progress of the Colonies in North America, from the Discovery of the Country to the Year 1776*, edited by Peter Force. Vol. 4. Washington DC, 1846.

Gorton, Samuel. *Simplicities Defence against Seven-Headed Policy*. London, 1646.

Grainger, Brett Malcolm. "Vital Nature and Vital Piety: Johann Arndt and the Evangelical Vitalism of Cotton Mather." *Church History* 81, no. 4 (2012): 852–72.

Grasso, Christopher. *Skepticism and American Faith: From the Revolution to the Civil War*. New York: Oxford University Press, 2018.

Graunt, John. *Natural and Political Observations, Mentioned in a Following Index, and Made upon the Bills of Mortality*. London, 1662.

Greene, Lorenzo Johnston. *The Negro in Colonial New England*. New York: Atheneum, 1968.

Gregory, Brad S. *The Unintended Reformation: How a Religious Revolution Secularized Society*. Cambridge, MA: Belknap Press of Harvard University Press, 2015.

Gribben, Crawford. *Evangelical Millennialism in the Trans-Atlantic World, 1500–2000*. Basingstoke: Palgrave Macmillan, 2011.

Gribben, Crawford. *The Puritan Millennium: Literature and Theology, 1550–1682*. Rev. ed. Milton Keynes: Paternoster, 2008.

Gronniosaw, James Albert Ukawsaw. *A Narrative of the Most Remarkable Particulars in the Life of James Albert Ukawsaw Gronniosaw, an African Prince, as Related by Himself*. 2nd ed. [Glasgow?], 1785.

Gura, Philip F. *A Glimpse of Sion's Glory: Puritan Radicalism in New England, 1620–1660*. Middletown, CT: Wesleyan University Press, 1986.

Gura, Philip F. "The Radical Ideology of Samuel Gorton: New Light on the Relation of English to American Puritanism." *William and Mary Quarterly* 36, no. 1 (1979): 78–100.

Guruswamy, Rosemary Fithian. "'Thou Hast the Holy Word': Jupiter Hammon's 'Regards' to Phillis Wheatley." In *Genius in Bondage: Literature of the Early Black Atlantic*, edited by Vincent Carretta and Philip Gould, 190–98. Lexington: University Press of Kentucky, 2001.

Gwyn, Douglas. "Quakers, Eschatology, and Time." In *The Oxford Handbook of Quaker Studies*, edited by Stephen W. Angell and Ben Pink Dandelion, 202–17. Oxford: Oxford University Press, 2013.

Gwyn, Douglas. "Seventeenth-Century Context and Quaker Beginnings." In *Early Quakers and Their Theological Thought, 1647–1723*, edited by Stephen W. Angell and Ben Pink Dandelion, 13–31. Cambridge: Cambridge University Press, 2015.

Haefeli, Evan. "Toleration and Empire." In *British North America in the Seventeenth and Eighteenth Centuries*, edited by Stephen Foster, 103–35. Oxford: Oxford University Press, 2013.

Hall, David D., ed. *The Antinomian Controversy, 1636–1638: A Documentary History*. 2nd ed. Durham, NC: Duke University Press, 1990.

Hall, David D. *The Puritans: A Transatlantic History*. Princeton, NJ: Princeton University Press, 2019.

Hall, Prince. *A Charge, Delivered to the African Lodge, June 24, 1797, at Menotomy*. [Boston], 1797.

Hammon, Jupiter. *America's First Negro Poet: The Complete Works of Jupiter Hammon of Long Island*. Edited by Stanley Austen Ransom Jr. Port Washington, NY: Kennikat Press, 1970.

Hammond, Henry. *Sermons*. London, 1675.

Hariot, Thomas. *A Briefe and True Report of the New Found Land of Virginia*. London, 1588.

Harrison, Peter. *The Bible, Protestantism, and the Rise of Natural Science*. Cambridge: Cambridge University Press, 2001.

Harrison, Peter. "Science and Secularization." *Intellectual History Review* 27, no. 1 (2017): 47–70.

Harrison, Peter. *The Territories of Science and Religion*. Chicago: Chicago University Press, 2015.

Hawks, Francis L., and William Stevens Perry, eds. *Documentary History of the Protestant Episcopal Church in the United States of America*. 2 vols. New York, 1863.

Helo, Ari. *Thomas Jefferson's Ethics and the Politics of Human Progress: The Morality of a Slaveholder*. New York: Cambridge University Press, 2014.

Hening, William Waller, ed. *The Statutes at Large; Being a Collection of All the Laws of Virginia, from the First Session of the Legislature in the Year 1619*. Vol. 3. Philadelphia, 1823.
Herschthal, Eric. "Antislavery Science in the Early Republic: The Case of Dr. Benjamin Rush." *Early American Studies* 15, no. 2 (2017): 274–307.
Hickman, Jared. *Black Prometheus: Race and Radicalism in the Age of Atlantic Slavery*. New York: Oxford University Press, 2017.
Hill, Christopher. *The World Turned Upside Down: Radical Ideas during the English Revolution*. London: Penguin Books, 1991.
Hill, Hamilton Andrews. *History of the Old South Church*. 2 vols. Boston, 1890.
Hoberman, Michael. *New Israel / New England: Jews and Puritans in Early America*. Amherst: University of Massachusetts Press, 2011.
Hopkins, Samuel. *Treatise on the Millennium*. Boston, 1854.
Hovey, Kenneth Alan. "Poe's Materialist Metaphysics of Man." In *A Companion to Poe Studies*, edited by Eric W. Carlson, 347–66. Westwood, CT: Greenwood Press, 1996.
Hutchins, Zachary. "Sewall's Secret: The Selling of More Than Two Dozen Africans." 2019. Unpublished.
Israel, Jonathan. *The Expanding Blaze: How the American Revolution Ignited the World, 1775–1848*. Princeton, NJ: Princeton University Press, 2019.
Israel, Jonathan. *Radical Enlightenment: Philosophy and the Making of Modernity, 1650–1750*. Oxford: Oxford University Press, 2003.
Jackson, Harry F. *Scholar in the Wilderness: Francis Adrian Van Der Kemp*. Syracuse, NY: Syracuse University Press, 1963.
Jackson, Maurice. *Let This Voice Be Heard: Anthony Benezet, Father of Atlantic Abolitionism*. Philadelphia: University of Pennsylvania Press, 2010.
Jacob, Margaret C. *The Secular Enlightenment*. Princeton, NJ: Princeton University Press, 2019.
Jacobs, Phoebe Lloyd. "John James Barralet and the Apotheosis of George Washington." *Winterthur Portfolio* 12 (1977): 115–37.
Jefferson, Thomas. "Letter to Benjamin Waterhouse." June 26, 1822. *Founders Online*. https://founders.archives.gov/documents/Jefferson/98-01-02-2905.
Jefferson, Thomas. "Letter to François Van Der Kemp." January 11, 1825. *Founders Online*. https://founders.archives.gov/documents/Jefferson/98-01-02-4857.
Jefferson, Thomas. "Letter to James Madison." September 6, 1789. *Founders Online*. https://founders.archives.gov/documents/Madison/01-12-02-0248.
Jefferson, Thomas. "Letter to John Cartwright." June 5, 1824. *Founders Online*. https://founders.archives.gov/documents/Jefferson/98-01-02-4313.
Jefferson, Thomas. "Letter to Levi Lincoln." October 25, 1802. *Founders Online*. https://founders.archives.gov/documents/Jefferson/01-38-02-0513.
Jefferson, Thomas. "Letter to William G. Munford." June 18, 1799. *Founders Online*. https://founders.archives.gov/documents/Jefferson/01-31-02-0112.
Jefferson, Thomas. "Letter to William Short" (October 31, 1819). In *Jefferson's Extracts from the Gospels: "The Philosophy of Jesus" and "The Life and Morals of Jesus,"* edited by Dickinson W. Adams, 387–91. Princeton, NJ: Princeton University Press, 1983.
Jefferson, Thomas. *Notes on the State of Virginia*. Philadelphia, 1788.
Jernegan, Marcus W. "Slavery and Conversion in the American Colonies." *American Historical Review* 21, no. 3 (1916): 504–27.
Johnson, Edward. *A History of New-England*. London, 1653.

Jordan, Winthrop D. *White over Black*. New York: Penguin Books, 1973.
Keith, George. *A Testimony against That False & Absurd Opinion Which Some Hold*. [Philadelphia], 1692.
Kennedy, Rick. *The First American Evangelical: A Short Life of Cotton Mather*. Grand Rapids, MI: William B. Eerdmans, 2015.
Kidd, Colin. *The Forging of Races: Race and Scripture in the Protestant Atlantic World, 1600–2000*. Cambridge: Cambridge University Press, 2006.
Kidd, Thomas S. "From Puritan to Evangelical: Changing Culture in New England, 1689–1740." PhD dissertation, University of Notre Dame, 2001.
Kidd, Thomas S. *The Great Awakening: The Roots of Evangelical Christianity in Colonial America*. New Haven, CT: Yale University Press, 2009.
Kidd, Thomas S. *The Protestant Interest: New England after Puritanism*. New Haven, CT: Yale University Press, 2004.
King, Miles. "Letter to Thomas Jefferson." August 20, 1814. *Founders Online*. https://founders.archives.gov/documents/Jefferson/03-07-02-0425.
Klingberg, Frank J., ed. *The Carolina Chronicle of Dr. Francis Le Jau, 1706–1717*. Berkeley: University of California Press, 1956.
Komline, David. "The Controversy of the Present Time: Arianism, William Whiston, and the Development of Cotton Mather's Late Eschatology." In *Cotton Mather and "Biblia Americana": America's First Bible Commentary. Essays in Reappraisal*, edited by Reiner Smolinski and Jan Stievermann, 439–59. Grand Rapids, MI: Baker Academic, 2011.
Kopelson, Heather Miyano. *Faithful Bodies: Performing Religion and Race in the Puritan Atlantic*. New York: New York University Press, 2014.
Lacey, Barbara E., ed. *The World of Hannah Heaton: The Diary of an Eighteenth-Century New England Farm Woman*. DeKalb: Northern Illinois University Press, 2003.
Laderman, Gary. *The Sacred Remains: American Attitudes towards Death, 1799–1883*. New Haven, CT: Yale University Press, 1996.
Lambert, Frank. "'I Saw the Book Talk': Slave Readings of the First Great Awakening." *Journal of African American History* 87, no. 1 (January 2002): 12–25.
Laqueur, Thomas Walter. *The Work of the Dead: A Cultural History of Mortal Remains*. Princeton, NJ: Princeton University Press, 2015.
Lewis, Rhodri. "William Petty's Anthropology: Religion, Colonialism, and the Problem of Human Diversity." *Huntington Library Quarterly* 74, no. 2 (June 2011): 261–88.
Ligon, Richard. *A True and Exact History of the Iland of Barbadoes*. London, 1657.
Lippard, George. *The Quaker City; or, The Monks of Monk-Hall*. 2 vols. Philadelphia, 1847.
Locke, John. *An Essay Concerning Human Understanding in Four Books*. London, 1694.
Locke, John. *The Reasonableness of Christianity as Delivered in the Scriptures*. London, 1695.
Lovelace, Richard F. *The American Pietism of Cotton Mather: Origins of American Evangelicalism*. Washington, DC: Christian University Press, 1979.
Loveman, Kate. "The Strange Finding Out of Moses His Tombe: News, Travel Narrative, and Satire." In *The Mysterious and the Foreign in Early Modern England*, edited by Helen Ostovich et al., 266–81. Newark: University of Delaware Press, 2008.
Mackie, John M. "Life of Samuel Gorton, One of the First Settlers of Warwick, in Rhode Island." In *Library of American Biography*, edited by Jared Sparks, 5:317–411. 2nd ed. Boston, 1864.
Maclear, J. F. "Anne Hutchinson and the Mortalist Heresy." *New England Quarterly* 54, no. 1 (1981): 74–103.

Mappen, Marc. "Anglican Heresy in Eighteenth Century Connecticut: The Disciplining of John Beach." *Historical Magazine of the Protestant Episcopal Church* 48, no. 4 (1979): 465–72.

Marshall, Peter. *Invisible Worlds: Death, Religion and the Supernatural In England, 1500–1700*. London: SPCK, 2017.

Martindell, Anne. *A Relation of the Labour, Travail and Suffering of That Faithful Servant of the Lord Alice Curwen*. [London], 1680.

Massing, Jean Michel. "From Greek Proverb to Soap Advert: Washing the Ethiopian." *Journal of the Warburg and Courtauld Institutes* 58 (1995): 180–201.

Matar, Nabil. *Islam in Britain, 1558–1685*. Cambridge: Cambridge University Press, 2009.

Mather, Cotton. *Advice from the Watch Tower*. Boston, 1713.

Mather, Cotton. *Agricola; or, The Religious Husbandman*. Boston, 1727.

Mather, Cotton. *The Angel of Bethesda*. Edited by Gordon Willis. Barre, MA: Barre Publications, 1972.

Mather, Cotton. *Awakening Thoughts on the Sleep of Death*. Boston, 1712.

Mather, Cotton. *Baptismal Piety*. Boston, 1727.

Mather, Cotton. *Biblia Americana: America's First Bible Commentary. A Synoptic Commentary on the Old and New Testaments*. Vol. 1: *Genesis*. Edited by Reiner Smolinski. Tübingen: Mohr Siebeck, 2010.

Mather, Cotton. *Biblia Americana: America's First Bible Commentary. A Synoptic Commentary on the Old and New Testaments*. Vol. 5: *Proverbs–Jeremiah*. Edited by Jan Stievermann. Tübingen: Mohr Siebeck, 2015.

Mather, Cotton. *Boanerges*. Boston, 1727.

Mather, Cotton. *Bonifacius*. Boston, 1710.

Mather, Cotton. *Brethren Dwelling Together in Unity*. Boston, 1718.

Mather, Cotton. *Christian Loyalty*. Boston, 1727.

Mather, Cotton. *Cœlestinus: A Conversation in Heaven, Quickened and Assisted, with Discoveries of Things in the Heavenly World*. Boston, 1723.

Mather, Cotton. *Coheleth. A Soul upon Recollection*. Boston, 1720.

[Mather, Cotton]. *A Collection of Some of the Many Offensive Matters Contained in a Pamphlet Entituled "The Order of the Gospel Revived."* Boston, 1701.

Mather, Cotton. *The Comfortable Chambers*. Boston, 1728.

Mather, Cotton. *Compassions Called For*. Boston, 1711.

Mather, Cotton. *Cotton Mather's "Problema Theologicum": An Authoritative Edition*. Edited by Jeffrey Scott Mares. *Proceedings of the American Antiquarian Society* 104, no. 2. Worcester, MA, 1995.

Mather, Cotton. *The Diary of Cotton Mather*. Edited by W. C. Ford. 2 vols. Boston: Massachusetts Historical Society, 1911.

Mather, Cotton. *A Faithful Man, Described and Rewarded*. Boston, 1705.

Mather, Cotton. *A Good Master Well Served*. Boston, 1696.

Mather, Cotton. *Hades Look'd Into*. Boston, 1717.

Mather, Cotton. *India Christiana*. Boston, 1721.

Mather, Cotton. "Latin Preface." In *Manuductio ad Ministerium: Directions for a Candidate of the Ministry*. Boston, 1726.

Mather, Cotton. *Light in Darkness*. Boston, 1724.

Mather, Cotton. *Magnalia Christi Americana; or, The Ecclesiastical History of New-England, from Its First Planting in the Year 1620. unto the Year of Our Lord, 1698*. London, 1702.

Mather, Cotton. *Manuductio ad Ministerium: Directions for a Candidate of the Ministry.* Boston, 1726.
Mather, Cotton. *A Midnight Cry.* Boston, 1692.
Mather, Cotton. *The Negro Christianized: An Essay to Excite and Assist the Good Work, the Instruction of Negro-Servants in Christianity.* Boston, 1706.
Mather, Cotton. *Reason Satisfied: And Faith Established.* Boston, 1712.
Mather, Cotton. *Selected Letters.* Edited by Kenneth Silverman. Baton Rouge: Louisiana State University Press, 1971.
Mather, Cotton. *Small Offers towards the Service of the Tabernacle in the Wilderness.* Boston, 1689.
Mather, Cotton. *Terra Beata.* Boston, 1726.
Mather, Cotton. *The Terror of the Lord: Some Account of the Earthquake That Shook New-England, in the Night, between the 29 and the 30 of October, 1727.* Boston, 1727.
Mather, Cotton. *Theopolis Americana: An Essay on the Golden Street of the Holy City.* Boston, 1710.
Mather, Cotton. *The Threefold Paradise of Cotton Mather: An Edition of "Triparadisus."* Edited by Reiner Smolinski. Athens: University of Georgia Press, 1995.
Mather, Cotton. *The Triumphs of the Reformed Religion, in America.* Boston, 1691.
Mather, Cotton. *The Widow of Naim.* Boston, 1728.
Mather, Cotton, and Mather, Increase. *Three Letters from New-England, Relating to the Controversy of the Present Time.* London, 1721.
Mather, Increase. *Meditations on the Glory of the Heavenly World.* Boston, 1711.
Mather, Increase. "To the Reader." In *God Brings to the Desired Haven*, by Thomas Prince. Boston, 1717.
Mather, Samuel. *A Funeral Discourse Preached on the Occasion of the Death of the High, Puissant and Most Illustrious Prince Frederick Lewis, Prince of Great-Britain.* Boston, 1751.
Mayhew, Experience. *Indian Converts: Or, Some Account of the Lives and Dying Speeches of a Considerable Number of the Christianized Indians of Martha's Vineyard, in New-England.* London, 1727.
Mayhew, Jonathan. *Practical Discourses on Occasion of the Earthquakes in November, 1755.* Boston, 1760.
Mayhew, Jonathan. *A Sermon Preached at Boston in New-England, May 26, 1751.* Boston, 1751.
Mbembe, Achille. *Critique of Black Reason.* Translated by Laurent Dubois. Durham, NC: Duke University Press, 2017.
McClure, Christopher Scott. "Hell and Anxiety in Hobbes's *Leviathan*." *The Review of Politics* 73 (2011): 1–27.
McDannell, Colleen, and Bernhard Lang. *Heaven: A History.* 2nd ed. New Haven, CT: Yale University Press, 2001.
McGiffert, Michael. *God's Plot: Puritan Spirituality in Thomas Shepard's Cambridge.* Rev. ed. Amherst: University of Massachusetts Press, 1994.
McGiffert, Michael. "Shepard, Thomas (1605–1649), New England Puritan Minister." *American National Biography Online.* Oxford University Press, 2000. https://www.anb.org/view/10.1093/anb/9780198606697.001.0001/anb-9780198606697-e-0100828.
Mede, Joseph. *The Works of the Pious and Profoundly-Learned Joseph Mede, B.D.* London, 1672.

Merchant, Carolyn. *The Anthropocene and the Humanities: From Climate Change to a New Age of Sustainability*. New Haven, CT: Yale University Press, 2020.

Merchant, Carolyn. *Radical Ecology: The Search for a Livable World*. 2nd ed. New York: Routledge, 2005.

Messamore, Everett. "Spiritualism and the Language of Universal Religion in Nineteenth-Century America." PhD dissertation, Ruprecht-Karls-Universität Heidelberg, 2018.

Middlekauff, Robert. *The Mathers: Three Generations of Puritan Intellectuals, 1596–1728*. Berkeley: University of California Press, 1999.

Milbank, John. "The Midwinter Sacrifice." In *The Blackwell Companion to Postmodern Theology*, edited by Graham Ward, 107–30. Oxford: Blackwell, 2001.

Milbank, John. "What Is Radical Orthodoxy?" University of Freiburg, 2015. http://www.unifr.ch/theo/assets/files/SA2015/Theses_EN.pdf. Last accessed September 3, 2020.

Miller, Perry. *The New England Mind: From Colony to Province*. Cambridge, MA: Belknap Press of Harvard University Press, 1983.

Miller, Perry. *The New England Mind: The Seventeenth Century*. Cambridge, MA: Belknap Press of Harvard University Press, 1982.

Moore, R. Laurence. "Religion, Secularization, and the Shaping of the Culture Industry in Antebellum America." *American Quarterly* 41, no. 2 (1989): 216–42.

Moorhead, James H. "The Erosion of Postmillennialism in American Religious Thought, 1865–1925." *Church History* 53, no. 1 (1984): 61–77.

More, Henry. "An Explanation of the Grand Mystery of Godliness." In *The Theological Works of the Most Pious and Learned Henry More, D. D.* London, 1708.

Morton, Nathaniel. *New-Englands Memoriall*. Boston, 1669.

Morton, Timothy. *Dark Ecology: For a Logic of Future Coexistence*. New York: Columbia University Press, 2016.

Morton, Timothy. *Humankind: Solidarity with Non-human People*. London: Verso, 2017.

Murphy, Andrew R. *Liberty, Conscience, and Toleration: The Political Thought of William Penn*. New York: Oxford University Press, 2016.

Murray, Hannah Lauren. *Liminal Whiteness in Early US Fiction: Interventions in Nineteenth-Century American Literature and Culture*. Edinburgh: Edinburgh University Press, 2021.

Nash, Gary B. *Quakers and Politics: Pennsylvania, 1681–1726*. New ed. Boston: Northeastern University Press, 1993.

National Funeral Directors Association. "Cremation Is Here to Stay: Aging Baby Boomers Proved Catalyst in Shift beyond Traditional Burial." nfda.org, July 15, 2019. https://www.nfda.org/news/media-center/nfda-news-releases/id/4395/cremation-is-here-to-stay-aging-baby-boomers-proved-catalyst-in-shift-beyond-traditional-burial.

Nelson, Dana D. *The Word in Black and White: Reading "Race" in American Literature, 1638–1867*. New York: Oxford University Press, 1994.

Neuman, Meredith Marie. *Jeremiah's Scribes: Creating Sermon Literature in Puritan New England*. Philadelphia: University of Pennsylvania Press, 2013.

New England Weekly Journal. February 24, 1729.

New-England Weekly Journal. March 2, 1730.

New-England Weekly Journal. March 9, 1730.

Norton, John. *Abel Being Dead Yet Speaketh*. London, 1658.

Noyes, John Humphrey. *The Berean: A Manual for the Help of Those Who Seek the Faith of the Primitive Church*. Putney, VT, 1847.

Noyes, Nicholas. *New-Englands Duty and Interest, to Be an Habitation of Justice, and Mountain of Holiness*. Boston, 1698.

Noyes, Nicholas. "The Rev. Nicholas Noyes to the Rev. Cotton Mather." In *Proceedings of the Massachusetts Historical Society*, 2nd Series, 9:484–85. Boston, 1866.

Nye, Philip, and Thomas Goodwin. "To the Reader." In *The Keyes of the Kingdom of Heaven and Power Thereof according to the Word of God*, by John Cotton. London, 1644.

Oberlin Evangelist. November 26, 1831.

O'Donnell, Patricia C. "This Side of the Grave: Navigating the Quaker Plainness Testimony in London and Philadelphia in the Eighteenth Century." *Winterthur Portfolio* 49, no. 1 (March 2015): 29–54.

Ogilby, John. *Africa.* London, 1670.

O'Neale, Sondra A. *Jupiter Hammon and the Biblical Beginnings of African-American Literature.* Metuchen, NJ: American Theological Library Association, 1993.

O'Neale, Sondra A. "A Slave's Subtle War: Phillis Wheatley's Use of Biblical Myth and Symbol." *Early American Literature* 21, no. 2 (1986): 144–65.

Paine, Thomas. *The Age of Reason.* London, 1794.

Paine, Thomas. *The Age of Reason: Part the Second.* London, 1795.

Palmer, Elihu. *An Enquiry Relative to the Moral & Political Improvement of the Human Species.* New York, 1797.

Palmer, Elihu. *Principles of Nature; or Developement of the Moral Causes of Happiness and Misery among the Human Species.* 2nd ed. New York, 1802.

Parr, Jessica M. *Inventing George Whitefield: Race, Revivalism, and the Making of a Religious Icon.* Jackson: University Press of Mississippi, 2015.

Pemberton, Ebenezer. *A Funeral Sermon on the Death of That Learned & Excellent Divine the Reverend Mr. Samuel Willard.* Boston, 1707.

Pemberton, Ebenezer. *A True Servant of His Generation Characterized, and His Promised State of Refreshment Assigned: A Sermon Preached on the Death of the Honourable John Walley Esq.* Boston, 1712.

Penn, William. *An Address to Protestants upon the Present Conjuncture in II Parts.* [London], 1679.

Penn, William. *A Brief Account of the Rise and Progress of the People Called Quakers.* London, 1694.

Penn, William. *The Frame of the Government of the Province of Pennsilvania in America.* 1682.

Penn, William. *The Invalidity of John Faldo's Vindication of His Book, Called "Quakerism No Christianity."* London, 1673.

Penn, William. *A Perswasive to Moderation to Church Dissenters, in Prudence and Conscience Humbly Submitted to the King and His Great Councel.* London, 1686.

Penn, William. *Quakerism, a New Nick-Name for Old Christianity.* London, 1672.

Perkins, William. *A Golden Chaine; or, The Description of Theologie Containing the Order of the Causes of Saluation and Damnation, according to Gods Word.* Cambridge, 1600.

Peterson, Mark A. "The Selling of Joseph: Bostonians, Antislavery, and the Protestant International, 1689–1733." *Massachusetts Historical Review* 4 (2002): 1–22.

Petty, William. *Several Essays in Political Arithmetick.* London, 1699.

Phelps, Elizabeth, Stuart. *The Gates Ajar.* Boston, 1878.

Pinheiro, John C. *Missionaries of Republicanism: A Religious History of the Mexican-American War.* New York: Oxford University Press, 2014.

Poe, Edgar Allan. *The Works of Edgar Allan Poe.* 10 vols. New York: Colonial Co., 1903.

Pooley, Roger. "Saltmarsh, John (d. 1647), Preacher and Religious Controversialist." *Dictionary of National Biography Online.* Oxford University Press, 2004. https://doi.org/10.1093/ref:odnb/24578.

Prince, George. *Elder John Prince of Hull, Mass.: A Memorial, Biographical & Genealogical.* Boston, 1888.

Prince, Thomas. *An Account of a Strange Appearance in the Heavens on Tuesday-Night, March 6. 1716: As It Was Seen over Stow-Market in Suffolk in England.* Boston, 1719.

Prince, Thomas. *Christ Abolishing Death and Bringing Life and Immortality to Light in the Gospel.* Boston, 1736.

Prince, Thomas. *Extraordinary Events the Doings of God, and Marvellous in Pious Eyes.* Boston, 1747.

Prince, Thomas. *A Funeral Sermon on the Reverend Mr. Nathanael Williams.* Boston, 1738.

Prince, Thomas. *God Brings to the Desired Haven.* Boston, 1717.

Prince, Thomas. *God Destroyeth the Hope of Man! A Sermon Occasion'd by the Inexpressible Loss in the Death of His Late Royal Highness Frederick Prince of Wales.* Boston, 1751.

Prince, Thomas. *It Being Earnestly Desired.* Boston, 1743.

Prince, Thomas. *Morning Health No Security against the Sudden Arrest of Death before Night.* Boston, 1727.

Prince, Thomas. *The Pious Cry to the Lord for Help When the Godly and Faithful Fail among Them.* Boston, 1746.

Prince, Thomas. "Preface." In *A Brief Discourse of concerning Futurities or Things to Come,* by William Torrey. Boston, 1757.

Prince, Thomas. *The Psalms, Hymns, and Spiritual Songs of the Old and New Testament, Faithfully Translated into English Metre.* Boston, 1758.

Prince, Thomas. *Sermon . . . : Upon the Death of the Honourable Samuel Sewall, Esq.* Boston, 1730.

Prince, Thomas. *Six Sermons by the Late Thomas Prince, A.M. One of the Ministers of the South Church in Boston.* Edinburgh, 1785.

Prince, Thomas. *The Sovereign God Acknowledged and Blessed, Both in Giving and Taking Away.* Boston, 1744.

Prince, Thomas. *Three Sermons on Death and Dying.* Prince Family Papers, 1724–1822, Mss Miscellaneous Boxes P. American Antiquarian Society. Worcester, MA.

Prince, Thomas. *The Vade Mecum for America; or, A Companion for Traders and Travellers.* Boston, 1731.

Reynolds, David S. "Deformance, Performativity, Posthumanism." *Nineteenth-Century Literature* 70, no. 1 (1 June 2015): 36–64.

Richards, Phillip M. "Nationalist Themes in the Preaching of Jupiter Hammon." *Early American Literature* 25, no. 2 (1990): 123–38.

Rivett, Sarah. *The Science of the Soul in Colonial New England.* Chapel Hill: University of North Carolina Press, 2011.

Rivett, Sarah, and Abram Van Engen. "Postexceptionalist Puritanism." *American Literature* 90, no. 4 (December 1, 2018): 675–92.

Rogers, John. *A Sermon Preached before His Excellency the Governour, the Honourable Council, and Representative of the Province of the Massachusetts-Bay in New England.* Boston, 1706.

Rubiés, Joan-Pau. "Hugo Grotius's Dissertation on the Origin of the American Peoples and the Use of Comparative Methods." *Journal of the History of Ideas* 52, no. 2 (1991): 221–44.

Rogers, P. G. *The Fifth Monarchy Men.* London: Oxford University Press, 1966.

Rush, Benjamin. *An Enquiry into the Influence of Physical Causes upon the Moral Faculty.* Philadelphia, 1786.

Rush, Benjamin. "Observations Intended to Favour a Supposition That the Black Color (as It Is Called) of the Negroes Is Derived from the Leprosy." *Transactions of the American Philosophical Society* 4 (1799): 289–97.

Saffin, John. "A Brief and Candid Answer to a Late Printed Sheet, Entituled, The Selling of Joseph." In *Notes on the History of Slavery in Massachusetts*, edited by George H. Moore, 251–56. New York, 1866.

Saltmarsh, John. *Sparkles of Glory, or Some Beams of the Morning-Star*. London, 1647.

Sancho, Ignatius. *Letters of the Late Ignatius Sancho, an African*. 3rd ed. London, 1784.

Scheick, William J. "Phillis Wheatley's Appropriation of Isaiah." *Early American Literature* 27, no. 2 (1992): 135–40.

Scherr, Arthur. "Thomas Jefferson versus the Historians: Christianity, Atheistic Morality, and the Afterlife." *Church History* 83, no. 1 (March 2014): 60–109.

Schlereth, Eric R. *An Age of Infidels: The Politics of Religious Controversy in the Early United States*. Philadelphia: University of Pennsylvania Press, 2013.

Schmidt, Leigh Eric. "'The Grand Prophet,' Hugh Bryan: Early Evangelicalism's Challenge to the Establishment and Slavery in the Colonial South." *South Carolina Historical Magazine* 87, no. 4 (1986): 238–50.

Schulz, Constance B. "'Of Bigotry in Politics and Religion': Jefferson's Religion, the Federalist Press, and the Syllabus." *Virginia Magazine of History and Biography* 91, no. 1 (January 1983): 73–91.

Schwartz, Hillel. *The French Prophets: The History of a Millenarian Group in Eighteenth-Century England*. Berkeley: University of California Press, 1980.

Seeman, Erik R. *Death in the New World: Cross-Cultural Encounters, 1492–1800*. Philadelphia: University of Pennsylvania Press, 2010.

Seeman, Erik R. "'Justise Must Take Plase': Three African Americans Speak of Religion in Eighteenth-Century New England." *William and Mary Quarterly* 56, no. 2 (April 1999): 393–414.

Seeman, Erik R. *Pious Persuasions: Laity and Clergy in Eighteenth-Century New England*. Early America. Baltimore: Johns Hopkins University Press, 1999.

Seeman, Erik R. *Speaking with the Dead in Early America*. Philadelphia: University of Pennsylvania Press, 2019.

Sensbach, Jon F. *Rebecca's Revival: Creating Black Christianity in the Atlantic World*. Cambridge, MA: Harvard University Press, 2006.

Sepinwall, Alyssa Goldstein. *The Abbé Grégoire and the French Revolution: The Making of Modern Universalism*. Berkeley: University of California Press, 2005.

Sewall, Samuel. "Appendix." In *Phaenomena Quaedam Apocalyptica ad Aspectum Novi Orbis Configurata; or, Some Few Lines towards a Description of the New Heaven as It Makes to Those Who Stand upon the New Earth*, 16–24. 2nd ed. Boston, 1727.

Sewall, Samuel. *Diary of Samuel Sewall*. 3 vols. Collections of the Massachusetts Historical Society. 5th Series. Vols. 5–7. Boston, 1878.

Sewall, Samuel. *The Letter-Book of Samuel Sewall*. 2 vols. Collections of the Massachusetts Historical Society. 6th Series. Vols. 1–2. Boston, 1886.

Sewall, Samuel. *Phaenomena Quaedam Apocalyptica ad Aspectum Novi Orbis Configurata. Or, Some Few Lines towards a Description of the New Heaven as It Makes to Those Who Stand upon the New Earth*. Boston, 1697.

Sewall, Samuel. *The Selling of Joseph: A Memorial*. Boston, 1700.

Shepard, Thomas. *The Parable of the Ten Virgins*. London, 1660.

Shepard, Thomas. *The Sincere Convert*. London, 1640.

Shepard, Thomas. *Subjection to Christ in All His Ordinances and Appointments, the Best Means to Preserve Our Liberty*. London, 1652.
Shepard, Thomas. *Theses Sabbaticæ*. London, 1650.
Shepard, Thomas. *A Treatise of Liturgies, Power of the Keyes, and of Matter of the Visible Church*. London, 1652.
Shepard, Thomas. *Wine for Gospel Wantons*. Cambridge, MA,, 1668.
Shields, David S. "Mental Nocturnes: Night Thoughts on Man and Nature in the Poetry of Eighteenth-Century America." *Pennsylvania Magazine of History and Biography* 110, no. 2 (April 1986): 237–58.
Shields, John C. *Phillis Wheatley's Poetics of Liberation: Backgrounds and Contexts*. Knoxville: University of Tennessee Press, 2008.
Shoemaker, Nancy. "How Indians Got to Be Red." *American Historical Review* 102, no. 3 (1997): 625–44.
Shoemaker, Nancy. *A Strange Likeness: Becoming Red and White in Eighteenth-Century North America*. New York: Oxford University Press, 2004.
Sidbury, James. *Becoming African in America: Race and Nation in the Early Black Atlantic*. New York: Oxford University Press, 2009.
Silva, Cristobal. *Miraculous Plagues: An Epidemiology of Early New England Narrative*. New York: Oxford University Press, 2011.
Silverman, Kenneth. *The Life and Times of Cotton Mather*. New York: Columbia University Press, 1985.
Sloterdijk, Peter. *In the World Interior of Capital: For a Philosophical Theory of Globalization*. Cambridge: Polity Press, 2013.
Smalbroke, Richard. *A Sermon Preached before the Incorporated Society for the Propagation of the Gospel in Foreign Parts*. London, 1733.
Smith, Gary Scott. *Heaven in the American Imagination*. New York: Oxford University Press, 2011.
Smith, Joseph. "Discourse, 5 January 1841, as Reported by William P. McIntire." *The Joseph Smith Papers*. Accessed August 16, 2020. https://www.josephsmithpapers.org/paper-summary/discourse-5-january-1841-as-reported-by-william-p-mcintire.
Smith, Joseph. "Revelation Book 1." *The Joseph Smith Papers*. Accessed August 16, 2020. https://www.josephsmithpapers.org/paper-summary/revelation-book-1/56.
Smith, Justin E. H. *Nature, Human Nature, & Human Difference: Race in Early Modern Philosophy*. Princeton, NJ: Princeton University Press, 2017.
Smith, Stanhope. *An Essay on the Causes of the Variety of Complexion and Figure in the Human Species*. Philadelphia: Robert Aitken, 1787.
Smolenski, John. *Friends and Strangers: The Making of a Creole Culture in Colonial Pennsylvania*. Philadelphia: University of Pennsylvania Press, 2012.
Smolinski, Reiner. "Apocalypticism in Colonial North America." In *The Encylopedia of Apocalypticism*, edited by Bernard McGinn et al., 3:36–71. New York: Continuum, 1998.
Smolinski, Reiner. "Caveat Emptor: Pre- and Postmillennialism in the Late Reformation Period." In *Millenarianism and Messianism in Early Modern European Culture*, vol. 3: *The Millenarian Turn*, edited by James E. Force and Richard H. Popkin, 145–69. Dordrecht: Springer Netherlands, 2001.
Smolinski, Reiner. "Introduction." In *The Threefold Paradise of Cotton Mather: An Edition of "Triparadisus,"* by Cotton Mather, 3–86. Athens: University of Georgia Press, 1995.
Smolinski, Reiner. "Israel Redivivus: The Eschatological Limits of Puritan Typology in New England." *New England Quarterly* 63, no. 3 (September 1990): 357–95.

Jeffrey S. Cramer, 281–316. New York: Library of America, 2001.

Thoreau, Henry David. *The Writings of Henry David Thoreau*. Edited by Bradford Torrey.

Van Engen, Abram C. *City on a Hill: A History of American Exceptionalism*. New Haven,

Vidal, Fernando. "Brains, Bodies, Selves, and Science: Anthropologies of Identity and the Resurrection of the Body." *Critical Inquiry* 28, no. 4 (June 2002): 930–74.

Wadsworth, Benjamin. *The Benefits of a Good, and the Mischiefs of an Evil, Conscience*. Boston, 1719.

Wadsworth, Benjamin. *Mutual Love and Peace among Christians*. Boston, 1701.

Walett, Francis G. "Shadrack Ireland and the 'Immortals' of Colonial New England." In *Sibley's Heir: A Volume in Memory of Clifford Kenyon Shipton*, 541–50. Publications of the Colonial Society of Massachusetts 59. Boston: Colonial Society of Massachusetts, 1982.

Walker, David. *Walker's Appeal in Four Articles*. 3rd ed. Boston, 1830.

Ward, Graham. "The Metaphysics of the Body." In *Apophatic Bodies: Negative Theology, Incarnation, and Relationality*, edited by Chris Boesel and Catherine Keller, 227–50. New York: Fordham University Press, 2010.

Warner, Margaret Humphreys. "Vindicating the Minister's Medical Role: Cotton Mather's Concept of the 'Nishmath-Chajim' and the Spiritualization of Medicine." *Journal of the History of Medicine and Allied Sciences* 36, no. 3 (1981): 278–95.

Warren, Wendy. *New England Bound: Slavery and Colonization in Early America*. New York: Liveright, 2017.

Washington, George. *Address of George Washington to the People of the United States, Announcing His Resolution to Retire from Public Life*. Providence, RI, 1796.

Waters, Brent. "Whose Salvation? Which Eschatology? Transhumanism and Christianity as Contending Salvific Religions." In *Transhumanism and Transcendence: Christian Hope in an Age of Technological Enhancement*, edited by Ronald Cole-Turner, 163–76. Washington, DC: Georgetown University Press, 2011.

Weber, Max. *The Protestant Ethic and the Spirit of Capitalism*. London: Routledge, 2001.

Weddle, Meredith Baldwin. *Walking in the Way of Peace: Quaker Pacifism in the Seventeenth Century*. New York: Oxford University Press, 2001.

Wesley, John. *Thoughts upon Slavery*. London, 1774.

Westerkamp, Marilyn J. "Anne Hutchinson, Sectarian Mysticism, and the Puritan Order." *Church History* 59, no. 4 (1990): 482–96.

Wheatley, Phillis. *Poems on Various Subjects, Religious and Moral*. Philadelphia, 1787.
Whiston, William. *A New Theory of the Earth, from Its Original to the Consummation of All Things*. 6th ed. London, 1755.
Whiston, William. *A Supplement to Mr. Whiston's Late Essay, towards Restoring the True Text of the Old Testament*. London, 1723.
Whitefield, George. *The Duty of a Gospel Minister*. Glasgow, 1741.
Whitefield, George. *An Exhortation to Come and See Jesus*. London, 1739.
Whitefield, George. *Five Sermons*. London, 1747.
Whitefield, George. *The Marriage of Cana*. Glasgow, 1741.
Whitefield, George. *The Nature and Necessity of Our New Birth in Christ Jesus, in Order to Salvation*. 3rd ed. London, 1738.
Whitefield, George. *A New Heart, the Best New Year's Gift*. London, 1740.
Whitefield, George. *The Power of Christ's Resurrection*. London, 1739.
Whitefield, George. *Some Remarks on a Late Pamphlet Intitled, The State of Religion in New-England*. Glasow [sic], 1742.
Whitefield, George. "To the Inhabitants of Maryland." In *Three Letters from the Reverend Mr. G. Whitefield*, 13–16. Philadelphia, 1740.
Whitefield, George. "An Unpublished Journal of George Whitefield." Edited by Earnest Edward Eells. *Church History* 7, no. 4 (1938): 297–345.
Whitefield, George. *The Wise and Foolish Virgins*. Edinburgh, 1740.
Whitefield, George. *The Works of the Reverend George Whitefield*. Vol. 2. London, 1771.
Willard, Samuel. *A Compleat Body of Divinity in Two Hundred and Fifty Expository Lectures on the Assembly's Shorter Catechism*. Boston, 1726.
Willard, Samuel. *Reformation the Great Duty of an Afflicted People*. Boston, 1694.
Williams, Roger. *The Bloudy Tenent, of Persecution, for Cause of Conscience*. London, 1644.
Williams, Roger. *A Key into the Language of America*. London, 1643.
Wilson, Thomas. *An Essay towards an Instruction for the Indians*. London, 1740.
Winchester, Elhanan. *A Course of Lectures, on the Prophecies That Remain to Be Fulfilled*. Vol. 3. London, 1789.
Winchester, Elhanan. "Letter to George Washington." *Founders Online*. August 15, 1791. https://founders.archives.gov/documents/Washington/05-08-02-0300.
Winiarski, Douglas L. *Darkness Falls on the Land of Light: Experiencing Religious Awakenings in Eighteenth-Century New England*. Chapel Hill: University of North Carolina Press, 2017.
Winship, Michael P. *Making Heretics: Militant Protestantism and Free Grace in Massachusetts, 1636–1641*. Princeton, NJ: Princeton University Press, 2002.
Winship, Michael P. *Seers of God: Puritan Providentialism in the Restoration and Early Enlightenment*. Baltimore: Johns Hopkins University Press, 2000.
Winslow, Edward. *Hypocrisie Unmasked*. London, 1647.
Winsor, Justin. *The Prince Library*. Boston: Alfred Mudge & Son, 1870.
Winthrop, James. *An Attempt to Translate the Prophetic Part of the Apocalypse of Saint John into Familiar Language*. Boston, 1794.
Winthrop, James. *A Systematic Arrangement of Several Prophecies Relating to Antichrist*. Boston, 1795.
Winthrop, John. *Winthrop's Journal, "History of New England", 1630–1649*. Edited by James Kendall Hosmer. 2 vols. New York: Scribners, 1908.
Wisner, William. "Letter to Thomas Jefferson." July 7, 1823. *Founders Online*. https://founders.archives.gov/documents/Jefferson/98-01-02-3618.

The Wonderful Narrative: or, A Faithful Account of the French Prophets. Boston, 1742.
Wood, Gordon S. *Friends Divided: John Adams and Thomas Jefferson.* New York: Penguin Press, 2017.
Woods, John A. "The Correspondence of Benjamin Rush and Granville Sharp 1773–1809." *Journal of American Studies* 1, no. 1 (1967): 1–38.
Wynne, John. *A Sermon Preached before the Incorporated Society for the Propagation of the Gospel in Foreign Parts,* London, 1725.
Young, B. W. "'The Soul-Sleeping System': Politics and Heresy in Eighteenth-Century England." *Journal of Ecclesiastical History* 45, no. 1 (1994): 64–81.
Zakai, Avihu. *Jonathan Edwards' Philosophy of History: The Re-enchantment of the World in the Age of Enlightenment.* Princeton, NJ: Princeton University Press, 2003.
Ziff, Larzer. *The Career of John Cotton: Puritanism and the American Experience.* Princeton, NJ: Princeton University Press, 1962.

Index

For the benefit of digital users, indexed terms that span two pages (e.g., 52–53) may, on occasion, appear on only one of those pages.

Act of Toleration (1689), 89
Adams, John, 13, 183–84, 206–8, 261–62n.21
An Address to the Negroes in the State of New-York (Hammon), 135–36
Advice from the Watchtower (Cotton Mather), 122–23, 248n.92
Aesop, 250n.116
African Methodist Episcopal Church, 140
Africans. *See* enslaved Africans; free Africans
The Age of Reason (Paine), 179–81
agrilogistics, 226–27
Alcott, William, 182–83, 213–14
Algonquian Indians, 100
Allen, Ethan, 200–1, 208
Alsted, Johann, 15–16
American Civil War, 182, 210–11, 214
American Colonization Society, 140
American Revolution. *See also* republicanism
  The Columbiad's depiction of, 185–86
  constraints on executive power and, 60–61
  Great Britain framed as "Antichrist" by some ministers during, 175–76
  models of human perfectibility and, 181–82
  resurrection as political metaphor and, 4–5, 184
  visions of secular progress and, 223–24
Ames, William, 231n.14
Angell, John, 48, 51–52
The Angel of Bethesda (Cotton Mather), 75, 80–82
Anglican Church. *See* Church of England
Anthropocene, the, 227–28
Antinomian Controversy, 9, 21–22, 28–29, 40. *See also* Hutchinson, Anne
Apess, William, 138, 253n.204
Apollos (New Testament), 117–18
The Apotheosis of George Washington (Barralet), 204
Appeal to the Coloured Citizens of the World (Walker), 141
Aquidneck settlement (Rhode Island), 28–29, 30–31, 51–52

Arianism, 85–86, 97–98, 242n.85
Ariès, Philippe, 222–23
Asad, Talal, 46–47
Ashurst, William, 116–17
Augustine (saint), 15, 66, 105, 230n.3
"Autumnal Tints" (Thoreau), 216–17

Backus, Isaac, 165
Baillie, Robert
  Congregationalist beliefs on resurrection criticized by, 17–20
  Congregationalist system of church government criticized by, 9, 16–17
  on Hutchinson, 18–19, 22
  millennialism and, 17, 18
Baily, John, 74–75
Ball, Charles, 139–40
Baptists, 48–49, 182
Barbados, 2–3, 55–56, 101, 104–5, 111, 124
Barclay, Robert, 52–53
Barlow, Joel
  Columbus depicted as forebearer of modern American democracy by, 189–90
  Columbus's first sight of North America compared to first sight of resurrection by, 188–89
  Congregationalist upbringing of, 186, 262–63n.41
  faith in internationalism and progress expressed by, 190–91
  on farming as means of eliminating racial difference, 197–98
  Federalist Party and, 186–87
  republicanism and, 190–91
  secular conceptions of the millennium used to depict American Republic by, 185–87, 188, 191
Barralet, John James, 204
Barton, Benjamin, 197
Baxter, Richard, 130, 162, 230n.17, 249n.110
Bayle, Pierre, 62
The Bay Psalm Book (Prince), 170–71

294 INDEX

Beach, John
  on enslaved Africans' potential salvation, 129
  on Jesus's resurrection, 127
  as missionary for Society for the Propagation of the Bible, 125–26
  mortalism condemned by, 126–27
  on political freedoms for Christian slaves, 129
  racial difference absent from millennial theology of, 11, 105–6, 128, 129–30, 198
  resurrection of the body absent from theology of, 11, 106, 127–30
  saints' immediate ascent into Heaven in theology of, 106, 128
  on Second Coming as end of life on earth, 127–28, 129–30
  slavery accepted by, 129
Beecher, Lyman, 260n.157
Belcher, Mary, 155, 157–58
Bercovitch, Sacvan, 71–72, 91
"Berenice" (Poe), 215
Biblia Americana (Cotton Mather), 65–66, 119
Bishop, George, 54–55
Block, Sharon, 103–4
Blount, Charles, 62
Blumenberg, Hans, 181
Bolt, John, 109
The Bones of Joseph (Colman), 98
Book of Common Prayer
  Savoy Conference (1661) and, 229 n7
Book of Common Prayer (Church of England), 1–2, 179
Book of Mormon, 176
Book of Sports, 234n.76
Borm, Johannes, 132–33
Boston (Massachusetts)
  arsons (1723) in, 109–110, 114
  city slave code (1723) in, 114
  as commercial center, 91
  earthquakes during eighteenth century in, 169, 171–73
  Great Awakening revivals in, 166–68
Brainerd, David, 167–68
Brattle Street Church (Boston, MA), 11, 94
Breen, Louise, 76–77
A Brief Discourse Concerning Futurities (Torrey), 148–49, 171–73
Brightman, Thomas, 15–16, 186
British Civil Wars (1638-53), 3–4, 16, 24, 36–37
Brooks, Joanna, 132, 251–52n.160
Brown, Charles Brockden, 198–99, 218
Brown, Vincent, 101–2

Bryan, Hugh, 133–34, 252n.170
Bulkeley, Peter, 25
Burnet, Thomas, 62, 145
Burnham, Michelle, 40–41
Butler, Jon, 163

Calamy, Edmund, 160
Calvinism, 13–14, 20, 24, 206, 207–8. *See also* Congregationalism; Puritans
Canada, 72, 91, 144
Cápac, Manco, 189
Cape Cod (Thoreau), 216–18
Casanova, José, 147–48
Catholicism
  as the Antichrist, 33–34, 45, 86–87, 96–97, 110–11, 171–72
  Beecher and, 260n.157
  funeral and burial practices in, 1–2
  Puritan beliefs regarding, 5, 8–9, 26, 33–34, 63
  relics and, 8–9
  salvation and resurrection beliefs in, 21, 26, 44, 50, 127
Cemeteries, 216–17, 222–23
Chaloner, Thomas, 66
changed saints
  Africans and Native Americans among the ranks of, 120–22
  biological and social needs of, 90–91
  The Conflagration's sparing of, 61, 84–85, 86–87
  geographical origins of, 97–98
  nationalities among, 61
  New Earth daily lives of, 86–87, 97, 120–21, 157–58, 172–73
  Nishmath-Chajim and, 82–83, 102
  racial difference and, 106
  raised saints' relationship with, 64–65, 80–83, 84–85, 88, 89–90, 95–96, 120–22, 145
  Second Coming of Jesus and, 95
Charles I (king of England), 152–53
Chauncy, Charles, 146–47, 160, 169, 256n.59
Christian History newspaper, 146–47, 160–61, 166
Chronological History of New England (Prince), 147, 170–71
Church of England
  Book of Common Prayer and, 1–2, 179
  evangelization of enslaved Africans and Native Americans by, 124–27 (*see also* The Society for the Propagation of the Gospel)
  Mather on, 68–69, 87–88
  mortalism and, 77–78, 126–27

psychopannychism and, 126–27
Puritans and Nonconformists persecuted by, 36–37, 87–88
Westminster Assembly and, 16–17
Church of Latter Day Saints, 176, 260n.168
Codrington, Christopher, 124
Cœlestinus (Cotton Mather), 80–81, 83
Coheleth (Cotton Mather), 75, 78
Colman, Benjamin
Brattle Street Church and, 94
on British imperialism and global improvement, 12–13, 96
on communion between the living and dead, 98
Davenport's criticisms of, 163–64
ecumenical cooperation between Protestant denominations promoted by, 145–46
on Enoch, 94–95
First Resurrection and, 94–95, 98–99
Hanover dynasty and, 96
human instincts celebrated by, 150–51
Mather and, 94–95, 97–98
memorial sermons of, 156–57
on millennial significance of Great Britain's wars against Catholic enemies, 157
on missionary efforts in North America, 96
on "moderate mirth," 151
moral value of commercial endeavor recognized by, 150
resurrection of the body and, 64, 95–96, 98–99
Second Coming of Jesus and, 95–96
warning about preaching imminence of millennium issued by, 97
Whitefield and, 164–65
The Columbiad (Barlow)
Columbus denied supernatural vision in, 188
Columbus depicted as forebearer of modern American democracy in, 189–90
Columbus's first sight of North America compared to resurrected believer's first sight of earth from heaven in, 188–89
faith in internationalism and progress expressed in, 190–91
global congress of secular millennium recounted in, 187
secular conceptions of the millennium used to depict American Republic in, 185–86
Comfortable Chambers (Cotton Mather), 75, 80
The Conflagration
changed saints spared in, 61, 84–85, 86–87
environmental destruction wrought by, 144, 145
Mather on, 61, 85–87, 90–91, 97, 120, 145

millennium following, 61, 145, 172–73
ministerial education and preparation for, 86–87
physico-theologians' scientific accounts of, 62, 145
Prince on, 144–45
Torrey on, 172–73
wicked people of Earth killed in, 61, 90–91
Winchester on, 176
Congregationalism. *See also* Puritans
Baillie's criticism of resurrection beliefs in, 17–20
church government structure in, 9, 16–17, 20–21, 62, 73
fractionalization into revivalist sects during eighteenth century within, 147, 164–65, 170
Great Awakening and Native American converts to, 131–32
the millennium and, 3, 18–19, 31
missionaries promoting, 104
ordained ministers' significant role in, 26, 47–48
slavery accepted within, 132
Connecticut, 69, 104, 169
Corrigan, John, 254n.11
Cotton, John
Antinomian Crisis and, 22
on believers' knowledge of their election, 29–30, 37–38
Congregationalist church government structure and, 16–17, 62
descendants of, 68
Familist sect and, 25
on financial transactions, 32
First Resurrection and, 72–73, 189
Hutchinson and, 23–24, 29
on individual conversion, 7, 9, 21, 28, 30–31, 32–33
resurrection of a millennial church and, 3, 7, 9, 19–20, 21, 28, 31–32, 38–39, 40, 51, 62, 184–85
resurrection of the body and, 28–29
on spiritual community, 30–33
Woodbridge's elegy for, 49–50
Coward, William, 77–78
Cromwell, Oliver, 3–4, 16
Croswell, Andrew, 163–66, 170
cryonics, 224–25
Cudworth, Ralph, 62, 75–76
Cuffe, Paul, 140
Cugoano, Ottobah, 11–12, 108–9, 137–38, 253n.198, 253n.200

cult of the dead, 182–84, 210
Curran, Andrew, 107
Cushman, Robert, 1–2

Danforth, Samuel, 67–68
The Danger of an Unconverted Ministry (Tennent), 163–64
Danish West Indies, 104–5, 132–33
Darby, John Nelson, 12–13, 176–77
Dashwood, Francis, 179
Davenport, James, 163–66, 169
Davenport, John, 25–26, 61, 67–68, 73–74
Davis, Andrew Jackson, 182–83, 212–14, 217–18, 268n.142
Day of Doom. *See* Doomsday
Death the Destroyer (Foxcroft), 156–57
Dickinson, Jonathan, 157
Doomsday
  Allen on, 200–1
  Baillie's description and, 18–19
  Colman's description of, 95
  fate of nations on, 59, 61
  fate of pagans who have not heard gospel on, 121–22
  fate of slaveholders on, 133–34
  resurrection of bodies of the elect on, 15, 24, 28, 62, 95
  "sacred time" concept and, 47
  Second Resurrection and, 72–73
  souls' reunion with bodies on, 100, 126–27
  Spiritualists and, 217–18
Douglass, Frederick, 108–9, 140–42
Downes, Paul, 265n.86
Dudley, Joseph, 91, 98
Dummer, William, 109–10
Dutton, Anne, 101, 134
Dwight, Theodore, 262–63n.41
Dwight, Timothy, 186–87
Dyer, Mary, 54–55

Eames, Thomas, 159–60
Edgar Huntly (Brown), 198–99
Edwards, Jonathan, 170, 173–74, 189, 208–9, 259n.139
Eire, Carlos, 20–21, 58, 230n.20
Eliot, John, 38, 66, 104–5, 107–8
The Endless Increase of Christ's Government (Prince), 174–75
English, George Bethune, 183–84
English Civil War. *See* British Civil Wars (1638–53)
English Independents, 16–17, 19–20, 32
Enoch (Book of Genesis), 94–95, 97
An Enquiry Into the Influence of Physical Causes upon the Moral Faculty (Rush), 194

enslaved Africans
  afterlife and resurrection beliefs among, 2–3, 100, 138–39
  burial restrictions regarding, 103
  Christian baptisms of, 6–7, 11, 104–5, 116
  Christian perspectives regarding salvation of, 101, 105–7, 108, 110, 112, 118–19, 120, 122–25, 129–31, 132–38
  Great Awakening and, 131–32
  Mather on the Christian education and conversion of, 105, 116–17, 118, 120, 122–23, 131
  missionary and evangelization efforts directed toward, 6–7, 11, 85–86, 101–2, 104, 120–21, 123–26, 130–33
  political freedoms following Christian conversion for, 128–32, 135–36
  whitening of bodies during resurrection of, 3, 6–7, 11, 82, 102–3, 105–6, 108–9, 111–13, 114–16, 117–19, 120–21, 122–23, 134–35, 137–38, 141–42, 198, 225–26
Erdozain, Dominic, 58
Erwin, John, 71–72
Ezekiel, Book of, 162–63

"The Facts in the Case of M. Valdemar" (Poe), 215–16
The Fall (Genesis), 12–13, 101, 153–54, 157–58
"The Fall of the House of Usher" (Poe), 215
Falque, Emmanuel, 224
Familists (Family of Love sect), 16, 19–20, 24–25, 49
Farman, Abou, 224–25
Fernel, Jean, 75–76
Fessenden, Tracy, 38
Field, Jonathan Beecher, 40–41
Fifth Monarchists, 16, 41, 97
Finley, Samuel, 193–94
Finney, Charles Grandison, 208–9
The First Fruits (Haidt), 132–33
First Resurrection
  allegorical readings of, 64, 111–12, 173, 189
  definition of, 3–4
  Finney on, 208–9
  Mather and, 10, 61, 64, 67–68, 70, 71, 72–74, 77, 89–90, 92, 98–99, 106, 120
  Mede's interpretation of, 69–70, 85, 97
  millennium following, 61
  Nonconformists' fate in, 89–90
  raised saints' rule over the world following, 15–16, 61, 63, 64–65, 69, 73–74, 84–85, 86–87, 88, 89–91, 120–22, 145, 172–73
  resurrection of the body and, 10, 15–16, 64

resurrection of the millennial church and, 31, 72–73
Revelation's description of, 3–4, 10, 15, 118–19
Second Coming of Jesus and, 61, 94–95
section of Heaven for souls awaiting, 79
Flavel, John, 166–67
Fleet, Thomas, 165–66
Fleetwood, William, 124–25
The Flood (Genesis), 12–13, 62, 151–52, 153–54, 157–58, 172–73
Flourens, Jean Pierre, 180–81
Fort William Henry, battle of, 171–72
Foucault, Michel, 225
Fowle, Daniel, 159
Fox, George
    authority of professional ministers contested by, 52
    Gorton and, 51–52
    inner light doctrine and, 21–22, 52–53
    memorial rings critiqued by, 53–54
    Quakers in Barbados and, 55–56
    resurrection of the body and, 54, 56–57
    salvation during life at moment of conversion affirmed by, 52
Foxcroft, Thomas, 12–13, 145–46, 150, 156–57, 164–65
Fox sisters, 209–10
Franklin, Benjamin, 13, 133–34, 179–81, 192
Frederick (prince of Wales), 152–53, 154–55, 156–57, 255n.36
free Africans
    as abolitionists, 137
    autobiographical accounts from, 132, 139–40
    Great Awakening and, 131–32
    Jefferson's rejection of citizenship for, 196–97
    missionary and evangelization efforts directed at, 104
    political and legal rights of, 103, 128–29
    "return to Africa" efforts and, 140, 196–97
    Sewall's concern about the presence in New England of, 113
French Prophets, 159–61, 169,
French Revolution, 184, 195, 205–6, 223–24
Freneau, Philip, 191–92, 202–4
Freud, Sigmund, 227

The Gates Ajar (Phelps), 210–12
George I (king of England), 88–89, 96–97
George II (king of England), 88–89
Georgia, 131
Gerbner, Katherine, 104–5
Gilbert, Amos, 208–9
Giles, Paul, 240n.31
Gillis, John, 38–39, 53

Gilman, Nicholas, 164–65
Glasson, Travis, 104–5
Godwyn, Morgan, 101, 130
Goetz, Rebecca, 104–5, 244n.1
Goodman, Nan, 60–61, 63–64, 85
A Good Master Well Served (Cotton Mather), 122–23
Goodwin, Thomas, 16–17
Gorton, Samuel
    Fox and, 51–52
    immortality of the individual independent from spiritual union with Christ rejected by, 45
    imprisonment of, 39–40
    mortalists criticized by, 46
    Morton's history of the Puritan colonies and, 49–52
    Quakers and, 48–49, 51–52
    religious institutions' legitimacy denied by, 9–10, 28–29, 38–40, 41–42, 48
    resurrection of the body rejected by, 5–6, 45
    resurrection of the Church rejected by, 5–6, 40, 43, 44–45, 51
    Rhode Island government roles of, 41–42
    sabbath-keeping practices critiqued by, 38–40
    sacred time concept rejected by, 9–10, 21–22, 40, 42–43, 47–48, 51
    salvation during life at moment of conversion affirmed by, 8, 17, 22, 40, 43, 48
    secularization and, 46–47
    separation of religious and civil spheres supported by, 41, 43–44, 46–47
    Shawomet settlement and, 40–42, 48
    spiritual significance of final hours of life rejected by, 45–47
    trial (1643) of, 40
Graunt, John, 155
Great Awakening
    Boston's revivals and, 166–68
    Congregationalism's fractionalization and, 147, 164–65, 170
    enslaved Africans and, 131–32
    New England's experiences in, 160–61, 169
    Prince and, 144, 146–47, 160–61, 165–68, 169–70, 175
    resurrection of the body and, 146–47
Gregory, Brad, 58
Gribben, Crawford, 17
Gronniosaw, James Albert Ukawsaw, 134–35
Gura, Philip, 231–32n.27
Guthrie, William, 166–67

Haefeli, Evan, 48–49, 236n.121

Haidt, Johann, 132–33
Hall, Prince, 108–9, 137–39
Hammon, Jupiter, 11–12, 134–36, 138–39
Hanoverian dynasty, 87–89, 96–97, 152–53
Hariot, John, 100
Harriot, Thomas, 2–3
Harrison, Peter, 58
Hastings, Selina, 132
Heaven
   Calvinist view of, 13–14
   immanent frame of human endeavor and, 148
   Jesus's ascent into, 83
   New Jerusalem and, 64–65, 84–85, 89–90
   Paul's description of his ascent to, 79–80
   Protestant beliefs regarding remoteness of, 6–7, 230n.17
   as raised saints' home during millennium, 88, 89–90
   reconstitution of earthly communities in, 22
   section for souls awaiting First Resurrection in, 79
   secularization and, 46
   souls' interaction in, 7, 63, 82–83
   Spiritualist views of, 13–14
   twenty-first century beliefs regarding, 14, 177–78
Hiacoomes, 101
Hickman, Jared, 140–42
History of the Work of Redemption (Edwards), 173
Hobbes, Thomas, 57–58, 64, 75–78, 83–84
The Holy Walk and Glorious Translation of Blessed Enoch (Colman), 94–95
Homer, 81–82
Hooker, Thomas, 68
Hopkins, Samuel, 189
"The House of Night" (Freneau), 203–4
Huguenots, 159. *See also* French Prophets
Hutchins, Zachary, 109–10, 114
Hutchinson, Anne
   church trial (1638) of, 23–26
   Congregationalist ministers criticized by, 26–27
   Cotton and, 23–24, 29
   death of, 28–29
   excommunication and exile from Boston of, 26–27, 28–29
   Holy Spirit's direct instruction and, 22–23
   on Jesus, 5–6, 9, 17–18, 26
   repudiation of worldly regimes endorsed by, 41
   on resurrection and marriage, 25
   resurrection of the body and, 5–6, 17–19, 23–24, 25–26, 27–28
   salvation during life affirmed by, 8, 9, 17, 22, 24–25, 27–28, 40
   the secular modern self and, 25–26, 27–28
   Shepard and, 23–26, 29
Hutchinson, William, 28–29, 40

Ibrahim Pasha, 183–84
immortality
   consciousness and, 14
   Enlightenment philosophy and challenges to concept of, 62
   immortalists and, 8, 161, 165–66, 168, 222–26
   Palmer's theory of "philosophical immortality" And, 201–2
   secular conceptions of the millennium and, 185
   the soul and, 74–75, 126–27
inner light doctrine (Quakerism), 21–22, 52–55, 57–58
Ireland, Shadrach, 165, 168
Irenaeus, 81–82
Isaiah, Book of, 109–10, 144, 172–73
Israel, Jonathan, 58

Jacob, Margaret, 58
Jacobite rising (1715), 96
Jamaica, 101–2, 111
"The Jamaica Funeral" (Freneau), 202–3
James, Book of, 42–43
Jamestown (Virginia), 1, 189
Jefferson, Thomas
   Adams and, 183–84, 206, 207, 261–62n.21
   on each generation's need for new laws, 222–23
   election of 1800 and, 179–80, 183–84
   on farmers and republicanism, 193
   free African citizenship rejected by, 196–97
   human perfectibility as a belief of, 193
   Jefferson Bible and, 179–80
   racist views of, 196
   religious beliefs of, 196, 204–6
   resurrection as political metaphor for, 183–84
   resurrection of the body rejected by, 13, 180–81, 193, 196
   Rush and, 196, 207
Jeremiah, Book of, 113, 122–23, 137–38
Jesus. *See also* Second Coming of Jesus
   ascension to Heaven of, 83
   Hutchinson on, 5–6, 9, 17–18, 26
   immortality of the soul and, 74–75

the millennium and rule by, 18
Quakers on, 56–57
resurrection of the body and, 17–18, 26, 47–48, 57, 83, 127, 207–8, 223–24
salvation of different races and nations and death of, 136–37
Jews, 17, 18, 73, 96, 105, 110–11, 175–76, 249n.101
Job (Old Testament), 153–54, 156–57
John, Gospel of, 172–73
Johnson, Edward, 26–27
Joseph (Book of Exodus), 98
Judgment Day. *See* Doomsday

Keith, George, 52–53, 57
King, Miles, 204–5
King, William, 1
King Philip's War, 103–4
Kopelson, Heather, 104–5

Lacy, John, 159–60
Laderman, Gary, 214
Lamech (Book of Genesis), 112, 151–52
La Peyrère, Isaac, 100–1
Laqueur, Thomas, 7, 222–23
The Laws of Health (Alcott), 213–14
Lazarus, 81–82, 132, 162–63
Le Jau, Francis, 124–25
Letter from a Gentleman in Boston (Chauncy), 160
"Ligeia" (Poe), 215
Ligon, Richard, 2–3
Lippard, George, 13–14, 182–83, 214, 218, 219–21
Locke, John, 62, 77–78, 83–84, 177–78, 239n.16, 241n.54
Luke, Gospel of, 67–68, 109

Magnalia Christi Americana (Mather)
on alchemy, 65–66
Bercovitch's interpretation of, 71–72
communion between the living and the dead and, 65–66, 68, 70, 78–79
on Davenport's church and public professions of faith, 73–74
dying of prominent Puritans recounted in, 66–67, 68
First Resurrection and, 66–68, 70, 71, 73–74, 77, 92, 98–99
immortality of the soul and, 74–75
Mede and, 70
on New England's future, 68–69, 70, 71, 72, 74

on relics, 66
resurrection of the body and, 67–68, 72
resurrection of the millennial church and, 72
Manuductio ad Ministerium (Cotton Mather), 86–88
Marrant, John, 132
Marshall, Peter, 7
Martin, Friedrich, 132–33
Massachusetts. *See also* New England
Baillie on Antinomian Crisis in, 22
burial practices in, 1
Great Awakening revivals in, 169
Mather on the government of, 10, 91
Puritan covenant theology and, 59–61
Quakers persecuted by, 51–52, 54–55
revocation of original charter in, 10, 62, 68–69
Shawomet settlement and, 43–44
materialism
Adams's critique of, 208
Enlightenment philosophy and, 98–99
Hobbes and, 75–76
resurrection of the body challenged in, 4, 13–14, 177–78
secularization and, 58
Mather, Cotton. *See also specific works*
belief in intelligent life other planets of, 174–75
Catholicism and, 63, 66, 86–87, 150
on Christian education and conversion of enslaved Africans, 105, 116–17, 118, 120, 122–23, 131
Colman and, 94–95, 97–98
communion between the living and the dead and, 63, 65–66, 68, 70, 77, 78–79, 80–81, 82–83, 99, 102
The Conflagration and, 61, 85–87, 90–91, 97, 120, 145
Congregationalist system of church government and, 73
death of, 80
The Enlightenment's influence on, 62
on enslaved Africans and salvation, 106–7, 120–21, 122–23
First Resurrection and, 10, 61, 64, 67–68, 70, 71, 72–74, 77, 89–90, 92, 98–99, 106, 120
Hanoverian dynasty and, 88–89
on Heaven, 79
immortality of the soul and, 74–75
Jews' conversion to Christianity predicted by, 73
Massachusetts's colonial government and, 10, 91

Mather, Cotton (*cont.*)
  materialism dismissed by, 83–84
  Mede's influence on, 69–70
  on ministers and party politics, 88
  missionaries and, 85–86, 107
  moral value of commercial endeavor recognized by, 150
  mortalism and psychopannychism condemned by, 78, 83–84
  on Native Americans in New England, 107
  New Earth predictions of, 84–85, 88, 89–92, 97, 120–22, 127
  on New England's millennial future, 68–70, 71, 72, 74, 91–94, 97–98
  New Jerusalem and, 89–90, 93
  on persecution of Nonconformists, 87–88, 89, 97–98
  pessimism about state of Protestantism in British Empire of, 85, 87–88, 89
  racism and, 115, 119–20, 122–23
  relics disparaged by, 66
  on resurrection and souls' interaction in Heaven, 7, 63, 82–83
  resurrection of the body and, 11, 63, 64, 67–68, 72, 75, 77, 78–79, 82–83, 84, 119, 127
  resurrection of the millennial church and, 3, 10–11, 72, 78–79
  Salem trials (1692) and, 75
  Second Coming of Jesus and, 61, 73, 86–87, 119–20
  Sewall and, 115
  on the slave trade, 105
  The Society for the Propagation of the Gospel and, 125–26
  whitening of bodies of color in resurrection and, 11, 82, 105–6, 117–18, 120–21, 122–23, 198
Mather, Increase, 61–62, 115, 149
Mather, Nathaniel, 67–68
Mather, Samuel, 153, 166–67
Matthew, Gospel of, 105, 234n.68
Mayhew, Experience, 101
Mayhew, Jonathan, 153, 171–72
Mbembe, Achille, 107
Mead, Matthew, 166–67
Mede, Joseph, 15–16, 69–70, 85, 97, 136–37
Merchant, Carolyn, 226
Methodists, 182
Methuselah (Book of Genesis), 151–52
Milbank, John, 223–24
the millennium. *See also* New Earth
  Conflagration preceding, 61, 145, 172–73
  Congregationalism and, 3, 18–19, 31
  Darby's predictions of Satan's tribulations preceding, 176
  exceptionalist millennialism and, 176
  First Resurrection and, 61
  Jesus's reign during, 18
  New Model Army and, 3–4
  secular conceptions of, 185–87, 188, 191
  Seven Years' War and increasing interest in, 148–49
  sin and, 11
  Whitefield on the imminence of, 163
Miller, Perry, 59–61, 63–64, 239–40n.26
Milton, John, 77–78
missionaries. *See also* The Society for the Propagation of the Gospel
  attitudes regarding racial difference and salvation among, 101–2
  enslaved Africans as conversion targets for, 6–7, 11, 85–86, 101–2, 104, 120–21, 123–26, 130–33
  Mather on, 85–86, 107
  Moravians and, 132–33
  Native Americans as target of, 11, 85–86, 96, 101–2, 104, 107–8, 110–11, 120–21, 124–25, 154–55
  Quakers as, 51–52, 104
  questions regarding political and social rights for Christian slaves among, 130–31
  resurrection of the body and, 131
  slavery of baptized Christians accepted by, 104–5
Mitchell, Jonathan, 67–68
A Modest Enquiry (Beach), 125–30
Moravian Church, 132–33, 245n.28
More, Henry, 62, 75–76
mortalism, 24, 46, 77–78, 83–84, 94–95, 126–27
Morton, Nathaniel, 49–52
Morton, Timothy, 226–28
Moss, Henry, 197

Narragansett Indians, 40–41
Native Americans
  afterlife and resurrection beliefs among, 2–3, 100, 140
  animism and, 226
  Christian perspectives regarding salvation of, 101, 107–8
  colonists' racial and cultural othering of, 103–4
  Great Awakening and, 131–32
  King Philip's War and, 103
  Mede's millennial interpretation of, 69–70

missionary and evangelization efforts directed toward, 11, 85–86, 96, 101–2, 104, 107–8, 110–11, 120–21, 124–25, 154–55
"nativist" movement of eighteenth century among, 140
proposed genealogies linking lost tribes of Israel to, 100–1, 105, 246–47n.54
The Negro Christianized (Cotton Mather), 116–19, 122–23
New Earth
America's place in, 85
Beach's rejection of the concept of, 127–28, 129–30
changed saints' lives on, 86–87, 97, 120–21, 157–58, 172–73
European colonization model for Mather's vision of, 90–91
Mather's predictions regarding, 84–85, 88, 89–92, 97, 120–22, 127
Sewall's predictions regarding, 111, 127
slavery eliminated on, 90–91, 111
Smith's predictions regarding, 176–77
time and space considerations on, 97
Torrey's predictions regarding, 172–74
New England. *See also specific colonies*
colonial burial and funeral practices in, 1–2
enslaved Africans in, 103, 109–10, 113–14, 116–17, 124, 125–26, 131–32
Great Awakening and, 160–61, 169
King Philip's War and, 103
Mather on the millennial future of, 68–70, 71, 72, 74, 91–94, 97–98
New Jerusalem and, 91
Sewall on the millennial future of, 111–12, 114–15
slave trade and, 93
New Jerusalem
Heaven and, 64–65, 89–90
Mather on, 89–90, 93
New England and, 91
as raised saints' millennial home, 89–90, 120–21
Revelation's description of, 93, 186
Satan's campaign to overthrow, 121–22
Sewall on, 110–12
unity and harmony in, 89–90, 93
New Lights, 125, 131–32, 146–47, 163, 168, 170
Newman, Samuel, 67–68
New Model Army, 3–4, 16, 50–51
New York (colony), 104–5, 124
Nishmath-Chajim ("breath of life," Cotton Mather)
clergy's role in society and, 76–77, 78–79
communion between raised saints and changed saints through, 82–83, 102
communion between the living and dead and, 80, 81–83
definition of, 64
individuals' physical appearances and, 81–82
physical health and, 75, 76–77
resurrection of the body and, 75, 77, 82–83, 84
soul and body linked through, 64, 75
transformative effect of grace and, 75–76
Nonconformists. *See also specific sects*
Arianism and, 85–86, 97–98
British government's exclusion from office of, 7, 89
First Resurrection and, 89–90
George II and, 88–89
Mather on the persecution of, 87–88, 89, 97–98
New Earth and, 11
Norton, John, 49, 68
Notes on the State of Virginia (Jefferson), 193–94, 196–97
Noyes, John Humphrey, 208–9, 267n.133
Noyes, Nicholas, 65, 70, 117–19
Nye, Philip, 16–17

Ogilby, John, 100
"On Being Brought from Africa to America" (Wheatley), 134–35
O'Neale, Sondra, 135–36
Oswego, battle of, 171–72
Ottoman Empire, 105, 184–85, 186
Overton, Richard, 77–78
Owen, Robert Dale, 208–10, 267n.130

Paine, Tom, 13, 179–81
Palmer, Elihu, 201–2, 208
Parker, Thomas, 67–68
Patterson, Orlando, 103
Paul the Apostle
ascent to Heaven described by, 79–80
evangelizing mission of, 117–18
immortality of the soul and, 74–75
resurrection of the body and, 127, 179–80, 194–95
Winthrop on literal interpretations of writings of, 185
Pemberton, Ebenezer, 12–13, 145–46, 150, 156–57
Penn, William, 52–54, 56–58, 237n.158
Pennsylvania, 53, 56, 194
Perkins, William, 162

Peter, Second Letter of, 145, 153
Petty, William, 155–56
Phaenomena Quaedam Apocalyptica (Sewall), 110–12, 114–15
Phelps, Elizabeth Stuart, 182–83, 210–12, 214
Philippians, Paul's Letter to, 157–58
Phips, William, 65–67
Plato, 81–82
A Plea for the West (Beecher), 260n.157
Plymouth colony, 69
Poe, Edgar Allan, 13–14, 182–83, 214–16, 218
Potter, John, 159–60
Predestination, doctrine of, 1–2, 20
Prentice, Sarah, 165, 168
Presbyterians, 16–17, 104
Priestly, Joseph, 207
Prince, Deborah, 166–67
Prince, Thomas
  belief in intelligent life other planets of, 174–75, 213
  on the body's vulnerability, 153–55, 157–58
  on British imperial power and Protestantism, 144, 147–48, 152
  Christian History newspaper and, 146–47, 160
  The Conflagration and, 144–45
  death of, 175–76
  on death of Frederick, Prince of Wales, 152–53, 154–55, 255n.36
  on earth's environmental degradation, 12–13, 146–47, 149, 151–55, 157–58, 165–66
  on geographical orientation, 143–44
  on God's total control of earth, 154
  Great Awakening and, 144, 146–47, 160–61, 165–68, 169–70, 175
  human instincts celebrated by, 150–51
  "immanent frame" of human endeavor and, 147–49
  immortalism condemned by, 161
  on individual conversion as a long-term process, 166–67
  Mather family and, 149–50
  moral value of commercial endeavor recognized by, 150, 158
  New Earth predictions of, 12–13, 146, 157–58, 173–74, 176–77
  notion of individual conversion as resurrection rejected by, 165–66, 168–69
  resurrection of the body and, 12, 146–47, 148–49
  Second Coming and, 148–49
  Sewall funeral sermon (1730) by, 143
  Shepard and, 166–68
  Tennent and, 161
  Torrey and, 171–73
  on the total number of global deaths, 155–56
  Whitefield and, 144, 146–47, 161, 164–65, 169
Prince Jr., Thomas, 146–47, 157–58, 160
Problema Theologicum (Cotton Mather), 72–73, 90
Pryer, Matthew, 55
Psalm 31:5, 74–75
Psalm 68:31, 135
Psalm 107:30, 149
psychopannychism, 77–78, 83–84, 126–27
purgatory, 6–7, 20, 58, 63, 77–78, 126–27
Puritans. *See also* Congregationalism
  beliefs regarding millennial fate of nations among, 59–60
  Catholicism and, 5, 8–9, 26, 33–34, 63
  clerical opinions regarding commerce among, 145–46
  communion between the living and the dead and, 63–64, 65–66, 68
  covenantal theology and, 59–61
  desacralization of relics and, 7–9
  funeral and burial practices among, 1–2, 7–8
  importance of Sunday worship and properly conducted ritual for, 36–37, 38–39
  predestination doctrine and, 1–2, 20
  resurrection as communal phenomenon for, 22
  resurrection of the body and, 5, 7, 8–9, 58
  resurrection of the church and survival of, 6–7, 43, 44–45
  resurrection of the historical Jesus and, 47–48
  secularization and, 7–9, 17, 20–21, 58, 59–60, 85
  spiritual significance of final hours of life for, 21–22, 47–48
Putney debates (1647), 50–51

The Quaker City (Lippard), 13–14, 218–21
Quakers
  British restrictions against, 56
  funeral and burial practices among, 53–54
  Gorton and, 48–49, 51–52
  inner light doctrine and, 21–22, 52–55, 57–58
  Keith's break with, 57–58
  Massachusetts Bay Colony's persecution of, 51–52, 54–55
  missionary work by, 51–52, 104
  resurrection of Jesus and, 56–57
  resurrection of the body and, 9–10, 52–54, 56–57

in Rhode Island, 48–49, 51–52
salvation during life at moment of conversion affirmed by, 8, 17, 19–20, 22, 52, 54, 57
significance of final hours of life and, 53–54

racial difference
Black perspectives on salvation and, 108–9, 137–39, 140–41
Christian perspectives on salvation and, 101–2, 105–8, 110, 112, 118–19, 120, 122–25, 128–31, 132–38, 140, 141–42
Enlightenment philosophy and, 107, 119–20
farming viewed as means of eliminating physical markers of, 197
notions of sin and salvation aligned with, 134–37
racism among colonists and, 103–4, 106–7, 108, 110, 113–14, 119–20, 122–23, 130, 196–97
radical black eschatologies and, 132, 138–42
Rush's description of Blackness as a "disease of the skin" and, 196–97
whitening of bodies of color at resurrection and, 3, 6–7, 11, 82, 102–3, 105–6, 108–9, 111–13, 114–16, 117–19, 120–21, 122–23, 134–35, 137–38, 141–42, 198, 225–26
Radical Orthodoxy movement, 223–24
raised saints. *See also* First Resurrection
changed saints' relationship with, 64–65, 80–83, 84–85, 88, 89–90, 95–96, 120–22, 145
Heaven as millennial home of, 88, 89–90
New Earth governed by, 15–16, 31, 61, 63, 64–65, 69, 73–74, 84–85, 86–87, 88, 89–91, 120–22, 145, 172–73
Nishmath-Chajim and, 82–83, 102
racial difference and, 106
resurrection of the Church and, 72, 77
Second Coming of Jesus and, 95
The Reasonableness of Christianity (Locke), 241n.54
Reason Satisfied and Faith Established (Cotton Mather), 75
Reason the Only Oracle of Man (Allen), 200–1
republicanism
Barlow's poetry and, 190–91
constraints on executive power and, 60–61
Jefferson on farmers and, 193
moral perfection and, 5–6, 180–81
resurrection as political metaphor and, 13, 190
resurrection of the body and, 201–2, 208
resurrection as political metaphor
American Revolution and, 4–5, 184

Jefferson and, 183–84
republicanism and, 13, 190
Washington's presidency and, 204
Winthrop (James) and, 184–85
resurrection of the body
Allen's rejection of, 200
colonial settlers' fears assuaged through belief in, 1–2, 4–5
conversion in Puritan theology and, 5, 7, 9
First Resurrection and, 10, 15–16, 64
Gorton and, 5–6, 45
Great Awakening and, 146–47
Hutchinson and, 5–6, 17–19, 23–24, 25–26, 27–28
Jefferson's rejection of, 13, 180–81, 193, 196
Jesus's resurrection and, 17–18, 26, 47–48, 57, 83, 127, 207–8, 223–24
Lippard and, 220–21
materialist challenges to, 4, 13–14, 177–78
Mather on, 11, 63, 64, 67–68, 72, 75, 77, 78–79, 82–83, 84, 119, 127
mortalism and, 24, 77–78, 83–84, 94–95, 126–27
Nishmath-Chajim and, 75, 77, 82–83, 84
Paine's rejection of, 179–80
Palmer's rejection of, 201–2
Phelps and, 211–12
Poe's short stories and, 215–16
Quakers and, 9–10, 52–54, 56–57
reinforcement of social order on Earth and, 6–7, 24, 57–58
republicanism and, 201–2, 208
Spiritualism and, 210
Thoreau and, 216–17
twenty-first century beliefs regarding, 14
whitening of bodies of color and, 3, 6–7, 11, 82, 102–3, 105–6, 108–9, 111–13, 114–16, 117–19, 120–21, 122–23, 134–35, 137–38, 141–42, 198, 225–26
resurrection of the Church
Brightman on, 15–16
Cotton and, 3, 7, 9, 19–20, 21, 28, 31–32, 38–39, 40, 51, 62, 184–85
First Resurrection and, 72–73
Gorton's rejection of, 5–6, 40, 43, 44–45, 51
individual conversion and, 7, 21
Mather and, 3, 10–11, 72, 78–79
Puritan survival and, 6–7, 43, 44–45
radicals' questioning of the claim of, 6–7, 16
raised saints and, 72, 77
Revelation, Book of
allegorical readings of, 184–85
on Babylon's fall, 137–38

Revelation, Book of (*cont.*)
  First Resurrection described in, 3–4, 10, 15, 118–19
  Last Judgment and, 184–85
  millennium described in, 15
  New Jerusalem described in, 93, 186
  resurrection of the body and, 10
  on satanic armies attempting to destroy Christendom, 69–70, 121–22
  Sewall's interpretation of, 110–11
Revolutionary War. *See* American Revolution
Rhode Island, 41–42, 48–49, 51–52
The Rising Glory of America (Freneau), 256n.53
Rivett, Sarah, 75–76
Roanoke colony (Virginia), 2–3
Robinson, William, 54–55
Rogers, Gamaliel, 159
Rogers, John, 59–61
Roman Catholicism. *See* Catholicism
Rush, Benjamin
  Blackness described as "disease of the skin" by, 196–97
  on education and moral progress, 194–95
  on the French Revolution, 195
  Jefferson and, 196, 207
  republican notions of resurrection and, 13
  Tennent and, 193–94
  on United States as moral laboratory, 194

saints. *See* changed saints; raised saints
Salem trials (1692), 75
Saltmarsh, John, 35–37, 50–51, 57–58
Saltmarsh Returned from the Dead (Gorton), 41–44, 45–46, 50–51
Sancho, Ignatius, 11–12, 108–9, 136–37, 138
Savage, Thomas, 23–24
Savoy Conference (1661), 229 n7
Schmidt, Carl, 181
Second Coming of Jesus
  Beach on the end of life of earth following, 127–28, 129–30
  Colman on, 95–96
  English Independents' beliefs regarding, 19–20
  First Resurrection and, 61, 94–95
  inner light doctrine and, 53, 54–55
  Mather on, 61, 73, 86–87, 119–20
  ministerial education in preparation for, 86
  Prince on, 148–49
  Puritan beliefs regarding, 19–20
  resurrection of the bodies of saints and, 148–49

secularization
  afterlife and, 46, 177–78
  death and, 8
  Gorton and, 46–47
  Hutchinson and, 25–26, 27–28
  "immanent frame" of human endeavor and, 147–49
  individuals' direct access to sources of transcendence and, 21–22, 27
  Locke and, 62
  materialism and, 58
  of the millennium concept, 185–86
  Puritanism and, 7–9, 17, 20–21, 58, 59–60, 85
  relationship between the dead with the living under, 14
  sacred history concept rejected under, 47
  the self and, 27–28, 53
  significance of final hours of life and, 46–47
  Sunday worship as means of halting, 36
  Taylor on, 7–8, 27, 47, 58
  temporal linearity and, 47
  Weber on, 7–8, 58
Seeman, Erik, 7, 182–83
The Selling of Joseph (Sewall), 110, 111–12, 113–14
sentimentalism, 7, 13–14, 214, 218
Sepinwall, Alyssa, 261n.14
Seven Years' War, 148–49, 171–72, 175–76, 185–86, 189
Sewall, Joseph, 109–10, 149, 163–65, 166–70
Sewall, Samuel
  arson against home (1723) of, 114
  black servants of, 113–14
  on Catholicism, 110–11
  First Resurrection and, 111–12
  Mather and, 115
  on missionaries' efforts among Native Americans, 110–11
  on Native Americans' genealogies, 105
  New Earth predictions of, 111, 127, 247n.63
  on New England's millennial future, 111–12, 114–15
  New Jerusalem described by, 110–12
  Prince's funeral sermon for, 143
  racist beliefs of, 110, 113–16, 130
  slave trade opposed by, 110, 111
  whitening of bodies of color through resurrection and, 3, 11, 105–6, 109, 111–13, 114–15, 120–21, 198
Shakers, 208–9
Shawomet settlement (Rhode Island), 40–42, 43, 48
Shepard, Thomas
  Antinomian Crisis and, 22

on believers' knowledge of their election, 29–30, 33–34, 35, 37–38
Congregationalist church government structure and, 62
death of, 66–67
on "double being" of saints, 34
Hutchinson and, 23–26, 29
on importance of pastoral guidance, 35, 37–38
on importance of spiritual community and Sunday worship, 35–39
on individual conversion and the resurrection of the church, 9, 21, 28
on man's birth into sin, 34
the millennial church and, 3
Prince and, 166–68
psychological ramifications of conversion studied by, 75–76
Shields, David, 203–4
Shoemaker, Nancy, 103–4
Sierra Leone, 140
Silva, Cristobal, 76–77
Sloterdijk, Peter, 147–48, 177–78
Smith, Joseph, 12–13, 176–77, 260n.168
Smith, Nat, 165
Smith, Ralph, 50
Smith, Stanhope, 197, 199
Smolinski, Reiner, 233n.61, 243n.99
The Society for the Propagation of the Gospel. *See also* Beach, John
beliefs regarding salvation of enslaved Africans among, 124–25
British imperial authority and, 123–24
enslaved Africans as target of proselytization of, 104, 123–25, 131
founding (1701) of, 139–40
Mather on, 125–26
millennial expectations of, 123–24
Native Americans as target of proselytization of, 104
slave plantation managed by, 124
slavery accepted by, 104–5, 124, 129, 132
Society of Friends. *See* Quakers
South Carolina (colony), 104–5, 124, 131, 133–34
Speedwell, 1
Spinoza, Baruch de, 58, 62
Spiritualism, 7, 13–14, 182–83, 209–18
Stansbury, Abraham, 205
Staynoe, Thomas, 121–22, 136–37
Stephenson, Marmaduke, 54–55
Stievermann, Jan, 71–72, 83, 119–20, 240n.31, 243n.99
Stiles, Ezra, 48, 51–52, 189

Stoddard, Solomon, 166–67
Stoughton, William, 59–61, 98
St. Thomas (Caribbean island), 132–33
Swedenborg, Emmanuel, 210–11
Sweet, John Wood, 101–2, 251n.157

Tackanash, 101
Taylor, Bron, 226
Taylor, Charles, 7–9, 21–22, 27–28, 47–48, 53, 58, 147–48, 222–23
Tennent, Gilbert
on Atlantic earthquakes of 1755, 171
on human corruption and the need for conversion, 168
New England's experience in the Great Awakening and, 161
Prince and, 161
on resurrection of the body and individual conversion, 12, 146–47, 161–63, 168–69
Rush and, 193–94
symbolic death and resurrection experienced by, 163
"unconverted" ministers criticized by, 163–64
Tennent, John, 163
Tennent, William, 163
Tertullian, 81–82
Test Act (1678), 89
Thacher, Peter, 80
Theopolis Americana (Cotton Mather), 91–93, 150
Thompson, Benjamin, 65, 70
Thoreau, Henry David, 13–14, 182–83, 214, 216–18
Thorowgood, Thomas, 100–1
Thoughts and Sentiments on the Evil and Wicked Traffic of the Slavery (Ottobah Cugoano), 137
Tillotson, John, 59
Toland, John, 62
Torrey, William, 148–49, 171–74
"To the University of Cambridge in New England" (Wheatley), 135
Traister, Bryce, 25–26, 238n.172
Triparadisus (Cotton Mather)
on America's place on New Earth, 91
on changed saints' lives on New Earth, 90–91
The Conflagration and, 97
First Resurrection and, 89–90
on human desire for immortality, 78
materialism dismissed in, 83–84
Nishmath-Chajim described in, 75, 80, 81–82
pessimism about fate of Protestantism in British Empire in, 89

Triparadisus (Cotton Mather) (*cont.*)
  on race and salvation, 120
  on raised saints' rule of New Earth, 84–85, 121–22
  on section of Heaven for souls awaiting First Resurrection, 79
Turrettini, François, 70–71

Vade Mecum (Thomas Prince), 143–44
Valeri, Mark, 150, 254n.11
van der Kemp, François, 180–81, 205–6, 266n.113
Vane, Henry, 26–27
Van Helmont, Jan Baptista, 75–76
Vidal, Fernando, 14, 239n.16
Virginia, 1–2, 103, 108, 246n.38
The Vision of Columbus (Barlow), 185–87, 189, 197–98. See also *The Columbiad* (Barlow)
Voltaire, 58, 204–5

Wadsworth, Benjamin, 151
Walden (Thoreau), 216–17
Walker, David, 108–9, 141–42
Walley, John, 156–57, 239n.25
Walley, Thomas, 67–68
Ward, Graham, 223–24
Warner, Margaret, 76–77, 78–79
War of 1812, 204–205
Washington, George, 189, 204
Watts, John, 79, 81–82
Weber, Max, 7–9, 20–21, 58
Weld, Thomas, 28–29
Wesley, John, 133–34
Westminster Assembly (1643–53), 16–17
Wheatley, Phillis, 11–12, 108–9, 132, 134–37
Wheelwright, John, 26–27
Whiston, William, 62, 112, 145

Whitefield, George
  on human corruption and the need for conversion, 168
  millennium's imminence preached by, 163
  on ministers' "experimental Acquaintance" with Jesus, 163–64
  New England's experience in the Great Awakening and, 160–61, 169
  people of color attracted to the preaching of, 131–32
  Prince and, 144, 146–47, 161, 164–65, 169
  on resurrection of the body and individual conversion, 12, 146–47, 161–63, 164–65, 168–69, 208
  slavery supported by, 132
  views of racial difference and salvation of, 108–9, 133–34
Whitehead, George, 52–53
Wieland (Brown), 198–99
Wigglesworth, Michael, 122
Willard, Samuel, 59–61, 156–57
William and Mary (king and queen of England), 62, 89
Williams, Nathanael, 174
Williams, Roger, 2–3, 41–42, 46–47, 100
Wilson, John, 23–24, 68
Wilson, Thomas, 124–25
Winchester, Elhanan, 176–77, 266n.107
Winiarski, Douglas, 165, 170
Winship, Michael, 51–52, 60–61, 63–64
Winslow, Edward, 67–68
Winthrop, James, 184–85
Winthrop, John, 17–18, 25, 28–29, 43–44
Wisner, William, 205
The Wonderful Narrative, 159–61
Woodbridge, Benjamin, 49–50
Woodbury, Richard, 164–66, 168

Young, Thomas, 200